T0186130

Lecture Notes in Computer Science   12851

More information about this subseries at http://www.springer.com/series/7408

Sotiris Moschoyiannis · Rafael Peñaloza ·
Jan Vanthienen · Ahmet Soylu ·
Dumitru Roman (Eds.)

Rules and Reasoning

5th International Joint Conference, RuleML+RR 2021
Leuven, Belgium, September 13–15, 2021
Proceedings

Springer

Editors
Sotiris Moschoyiannis (iD)
University of Surrey
Guildford, UK

Jan Vanthienen (iD)
KU Leuven
Leuven, Belgium

Dumitru Roman
SINTEF/University of Oslo
Oslo, Norway

Rafael Peñaloza
University of Milano-Bicocca
Milano, Italy

Ahmet Soylu
OsloMet – Oslo Metropolitan University
Oslo, Norway

ISSN 0302-9743   ISSN 1611-3349   (electronic)
Lecture Notes in Computer Science
ISBN 978-3-030-91166-9   ISBN 978-3-030-91167-6   (eBook)
https://doi.org/10.1007/978-3-030-91167-6

LNCS Sublibrary: SL2 – Programming and Software Engineering

This Springer imprint is published by the registered company Springer Nature Switzerland AG
The registered company address is: Gewerbestrasse 11, 6330 Cham, Switzerland

Preface

These are the proceedings of the 5th International Joint Conference on Rules and Reasoning (RuleML+RR 2021). RuleML+RR merged the efforts of two well-established conference series: the International Web Rule (RuleML) symposia and the Web Reasoning and Rule Systems (RR) conferences.

The RuleML symposia have been held since 2002 and the RR conferences since 2007. The RR conferences have been a forum for discussion and dissemination of new results on web reasoning and rule systems, with an emphasis on rule-based approaches and languages. The RuleML symposia were devoted to disseminating research, applications, languages, and standards for rule technologies, with attention to both theoretical and practical developments, to challenging new ideas, and to industrial applications. Building on the tradition of both RuleML and RR, the joint conference series RuleML+RR aims at bridging academia and industry in the field of rules, and at fostering the cross-fertilization between the different communities focused on the research, development, and applications of rule-based systems. RuleML+RR aims at being the leading conference series for all subjects concerning theoretical advances, novel technologies, and innovative applications about knowledge representation and reasoning with rules.

To leverage these ambitions, RuleML+RR 2021 was organized as part of the event Declarative AI 2021: Rules, Reasoning, Decisions, and Explanations, that was held during September 13–15, 2021. This event was hosted by KU Leuven, Belgium. With its general topic "Declarative Artificial Intelligence" a core objective of the event was to present the latest advancements in AI and rules, rule-based machine learning, reasoning, decisions, and explanations and their adoption in IT systems. To this end, Declarative AI 2021 brought together co-located events with related interests. In addition to RuleML+RR this included DecisionCAMP 2021 and the Reasoning Web Summer School (RW 2021).

The RuleML+RR conference included three subevents:

1. Doctoral Consortium – an initiative to attract and promote student research in rules and reasoning, with the opportunity for students to present and discuss their ideas, and benefit from close contact with leading experts in the field.
2. International Rule Challenge – an initiative to provide competition among work in progress and new visionary ideas concerning innovative rule-oriented applications, aimed at both research and industry.
3. Industry Track – a forum for all sectors of industry and business (as well as the public sector) to present, discuss, and propose existing or potential rule-based applications.

The program of the main track of RuleML+RR 2021 included the presentation of 17 full research papers and two short papers. These contributions were carefully selected by the Program Committee (PC) from 39 high-quality submissions to the event. Each paper was carefully reviewed and discussed by at least three members of the PC. The technical program was then enriched with the additional contributions from its subevents as well as from DecisionCAMP 2021, a co-located event aimed at practitioners.

At RuleML+RR 2021 and DecisionCAMP 2021, two invited keynotes were presented by experts in the field:

- Ryan Urbanowicz (University of Pennsylvania, USA): Interpretable Machine Learning with Rule-based Modeling
- Alon Halevy (Facebook AI, USA): Symbolic AI in a Machine Learning World

The chairs sincerely thank the keynote speakers for their contribution to the success of the event. The chairs also thank the Program Committee members and the additional reviewers for their hard work in the careful assessment of the submitted papers. Further thanks go to all authors of contributed papers for their efforts in the preparation of their submissions and the camera-ready versions within the established schedule. Sincere thanks to the chairs of the Doctoral Consortium, the Rule Challenge, and the Industry Track, and to the chairs of all co-located Declarative AI 2021 events. The chairs finally thank the entire organization team including the Publicity, Proceedings, and Sponsorship Chairs, who actively contributed to the organization and the success of the event.

A special thanks goes to all the sponsors of RuleML+RR 2021 and Declarative AI 2021: Artificial Intelligence Journal, Springer, Leuven.AI, DMCommunity, KU Leuven, University of Surrey, University of Milano-Bicocca, RuleML Inc, RR Association. A special thanks also goes to the publisher, Springer, for their cooperation in editing this volume and publication of the proceedings. We are grateful to the sponsors of the RuleML+RR 2021 as they also contributed towards the awards: the best paper award, the best presentation award, the best student paper award, the Rule Challenge award, and the Harold Boley award for the most promising paper.

September 2021

Sotiris Moschoyiannis
Rafael Peñaloza
Jan Vanthienen
Ahmet Soylu
Dumitru Roman

Organization

General Chair

Jan Vanthienen — KU Leuven, Belgium

Program Chairs

Sotiris Moschoyiannis — University of Surrey, UK
Rafael Peñaloza — University of Milano-Bicocca, Italy

Doctoral Consortium Chairs

Anna Fensel — University of Innsbruck, Austria
Joost Vennekens — KU Leuven, Belgium

Rule Challenge Chairs

Alireza Tamaddoni Nezhad — University of Surrey, UK
Ahmet Soylu — Oslo Metropolitan University, Norway

Industry Track Chairs

Nicolay Nikolov — SINTEF AS, Norway
Ioan Toma — Onlim, Austria

Proceedings Chairs

Dumitru Roman — SINTEF AS/University of Oslo, Norway
Ahmet Soylu — Oslo Metropolitan University, Norway

Program Committee

Leopoldo Bertossi — Carleton University, Canada
Mehul Bhatt — Örebro University, Sweden
Meghyn Bienvenu — French National Center for Scientific Research, France
Andrea Billig — Fraunhofer FOKUS, Germany
Juliana Bowles — University of St Andrews, UK
Francesca Buffa — University of Oxford, UK
Pedro Cabalar Fernández — University of A Coruña, Spain
Iliano Cervesato — Carnegie Mellon University, Quatar
Robert Ching-Hsien Hsu — Asia University, Taiwan
Horatiu Cirstea — Inria, France

Stefania Costantini	University of Aquila, Italy
Giovanni De Gasperis	Università degli Studi dell'Aquila, Italy
Marc Denecker	KU Leuven, Belgium
Juergen Dix	Clausthal University of Technology, Germany
Wolfgang Faber	Alpen-Adria-Universität Klagenfurt, Austria
Mohamad Amine Ferrag	Guelma University, Algeria
Thom Fruehwirth	University of Ulm, Germany
Tiantian Gao	Stony Brook University, USA
Giancarlo Guizzardi	Free University of Bozen-Bolzano, Italy
Ryszard Janicki	McMaster University, Canada
Matthew Karlsen	University of Surrey, UK
Tomáš Kliegr	Prague University of Economics and Business, Czech Republic
Matthias Klusch	German Research Center for Artificial Intelligence, Germany
Anna Kobusinska	Poznan University of Technology, Poland
Michael Kohlhase	FAU Erlangen-Nürnberg, Germany
Roman Kontchakov	Birkbeck, University of London, UK
Manolis Koubarakis	University of Athens, Greece
Paul Krause	University of Surrey, UK
Markus Krötzsch	TU Dresden, Germany
Domenico Lembo	Sapienza University of Rome, Italy
Maurizio Lenzerini	Sapienza University of Rome, Italy
Francesca Lisi	University of Bari, Italy
Thomas Lukasiewicz	University of Oxford, UK
Leandros Maglaras	De Montfort University, UK
Nurulhuda A. Manaf	National Defence University of Malaysia, Malaysia
Marco Manna	University of Calabria, Italy
Marco Maratea	University of Genoa, Italy
Angelo Montanari	University of Udine, Italy
Sotiris Moschoyiannis	University of Surrey, UK
Grzegorz J. Nalepa	AGH University of Science and Technology, Poland
Alireza Tamaddoni Nezhad	University of Surrey, UK
Magdalena Ortiz	TU Vienna, Austria
Jeff Pan	University of Aberdeen, UK
Monica Palmirani	University of Bologna, Italy
Adrian Paschke	Free University of Berlin, Germany
Rafael Penaloza	Free University of Bozen-Bolzano, Italy
Andreas Pieris	University of Edinburgh, UK
Luca Pulina	University of Sassari, Italy
Jan Rauch	Prague University of Economics and Business, Czech Republic
Sebastian Rudolph	TU Dresden, Germany
Emanuel Sallinger	University of Oxford, UK
Konstantin Schekotihin	Alpen Adria-Universität Klagenfurt, Austria
Stefan Schlobach	Vrije Universiteit Amsterdam, The Netherlands

Umberto Straccia	ISTI - CNR, Italy
Rolf Schwitter	Macquarie University, Australia
Theresa Swift	Coherent Knowledge, USA
Giorgos Stamou	National Technical University of Athens, Greece
Giorgos Stoilos	Athens University of Economics and Business, Greece
Ahmet Soylu	Oslo Metropolitan University, Norway
Sergio Tessaris	Free University of Bolzen-Bolzano, Italy
Kia Teymourian	Boston University, USA
Nikos Triantafyllou	National Technical University of Athens, Greece
Anni-Yasmin Turhan	TU Dresden, Germany
Ryan Urbanowicz	Pennsylvania State University, USA
Riccardo Zese	University of Ferrara, Italy

Additional Reviewers

Loan Ho
Sascha Rechenberger
Mantas Simkus
Falco Nogatz
Laura Pandolfo

Sponsors

Abstracts of Kenote Speakers

Interpretable Machine Learning
with Rule-Based Modeling

Ryan J. Urbanowicz

University of Pennsylvania, Philadelphia, PA 19104, USA
ryanurb@upenn.edu

Abstract. Explainability has become achievable for most machine learning methodologies, but interpretability remains the gold standard for model transparency [1]. Unlike explainability, interpretability is a property that is unique to specific machine learning methods based on how models are represented and constrained. Unfortunately, methods regarded as interpretable, e.g. decision trees, may not achieve the same level of predictive performance, particularly when applied to problems with complex underlying patterns of association. Rule-based machine learning with algorithms such as 'Learning Classifier Systems' (LCS) offer an attractive alternative to other popular ML modeling techniques [2,3]. They have been demonstrated to be able to model extremely complex associations as well as provide opportunities to do so in an inherently interpretable manner [4]. This makes their application particularly promising in fields such as medicine, where achieving high predictive performance must be paired with model transparency to foster trust, promote knowledge discovery, identify/avoid sources of bias, and maintain accountability [5]. Learning classifier systems utilize an evolutionary algorithm search to discover a set of human-readable IF:THEN rules that collectively comprise the trained model. This allows them to capture simple as well as complex associations with outcome including epistatic feature interactions and heterogeneous associations, i.e. subgroups of instances within which a distinct feature or set of features are predictive of outcome [2]. This talk examines the unique properties of learning classifier system algorithms, as well as a variety of strategies that have been proposed to improve and facilitate their interpretability with respect to understanding individual predictions, model feature importance, and characterizing underlying patterns of associations.

Keywords: Machine learning · Interpretable · Explainable · Learning classifier systems

References

1. Rudin, C.: Stop explaining black box machine learning models for high stakes decisions and use interpretable models instead. Nat. Mach. Intell. **1**(5), 206–215 (2019)
2. Urbanowicz, R.J., Browne, W.N.: Introduction to learning classifier systems. Springer (2017)
3. Urbanowicz, R.J., Moore, J.H.: Learning classifier systems: a complete introduction, review, and roadmap. J. Artif. Evol. Appl. (2009)

4. Urbanowicz, R.J., Moore, J.H.: ExSTraCS 2.0: description and evaluation of a scalable learning classifier system. Evol. Intell. **8**(2), 89–116 (2015)
5. Urbanowicz, R.J., Andrew, A.S., Karagas, M.R., Moore, J.H.: Role of genetic heterogeneity and epistasis in bladder cancer susceptibility and outcome: a learning classifier system approach. J. Am. Med. Inf. Assoc. **20**(4) 603–612 (2013)

Symbolic AI in a Machine Learning World

Alon Halevy

Facebook, USA
ayh@fb.com

Abstract. The key technical problems that online social networks focus on today are detecting policy violating content (e.g., hate speech, misinformation) and ranking content to satisfy their users' needs. By nature, these problems are somewhat vague and need to handle multi-modal content in many languages, and therefore do not naturally lend themselves to AI techniques based on declarative representations and reasoning. However, the machine learning techniques that are employed also have some drawbacks, such as the fact that it is hard to update their knowledge efficiently or to explain their results. In this talk I will outline a few opportunities where methods from symbolic AI, combined appropriately into the machine learning paradigm, can ultimately have an impact on our goals. As one example, I will describe Neural Databases, a new kind of database system that leverages the strength of NLP transformers to answer database queries over text, thereby freeing us from designing and relying on a database schema.

Contents

Technical Communication Papers

Full Papers

Policy-Based Automated Compliance Checking

Anas Al Bassit⬚, Katsiaryna Krasnashchok(✉)⬚, Sabri Skhiri⬚,
and Majd Mustapha⬚

EURA NOVA, 1435 Mont-Saint-Guibert, Belgium
{anas.albassit,katherine.krasnoschok,sabri.skhiri,
majd.mustapha}@euranova.eu

Abstract. Under the GDPR requirements and privacy-by-design guidelines, access control for personal data should not be limited to a simple role-based scenario. For the processing to be compliant, additional attributes, such as the purpose of processing or legal basis, should be verified against an established data processing agreement or policy. In this paper, we propose an automated policy-based compliance checking model and implement it using SHACL. We provide the preliminary performance evaluation results and offer optimizations. We also define the procedure for handling conflicts in policies, resulting from the natural language description of the compliance rules. Our method combines a data model with compliance checking within the Semantic Web framework, generating what we call an operational model and promoting interoperability.

Keywords: Privacy · Compliance · SHACL · Reasoning · GDPR

1 Introduction

The requirement for compliance with data protection regulations, such as the General Data Protection Regulation (GDPR), can lead to difficulties in the implementation of business applications, making privacy-by-design solutions increasingly more appealing. A Controller can obtain personal data from Data Subjects, supported by different documents, such as privacy policies or data processing agreements, describing the rules of processing. To be compliant, business processes need to conform to these rules, given that the rules themselves do not violate the GDPR. And for automating the compliance, the rules and the business requests need to be encoded in a machine-readable way. In this paper, we introduce an automated compliance checking model, based on natural language privacy policies and other related documents. This work is developed within the ASGARD research project, in particular, its RUNE track, focusing on privacy by design. According to the GDPR compliance framework proposed by [9], our

Supported and funded by the Walloon region, Belgium. ASGARD project, convention number 8175.

S. Moschoyiannis et al. (Eds.): RuleML+RR 2021, LNCS 12851, pp. 3–17, 2021.
https://doi.org/10.1007/978-3-030-91167-6_1

model aims to solve the Operational Compliance task – the last of the three key tasks in the data supply chain. We employ Semantic dAta priVacy modEl (SAVE) [12] – our recently proposed conceptual model, for the machine-readable representation of policies and rules in written documents. The contributions of this work are the following: (i) we formalize an implementation-independent compliance checking model for SAVE policies; (ii) we implement the model using Shapes Constraint Language and its Advanced Features (SHACL-AF)[1] and provide preliminary evaluation; (iii) we support interoperability by operating within the Semantic Web framework with declarative compliance rules; (iv) we ensure explainability by providing exhaustive answers to compliance requests; (v) comparing to related works that mainly deal with permissions, our model can handle prohibitions, since both concepts occur in privacy policies and related contracts. Even though data protection regulation implies general prohibition (whatever is not permitted is prohibited), we use prohibitions to indicate when a personal data request is *explicitly* prohibited by the policy, as opposed to *implicitly* prohibited, i.e., not permitted. This makes the model transparent and close to the source (written policies), but also introduces conflicts into the policies. Therefore, we also present an algorithm for conflict detection and resolution.

The paper is structured as follows: in Sect. 2 we discuss recent solutions for automated compliance. Our compliance checking method is formalized in Sect. 3. The SHACL-based model and its preliminary evaluation are presented in Sect. 4. Finally, Sect. 5 concludes our work and outlines future plans.

2   Related Work

Regulatory compliance became popular in industry and academia in recent years. Remarkable works have emerged in modeling legal and privacy rules and automating compliance. In this section, we present an overview of the latest approaches with a special focus on the ones using Semantic Web technologies.

The SPECIAL[2] project covers an umbrella of use-cases regarding compliance of processing activities, and features extensive use of Semantic Web. Compliance algorithms, formalized within the project [5,6,11], use OWL reasoning, in addition to incorporating the SANSA stack [14] for distributed reasoning [20]. In [7] another approach to compliance reasoning was developed using ODRL and Answer Set Programming. SPECIAL's focus differs from RUNE and mainly lies in policies created by users (consent) or stakeholders (usage policies), as opposed to written policies, and thus it does not need to handle prohibitions or conflicts that occur in such documents. SERAMIS[3] is another project where ODRL is extended to describe the legislative model [1], however, its compliance assessment is partly manual and performed through questionnaires. The MIREL[4] project developed a GDPR-based ontology – PrOnto [17]. In this project, deontic

---

[1] https://www.w3.org/TR/shacl-af/.

[2] https://www.specialprivacy.eu/publications/scientific-publications.

[3] https://cordis.europa.eu/project/id/612052.

[4] https://www.mirelproject.eu/.

rules are represented in LegalRuleML [2], and then transformed into Defeasible Logic theory where legal reasoning takes place [13]. The DAPRECO[5] project uses PrOnto to express legal rules from the GDPR and applies RIO logic to extend business processes and encode data protection rules [3,4]. DPMF [19] is the recent privacy framework that provides a comprehensive description of business processes and semi-automated compliance assessment, with plans to involve Semantic Web in the future. The core of MIREL, DAPRECO and DPMF is legal reasoning and GDPR compliance, which is different from our policy-based compliance. Yet, it is worth noting that in their latest work [18], authors of DAPRECO experiment with SHACL to express RIO logic for compliance, which indicates interest in SHACL in privacy and legal domains. The BPR4GDPR[6] project uses a compliance ontology to evaluate business processes, defines prevention rules for incompatible purposes, and performs process mining to find misuses regarding the defined policies [15]. BPR4GDPR deals with workflows, while RUNE considers processing actions to be independent, thus simplifying the problem and the compliance reasoning. Similarly to most of the aforementioned works, we operate within the Semantic Web framework. Implementation-wise, our approach is close to $SHACL_{ARE}$ [8], where SHACL is used for checking compliance of business process logs against automatically mined constraints. In addition to constraints, our model uses SHACL-AF inference rules, which allow us to generate detailed answers to data processing requests, including partial compliance.

3   Policy-Based Compliance Checking

Since we work with machine-readable privacy *policies*, we refer to our compliance as *policy-based*, distinguishing it from GDPR compliance, where the rules encode the GDPR norms. At this stage, we assume that our input policies are GDPR-compliant, and we verify the compliance of incoming requests to these policies. Hence, we define compliance checking as follows: given a request for personal data processing, verify if it is permitted, according to a policy. This definition is the basic compliance checking operation in our model. On the other hand, our conceptual model captures both permissions and prohibitions[7]. Therefore, we can provide more detailed answers to compliance requests, such as: processing is *permitted*, *explicitly prohibited* (by the policy), *implicitly prohibited* (neither permitted, nor prohibited), and even *partially permitted/prohibited*, when certain parts of the request are compliant, but not the whole request.

3.1   The Conceptual Model for Privacy Policies

In our approach, we build upon SAVE [12] – a semantic conceptual model developed for the RUNE project, that merges two latest privacy ontologies and

---

[5] https://www.fnr.lu/projects/data-protection-regulation-compliance/.

[6] http://www.bpr4gdpr.eu/.

[7] Obligations and related technical/organisational measures are also captured in SAVE, but, at this phase, not considered for compliance checking.

provides a fine-grained representation of privacy policies and data processing agreements, which can be leveraged for automated compliance checking. In this section, we explain the elements of SAVE that are essential for our model.

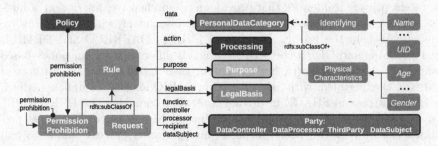

Fig. 1. A fragment of the SAVE model relevant for compliance checking. Each solid-border block is a SAVE taxonomy. For illustration, part of the `PersonalDataCategory` taxonomy is shown. The last level represents *leaves*.

Figure 1 shows the structure of a SAVE policy, consisting of rules[8]: a rule is defined by its deontic type (permission or prohibition), and by a set of attributes with their values. The currently supported attributes are: *action*, *data*, *purpose*, *legalBasis*, *controller*, *processor*, *recipient* and *dataSubject*. The values are assigned from the respective SAVE taxonomy – partially ordered set (*poset* [10]) of concepts. SAVE allows nested rules (the rule and its exception), however, our conflict resolution method effectively flattens the rules (see Sect. 3.3).

IMDBPolicy a Policy ; permission Permission1 ; prohibition Prohibition8 .

Permission1 a Permission ;
  action Collect, Use ;
  data Name, Age, Gender ;
  purpose CustomerCare, PersonalisedAdvertising ;
  controller IMDB ;
  dataSubject IMDBUser .

Prohibition8 a Prohibition ;
  action Use ;
  data Identifying ;
  purpose PersonalisedAdvertising ;
  controller IMDB ;
  dataSubject IMDBUser .

Fig. 2. IMDB SAVE policy excerpt (prefixes omitted due to space limitations)

To illustrate an example of a SAVE policy, we take two rules from the policy[9] in [12], extracted from the IMDB Privacy Notice[10]. The policy on Fig. 2 consists of `Permission1` and `Prohibition8` (edited for this example). The permission states that *IMDB* (controller), may *Collect* and *Use IMDBUser*'s *Name*, *Gender* and *Age*, for *CusomerCare* and *PersonalisedAdvertising* purposes. `Prohibition8` forbids the *Use* of data subject's *Identifying* data for

---

[8] The full SAVE model: http://rune.research.euranova.eu#resulting-model.
[9] http://rune.research.euranova.eu/demo/Policy.html.
[10] Archived version of the IMDB policy can be found here.

PersonalisedAdvertising. An attribute can be assigned a subset of concepts from the respective taxonomy. Such structure is compact and close to the rule description in the text: one sentence or paragraph can combine multiple actions, data types, purposes, etc., meaning all of them are allowed/prohibited. Moreover, in a rule attributes may be missing, i.e., not mentioned in the text. In such cases, the root of the corresponding taxonomy (*greatest* element of its poset) is assumed. The structure of a *Request* is identical to *Rule*, hence, our model also allows requests with multiple values for an attribute, i.e., all of them are requested.

3.2   Formalization

In this section, we formalize our compliance checking method. By providing clear definitions of terms, operators and algorithms we aim to ensure implementation-independent coherence of our model.

Any SAVE concept that can be assigned as a value of an attribute is called a Data Processing Term (DPT). There are two kinds of DPTs:

- Hierarchical DPTs belong to the following posets: Processing Actions (A), Purposes (P), Personal Data Categories (D), Legal Bases (B). These terms are pre-defined by the corresponding taxonomies in SAVE (see footnote 8).
- Constant DPTs are the following: Controllers (C), Processors (R), Third Parties (T), Data Subjects (S). Their values depend on the concrete policy.

The set of all DPTs of every attribute type is denoted by $\Omega = \{A \cup P \cup D \cup B \cup C \cup R \cup T \cup S\} = \{\bigcup \Omega_i | \ i \in \{1, \ldots, 8\}\}$. Hierarchical DPT sets are partially ordered (posets), according to `subClassOf` relationship, and thus support comparison operators $\{\neq, =, <, >, \leq, \geq\}$. For example, if we consider a part of the D taxonomy from Fig. 1, we can extract many predicates: *Name* $\leq$ *Identifying*, *PhysicalCharacteristics* $>$ *Age*, etc. Constant DPTs are seen as hierarchies of two levels: the root covering the DPT type (*greatest* element of the poset) and the *leaves* – individual values, defined by the policy. Thus, the same comparison operators are applicable. For instance, *IMDB* $\in C$ in our example policy is defined as an instance of *DataController*, i.e., *IMDB* $<$ *DataController*. From here on, in our definitions we do not distinguish between the two kinds. We do, however, distinguish between attribute types: the DPT operators are only defined for the subsets of the same poset, i.e. $X_1, X_2 \subseteq \Omega_i \mid i \in \{1, \ldots, 8\}$. Further on, the notation Ω_i indicates elements or subsets of the same type.

The union(+) operator is defined between DPTs and sets of DPTs, as a rule can contain one or more DPT as the attribute value.

$+ (X_1, X_2)$ read the union of X_1 and X_2 – commutative, associative, idempotent

$$\forall x_1, x_2 \in \Omega_i \ (x_1 + x_2 = x_1) \leftrightarrow (x_2 \leq x_1) \tag{1}$$

The $(+)$ operator follows the standard properties of set union. In addition, (1) states that the union of two comparable elements is equal to the bigger element of the pair, thus *merging* the two elements. In the definitions that follow, we take advantage of this property: all operations are defined for sets of DPTs in their *compact* form, i.e., there are no two elements in the set that can be merged.

The $leaf(x)$ operator tells us if the DPT (in a set of one) represents the last level in the hierarchy of the poset, i.e., one of its *minimal* elements:

$$\forall X_1 \subseteq \Omega_i \; leaf(X_1) \to \forall X_2 \subseteq \Omega_i \; (|X_1| = 1 \land |X_2| = 1 \; \land (X_1 + X_2 = X_1) \leftrightarrow (X_2 = X_1)) \quad (2)$$

The part-of ($\sqsubseteq$) operator between DPT sets follows the subsumption relation:

$\sqsubseteq (X_1, X_2)$ read X_1 is part-of X_2 − reflexive, transitive and antisymmetric

$$\forall x_1, x_2 \in \Omega_i \; (x_1 \sqsubseteq x_2 \leftrightarrow x_1 \leq x_2) \tag{3.1}$$

$$\forall X, Y \subseteq \Omega_i \; (X \sqsubseteq Y \leftrightarrow \forall x \in X \; \exists y \in Y (x \leq y)) \tag{3.2}$$

$$\forall X_1 \subseteq \Omega_i (leaf(X_1) \leftrightarrow \forall X_2 \subseteq \Omega_i (X_2 \sqsubseteq X_1 \to X_2 = X_1)) \tag{3.3}$$

Let us call a Data Processing Sentence (DPS) a tuple (a, p, d, b, c, r, t, s) where each element is a subset of DPTs of the corresponding type that forms the value of the respective attribute: $a \subseteq A$, $p \subseteq P$, $d \subseteq D$, $b \subseteq B$, $c \subseteq C$, $r \subseteq R$, $t \subseteq T$, $s \subseteq S$. The set of all possible DPS is denoted by Θ. $\varepsilon(Y, x)$ expresses the relation between DPTs and a DPS and is defined as the maximal subset $Y \subseteq \Omega_i$, belonging to the DPS x, i.e., the full value of an attribute. $simple(x)$ defines if a DPS x contains at most one DPT of each type − at most one *action*, *data*, etc. And finally, $at(x)$ defines an *atomic* DPS x, containing at most one DPT of each type that is also a *leaf*.

Similar to DPTs, a union operator can be defined for DPSs. To merge two DPSs, their attribute values must be equal except for at most one attribute:

$+ (x_1, x_2)$ read the union of x_1 and x_2 − idempotent, commutative

$x_1, x_2, x_3 \in \Theta \quad Y_1, Y_2 \subseteq \Omega_i \quad Z_1, Z_2 \subseteq \Omega_j \quad V_1, V_2 \subseteq \Omega_k \quad j \neq k$

$$\forall x_1, x_2 \; \exists \; x_3 \; (x_1 + x_2 = x_2 + x_1 = x_3) \leftrightarrow$$
$$\forall Y_1, Y_2 (Y_1 \; \varepsilon \; x_1 \land Y_2 \; \varepsilon \; x_2 \to Y_1 + Y_2 \; \varepsilon \; x_3) \land \neg \exists Z_1, Z_2, V_1, V_2 \tag{4.1}$$
$$(Z_1 \; \varepsilon \; x_1 \land V_1 \; \varepsilon \; x_1 \land Z_2 \; \varepsilon \; x_2 \land V_2 \; \varepsilon \; x_2 \; \land Z_1 \neq Z_2 \land V_1 \neq V_2)$$

$$\forall x_1, x_2 (x_1 + x_2 = x_1 \leftrightarrow x_1 + x_2 = x_2 \leftrightarrow x_1 = x_2) \tag{4.2}$$

Union of DPSs, unlike union of DPTs, is non-associative. To demonstrate that, let us take four DPSs, each consisting of three attributes, for simplicity − *action* (a), *data* (d) and *purpose* (p) − and evaluate some expressions:

$x_1(a : Store, d : Age, p : Security)$ $x_3(a : \{Store, Use\}, d : Name, p : Security)$

$x_2(a : Store, d : UID, p : Security)$ $x_4(a : Use, d : \{Age, UID\}, p : Security)$

$x_1 + x_2 = x_2 + x_1 = (a : Store, d : \{Age, UID\}, p : Security)$

$x_1 + x_3$: not valid − action and data are not equal between x_1 and x_3

$(x_1 + x_2) + x_4 = (a : \{Store, Use\}, d : \{Age, UID\}, p : Security)$

$x_1 + (x_2 + x_4)$: not valid − action and data are not equal for x_2 and x_4

Finally, the part-of operator is also defined between two DPSs:

$\sqsubseteq (x_1, x_2)$ read x_1 is part-of x_2 – reflexive, transitive and antisymmetric

$$\forall x_1, x_2 \in \Theta(x_1 \sqsubseteq x_2 \leftrightarrow \forall i \in \{1, \dots, 8\} \; \forall Y_1 Y_2 \in \Omega_i (Y_1 \; \varepsilon \; x_1 \wedge Y_2 \; \varepsilon \; x_2 \rightarrow Y_1 \sqsubseteq Y_2)) \qquad (5)$$

DPS covers the structure of SAVE permissions, prohibitions and requests. $M \subseteq \Theta$ denotes the set of permissions in a given policy, $H \subseteq \Theta$ – the set of prohibitions, and $Q \subseteq \Theta$ – the set of possible requests. To be compliant, a request q has to conform to at least one permission in M and to not fall under any prohibition in H:

$$check(q, M, H) \;_{def} = \forall x \in Q(at(x) \wedge x \sqsubseteq q \rightarrow \exists m \in M(x \sqsubseteq m) \wedge \neg \exists h \in H(x \sqsubseteq h)) \qquad (6)$$

Request Example 1. Let us return to our running example from Fig. 2. For simplicity, we will use *action*, *data* and *purpose* attributes to encode the policy $\{M = m_1, H = h_8\}$, and introduce a request q_1:

$q_1(a : \{Collect, Analyse\}, d : Gender, p : PersonalisedAdvertising)$
$m_1(a : \{Collect, Use\}, d : \{Name, Age, Gender\}, p : \{CustomerCare, PersonalisedAdvertising\})$
$h_8(a : Use, d : Identifying, p : PersonalisedAdvertising)$

For q_1 to be permitted, it should be checked against the policy following (6). The first step is to **normalize** the request, i.e., break it down into *atomic subrequests* q_{1i}, where $at(q_{1i}) \wedge q_{1i} \sqsubseteq q_1$, following the SAVE hierarchies. Then, the *check* function is applied. As a result, q_1 is compliant with the policy:

$q_1(a : \{Collect, Analyse\}, d : Gender, p : PersonalisedAdvertising) =$
$\{q_{11}(a : Collect, d : Gender, p : PersonalisedAdvertising),$
$q_{12}(a : Analyse, d : Gender, p : PersonalisedAdvertising)\}$
$check(q_1, M, H) : q_{11} \sqsubseteq m_1 \wedge q_{12} \sqsubseteq m_1 \quad (Analyse < Use)$

3.3   Conflict Detection and Resolution

A conflict occurs when a permission and a prohibition "intersect", i.e., there is at least one atomic DPS part-of one rule that is also part-of the other:

$$\forall m \in M, \forall h \in H \; conflict(m, h)_{def} = \exists x \in \Theta(at(x) \wedge x \sqsubseteq m \wedge x \sqsubseteq h) \qquad (7)$$

Request Example 2. Let us run the *check* for the new q_2 asking for *Name*:

$q_2(a : \{Collect, Analyse\}, d : Name, p : PersonalisedAdvertising) =$
$\{q_{21}(a : Collect, d : Name, p : PersonalisedAdvertising),$
$q_{22}(a : Analyse, d : Name, p : PersonalisedAdvertising)\}$
$check(q_2, M, H) : q_{21} \sqsubseteq m_1 \wedge q_{22} \sqsubseteq m_1 \wedge q_{22} \sqsubseteq h_8 \quad (Analyse < Use \wedge Name < Identifying)$

As seen from the check, q_2 is not compliant. We also see that m_1 and h_8 contain a common DPS q_{22} and thus are in a conflict. In a SAVE policy conflicts can occur between separate rules (due to ambiguity of terms in the text), or as a result of nesting rules. In both cases, we treat it as a conflict. We use strict partial order operators $\{<, >\}$ to state which rule is stronger. With nested rules we can assume that the exception > main rule, but in other situations we expect a legal expert (a Data Protection Officer) to make final decisions.

Algorithm 1 defines our conflict detection and resolution method. First, we normalize rules of one type, either permissions or prohibitions. The *normalize* function breaks down a rule's attribute values into leaves and creates atomic DPSs by generating their combinations. Next, for each permission/prohibition pair we check if there is an atomic DPS that is part-of both rules (*conflict* (7)). If it is the case, the other conflicting rule is normalized. The resolution process, as mentioned earlier, is based on a strict partial order over the rules. Following this order, the weaker DPSs are identified and removed from the normalized rules (lines 5−10, where *conflict* applied to atomic DPSs actually checks for their equality). Finally, the DPSs are transformed back into their compact form by applying union (+) until there is no merge possible (*denormalize*, lines 11 − 12). The resulting conflict-free policy is then used in our compliance checking procedure, able to indicate the exact parts of the request that are permitted, explicitly prohibited, and implicitly prohibited (not explicitly permitted).

Algorithm 1: Conflict detection/resolution

Input : Policy $\{M, H\}$; $conflict(m, h)$ defined; partial order $\{<, >\}$ defined.
Output: Final conflict-free policy $\{M, H\}$.

```
1  M_norm = normalize(M) ;                                    ▷ normalize only M (or only H)
2  forall the m_norm ∈ M_norm, h ∈ H do
3  │  if conflict(m_norm, h) then
4  │  │  h_norm = normalize(h) ;                              ▷ normalize the conflicting DPS
5  │  │  forall the m_at ∈ m_norm, h_at ∈ h_norm do
6  │  │  │  if conflict(m_at, h_at) then
7  │  │  │  │  if m_at > h_at then h_norm = h_norm \ h_at;
8  │  │  │  │  else m_norm = m_norm \ m_at;
9  │  │  end
10 │  end
11 │  M = M \ m ∪ denormalize(m_norm);                        ▷ remove original DPS
12 │  H = H \ h ∪ denormalize(h_norm);                        ▷ and add conflict-free ones
13 │  end
14 end
15 return M, H
```

In Request Example 2 we established that q_{22} indicates *the presence* of a conflict between m_1 and h_8. Upon analyzing the rules, we see that the full conflict is expressed by the DPS $(a : Use, d : Name, p : PersonalisedAdvertising)$, comprising four atomic DPSs (after normalizing Use). If we assume that $h_8 > m_1$, then, following Algorithm 1, the conflict-free permission looks as follows:

$m_{11}(a : Collect, d : \{Name, Age, Gender\}, p : \{CustomerCare, PersonalisedAdvertising\})$
$m_{12}(a : Use, d : \{Age, Gender\}, p : \{CustomerCare, PersonalisedAdvertising\})$
$m_{13}(a : Use, d : Name, p : CustomerCare)$

3.4   Compliance Checking of a Request

The compliance checking procedure (Algorithm 2) follows the definition (6). It can detect partial compliance and provide a detailed compliance report. This improves explainability of our approach, which would not be possible without the normalization of requests. However, normalization of a DPS can cause combinatorial explosion in number of resulting atomic DPSs, making it a potential performance bottleneck. For example, the "worst case" request containing the roots of SAVE taxonomies is normalized into about 10^7 atomic DPSs – combinations of every leaf of each taxonomy. This problem can be handled with application-dependent solutions: for instance, we can impose restrictions on the structure of the policies and/or requests, as in [5], or find a way to check multiple subrequests at once. In our implementation, we adopt the latter suggestion.

Algorithm 2: Compliance checking

Input : Conflict-free policy $\{M, H\}$; Request q
Output: $answer \in \{"granted", "prohibited", "part\text{-}granted", "not\ granted"\}$;
          q_{prm} – permitted subrequests; q_{nprm} – non-permitted; q_{prh} – prohibited;
1 $q_{prm} = \emptyset; q_{nprm} = \emptyset; q_{prh} = \emptyset; q_{norm} = normalize(q)$;
2 **forall the** $q_i \in q_{norm}$ **do**
3   **forall the** $x \in M \cup H$;   ▷ each DPS in the policy
4   **do**
5   **if** $q_i \sqsubseteq x$;   ▷ subrequest is part-of the DPS
6   **then**
7   **if** $x \in M$ **then** $q_{prm} = q_{prm} \cup \{q_i\}$;
8   **else** $q_{prh} = q_{prh} \cup \{q_i\}$;
9   **end**
10   **end**
11   **if** *not* $(q_i \in q_{prm}$ *or* $q_i \in q_{prh})$ **then** $q_{nprm} = q_{nprm} \cup \{q_i\}$;
12 **end**
13 **if** $q_{nprm} = \emptyset$ *and* $q_{prh} = \emptyset$ **then return** "granted", $q_{prm}, q_{nprm}, q_{prh}$;
14 **else if** $q_{prm} = \emptyset$ *and* $q_{prh} \neq \emptyset$ **then return** "prohibited", $q_{prm}, q_{nprm}, q_{prh}$;
15 **else if** $q_{prm} \neq \emptyset$ **then return** "part-granted", $q_{prm}, q_{nprm}, q_{prh}$;
16 **else return** "not granted", $q_{prm}, q_{nprm}, q_{prh}$;

---

4 SHACL-Based Compliance Model

A compliance check can be seen as semantic *validation* of a request against defined rules – *constraints*, which motivated us to use SHACL-AF as the "engine" of our model. Notably, SHACL has recently been gaining interest in privacy and compliance research [8,18], but has not yet been used as the inference tool for policy-based compliance. Figure 3 shows our compliance checking system. The Preprocessing module is invoked upon policy creation and includes automated conflict detection, expert-assisted resolution, automated denormalization and generation of SHACL compliance rules. The combination of SAVE and SHACL gives us an *operational* model, where compliance is encoded in a structured and unambiguous way. The Compliance Checking module is invoked upon request and consists of request preprocessing and compliance checking components. The first step is necessary for handling various kinds of requests, created by a user, or generated by an application. These "raw" requests may mention metadata and data sources (tables, columns), and need to be transformed into SAVE requests. We leave out of the scope of this work the mapping of data sources to SAVE concepts and assume that such mapping (Business Catalog) is available. We also plan to use external access control tools to handle user/role privileges.

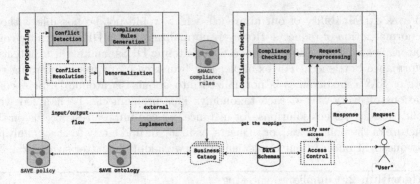

Fig. 3. SAVE/SHACL policy-based compliance checking model

4.1 SAVE-to-SHACL Translation

Coming back to our example in Fig. 2, we show the translation of `Permission1` into SHACL on Fig. 4, that can act as a template for any rule. The template was developed by mapping the semantics of our operators, in particular, part-of (3,5), to SHACL constraints, and Algorithm 2 to inference rules. Each SAVE attribute is converted into `sh:property` condition, and each DPT in it becomes either `sh:class` (hierarchical DPT) or `sh:hasValue` (constant DPT). By definition, `sh:class` (see footnote 1) checks if subject is an instance of the object class, following `rdf:type/rdfs:subClassOf*` property path, which corresponds to checking if the subject DPT is part-of (3) object DPT (`sh:hasValue` is a special case of (3) applied to constant DPTs, as they are checked by value). Multiple values are combined with `sh:or`. Each rule in the policy is encoded and added to the policy shapes graph. The graph assumes an input of the initial request and its atomic subrequests generated by normalization. The check is performed in two steps (controlled by `sh:order`): (i) each subrequest is checked against each rule: if it satisfies every `sh:condition` (part-of (5) returns *true*), new triples are inferred; (ii) the `answer` for the parent request is inferred in a separate SHACL rule, by counting how many subrequests were permitted/prohibited.

4.2 Implementation and Evaluation

In order to evaluate our approach, we implemented the first version of our model[11], using TopBraid SHACL API and Apache Jena[12]. This version works with valid SAVE requests, so the only preprocessing performed on a request is normalization. To address the combinatorial explosion problem (see Sect. 3), we developed two compliance checking procedures. The SHACL-Core procedure

---

[11] The source code: https://github.com/euranova/shacl-compliance. A light demo: https://rune-278710.ew.r.appspot.com/save/compliance.

[12] https://github.com/TopQuadrant/shacl; https://jena.apache.org/.

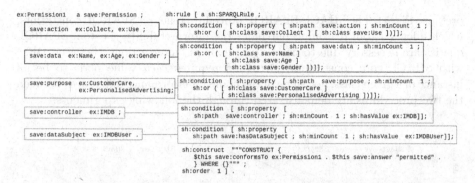

Fig. 4. Translation of IMDB `Permission1` into the SHACL rule. Prefixes: `save` – for SAVE terms, `sh` – for SHACL terms, `ex` – for policy-specific values.

translates each SAVE rule into a SHACL `SPARQLRule` using core constraints (following example on Fig. 4). It normalizes the request, creates the atomic subrequests, sends the subrequests and the parent request in a batch to SHACL engine and receives the result. Alternatively, the SHACL-SPARQL procedure does not "materialize" each subrequest. Instead, it combines all atomic subrequests into one using `RDFList` structures, and performs the check on all of them at once, by inferring "intersections" – common DPSs between the request and the rules – using custom SPARQL constraints (also based on `rdf:type/rdfs:subClassOf*` property path). Request Example 3 depicted on Fig. 5 shows the difference in expressing and validating normalized requests between the two procedures.

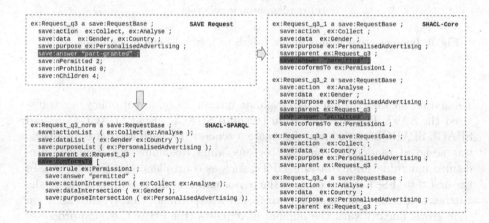

Fig. 5. Request normalization and answers for the two procedures

The two compliance checking procedures have their benefits and drawbacks. While both implementations use SPARQL to construct inferred triples, SHACL-Core expresses constraints declaratively, making them relatively easy to interpret (see Fig. 4). The SHACL-SPARQL procedure relies on SPARQL constraints, which allow custom reasoning but hider the interpretability. Custom SPARQL queries are necessary due to inability to express "intersections" between DPSs with SHACL core constraints (sh:class requires *each* value node to be an instance of a given class, not *some* of the nodes). Performance differences between the two procedures are demonstrated through the following experiments.

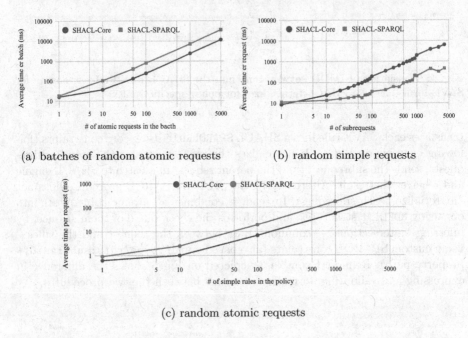

(a) batches of random atomic requests   (b) random simple requests

(c) random atomic requests

Fig. 6. Inference time evaluation on IMDB policy (a, b) and random policies (c)

Evaluation on IMDB Policy. To evaluate our model on a real policy, we translated the SAVE IMDB policy from [12] into SHACL, using SHACL-Core and SHACL-SPARQL procedures. To create a request, for each attribute, one DPT was assigned randomly from the corresponding taxonomy (or from the predefined individuals, for constant DPTs, such as controllers, processors, etc.). In the first test (Fig. 6a), we compare the performance of the two procedures on the batches of atomic requests. It is clear from the experiment that (i) the execution time grows linearly with the number of requests (the SHACL engine processes shapes consecutively); and (ii) the SHACL-SPARQL procedure performs significantly worse than the SHACL-Core on atomic requests. Due to heavy usage of custom SPARQL constraints in the SHACL-SPARQL method, the inference on a single request is slow, compared to core constraints. And since all requests in the batch are separate (and not subrequests of one request), we cannot combine them and check simultaneously, thus we lose the advantage of the SHACL-

SPARQL version. In a production system, SHACL-Core procedure is suitable for fine-grained requests, using lower levels of SAVE taxonomies.

On the other hand, Fig. 6b shows the benefits of the SHACL-SPARQL procedure. In this test a batch of simple, not necessarily atomic, requests, was generated and the performance of both implementations was measured depending on the number of subrequests. As expected, with few subrequests (less than 10), SHACL-Core performs better. However, very soon the amount of subrequests processed consecutively makes it slower than the SHACL-SPARQL alternative. For comparison, the "worst case" request (about 10^7 subrequests) is processed by the SHACL-SPARQL procedure in about 5 min, while SHACL-Core would take roughly 16 h (estimated, with the average subquery execution time of 4ms). The SHACL-SPARQL procedure does not check each subrequest separately, thus, its performance is less affected by the number of subrequests than by the number of SPARQL queries triggered by the SHACL engine, which, in its turn, depends on whether the request "intersects" with the policy rules or not. This explains the uneven performance of SHACL-SPARQL: when the request does not "intersect" with any rule, the response is obtained faster.

Evaluation on Random Policies. The IMDB policy used in the previous experiments contains 23 compact rules, or 222 *simple* rules. To evaluate our system on policies of different sizes, we randomly generated simple rules (similarly to requests), combined them into policies, and ran batches of 100 random atomic requests against them. Figure 6c shows that, due to SHACL engine validating the shapes consecutively, the execution time increases with the size of the policy, albeit slower than with the number of requests. It can serve as evidence in favor of using compact rule representation to potentially speed up the inference. To test this hypothesis, we plan additional experiments evaluating simple vs. compact policy representations.

5   Conclusion and Future Work

In this paper, we introduced an automated compliance checking model based on the SAVE conceptual model for privacy policies. We formalized the model in an application-independent manner and provided implementation with SHACL-AF. To the best of our knowledge, it is the first application of SHACL-AF inference rules for automating compliance based on policies. Encoding the compliance rules declaratively provides us with a self-contained interoperable model, where conceptual rules are enriched with compliance logic in SHACL. Our compliance model keeps the policies compact and close to their textual representation, and our conflict resolution method provides conflict-free co-existence of permissions and prohibitions. Finally, the proposed SHACL-SPARQL procedure aims to mitigate the combinatorial explosion of subrequests introduced by the model.

One of the goals of our model is facilitating the adoption of SAVE in the Semantic Web community. Currently, we are building upon the first version to continue implementation of components, such as conflict resolution, and evaluation of the model, as well as testing various optimization techniques, in particular, optimizations of SPARQL constraints. The next steps include adding obligations and technical/organisational measures from SAVE, as well as incorporating selected model constraints from the DPMF [19] into our model, in order to enrich its validation capabilities. Additionally, we consider employing ODIN [16] for linking data sources to SAVE concepts, as well as integration with metadata and access control tools. And finally, within the scope of the RUNE project, work on the SAVE model continues, specifically, the development of methods of automated rule extraction from written policies and data processing agreements.

References

1. Agarwal, S., Steyskal, S., Antunovic, F., Kirrane, S.: Legislative compliance assessment: framework, model and GDPR instantiation. In: Medina, M., Mitrakas, A., Rannenberg, K., Schweighofer, E., Tsouroulas, N. (eds.) APF 2018. LNCS, vol. 11079, pp. 131–149. Springer, Cham (2018). https://doi.org/10.1007/978-3-030-02547-2_8
2. Athan, T., Governatori, G., Palmirani, M., Paschke, A., Wyner, A.: LegalRuleML: design principles and foundations. In: Faber, W., Paschke, A. (eds.) Reasoning Web 2015. LNCS, vol. 9203, pp. 151–188. Springer, Cham (2015). https://doi.org/10.1007/978-3-319-21768-0_6
3. Bartolini, C., Calabró, A., Marchetti, E.: Enhancing business process modelling with data protection compliance: an ontology-based proposal. In: ICISSP, pp. 421–428 (2019). https://doi.org/10.5220/0007392304210428
4. Bartolini, C., Lenzini, G., Santos, C.: An agile approach to validate a formal representation of the GDPR. In: Kojima, K., Sakamoto, M., Mineshima, K., Satoh, K. (eds.) JSAI-isAI 2018. LNCS (LNAI), vol. 11717, pp. 160–176. Springer, Cham (2019). https://doi.org/10.1007/978-3-030-31605-1_13
5. Bonatti, P.A., Ioffredo, L., Petrova, I.M., Sauro, L., Siahaan, I.R.: Real-time reasoning in OWL2 for GDPR compliance. Artif. Intell. 103389 (2020). https://doi.org/10.1016/j.artint.2020.103389
6. Bonatti, P.A., Petrova, I.M., Sauro, L.: A richer policy language for GDPR compliance. In: Simkus, M., Weddell, G.E. (eds.) Proceedings of the 32nd International Workshop on Description Logics, Oslo, Norway, 18–21 June 2019. CEUR Workshop Proceedings, vol. 2373. CEUR-WS.org (2019). http://ceur-ws.org/Vol-2373/paper-5.pdf
7. De Vos, M., Kirrane, S., Padget, J., Satoh, K.: ODRL policy modelling and compliance checking. In: Fodor, P., Montali, M., Calvanese, D., Roman, D. (eds.) RuleML+RR 2019. LNCS, vol. 11784, pp. 36–51. Springer, Cham (2019). https://doi.org/10.1007/978-3-030-31095-0_3
8. Di Ciccio, C., Ekaputra, F.J., Cecconi, A., Ekelhart, A., Kiesling, E.: Finding non-compliances with declarative process constraints through semantic technologies. In: Information Systems Engineering in Responsible Information Systems, pp. 60–74 (2019). https://doi.org/10.1007/978-3-030-21297-1_6
9. Hamdani, R.E., Mustapha, M., Amariles, D.R., Troussel, A., Meeùs, S., Krasnashchok, K.: A combined rule-based and machine learning approach for automated GDPR compliance checking. In: Proceedings of the Eighteenth International Conference on Artificial Intelligence and Law, pp. 40–49. ICAIL 2021, Association

for Computing Machinery, New York, NY, USA (2021). https://doi.org/10.1145/3462757.3466081

10. Joslyn, C.: Poset ontologies and concept lattices as semantic hierarchies. In: Wolff, K.E., Pfeiffer, H.D., Delugach, H.S. (eds.) ICCS-ConceptStruct 2004. LNCS (LNAI), vol. 3127, pp. 287–302. Springer, Heidelberg (2004). https://doi.org/10.1007/978-3-540-27769-9_19

11. Kirrane, S., et al.: A scalable consent, transparency and compliance architecture. In: Gangemi, A. (ed.) ESWC 2018. LNCS, vol. 11155, pp. 131–136. Springer, Cham (2018). https://doi.org/10.1007/978-3-319-98192-5_25

12. Krasnashchok, K., Mustapha, M., Al Bassit, A., Skhiri, S.: Towards privacy policy conceptual modeling. In: Dobbie, G., Frank, U., Kappel, G., Liddle, S.W., Mayr, H.C. (eds.) ER 2020. LNCS, vol. 12400, pp. 429–438. Springer, Cham (2020). https://doi.org/10.1007/978-3-030-62522-1_32

13. Lam, H.P., Hashmi, M.: Enabling reasoning with LegalRuleML. Theory Pract. Log. Program. **19**(1), 1–26 (2019). https://doi.org/10.1017/S1471068418000339

14. Lehmann, J., et al.: Distributed semantic analytics using the SANSA stack. In: d'Amato, C. (ed.) ISWC 2017. LNCS, vol. 10588, pp. 147–155. Springer, Cham (2017). https://doi.org/10.1007/978-3-319-68204-4_15

15. Lioudakis, G.V., et al.: Facilitating GDPR compliance: the H2020 BPR4GDPR approach. In: Pappas, I.O., Mikalef, P., Dwivedi, Y.K., Jaccheri, L., Krogstie, J., Mäntymäki, M. (eds.) I3E 2019. IAICT, vol. 573, pp. 72–78. Springer, Cham (2020). https://doi.org/10.1007/978-3-030-39634-3_7

16. Nadal, S., Rabbani, K., Romero, O., Tadesse, S.: ODIN: a dataspace management system. In: Suárez-Figueroa, M.C., Cheng, G., Gentile, A.L., Guéret, C., Keet, C.M., Bernstein, A. (eds.) Proceedings of the ISWC 2019 Satellite Tracks (Posters & Demonstrations, Industry, and Outrageous Ideas) co-located with 18th International Semantic Web Conference (ISWC 2019), Auckland, New Zealand, 26–30 October 2019. CEUR Workshop Proceedings, vol. 2456, pp. 185–188. CEUR-WS.org (2019). http://ceur-ws.org/Vol-2456/paper48.pdf

17. Palmirani, M., Martoni, M., Rossi, A., Bartolini, C., Robaldo, L.: Pronto: Privacy ontology for legal reasoning. In: Ko, A., Francesconi, E. (eds.) Electronic Government and the Information Systems Perspective - 7th International Conference, EGOVIS 2018, Regensburg, Germany, September 3–5, 2018, Proceedings. Lecture Notes in Computer Science, vol. 11032, pp. 139–152. Springer (2018). https://doi.org/10.1007/978-3-319-98349-3_11

18. Robaldo, L.: Towards compliance checking in reified I/O logic via SHACL. In: Proceedings of the Eighteenth International Conference on Artificial Intelligence and Law, pp. 215–219. ICAIL 2021, Association for Computing Machinery, New York, NY, USA (2021). https://doi.org/10.1145/3462757.3466065

19. Sion, L., Dewitte, P., Van Landuyt, D., Wuyts, K., Valcke, P., Joosen, W.: DPMF: a modeling framework for data protection by design. Enterp. Modell. Inf. Syst. Archit. (EMISAJ) **15**, 10–1 (2020). https://doi.org/10.18417/emisa.15.10

20. Westphal, P., Fernández, J.D., Kirrane, S., Lehmann, J.: SPIRIT: a semantic transparency and compliance stack. In: Khalili, A., Koutraki, M. (eds.) Proceedings of the Posters and Demos Track of the 14th International Conference on Semantic Systems co-located with the 14th International Conference on Semantic Systems (SEMANTiCS 2018), Vienna, Austria, 10–13 September 2018. CEUR Workshop Proceedings, vol. 2198. CEUR-WS.org (2018). http://ceur-ws.org/Vol-2198/paper_119.pdf

Correctness of Automatically Generated Choreography Specifications

Nurulhuda A. Manaf(✉)(iD), Nor Najihah Zainal Abidin(✉)(iD),
and Nur Amalina Jamaludin(✉)

National Defence University of Malaysia (NDUM), 53000 Kuala Lumpur, Malaysia
{nurulhuda,amalinajamaludin}@upnm.edu.my, 3201334@alfateh.upnm.edu.my

Abstract. The service choreography approach has been proposed for the declarative specification of multi-party conversations between participant services, in service-oriented applications and web transactions. Constraint solvers such as Alloy Analyzer can be used for the automated generation and verification of declarative choreography specifications. This presumes a mapping between the declarative specification of business rules in *Semantics of Business Vocabulary and Rules* (SBVR), an OMG standard for specifying business models in structured English, and the *Alloy Analyzer* which is a SAT based constraint solver. This paper is concerned with the correctness of such mapping between the generated instance (choreography) in Alloy and the global graph obtained as a direct visual representation of the SBVR model specification.

Keywords: Declarative specification · Service choreography · SBVR · Constraints · Model transformation · Mapping correctness

1 Introduction

The service choreography approach [37] coordinates the collaboration of distributed systems across autonomous participant services [33]. Choreography focuses mainly on prescribing the ordering of the message exchange between services, according to agreed global constraints. It is key to realising value added service chains in ecosystem oriented architectures [19].

The OMG standard *Semantics of Business Vocabulary and Rules* (SBVR) [30] intends to express complex business requirements declaratively. Recent works [1,5,15,17] advocate SBVR for specifying business models. They tend to capitalise on the fact SBVR specifies rules in natural language, which the end-user to validate the specification directly, and at the same time describes them in formal logic, which is beneficial for verification.

In previous work, we have applied SBVR and its supplement, the *Date-Time Vocabulary* (DTV) [32], for specifying service choreographies [1,17]. An

This research is funded by Malaysian Ministry of Higher Education under the Fundamental Research Grant Scheme (FRGS) /1/2018/ICT01/UPNM/03/1.

© Springer Nature Switzerland AG 2021
S. Moschoyiannis et al. (Eds.): RuleML+RR 2021, LNCS 12851, pp. 18–32, 2021.
https://doi.org/10.1007/978-3-030-91167-6_2

application to commuter journeys was given in [14]. Further, the *SBVR2Alloy* compilation tool [16] has been built that can automatically generate the service choreography, corresponding to the input SBVR model. An Alloy model [1] describes a set of constraints in terms of structure. It generates an analysis automatically and produces an instance structure of model that satisfies the ordering of constraints in a service choreography.

In addition to verifying conformance to message ordering constraints, the *Alloy Analyzer* constraint solver [13] can be used to perform realisability checks and assert static constraints on the generated choreography.

In this paper, the focus is on the correctness of the mapping between the input SBVR model capturing the business rules and the Alloy model [13] used to generate the corresponding choreography, and verify for realisability.

The main contribution of this paper is a method for checking the correctness of the mapping between (a) the model transformation from SBVR into Alloy [16], and (b) the generated global view [4,9,36] which is a visual representation translating from the corresponding SBVR model. Both models describe the global behaviours and the complex interactions in the choreography specification.

This paper is laid out as follows. Section 2 introduces basic handling of constraints in SBVR as well as the mapping of the SBVR model onto the Alloy model. Section 3 describes the semantics of the global view represented in the visual representation, and shows how the mechanism applies for transforming the SBVR model into the global view, and the correctness of the conformance mapping. Section 4 discusses related work and Sect. 5 contains some conclusions and future work.

2   Mapping an SBVR Model onto an Alloy Model

In this section, a brief introduction to the OMG standard SBVR is provided and the development of an SBVR model is outlined. We then describe how the SBVR model is mapped onto the Alloy Model, using *Alloy Analyzer*.

2.1   An OMG Standard SBVR

The OMG standard SBVR [30] provides a means to express business concepts and rules in natural language for different types of business activities. SBVR rules are expressed in Structured English (SBVR - SE) [30] which is formed by means of semantic formulations. The SBVR rules describe the meaning of business rules by composing the logical formulation which is in the form of the combination of atomic formulation (e.g., Fact Types), modality (i.e., obligation, prohibition, etc.), logical operation (i.e., OR, XOR, AND, etc.), and the quantification (e.g., exactly one, at least one, etc.). This combination produces a constructive rule, e.g., *It is obligatory that each rental car is owned by at least one branch.* The deontic modality, i.e., 'obligatory' on the constraint defined by the rule. The quantification, 'each' and 'at least one' effect restriction of the rental car belonging. Furthermore, 'is owned by' is the designation for the Fact Type which makes an assertion on the corresponding Terms (rental car and branch).

2.2   SBVR Model for Service Choreography

The SBVR model prescribes a set of global constraints from informal requirements, namely an agreed contract of common rules that govern the allowed interactions and the ordering of services interaction. The structure of the rules is based on the semantic formulations that are used in the SBVR standard [30] and supplemented by the DTV [32].

Figure 1 represents the overall picture of how an SBVR model is built for service choreography. A set of terms and a set of fact types in SBVR is essential for constructing the rules. Then two main components, participants and events, play an important role in modelling choreography. Each designated participant involved in the multi-party conversation (i.e. participant), each designated event characterises the occurrence of event (messages exchange) performed by the participant(s) (i.e. event), and static constraints specify the domain specific constraints for each participant and event, are defined as Term, e.g. **Term: participant 1**, **Term:** participant 2, **Term:** event 1, **Term:** static 1 as shown in the figure.

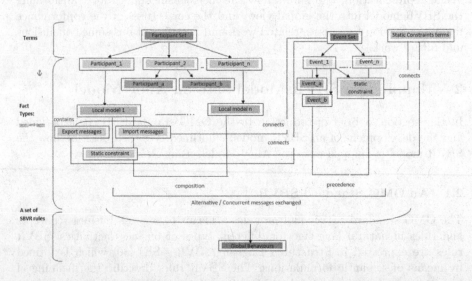

Fig. 1. Coordinating SBVR model for service choreography

The Fact Types (FT) of the SBVR model for specifying the participant set (e.g. **FT:** participant2 includes participant) and the event set (e.g. **FT:** event1 includes event) applied Set Definition in SBVR standard. On the other hand, "term verb term" has been used to specify the static constraints and the messages exchange including the export and the import messages. It is important to represent the local behaviour of each participant.

These SBVR rules capture the specification of the ordering of services interaction where the time notion of precedence, 'immediately precedes', by DTV [32], is advocated. Differently, the SBVR rules for specifying the complex interactions: concurrent and alternatives interactions apply the logical operators (AND, XOR, and OR) in the SBVR standard. The interested reader might refer [1,16] for further explanation.

2.3   Mapping the SBVR Model into the Alloy Model

Alloy analyzer is based on a logic which provides the structures representing relations. Alloy model consists of a module containing a number of signatures and abstract signatures. Signatures represent terms, while abstract signatures describe the participant set and the event set in the SBVR model. Table 1 shows participant1 is a member of the participant. Furthermore, Rule 1 illustrates a nesting of event1. Each signature and abstract signature introduce fields which are captured by relations. These fields denote *verb* interconnecting with Terms in each FT. It is used to specify the import and the export messages by/from the participant(s) (see Table 1).

The multiplicities in Alloy are applied to illustrating the accurate meaning of the complex interactions as well as the ordering of messages exchanged in the choreography. The combination of signature, multiplicities, and field are the basis of the development of SBVR rule in Alloy. In addition, facts and predicates in Alloy are deployed to constrain a certain case.

Rule 1 represents the general form of rule capturing the alternative interaction concerns on the sending (receiving) of the choices of events which is emphasised by specifying the logical operation **or ... but not all**. In Alloy, fact is exploited to ensure the explicit choices is defined (only one of the events will be true). Lone multiplicity (it can be true or false) is declared for each subsignature of event 1. Fact is applied for translating Rule 2 too. Rule 2 constrains at least one of the events is selected by the participant1. Rule specifies the alternative interaction encapsulates inclusive choices (OR) of the events. Hence, lone multiplicities instead of one multiplicity associated on event 1 and event 2 are mapped from each corresponding verbs 1 and verbs 2 that connect with the signature participant1.

Rules 3–4 specify the allowed orderings of the messages exchange when the multi-party conversation takes place. Rule 3 demonstrates there is no occurrence of an event after event 1 and before event 2. A notion of *immediately precedes* definition is advocated from DTV [32]. Rule is translated into Alloy by defining a signature of the initial event which is mapped to the field 'immediatelyprecedes' associating with the event occurs immediate after.

Table 1. Mapping of SBVR2Alloy model

SBVR model	Alloy model
Terms	**signature**
Term:participant1;	sig participant1{};
Term:event1;	sig event1{};
Term:static1;	sig static1{};
Term:T1;	sig T1{};
FT : participant and event set	**abstract signature**
Fact Type: participant *includes* participant1;	abstract sig participant{}
	one sig participant1 extends participant{}
Fact Type: event *includes* event1;	abstract sig event{}
	one sig event1 extends event{}
FT : messages exchange and static constraint	**field (relation)**
Fact Type: participant1 *verbs* event1	one sig participant1 extends participant{verbs1: one event1,
Fact Type: participant1 *verbs1* static1	verbs: one static1}
Rules : complex interaction	**field (relation), fact, and multiplicities**
Rule 1: It is obligatory that the participant1 *verbs*	one sig participant1 extends participant{verbs: one event1}
exactly one event1 that *includes* exactly one eventa	abstract sig event1 extends event {at: one t1_event1}
or exactly one eventb **but not both**	{(event1 = eventa and no eventb)
at exactly one T	or (event1 = eventb and no eventa)}
	lone sig eventa extends event1{}
	lone sig eventb extends {}
Rule 2: It is obligatory that the participant1 *verbs*	one sig participant1 extends participant{verbs1: lone event1,
exactly one event1 **or** exactly one event2,	verbs2: lone event2}
at exactly one T	{ #verbs1 = 1 or #verbs2 = 1}
	lone sig event1 extends event {at: one t1_event1}
	lone sig event2 extends event {at: one t1_event2}
Rules : the ordering of messages exchange (events)	**field (relation), fact, and multiplicities**
Rule 4: : It is obligatory that exactly one event1 *immediately precedes* exactly one event2	one sig event1 extends event {immediatelyprecedes: one event2
Rule 6: It is obligatory that exactly one T1 *immediately precedes* exactly one T2	one sig T1 extends Time {immediatelyprecedes: one T2}

In modelling services interaction, there is the case when no indication to inform which interaction is performed initially as in the FTs specification: participant1 sends event1; participant2 receives event1. As the solution, the principal concept in the DTV, a notion of time understood as in the construct occurrence at time interval is applied. Hence the following time declarations as well as Rule 4 are used. 1. participant1 sends event1 at T1; 2. participant2 receives event1 at T2. The same mechanism for translating Rule 4 and Rule 5 is applied for transforming Rule 6 into Alloy.

3   Correctness of SBVR2Alloy Model

In this section, we outline the main aspects for ensuring the correctness of the mapping, which draws upon the semantics of global view.

3.1   Global View of Choreography

The semantics of global view of choreography [36], which is given as a visual representation (graph), is proposed for checking the correctness of the mapping between the SBVR model and Alloy model, built in Alloy Analyzer. Our interest in this approach is on its visual representation and its compatibility with our choreography model, characterising the behaviour from the specifications to capture the complex interactions in the business model.

The coordination of services interaction between participants in global view is modelled with representing the interactions between the participant 1 and the participant 2 who is sending and receiving message, m, respectively. This interaction denoted by $P1 \rightarrow P2 : m$.

A *global choreography (g-choreography)* denoted by G is derived by the semantics: i. $G ::= 0$ (no interaction); ii. $p_1 \rightarrow p_2 : m$ (a simple interaction between two participants p_1 and p_2); iii. $G; G'$ (sequential of two g-choreographies) iv. $G|G'$ (parallel between two Gs) v. $G + G'$ (choices of Gs). This can be illustrated respectively in the following figure. Each graph in Fig. 2, $\bigcirc$ represents the initial state, $\bigcirc$ represents the final state, while $\diamondsuit$ depicts the alternative interaction in the branching graph and $\square$ represents the concurrent interaction in the parallel graph.

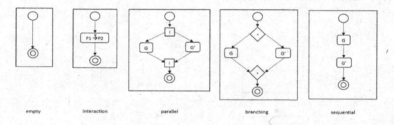

Fig. 2. Global view graph as a visual representation

As discussed previously, an SBVR model consists of several rules specifying the complex interactions involved in the choreography. To build a global view, the following SBVR rules are considered as an illustrative example of the specification to show a single interaction between participant 1 and participant 2 (Rule 1 and Rule 2), subsequently participant 2 and participant 3 (Rule 3 and Rule 4), and the ordering of both interactions (Rule 5). Verbs associated with the event and particularly with T1 in the rule, illustrate the intended participant will be sending the event, conversely, verbs associated with the event which is mapped with T2, specify the intended participant will be receiving the event. In real, verb can be any vocabularies representing the same meaning of sending and receiving.

Rule 1: It is obligatory that the participant 1 verb1 exactly one event 1 at exactly one T1

Rule 2: It is obligatory that the participant 2 verb2 exactly one event 1 at exactly one T2

Rule 3: It is obligatory that the participant 2 verb3 exactly one event 2 at exactly one T1

Rule 4: It is obligatory that the participant 3 verb4 exactly one event 2 at exactly one T2

Rule 5: It is obligatory that exactly one event 1 immediately precedes exactly one event 2

Rule 6: It is obligatory that exactly one T1 of event 1 immediately precedes exactly one T2 of event 1

Rule 7: It is obligatory that the T1 of event 2 immediately precedes exactly one T2 of event 2

The declarations of time as depicted in Rule 6 and Rule 7 are a solution to indicate and to inform which interaction is performed initially. For instance, Rule 6 relates with Rule 1 emphasising the participant 1 initiates the interaction by sending the event 1 which is followed by participant 2 who will be receiving the event 1 immediate after (the interrelated between Rule 2 and Rule 7).

The following figure illustrates the possible visual representation from the above specification of SBVR model.

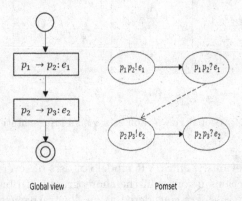

Global view   Pomset

Fig. 3. Visual representation of global view and pomset for SBVR model (Rule 1–Rule 5)

$p_1 \rightarrow p_2 : e_1$ and $p_2 \rightarrow p_3 : e_2$ in Fig. 3 illustrates the specification of SBVR model for Rule 1–2 and Rule 3–4, respectively. The down arrow in between those interactions showing the sequential reflects the specification of Rule 5.

Pomset of Choreography [36] is an injection of g-choreographies to capture the causal dependencies of the services interactions in choreographies. It illustrates the transition of one interaction - by sending and receiving of the message, to another interaction - by sending and receiving of the other message. In pomset, semantic is labelled by actions: ! represents sending, i.e. $p1p2!e1$ specifies the sending of message $e1$ from $p1$ to $p2$; ? represents receiving, i.e. $p1p2?e1$ describes the receiving of message $e1$ by $p2$.

The use of pomset enables to visualise the notion of time in SBVR model to specify the ordering of sending (receiving) the same event as declared in Rule 6–7 (see Fig. 3). Simple arrows in Fig. 3 illustrates the aforementioned ordering, on the other hand the dotted arrow shows the dependency between those two interactions capturing the sequential composition.

The following rules are the specification for illustrating the complex interactions in SBVR model : the alternative interaction by defining OR over the event terms. This means, by referring to Rule 8, the participant 1 has the possibilities to select at least one of the events (OR) to perform the interaction. The receiver, participant 2 will perform the correspond events as sent by the sender (Rule 9). Rule 8–9 and Rule 10–11 describe two interactions that must be happened in order as defined in Rule 12.

Rule 8: It is obligatory that the participant 1 verb1 exactly one event 1 or exactly one event 2, at exactly one T1

Rule 9: It is obligatory that the participant 2 verb2 exactly one event 1 or exactly one event 2, at exactly one T2

Rule 10: It is obligatory that the participant 2 verb3 exactly one event 3 at exactly one T1

Rule 11: It is obligatory that the participant 3 verb4 exactly one event 3 at exactly one T2

Rule 12: It is obligatory that exactly one event 1 or exactly one event 2 immediately precedes exactly one event 3

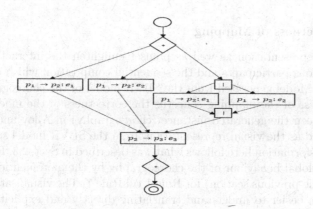

Fig. 4. Visual representation of global view for SBVR model (Rule 8–Rule 12)

Figure 4 describes the specified SBVR rules (Rule 8–12) applying the visual representation of global view. Rule 8 and Rule 9 has depicted with the fork (as branches). The first fork shows only the event 1 is chosen, the second fork represents only the event 2 is sent and is received by the participant 1 and participant 2, respectively, the last fork illustrates whenever both of the events are selected to be executed by the participants concurrently. Here, the parallel graph is applied. Rule 10–11 are specified as a single interaction, $p_2 \rightarrow p_3 : e_3$ occurs immediately after the previous interaction. This shows the sequential as declared in Rule 12.

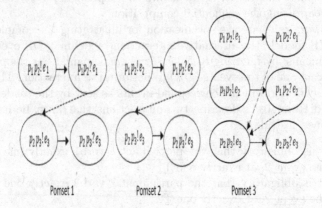

Fig. 5. Pomsets showing Rule 8–12

Figure 5 contains three pomsets defines three choices of interactions showing causal dependencies. Pomset 3 describes the occurrence of the event 1 and the event 2 at the same time which are sent by the participant 1 and received by the participant 2.

3.2   Correctness of Mapping

The visual representation as well as pomset enlighten the interactions among the autonomous participants and the sequential composition which corresponds to the Alloy Model generated from the SBVR model of the choreography.

Correctness of the mapping concerns the correctness of the model transformation between the generated instance (choreography) in Alloy and the global view obtained as the visual representation, from the SBVR model specification.

The transformation here follows what was described in Sect. 2.3. Figure 6 represents the global behaviour of the choreography by the aforementioned specifications (in the previous section) for Rule 1 till Rule 7. The visualisation in Alloy making them easier to understand translating directly and explicitly from the specified SBVR rules. As shown in figure, the yellow box stated participant1 is pointed (arrow: verb1) to the event1 which is mapped to T1_E1 with the arrow stated: at. This reflected the specified Rule 1. A similar mechanism is used to specify Rule 2–4. The ordering of the interactions between the message exchange of event 1 by participant 1 and participant 2, and the message exchange of the event 2 by the participant 2 and the participant 3, is depicted using a simple arrow states immediately precedes. It is pointed from the event1 to the event2. This described the specified Rule 5.

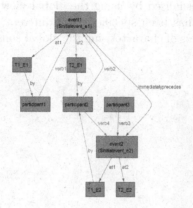

Fig. 6. The generated Alloy model for choreography from SBVR model (Rule 1–Rule 7)

Rule 6 and Rule 7 are depicted in Alloy as in Fig. 7. From the visualisation, it can be seen who takes the action initially and perform the next action in each interaction afterwards.

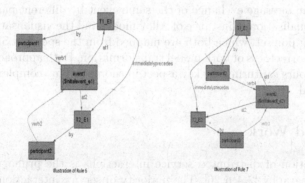

Fig. 7. The illustration of Alloy for Rule 6–7

The following figure illustrates the generated choreography in Alloy model via transforming from the specification of SBVR model (Rule 8–12). Alloy does generate all possible executions it does not output them all in one graph, instead it includes a "Next" feature on its interface that allows the user to go through the possible executions one at a time. Therefore, it is not possible to show them all in one figure. Hence, there are three possibilities to present the alternative interaction encapsulates OR over two events, event 1 and event 2. The first graph indicates the participant 1 and the participant 2 execute the interaction by choosing the event 1 only, the second graph shows only the event 2 is selected, while the last graph represents both events are chosen concurrently. The similar illustration has been visualised by using the global view as depicted in Fig. 4. Even both approaches has been specified with different semantics, the output represents the correctness of characterising the global constraints from the specification.

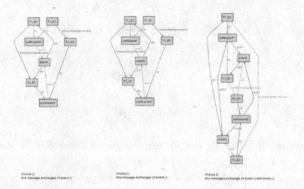

Fig. 8. The illustration of Alloy for the complex interaction OR over the event terms

Figure 8 also illustrates the visualisation of pomset in Fig. 5. Both present the ordering of the message exchange of the same event by different participants.

All the visualisation of instance of Alloy model and the visualisation of global view including pomset, which both are mapped from the specified SBVR model, checking the correctness of both model transformation. Both approaches describe global behaviours capturing the key aspect in choreography: complex interaction and sequential.

4   Related Work

The coordination of distributed service interactions is the primary concern of service choreography [2,4,6,26]. The majority of service interaction approaches have been provided for graphically defining service choreographies. Business Process Model and Notation (BPMN) [8,26,28] is user friendly choreographic models, represented graphically using notation but combine different semantics. The characteristics of BPMN is similar to Unified Modeling Language (UML). UML is a widely-known standard specification language for constructing service interactions [31]. Another language for choreography specification is Web Services Choreography Description Language (WS-CDL) [18]. WS-CDL proposes a metamodel-driven transformation technique consisting of a collection of

Atlas Transformation Language (ATL) rules which refines WS-CDL choreographies towards executable Business Process Execution Language for Web Services (WS-BPEL) orchestrations. However, WS-CDL is unable to acknowledge and establish a way for verifying conformance to choreography specifications [21].

Moreover, the work on a declarative approach to service interaction coordination is sparse. e.g., [3,12,22]. The focus seems to be more on reasoning about the consistency of the rule set, which of course is an important aspect of verification, and less on explicitly capturing the orderings in terms of observable message exchanges. The work on DecSerFlow [8] includes a graphical interface for user interaction but this is proprietary notation. In contrast, our approach uses SBVR for this purpose, which was developed with the business user in mind and is a standard maintained by OMG.

The OMG defined Decision Model and Notation (DMN) [29] is a design language and basic notation for describing decision rules. It is another well-known standard specification language for modelling service interactions and providing graphical notations that are easy to understand [7,10]. In the same way that BPMN does for business processes, it provides an integrated notation for decision management. However, for each intermediate step, DMN proposes a long technical noun phrase, whereas SBVR stays much closer to what business people actually say. It can be argued that when compared to DMN, SBVR uses more natural business language.

Global graph represents as the global view of the choreography where multiple participants interact with each other [11]. Examples of similar approaches that applied global graph as the global view can be found in [9]. The counterexamples were visualised by global graph and identifies the possible misbehaviours from the message-passing systems. Moreover, [20] formalise the global view of the choreography for reversible computations approach. Additional work by [27] deals with synthesising the global graph which illustrates the universal structure of communications from CFSM. Although our approach are similar, our main concern of applying global graph are different as we applied visual representation as the global graph to perform the conformance mapping correctness of SBVR model into Alloy model.

5   Conclusion and Future Work

SBVR and Date-Time Vocabulary is used to specify business models in a declarative manner. Alloy Analyzer, a SAT constraint solver, provides an automated means to generate and verify the realisability of the choreography generated from the SBVR model. Hence, a transformation from the SBVR model to the Alloy model has been developed.

The correctness of the conformance mapping has been described in this paper. The correctness is conformed between the generated choreography in Alloy model transforming from the specification of SBVR model and the visual representation of the global view translating from the corresponding SBVR model. The correctness is concerned when the generated choreography models capture all global behaviours particularly in terms of the global ordering constraints and the complex interactions describing alternative (choice) and parallel (concurrent) interactions.

In order to enable end-users to participate in the development of the SBVR model on their own and then transform the SBVR model into the Alloy model automatically, the SBVR2Alloy tool [16] has been developed. It can be used to express complex rules, with a focus on capturing constraints on the orderings of service interactions, including concurrent interactions [23]. The tool can be extended to include less common features of SBVR and indeed this is part of the future work planned. It could be used to impress the distinction between *obligation* and *prohibition* on a message being received. This also brings in faulty channels or erroneous communication which in turn points to the need for transactional guarantees [24,34] in choreographies of ecosystem composed services [25,35]. The ultimate goal is an automated tool for modelling business rules but also executing the corresponding SBVR model and offering a preview of all possible executions to both modellers and end-users so that the business model can be adapted or extended to better match the business need.

References

1. Manaf, N.A., Moschoyiannis, S.: Generating choreographies from SBVR models. In: AIP Conference Proceedings, vol. 2184, p. 060062. AIP Publishing LLC (2019)
2. Ataee, S.M., Bayram, Z.: An improved abstract state machine based choreography specification and execution algorithm for semantic web services. Sci. Program. **2018**, 4094951:1–4094951:20 (2018)
3. Autili, M., Tivoli, M.: Distributed enforcement of service choreographies. In: Int'l Workshop on Foundations of Coordination Languages and Self-Adaptive Systems (FOCLASA), pp. 18–35 (2014)
4. Autili, M., Inverardi, P., Tivoli, M.: Choreography realizability enforcement through the automatic synthesis of distributed coordination delegates. Sci. Comput. Program. **160**, 3–29 (2018)
5. Bajwa, I.S., Lee, M.G., Bordbar, B.: SBVR business rules generation from natural language specification. In: AAAI: AI for Business Agility, pp. 2–8 (2011)
6. Bhattacharyya, A., Chittimalli, P.K., Naik, R.: Relation identification in business rules for domain-specific documents. In: Proceedings of the 11th Innovations in Software Engineering Conference, pp. 14:1–14:5. ACM (2018)
7. Calvanese, D., Dumas, M., Laurson, Ü., Maggi, F.M., Montali, M., Teinemaa, I.: Semantics, analysis and simplification of DMN decision tables. Inf. Syst. **78**, 112–125 (2018)
8. Corradini, F., Fornari, F., Polini, A., Re, B., Tiezzi, F.: A formal approach to modeling and verification of business process collaborations. Sci. Comput. Program. **166**, 35–70 (2018)
9. Guanciale, R., Tuosto, E.: Pomcho: a tool chain for choreographic design. Sci. Comput. Program. **202**, 102535 (2021)
10. Hasic, F., Vanthienen, J.: Complexity metrics for DMN decision models. Comput. Stand. Interfaces **65**, 15–37 (2019)
11. Honda, K., Yoshida, N., Carbone, M.: Multiparty asynchronous session types. J. ACM **63**(1), 9:1–9:67 (2016)

12. Jacquet, J.-M., Linden, I., Staicu, M.-O.: On the introduction of time in distributed blackboard rules. In: Canal, C., Villari, M. (eds.) ESOCC 2013. CCIS, vol. 393, pp. 144–158. Springer, Heidelberg (2013). https://doi.org/10.1007/978-3-642-45364-9_13

13. Jackson, D.: Software Abstractions - Logic, Language, and Analysis. Revised Edition, The MIT Press, Cambridge (2012)

14. Karlsen, M.R., Moschoyiannis, S.: Learning condition–action rules for personalised journey recommendations. In: Benzmüller, C., Ricca, F., Parent, X., Roman, D. (eds.) RuleML+RR 2018. LNCS, vol. 11092, pp. 293–301. Springer, Cham (2018). https://doi.org/10.1007/978-3-319-99906-7_21

15. Levy, F., NazarenkoF, A.: Formalization of natural language regulations through SBVR structured English - (tutorial). In: Theory, Practice, and Applications of Rules on the Web - 7th International Symposium, RuleML, pp. 19–33 (2013)

16. Manaf, N.A., Antoniades, A., Moschoyiannis, S.: SBVR2Alloy: an SBVR to alloy compiler. In: 10th IEEE Conference on Service-Oriented Computing and Applications, SOCA 2017, pp. 73–80. IEEE Computer Society (2017)

17. Manaf, N.A., Moschoyiannis, S., Krause, P.J.: Service choreography, sbvr, and time. In: Proceedings of the 14th International Workshop on Foundations of Coordination Languages and Self-Adaptive Systems, FOCLASA. EPTCS, vol. 201, pp. 63–77 (2015)

18. Mansour, K.S., Hammal, Y.: ATL based refinement of WS-CDL choreography into BPEL processes. In: Chikhi, S., Amine, A., Chaoui, A., Saidouni, D.E. (eds.) MISC 2018. LNNS, vol. 64, pp. 329–343. Springer, Cham (2019). https://doi.org/10.1007/978-3-030-05481-6_25

19. Marinos, A., Moschoyiannis, S., Krause, P.: Towards a RESTful infrastructure for digital ecosystems. Int. J. Electron. Bus. 9 (2011)

20. Mezzina, C.A., Tuosto, E.: Choreographies for automatic recovery. CoRR abs/1705.09525 (2017)

21. Montali, M.: Specification and Verification of Declarative Open Interaction Models: A Logic-Based Approach, vol. 56. Springer Science & Business Media, Heidelberg (2010)

22. Montali, M., Pesic, M., Aalst, W.M.V.D., Chesani, F., Mello, P., Storari, S.: Declarative specification and verification of service choreographiess. ACM Trans. Web (TWEB) 4(1), 1–62 (2010)

23. Moschoyiannis, S., Krause, P., Shields, M.W.: A true-concurrent interpretation of behavioural scenarios. ENTCS 203(7), 3–22 (2009). eTAPS - FESCA

24. Moschoyiannis, S., Razavi, A., Krause, P.: Transaction scripts: making implicit scenarios explicit. ENTCS 238(6), 63–79 (2010). eTAPS - FESCA

25. Moschoyiannis, S., Shields, M.W.: A set-theoretic framework for component composition. Fund. Inform. 59, 373–396 (2004)

26. Muram, F.U., Javed, M.A., Tran, H., Zdun, U.: Towards a framework for detecting containment violations in service choreography. In: IEEE International Conference on Services Computing, SCC, pp. 172–179. IEEE Computer Society (2017)

27. Ng, N., Yoshida, N.: Static deadlock detection for concurrent go by global session graph synthesis. In: Zaks, A., Hermenegildo, M.V. (eds.) Proceedings of the 25th International Conference on Compiler Construction, CC 2016, Barcelona, Spain, 12–18 March 2016, pp. 174–184. ACM (2016)

28. OMG: Business Process Model and Notation (BPMN), vol. Version 2.0. OMG document formal/2011-01-03. http://www.omg.org/spec/BPMN/2.0/

29. OMG: Decision Model and Notation (DMN), vol. Version 1.3. OMG document formal/2021-01-01. https://www.omg.org/spec/DMN

30. OMG: Semantics of Business Vocabulary and Business Rules (SBVR), vol. Version 1.5. OMG document formal/dtc/2019-10-02. https://www.omg.org/spec/SBVR/1.5/PDF

31. OMG: Unified Modeling Language (UML), vol. Version 2.5.1. OMG document formal/2017-12-05. https://www.omg.org/spec/UML/

32. OMG: Date-Time Vocabulary (DTV), Version 1.3. OMG document formal/dtc/2016-02-20. http://www.omg.org/spec/DTV/1.3/Beta2 (2017)

33. Papazoglou, M.P., Georgakopoulos, D.: Introduction: service-oriented computing. Commun. ACM **46**(10), 24–28 (2003)

34. Razavi, A., Moschoyiannis, S., Krause, P.: Concurrency control and recovery management for open e-business transactions. In: Communicating Process Architectures 2007, vol. 65, pp. 267–285 (2007)

35. Razavi, A.R., Moschoyiannis, S., Krause, P.: A scale-free business network for digital ecosystems. In: IEEE Int'l Conference on Digital Ecosystems and Technologies, pp. 241–246 (2008)

36. Tuosto, E., Guanciale, R.: Semantics of global view of choreographies. J. Log. Algebraic Methods Program. **95**, 17–40 (2018)

37. W3C: Web Services Choreography Description Language (WS-CDL). W3C Working Group (2006). http://www.w3.org/TR/ws-cdl-10-primer/

Conflict-Free Access Rules for Sharing Smart Patient Health Records

Matthew Banton(✉) , Juliana Bowles(✉) , Agastya Silvina(✉) ,
and Thais Webber(✉)

School of Computer Science, University of St Andrews, St Andrews KY16 9SX,
Scotland, UK
{mb471,jkfb,as362,tcwds}@st-andrews.ac.uk

Abstract. With an increasing trend in personalised healthcare provision across Europe, we need solutions to enable the secure transnational sharing of medical records, establishing granular access rights to personal patient data. Access rules can establish what should be accessible by whom for how long, and comply with collective regulatory frameworks, such as the European General Data Protection Regulation (GDPR). The challenge is to design and implement such systems integrating novel technologies like Blockchain and Data Lake to enhance security and access control. The blockchain module must deal with adequate policies and algorithms to guarantee that no data leaks occur when authorising data retrieval requests. The data lake module tackles the need for an efficient way to retrieve potential granular data from heterogeneous data sources. In this paper, we define a patient-centric authorisation approach, incorporating a structured format for composing access rules that enable secure data retrieval and automatic rules conflict checking.

Keywords: Healthcare systems · Patient health records · Blockchain · Data lake · Access rules

1 Introduction

Healthcare data systems have evolved from just systems for managing and organising health records to become trustworthy and secure platforms that deal with multiple sources data integration, transformation, and analytics [13]. Their ultimate purpose is to both support organisational decision making as well as medical professionals in clinical decisions, personalised treatments, overall services quality, and efficiency improvement [3].

Patient Health Records (PHR) contain crucial information to enable better clinical decisions such as the patient's medical history, past and ongoing treatments, prescribed medications, exams, and more recently, even data coming from home environment and health tracking technologies. PHR is an essential part

This research is funded by the EU H2020 project Serums (Securing Medical Data in Smart Patient-Centric Healthcare Systems), grant code 826278.

in any healthcare data system, however adhering to different storage and access control policies for different jurisdictions and organisations, as well as the EU General Data Protection Regulation[1] (GDPR), makes creating a single healthcare platform difficult [21]. Data Lakes are an emergent technology that can aid with these challenges. It can manage the retrieval of diverse medical data, and place it in different repositories, enabling a myriad of strategies for data aggregation, through specialised database queries and processes [17]. However, Data Lakes do not support another crucial requirement of such platform, that being how one can securely provide access to legitimate healthcare providers, with decreased likelihood of data leaks or breaches [24].

This drives the proposal of fine-grained access control strategies within such systems to increase patients control over their own medical data while still establishing the same level of access control practised in healthcare organisations [24]. Recently, blockchain technology has emerged in the healthcare domain as a way to ensure data integrity and increase security and trust in verifiable data sharing transactions, preventing tampering as well as increasing the transparency in communications between patients and healthcare professionals [2, 19, 24].

The EU project Serums[2] [5, 8, 20, 26] proposes the design of a rule-based authorisation mechanism, blending blockchain and data lake technologies, in a secure patient-centric data sharing platform. The project deals with modern challenges such as the size, complexity and variety of data format present in patient health records, which demand solutions that efficiently unifies these formats into an extensible and flexible standard, and ensures interoperability between data systems placed in different locations.

The Serums Smart Patient Health Record (SPHR) is the unified format proposed to integrate distributed sources of patient information registered in Europe [8, 20]. The SPHR contains metadata, linking the patient medical history in a structured way in the data lake, built across authorised healthcare providers and approved health data sources. Based on the metadata, Serums provides an interface for users to create access rules. Thus, users can easily define who (professional or organisation) is allowed to access what (granular medical metadata), from whom (which patient), and when (rule expiration date) through the creation of collective and individual access rules. Conflicting rules may occur checking grantee, expiration date of the rules, overlapping metadata, and the action established by the rules (i.e., grant or deny access). A conflict-free state of the rules set for an individual can be reached using a strategy for conflict detection as well as assumptions to minimise and resolve these conflicts.

This paper presents the pathways in Serums that enable the integration of the scalable Serums data lake tied to a blockchain network to securely retrieve medical data, in a unified manner, and following established access rules for its users. We describe the access rules schema highlighting a structured way to define and validate them within the healthcare system.

---

[1] Information on GDPR can be found at https://gdpr-info.eu/.

[2] For more information on Serums project please refer to www.serums-h2020.org.

The paper is structured as follows. Section 2 brings related work on blockchain for access control in healthcare data sharing systems. Section 3 describes the Serums platform with focus on the data sharing principles, authorisation mechanism and the pathway to secure SPHR retrieval in the system. Section 4 focus specifically on the access rules design, its structured format, and the subsequent logic-based formalisation. We demonstrate the access rules application through a patient journey, and the expected conflicts that may arise on real-time rules verification. Section 5 concludes this paper highlighting the paper contribution and future work towards enabling a rule-based multinational data sharing platform for healthcare provision in Europe.

2   Related Work

Blockchain allows the creation of transparent and secure user authorisation mechanisms since it can improve access control whilst recording a trail for auditing, especially in case of data breach investigations [19]. A recent survey [24] categorises the strategies to securely share confidential medical records and describes the characteristics of blockchain-based mechanisms employed in several healthcare platforms, so these records can be shared within and across multiple authorised healthcare providers.

We compare Serums to earlier contributions in the literature that specifically exploited the Hyperledger Fabric technology [1] to develop different authorisation mechanisms [2,14,16,18,25] and focus on the design of efficient permissioned blockchains for secure medical data sharing. They are similar to Serums since they also exploit the inherent secure-by-design feature of blockchain to provide tamper-proof logs for transactions over medical records. Moreover, they all construct a particular data retrieval infrastructure with underlying authorisation mechanisms to enable different functions to different user roles.

Serums highlights two essential aspects on access control strategy and patient-centric approach: (i) level of patient control over data and (ii) security measures applied to the access of confidential medical data. We selected two recent contributions in the literature [18,25] to trace a brief comparison with Serums design and their rule-based approach to define users access privileges.

Tanwar, Parekh and Evans (2020) [25] propose an architecture to authenticate and authorise users in a PHR sharing system. Patients register on a blockchain and control their own node, as well as who may access that node (using an algorithm), allowing them to grant and revoke access over the medical data to professionals. Similar to Serums, the architecture follows a patient-centric approach that allows patients to decide about access privileges. For instance, Serums also allows professionals to trigger requests to access the medical records of patients, and patients are responsible to agree or deny them. In both platforms, these requests are controlled and logged by their blockchain.

However, Serums prioritises that medical data is not stored on-chain. While the advantages of storing data on-chain are stated by the authors [25], there are also disadvantages, first being that data cannot be deleted from the chain (which may run into issues with legislation, especially the so called "Right to be forgotten" on GDPR). Secondly, blockchain blocks are typically not large enough to store the variety of data needed (images such as X-Rays and video files such as Ultrasounds) [18]. Serums stores access rules on-chain, which determine who may access the patient data. This brings many benefits such as providing assurance of who, where and when data is accessed, but also allows users to request their data is deleted in line with their rights in the legislation.

Guo *et al.* [18] maintain the data off-chain, focusing on blockchain to verify the integrity of the data. Additionally, this solution uses customised Access Control Lists (ACLs) which define what users are allowed to do. When receiving a request for a patients PHR, the blockchain accesses the relevant ACL to determine if the user has the relevant permissions. Upon confirmation, the chain releases a single use URL directing the user to the data, as well as a hash of that data. The hash ensures that the data the blockchain is directing to is the same as the data that is eventually retrieved, ensuring integrity.

Serums allows creation of highly granular access rules to medical records by patients and organisations since it introduces the concept of flexible data tags. Similar to [18], Serums data lake component efficiently process data requests based on these tags securely linked to the original data sources. One of the challenges imposed by this feature is that conflicts between rules can arise such as defining different actions over same tags for a pair patient/grantee, when inserting a new rule; and after conflict detection, an action must be taken by the rule creator to resolve it.

Recently, Cui *et al.* [11] developed an example of conflict resolution for Software Defined Networking forwarding rules. They use a three-step process, finding related rules (i.e., any rule with the same source and destination addresses), finding any conflicts (i.e., when the action of two matching rules would be different), and then resolving the conflict. In this related work, conflicts are resolved based upon priority, which is based upon the network function that has generated the rule (security functions having higher priority), as well as the priority of function that generated it. For Serums, the key point is to provide an easy way to patients access their own medical data and update the access privileges given to professionals, especially when they are abroad and seeking to share medical records. Users can create customised access rules to allow professionals to access the medical information. Only that these conflicts may arise when different actions (allow/deny) are defined to the same grantee and set of tags. In this sense, Serums does not use priorities to process rules as [11], but instead requires that users themselves choose the valid rule to be stored in case of detected conflict.

3   Serums Data Sharing Platform Design

Serums platform allow patients to: (i) retrieve their own confidential medical records (i.e., SPHR) containing data from the diverse healthcare providers, as well as (ii) define data access rules to professionals and organisations. Serums should as well enable organisations enrolled in the platform to create and update the patients access rules for their own professionals, in such a way they comply with the GDPR as well as with their policies and current legislation on medical data sharing for lawful data processing [21].

Serums architecture (Fig. 1) presents the Smart Health Centre System (SHCS) which comprises of a web-based front-end [5] to allow users to retrieve health records (SPHR) [9,10]; as well as a backend with integrated APIs to communicate with each internal module and with external data sources (e.g. hospitals, health-care organisations, data systems). SPHR metadata (tags) are labels to medical data sources provided by each organisation in the process of their registering to Serums. An SPHR retrieval request triggers a Serums API call to the data lake, which checks the private and permissioned blockchain state [6,20,26] for access privileges (i.e., access rules in place) for the authenticated user.

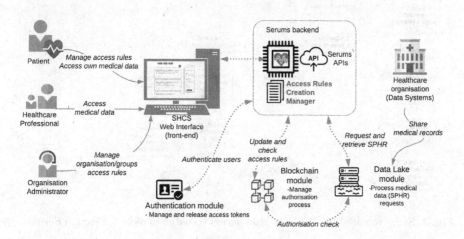

Fig. 1. Serums platform enables custom access rules creation and SPHR retrieval.

A user-friendly interface enables authorised users to easily create and update a set of access rules related to the patient's SPHR, which are secured through the blockchain [5]. Thus, the blockchain contribution to Serums backend is two-fold: first, related to data confidentiality and privacy, blockchain efficiently stores access rules defined by users allowing only authorised individuals to access patients records information; second, the ability to effectively track and audit users interactions within the system.

The customisation of access rules by an individual (patient or admin) assigns permissions to authorised users referring to selected SPHR entries (named data tags), within a specified timeframe. Every time a user attempts to access a patient record (SPHR) in the Serums data lake, the access privileges are checked by the blockchain, and the users can only access the granular SPHR data tags referred to in their own set of access rules. Rules defined by users operate with an underlying logic-based approach that enable the automatic update of their access permissions over data tags and further conflict detection.

A conflict can be defined as whenever a new access rule, checked against the existent set of rules, would state privileges to the same user but in overlapping time frames, or when it contradicts another access rule in place to a user (i.e., denies it). In Serums, the verification of access rules conflicts follows an algorithmic solution (refer to Sect. 4) that ensures the storage of a conflict-free set of rules on the blockchain after any request of rule update by authorised users.

Blockchain always stores an initial set of rules for the users; for example, a user patient, as the data owner, has access to all tags available for them in the data lake to retrieve. Medical professionals will also have rules in place giving them access to patient data, according to local organisational policies.

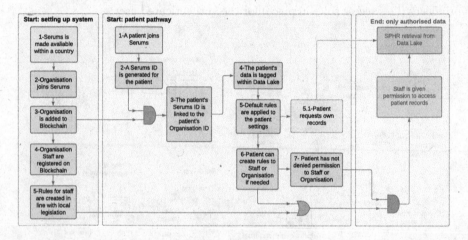

Fig. 2. Steps required for a user to gain access to patients records through Serums.

Figure 2 outlines a diagram with the steps required for a professional to gain access to patient data. The flow in the diagram can be separated into the organisation pathway and the patient pathway to be enabled in the system. Setting up the system follows five basic sequential steps: from the point Serums must be offered within the European country the healthcare organisation operates, to the point organisation staff are registered on the blockchain. Then, standard access rules are defined in line with local legislation and organisational policies.

These initial steps (on Fig. 2) only allow a medical professional to login into the system, but do not define any authorisation to access medical data, or even have the medical data available to upload. Many systems based on permissioned blockchains include a step that imports data from patients into the system [17, 25] as part of the organisational setup, assuming the organisation is only going to be using its system for all data management. However, the focus of Serums platform is to allow professionals to access patient data from other European healthcare organisations, and not to replace their data management system entirely.

The data importation is a part of the patient pathway (see Fig. 2). First, when patients join Serums they automatically receive a unique Serums ID. This is separate to the username the patient decides as login detail when joining Serums. Second, the patients Serums ID is then linked to the organisation's Serums ID, the one the patient is joining at (setting up system pathway required). Then, the organisational access rules based on policies and legislation can be applied to the patient, and then patient data uploaded to Serums. This allows professionals (of that organisation) to access the patient data using Serums, as well as allowing the patient to access their own medical data available through the SPHR.

From this step forward, the patient can create new access rules as they see fit. For example, they may allow other organisation staff to access their data even if the default rules would not normally allow it, or they can prevent certain staff from accessing any medical records, should that be something they wish.

Assuming that a medical professional has been given permission to access the records (either from default organisational rules, or from a patient's custom rule) and the patient has not denied them access, then that medical professional can access the patient's data. From this point, it is straightforward to allow another organisation (or particular medical professional) to access their medical data, through the creation of a new custom rule using the professional or the organisation Serums ID.

4   Serums Access Rules Design

Serums users must first login successfully to the system to have access to specific functionalities (i.e., create or update an access rules to a professional, retrieve SPHR data, visualise data analytics, and other functionalities [20]), according to their roles in the system (e.g., patient, administrator, doctor, nurse, etc.).

A Serums user with the appropriate operational privilege (i.e., admin) can manipulate (create/read/update/delete) rules for users within the Serums front-end. Organisational rules created by administrators affect all patient records that pertain to an organisation, considering current legislation to specify the grantees, since patient registration on Serums. Also, patients can directly create access rules to authorised organisations and professionals in the Serums front-end. Access rules are defined with a given *validity* for its persistence in the system. The temporal duration of rules must be explicitly defined, i.e., each rule must specify a *time limit* from rule creation to an expiration date.

Access rules are defined over *tags* that categorise the medical data provided by authorised organisations to the Serums data lake. Serums itself, in this platform version, does not check the medical data provided for appropriate tagging, beyond the basic check performed to ensure data is in the correct format. Serums data lake retrieves all authorised pieces of information according to the rules defined over these data tags. Organisations can always add new tags, whenever they include new systems or applications in their healthcare settings.

The rules are stored in the blockchain right after their creation (or update) takes place, provided no conflict is detected with existent rules, i.e., new access rules are checked against existing ones. A conflict exists where similar rules (from the same grantee and set of tags) establish contrasting privileges (like granting or denying access, overlapping time frames, etc.). If a conflict is detected then the user will be notified and asked to take an action to choose which rule should be stored, or accept an amended rule to ensure there is no conflict. In a proof-of-concept platform version, we propose this format for access rules representation and for automatic conflict detection when creating (or updating) rules, thus users can take action to store only conflict-free rules in the blockchain.

4.1 Serums Access Rules Format

Let Act be a set of actions, Id_S denote a set of identifiers indexed by a sort in S where sorts correspond to granters and grantees, that is, S is a disjoint union where $S = S_G \uplus S_R$. Let T be a set of tags. Following we show examples of considered actions, sorts S_G and S_R, data tags, and rule creators.

$$
\begin{aligned}
\textbf{Actions} &: \text{allow}, \text{deny} \\
\textbf{Granters} &: \text{patient}, \text{organisation} \\
\textbf{Grantees} &: \text{nurse}, \text{doctor}, \text{consultant}, \text{organisation}, \text{department} \\
\textbf{Tags} &: \text{consultation}, \text{treatment}, \text{test}, \text{device}, \\
&\quad \text{medication}, \text{personal}, \text{chemotherapy}, \\
&\quad \text{comorbodities}, \text{hospitalisation}, \text{symptoms} \\
\textbf{Rule creators} &: \text{organisation administrator}, \text{patient}
\end{aligned}
$$

In particular, we assume that a granter sort can be *patient* or *organisation*, $S_G = \{p, o\}$. Similarly, sorts for grantees are $S_R = \{n, d, c, o\}$. We also note that in this context an organisation can be a hospital, general practice, clinic, etc. The organisation administrators can create the access rules commonly applied to staff in their local systems with patient consent.

Definition 1. *An access rule r is a tuple $r = (g, \alpha, R, D, \Gamma)$ where*

- $g \in Id_G$ is a grantee,
- $\alpha \in Act$ is an action,
- $R \subseteq Id_R$ is a subset of granters where necessarily $g \notin R$,
- $D = (d_1, d_2) \subseteq \mathbb{N} \times \mathbb{N}$ is the time interval indicating when the rule is valid where necessarily $d_1 \leq d_2$, and
- $\Gamma \subseteq T$ is a subset of tags.

We note that even though our implementation uses epoch times to represent dates, it suffices to think about these as natural numbers in this context. The time interval $(d_1, d_1) \cdot$ or (d_1, inf) can be used to indicate that a rule is valid forever. In addition, implicit in a rule is the user creating it, so if $g \in Id_p$ then this is a rule created by a patient, and if $g \in Id_o$ then we have a rule created by the organisation for all patients. One example of a possible rule is $r_1 = (p_1, allow, \{d_1, d_2\}, (t_1, t_2), \{treatment, medication\})$ where patient $p_1 \in$

Id_p allows doctors $d_1, d_2 \in Id_d$ to have access to all 'treatment' and 'medication' records that p_1 received in the time interval (t_1, t_2).

When rules are defined for the same grantee, their combined effect represent the complete access allowed (or denied) over the selected subset of tags.

Assume the complete set of rules to be given by $\mathcal{R}$. A set of rules R for grantee g is correct if and only if there are no rules in R that conflict with each other, that is, $\forall r_1, r_2 \in R, \neg(r_1 \perp r_2)$. Conflict can arise when different actions are placed, for instance simultaneously allowing and denying access over the same data tags and grantee for intersecting time periods. When rules are in conflict, the conflict is highlighted to the user on time of creation, with a request issued by the system for the user to choose which rule should be stored in the blockchain. Whenever possible, system can suggest a conflict-free amended rule.

To check rule consistency automatically and find the set of rules that should be used we can adopt a similar approach to others that have used Satisfiability Modulo Theories (SMT) solvers such as Z3 [22], as well as recommendations to resolve those conflicts [4]. Thus, to help move towards a more user-centric approach, we use a straightforward Z3 coding to identify potential conflicts in rules using our proposed format. We allow the user to select which rule should be applied in case of conflict, defining the next current conflict-free set of rules to be stored in the blockchain.

4.2   Access Rules Application Example

This section explores the access rules creation process within a use case description originated from a patient journey in real-world hospitals in Edinburgh (HE), Barcelona (HB) and Maastrich (HM). A patient journey example includes collection of personal information in several cross-country organisations such as their appointments in GP practices, interactions with professionals, scheduled treatments in hospitals, home care visits, prescribed medications, and the use of a smart device for toxicity data collection [23], just to name a few.

We divide the patient journey description into several points (P_i), and exemplify the creation of access rules and conflicts that can arise from their creation and update in a period of time.

P1. *A hypothetical breast cancer patient will start chemotherapy at HE, in Scotland. A treatment plan and regimen has been established (this will be over several months with treatment in hospital every three weeks). The patient also has a comorbidity. As any cancer patient on chemotherapy, she might have a higher toxicity level as a result [15,23], but it is important to guarantee that the level does not go above 3. Toxicity levels range from 0 (no toxicity) to 5 (so high it causes death).*

From P1 we can generate a set of rules at organisation (hospital) level, which follows Scottish local regulation, where professionals and staff from the hospital (HE) will be granted permission to access all data tags concerning the patient, for example. During her first visit to the HE, the patient is registered in the system and a Serums identity is created (refer to the patient pathway in Fig. 2). After the patient enrolment, with patient consent, the organisation can create access rules linked to the patient and to the respective professionals.

In the UK, the principle of *implied consent* is one that operates in the process of patient referrals, for instance, from a General Practitioner (GP) to a Specialist within a hospital. This assumes the patient consent to the sharing of personal information, within the National Healthcare System (NHS), at the time the referral is made and for any subsequent treatment relating to the referral. Thus, the organisation can create the following access rule r_1 for the patient based on the local legislation and hospital policies once the patient is registered in Serums.

$$r_1 = (p_1, allow, \{d_1, d_2, n_1\}, (t_1, t_2), T)$$

In this rule example, p_1 is the Serums ID to refer to the patient, and $d_1, d_2 \in Id_d$ and $n_1 \in Id_n$ are doctors and a nurse working at HE; t_1 is the referral date and T denotes all tags. The creator of the rule (in this case, the admin) is explicitly stored on the blockchain component for auditing purposes, however this is not shown in the tuple to simplify the presentation.

The tags provided by the organisation (HE) to be shared as SPHR, for example, are in the set $T =$ {consultation, treatment, test, medication, personal, chemotherapy, comorbidities, hospitalisation, symptoms, device}. As mentioned before, the organisation can also create a set of access rules based on Scottish legislation and compliant with GDPR at time of patient enrolment in Serums. Moreover, we can assume that the patient creates an additional rule r_2 that enables a further doctor $d_3 \in Id_d$ from a different healthcare organisation (her GP) to access the information about her chemotherapy treatment. Her GP is registered as a Serums user by that different organisation, also enrolled in Serums.

$$r_2 = (p1, allow, \{d_3\}, (t1, t2), \{chemotherapy\})$$

It is worth mentioning that Serums allows the creation of rules standing by the same grantee, tags, and grant action but with different (or extended) validity when checked against an existent rule. Once validity expires, the rule is not included in the information retrieval process since blockchain only returns authorised tags of valid rules.

P2. *Patient p_1 aims to give consent to sharing data in between treatment visits via the Cancer Data Gateway and the patient portal. Through a new access rule, she determines who in the medical team sees this information. The oncologist/nurse and her GP.*

In between treatments the patient is sharing symptoms information to both the doctors and nurse at HE and her GP.

$$r_3 = (p1, allow, \{d_1, d_2, n_1, d_3\}, (t1, t2), \{symptoms\})$$

P3. *Via a user-friendly web application with questionnaires provided by the hospital, e.g., the patient can provide information on symptoms daily during her treatment. Serious reported symptoms can be picked up by the clinical team and acted upon immediately.*

P4. *Combined health data can help clinicians adapt treatments better to the patient as an individual which results in controlled toxicity levels and improved health outcomes [23]. It uses data from several patients treated over the years with comparable characteristics.*

From P3, we exemplify that organisations can always provide new data tags to be linked in Serums, e.g., *symptoms*, to include data from this specific system, and from several other in-house applications. In addition, further rules have to be defined to guarantee that oncologists (d_1, d_2), nurse (n_1) and patient's GP (d_3), all have access to any additional important information, as mentioned in P4, where $R = \{d_1, d_2, n_1, d_3\}$.

$$r_4 = (p1, allow, R, (t_1, t_2), \{personal, comorbidities, hospitalisation\})$$

P5. *During the recovery at home between treatments there are signs that toxicity levels are high or that the condition of the patient is deteriorating.*

P6. *One of the members of the clinical team (oncologist, nurse or GP) notices in the system that there are irregularities in the patient's data [23] and phones the patient to intervene.*

P7. *During the phone call a decision is made for the GP/nurse to visit the patient at home and provide some additional medication to alleviate symptoms. Admission to hospital is not necessary. The patient improves. After a few weeks, patient comes to the HE to receive the next chemotherapy treatment.*

None of the points from P5 to P7 require the creation of new access rules. However, these can be steps of vital importance for the patient's improvement, considering the professionals clinical opinion, thus avoiding an unnecessary admission to the hospital. This would be difficult without the right people having access to the right information in a timely manner.

P8. *Patient p_1 has decided to visit her daughter that lives in Barcelona. As she is undergoing chemotherapy and to prevent potential problems, she gets in touch with an oncologist at a hospital in Barcelona (HB) so that he can evaluate her case.* In order to do so, the oncologist needs access to the information on her treatment. Consequently, p_1 creates a new access rule to allow the oncologist to access her information for two days, so he can evaluate the situation.

Thus, from P8, the patient would be creating the following rule with time validity (t3, t4) regarding the HB oncologist:

$$r_5 = (p1, allow, \{o_1\}, (t_3, t_4), \Gamma)$$

with $\Gamma = \{personal, comorbidities, hospitalisation, chemotherapy, medication\}$ and $o_1 \in Id_d$ the oncologist working at HB.

P9. *For unrelated reasons, the patient decides to cancel the trip and creates a new rule to deny the access to the doctor.*

The next rule r_6 is an example of a rule to comply with point P9 revoking access rights to the oncologist from HB. It should be noted that the patient could also update rule r_5 to deny access again, either approach will work, and would have the same end result.

$$r_6 = (p1, deny, \{o_1\}, (t_3, inf), \Gamma)$$

P10. *Let us now imagine that later the patient decides to move to Maastrich, in the Netherlands, and registers at the local hospital (HM).*

The hospital (HM) follows Dutch regulations that establish that only the doctor and nurse responsible for her case can have access to her Dutch records. Thus, this organisation creates rules concerning the local tags they have. In that case, the patient herself can decide if she wishes to share her previous Scottish medical history with additional staff and/or other EU organisations. Through Serums she can create these new rules and allow new clinical staff (not only the ones assigned to her case at HM) to access to her present and previous records.

From P10, we also emphasise how Serums treats new rules that operate in a similar manner to previous rules, i.e., having established the same action but over a different set of tags for a particular pair granter-grantee. For example, consider a patient (p_2) initially allowing a particular doctor (d_1) to access personal detail, chemotherapy, treatment, and tests information. A couple of months after, the patient gives access to the same doctor to personal details, chemotherapy, device information, and tests. It could just be a result of the patient acquiring a health tracking device, or doctor requesting further access, or it could only be the patient forgetting they already have given the doctor access to data, and then giving more (or less) than it is needed. The access rules (r_7, r_8) are as follows:

$$r_7 = (p2, allow, d_1, (t1, t2), \{personal, chemotherapy, treatment, test\})$$

$$r_8 = (p2, allow, d_1, (t1, t2), \{personal, chemotherapy, device, test\})$$

In this case, the system detects a potential conflict, and return an amended possible rule, with no conflict to be stored. The result indicates that the patient is only giving extra permissions to a doctor.

$$r_8' = (p2, allow, d_1, (t1, t2), \{device\})$$

However, the patient will be notified on the current allowances to be sure that the rules contain the tags set she is willing to allow access to at that moment. Using Boolean algebra, we can see that this effectively mean the particular doctor has the following rule in place:

$$r_8'' = (p2, allow, d_1, (t1, t2), \{personal, chemotherapy, treatment, device, test\})$$

Serums can inform the patient that the doctor have access to the treatment information contained in the conflicting rule (r_7), which was not included in the patients new rule (r_8), and ask for additional confirmation that the amend (r_8'') is what the patient actually desires to share.

This use case illustrated the application of a straightforward format of access rules in different situations that can occur in a patient journey. The logic approach eases the integration of a user-friendly interface for users to define sets of conflict-free access rules to medical records.

5   Conclusion

The core of this work is to explore the requirements for access rules and to experiment on a structured format for representing and checking these rules. The advantage of having this format is to facilitate formal verification of the Serums blockchain-based authorisation mechanism. It enables us to tackle conflict resolution using SMT solvers and constraint solvers, as done in [4,7], for finding, respectively, the optimal treatment plan (in case of conflicts in medical recommendations for patients with multiple chronic conditions) and optimal medication combinations.

We have built a high-level model of data access authorisation. The proposed rules format can support individual (and collective) access rules definition in such a way users can easily define who is allowed to access what (through data tags), from whom (which patient), and when (time boundaries). Further definitions of conflict resolution will be done to take into consideration not only the overlapping tags, but also other important aspects of legislation by country and extended versions of the parameters in the rules. We proposed an initial concept of tags that can be formally expanded as we evaluate further use cases. The rule format also enables us to tackle and conform to important security issues such as access rights to medical data and governing policies.

In future work, we aim the integration of a user-friendly interface in natural language for defining rules, the validation and formal verification [12] of the structures built in the blockchain and data lake modules, as well as coding further real-world use cases.

References

1. Androulaki, E., et al.: Hyperledger fabric: a distributed operating system for permissioned blockchains. In: Proceedings of the Thirteenth EuroSys Conference, pp. 1–15 (2018). https://doi.org/10.1145/3190508

2. Azaria, A., Ekblaw, A., Vieira, T., Lippman, A.: Medrec: using blockchain for medical data access and permission management. In: 2016 2nd International Conference on Open and Big Data (OBD), pp. 25–30. No. 16337137 in OBD, IEEE, New York, NY, USA (2016). https://doi.org/10.1109/OBD.2016.11
3. Bardhan, I.R., Thouin, M.F.: Health information technology and its impact on the quality and cost of healthcare delivery. Decis. Support Syst. **55**(2), 438–449 (2013). https://doi.org/10.1016/j.dss.2012.10.003
4. Bowles, J., Caminati, M., Cha, S., Mendoza, J.: A framework for automated conflict detection and resolution in medical guidelines. Sci. Comput. Program. **182**, 42–63 (2019). https://doi.org/10.1016/j.scico.2019.07.002
5. Bowles, J., Mendoza-Santana, J., Webber, T.: Interacting with next-generation smart patient-centric healthcare systems. In: UMAP 2020 Adjunct: Adjunct Publication of the 28th ACM Conference on User Modeling, Adaptation and Personalization, pp. 192–193. ACM, New York, NY, USA (July 2020). https://doi.org/10.1145/3386392.3399561
6. Bowles, J., Webber, T., Blackledge, E., Vermeulen, A.: A blockchain-based healthcare platform for secure personalised data sharing. Stud. Health Technol. Inform. Public Health Inform. **281**, 208–212 (2021). https://doi.org/10.3233/SHTI210150
7. Bowles, J.K.F., Caminati, M.B.: Balancing prescriptions with constraint solvers. In: Liò, P., Zuliani, P. (eds.) Automated Reasoning for Systems Biology and Medicine. CB, vol. 30, pp. 243–267. Springer, Cham (2019). https://doi.org/10.1007/978-3-030-17297-8_9
8. Bowles, J.K.F., Mendoza-Santana, J., Vermeulen, A.F., Webber, T., Blackledge, E.: Integrating healthcare data for enhanced citizen-centred care and analytics. Stud. Health Tech. Inf. **275**, 17–21 (2020). https://doi.org/10.3233/SHTI200686
9. Constantinides, A., Belk, M., Fidas, C., Pitsillides, A.: Design and development of the Serums patient-centric user authentication system. In: UMAP 2020 Adjunct: Adjunct Publication of the 28th ACM Conference on User Modeling, Adaptation and Personalization, pp. 201–203. ACM, New York, NY, USA (July 2020). https://doi.org/10.1145/3386392.3399564
10. Constantinides, A., Fidas, C., Belk, M., Pietron, A.M., Han, T., Pitsillides, A.: From hot-spots towards experience-spots: leveraging on users' sociocultural experiences to enhance security in cued-recall graphical authentication. Int. J. Hum. Comput. Stud. **149**, 102602 (2021). https://doi.org/10.1016/j.ijhcs.2021.102602
11. Cui, J., Zhou, S., Zhong, H., Xu, Y., Sha, K.: Transaction-based flow rule conflict detection and resolution in SDN. In: 2018 27th International Conference on Computer Communication and Networks (ICCCN), pp. 1–9 (2018). https://doi.org/10.1109/ICCCN.2018.8487415
12. David, A., Larsen, K.G., Legay, A., Mikučionis, M., Poulsen, D.B.: UPPAAL SMC tutorial. Int. J. Softw. Tools Technol. Transf. **17**(4), 397–415 (2015). https://doi.org/10.1007/s10009-014-0361-y
13. Dhayne, H., Haque, R., Kilany, R., Taher, Y.: In search of big medical data integration solutions - a comprehensive survey. IEEE Access **7**, 91265–91290 (2019). https://doi.org/10.1109/ACCESS.2019.2927491
14. Dubovitskaya, A., Xu, Z., Ryu, S., Schumacher, M., Wang, F.: Secure and trustable electronic medical records sharing using blockchain. In: AMIA Annual Symposium Proceedings, vol. 2017, p. 650. American Medical Informatics Association (2017). https://www.ncbi.nlm.nih.gov/pmc/articles/PMC5977675/
15. Extermann, M., et al.: Predicting the risk of chemotherapy toxicity in older patients: the chemotherapy risk assessment scale for high-age patients (crash) score. Cancer **118**(13), 3377–3386 (2012). https://doi.org/10.1002/cncr.26646

16. Fan, K., Wang, S., Ren, Y., Li, H., Yang, Y.: Medblock: efficient and secure medical data sharing via blockchain. J. Med. Syst. **42**(8), 1–11 (2018). https://doi.org/10.1007/s10916-018-0993-7

17. Gavrilov, G., Vlahu-Gjorgievska, E., Trajkovik, V.: Healthcare data warehouse system supporting cross-border interoperability. Health Inform. J. **26**(2), 1321–1332 (2020). https://doi.org/10.1177/1460458219876793

18. Guo, H., Li, W., Nejad, M., Shen, C.C.: Access control for electronic health records with hybrid blockchain-edge architecture. In: 2019 IEEE International Conference on Blockchain (Blockchain), pp. 44–51. IEEE (2019). https://doi.org/10.1109/Blockchain.2019.00015

19. Hölbl, M., Kompara, M., Kamišalić, A., Nemec Zlatolas, L.: A systematic review of the use of blockchain in healthcare. Symmetry **10**(10), 470 (2018). https://doi.org/10.3390/sym10100470

20. Janjic, V., Bowles, J.K.F., Vermeulen, A.F., et al.: The serums tool-chain: ensuring security and privacy of medical data in smart patient-centric healthcare systems. In: 2019 IEEE International Conference on Big Data, pp. 2726–2735. IEEE, New York, NY, USA (December 2019). https://doi.org/10.1109/BigData47090.2019.9005600

21. Larrucea, X., Moffie, M., Asaf, S., Santamaria, I.: Towards a gdpr compliant way to secure european cross border healthcare industry 4.0. Comput. Stand. Interfaces **69**, 103408 (2020). https://doi.org/10.1016/j.csi.2019.103408

22. de Moura, L., Bjørner, N.: Z3: an efficient SMT solver. In: Ramakrishnan, C.R., Rehof, J. (eds.) TACAS 2008. LNCS, vol. 4963, pp. 337–340. Springer, Heidelberg (2008). https://doi.org/10.1007/978-3-540-78800-3_24

23. Silvina, A., Bowles, J., Hall, P.: On predicting the outcomes of chemotherapy treatments in breast cancer. In: Riaño, D., Wilk, S., ten Teije, A. (eds.) AIME 2019. LNCS (LNAI), vol. 11526, pp. 180–190. Springer, Cham (2019). https://doi.org/10.1007/978-3-030-21642-9_24

24. Sookhak, M., Jabbarpour, M.R., Safa, N.S., Yu, F.R.: Blockchain and smart contract for access control in healthcare: a survey, issues and challenges, and open issues. J. Netw. Comput. Appl. **178**, 102950 (2021). https://doi.org/10.1016/j.jnca.2020.102950

25. Tanwar, S., Parekh, K., Evans, R.: Blockchain-based electronic healthcare record system for healthcare 4.0 applications. J. Inf. Secur. Appl. **50**, 102407 (2020). https://doi.org/10.1016/j.jisa.2019.102407

26. Webber, T., Santana, J.M., Vermeulen, A.F., Bowles, J.K.F., et al.: Designing a patient-centric system for secure exchanges of medical data. In: Gervasi, O. (ed.) ICCSA 2020. LNCS, vol. 12254, pp. 598–614. Springer, Cham (2020). https://doi.org/10.1007/978-3-030-58817-5_44

Structuring Rule Sets Using Binary Decision Diagrams

Florian Beck[✉], Johannes Fürnkranz, and Van Quoc Phuong Huynh

Institute for Application-oriented Knowledge Processing (FAW),
Johannes Kepler University, Linz, Austria
{fbeck,juffi,vqphuynh}@faw.jku.at

Abstract. Over the years we have seen considerable progress in learning rule-based theories. However, all state-of-the-art rule learners still learn descriptions that directly relate the input features to the target concept and are not able to discover intermediate concepts which might result in a more compact and interpretable theory. An analogous observation can also be made in electronic design automation where the task is to find the minimal representation of a Boolean function: if the representation is not limited to two levels, even smaller circuits can be found. In this paper, we consider binary classification tasks as multi-level logic optimization problems. We take DNF descriptions of the positive class, as obtained by state-of-the-art rule learners, and generate binary decision diagrams with the equivalent expression as the rule set. Finally, a new rule-based theory is extracted from the BDD, which includes new intermediate concepts and is therefore better structured than the original DNF rule set. First experiments on small artificial datasets indicate that intermediate concepts can be reliably detected, and the size of the resulting representations can be compressed, but a first study on a simple real-world dataset showed that the found structures are too complex to be interpretable.

Keywords: Inductive rule learning · Learning in logic · Binary decision diagrams · Multi-level logic optimization

1 Introduction

One of the big unsolved problems in inductive rule learning is the invention of new intermediate concepts. This line of work has been known as *constructive induction* [15] or *predicate invention* [30], but surprisingly, it has not received much attention since the classical works in inductive logic programming in the 1980s and 1990s. Most of the approaches are tailored towards learning from small datasets, often single examples, making use of additional knowledge, e.g., in the form of rule templates [21]. Kramer [14] provides an excellent recent summary of work in this area, also pointing out essentially the above-mentioned research gap.

© Springer Nature Switzerland AG 2021
S. Moschoyiannis et al. (Eds.): RuleML+RR 2021, LNCS 12851, pp. 48–61, 2021.
https://doi.org/10.1007/978-3-030-91167-6_4

A straight-forward way for inventing new concepts is the use of a wrapper that scans for regularly co-occurring patterns in rules, and use them to define new intermediate concepts which allow to compress the original theory [25, 33]. For rules that have been obtained from decision trees [27], each path from the root vertex to the leaf can be interpreted as a rule. If two paths have common arcs, their corresponding rules share part of their conditions as well. From these, we can create a new concept that is used in two or more rules. However, by creating concepts in this way, we will only obtain conjunctive expressions as intermediate concepts. This is a severe limitation, as it can only re-inforce the learning of rules that have been found in previous iterations, so that they can be more quickly found with the learned conjunctive short-cuts.

In general, conjunctions can be described efficiently by decision trees, while disjunctive concepts may suffer from the well-known replication problem [24], i.e., the problem that the same subtree would have to be learned in multiple parts of the tree. This problem can be handled efficiently by decision graphs, a generalization of decision trees [23]. They additionally contain joins, where two (or more) vertices have a common child. This specifies that two subsets have some common properties, and hence can be considered as a disjunctive intermediate concept. Much more rewarding would therefore be a method that allows to extract disjunctive descriptions of possible subconcepts from learned rule sets. In this short paper, we will thus present a new approach how to extract rule-based theories with both conjunctive and disjunctive intermediate concepts. We focus on binary decision diagrams (BDDs) as a subgroup of decision graphs, which are well-known in the field of electronic design automation, and show they can be used for extracting meaningful disjunctive subconcepts from learned rule sets.

The paper is structured as follows: Sect. 2 gives a brief introduction into BDDs and presents related work. Subsequently, Sect. 3 explains our rule set structuring algorithm based on an illustrative example. In Sect 4, we apply the approach both on artificial and on some real-world datasets. We conclude in Sect. 5 and discuss possible improvements to make the presented approach applicable to a wider variety of datasets.

2   Preliminaries and Related Work

A *binary decision diagram* (BDD) is a rooted, directed acyclic graph. Each non-terminal vertex v is labeled by a variable $var(v)$ and has arcs directed toward two children: $lo(v)$ corresponding to the case where the variable is assigned 0 and $hi(v)$ corresponding to the case where the variable is assigned 1. Each terminal vertex is labeled 0 or 1 [7]. Two example BDDs describing the parity concept are shown in Fig. 1. The resulting truth table of both diagrams is equivalent, however, the specific case of a binary decision tree in Fig. 1a needs more non-terminal and terminal vertices than the BDD in Fig. 1b. In fact, Fig. 1b shows a reduced ordered BDD (ROBDD), which merges duplicate non-terminal and non-terminal vertices and eliminates redundant vertices v with $hi(v) = lo(v)$.

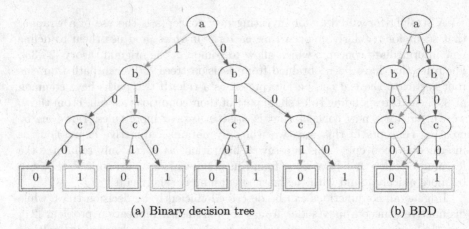

(a) Binary decision tree   (b) BDD

Fig. 1. Binary decision tree and BDD for the parity problem. Each non-terminal vertex is labeled with the variable to check and has two outgoing arcs: the green one if the value is 1 and the red one if it is 0. The terminal vertices labeled with 0 (1) correspond to an even (odd) parity. (Color figure online)

Furthermore, each path through the diagram traverses the variables in the same order, which makes ROBDDs to a canonical representation of Boolean formulas for a given variable order. In the following, when speaking of BDDs, we will assume them to be reduced and ordered (i.e., ROBDDs).

BDDs are mainly used in the field of electronic design automation during the process of logic synthesis. The task is to find a minimal digital circuit with the desired behavior defined by e.g. a Boolean formula, which is known as logic minimization. First approaches in the 1980s, such as the ESPRESSO algorithm [5], delivered efficient solutions for the minimization on two levels, while a few years later algorithms and systems for multi-level logic optimization were designed, e.g. MIS [6]. More recently, with and-inverter-graphs (AIG) a new scalable representation is used in synthesis and verification tasks [2].

In the 1990s, decision diagrams were also applied to machine learning under the name of decision graphs. Reduced ordered decision graphs (RODG) were combined with the minimum description length principle to trade off between accuracy in the training set and complexity of the description [22]. Oblivious, read-once decision graphs (OODG) [13] extend RODGs by not being limited to binary tests, which is crucial for many real-world datasets. The combination of logic synthesis and machine learning, in particular the trade-off between exactness and generalization, is currently still being researched [28].

Roughly parallel to this, on the side of symbolic machine learning, first approaches to restructure rule sets developed. For example, DUCE was a machine learning system which is able to restructure a knowledge base by suggesting and interactively refining high-level domain features [19]. Surprisingly, this topic known as constructive induction or predicate invention has not received much attention since then. Recent research approaches the problem from deep learning,

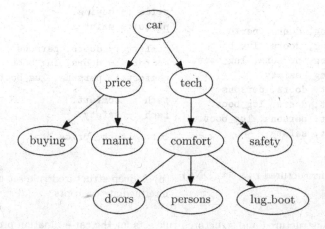

Fig. 2. Concepts in the car-evaluation dataset, cf. [3]

with formalisms like sum-product-networks (SPN) [26] or binary neural networks (BNN) [8], which also have a declarative interpretation, but, however, are not constructed to be minimal and interpretable like traditional rule sets.

3   Rule Set Structuring

Like decision trees, BDDs can be used to generate sets of rules. Each path in a decision tree or diagram can be converted to a rule with attribute-value pairs (derived by vertex resp. arc) as conditions, whereas the head of the rule is given by the leaf. If two paths overlap, then the corresponding rules will share conditions as well, though, this is not necessarily the case the other way around. While this holds for both decision trees and diagrams, the number of arcs only used in a single path can be significantly higher in decision trees than in BDDs, like, e.g., in Fig. 1. The main difference between the two data structures is that BDDs allow vertices to have an indegree $deg^-(v)$ of more than 1. In such 'join' vertices, two or more different incoming paths can share their remaining arcs until the leaf is reached. Therefore, we can define a new *disjunctive concept* for all incoming paths ending there and starting either from the root vertex or another 'join' vertex. If some of the incoming paths have at least two arcs in common, we can additionally define a *conjunctive concept*. In Fig. 1b, both vertices labeled with c have $deg^-(v) = 2$. The left one combines the paths $a = 0 \wedge b = 1$ and $a = 1 \wedge b = 0$ to a new disjunctive concept for parity $odd \leftarrow (a = 0 \wedge b = 1) \vee (a = 1 \wedge b = 0)$, the right one analogously for *even*. These concepts can be reused in the rules for the terminal vertex labeled with 1: $parity \leftarrow (even \wedge c = 0) \vee (odd \wedge c = 1)$.

To demonstrate the functionality of the proposed method, we will apply it on a sample dataset dealing with the evaluation of cars. Our car-evaluation dataset is inspired by the dataset presented in [3], where it was used as an

```
                                    price :- buying.
car :- buying, doors, persons.      price :- maint.
car :- buying, doors, lug_boot.
car :- buying, persons, lug_boot.   comfort :- doors, persons.
car :- buying, safety.              comfort :- doors, lug_boot.
car :- maint, doors, persons.       comfort :- persons, lug_boot.
car :- maint, doors, lug_boot.
car :- maint, persons, lug_boot.    tech :- comfort.
car :- maint, safety.               tech :- safety.

                                    car :- tech, price.
```

(a) A flat unstructured rule set (DNF)   (b) A deep structured rule set using three intermediate concepts

Fig. 3. Unstructured and structured rule sets for the car-evaluation problem.

example dataset for tree-structured criteria in the field of multi-attribute decision making. The structure of the criteria is adopted unchanged and shown in Fig. 2. According to this tree, the quality of cars is measured by two main groups of criteria: price and technical characteristics. The price is determined by buying and maintenance price. Technical characteristics are decomposed into safety and comfort, which further depends on number of doors, number of persons that fit in the car and size of the luggage boot.

While the number and structure of the attributes remain unchanged, we restrict the domain of each attribute to the values acceptable (acc) and unacceptable (unacc). In particular, the target attribute will be limited to these two values as well, so that the dataset can be transformed easily into a binary classification problem. For convenience, we abbreviate the condition x=acc as x and x=unacc as \+ x for every attribute x.

Figure 3b shows the structured rule set that defines the resulting domain. However, the resulting minimal DNF, shown in Fig. 3a already consists of 22 literals, while the rule set with intermediate concepts only consists of 12. Therefore, classical rule learners would have to learn longer rules for a perfect theory than they would be if we learn intermediate concepts. In general, the number of terms in both a CNF and DNF can grow exponentially (see [18]).

Our goal is now to find a rule representation close to the one defined in Fig. 3b using a BDD. We could start off with a DNF expression that describes all acceptable combinations of the $2^6 = 64$ possible samples and transform this Boolean formula to a BDD. To this end, we use the Python library PBDD[1], which can not only build BDDs in an efficient way (cf. [4]), but also provides the option to find the best variable ordering (see [29]).

With this, the DNF of Fig. 3a, which is also the output of all rule learners that we tried, can be converted to the BDD shown in Fig. 4a. The concepts detected with the identification of all 'join' vertices are listed in the rule set in

---

[1] https://github.com/tyler-utah/PBDD.

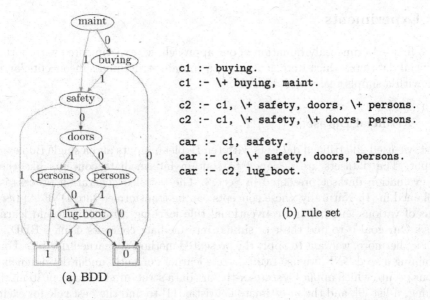

```
c1 :- buying.
c1 :- \+ buying, maint.

c2 :- c1, \+ safety, doors, \+ persons.
c2 :- c1, \+ safety, \+ doors, persons.

car :- c1, safety.
car :- c1, \+ safety, doors, persons.
car :- c2, lug_boot.
```

(b) rule set

(a) BDD

Fig. 4. BDD and a derived rule set for the car-evaluation dataset. Concept c1 corresponds to the vertex labeled with safety, c2 to the vertex labeled with lug_boot and car to the terminal vertex labeled with 1.

Fig. 4b. Instead of originally three intermediate concepts with eight rules, we now found only two intermediate concepts with seven rules in total. However, the detected concepts are similar to the original ones: c1 is identical to price when simplifying the second rule and c2 is close to comfort. The tech concept is merged into the final car concept and is thus not listed explicitly. To conclude, by the invention of concepts, the presented approach was able to find a DNF-equivalent rule set which is better structured and uses less rules.

In general, it will not be feasible to use a DNF expression that represents a disjunction of all positive samples as the input for computing the BDD. This approach presumes that the data is noise-free and complete, since all test samples that are not identical to a known positive sample are considered as negative, i.e., it does not generalize at all. Traditional approaches in logic synthesis like Karnaugh maps [12] and the Quine-McCluskey algorithm [16] can cope with the non-completeness by explicitly considering feature combinations that do not appear in the training set as "don't cares" and treating them arbitrarily either as positive or negative samples. However, in machine learning the training set is usually only a tiny fraction of the whole feature space, which makes it impossible to explicitly evaluate all "don't cares".

However, in order to overcome this problem of overfitting, we can shift the task of generalization to a rule learner, which is able to learn a small and general rule set from the input data, thereby also dealing with possible noise in the data. The learned rule set can the be used as input for the BDD creation. These experiments will be described in the next section.

4   Experiments

For a first experimental evaluation of our approach, we experimented with both, artificial datasets, which were generated to contain structured subconcepts, and also with a simple real-world datasets.

4.1   Artificial Datasets

First, we used 20 artificial datasets with ten Boolean inputs and a single Boolean output. The datasets are designed to contain intermediate concepts like the car-evaluation dataset presented in Sect. 3. The detailed generation process is explained in [1]. Naturally, these concepts can be transformed into DNF expressions of various lengths, and conventional rule learning algorithms would learn these. Our goal is to find these or similar intermediate concepts using a BDD.

Furthermore, we want to apply the presented method on learned rule sets. For obtaining a seed DNF, we use LORD, a rule learner currently under development in our group, which applies a state-of-the-art data structure for frequent itemset mining, n-list [9], and the m-estimate heuristic [11] to find the best rule for each training example via a greedy method. These local best rules are collected and then filtered to form a rule-based classifier. As it learns the best rule for each training example, the produced rule sets are typically larger (but often also more accurate) than the sparse rule sets learned by conventional learners, and often contain several variants of similar rules. For this reason, it seemed like a perfect choice for our exploration of the use of BDDs for structuring rule sets.

For both settings, we compare the number of rules $|R|$ and concepts $|C|$ in the DNF resp. flat rule set with the corresponding numbers $|R'|$ and $|C'|$ in the rule set extracted from the generated (RO)BDD. Obviously, for the DNF representations $|C| = 0$ for all datasets by definition. Furthermore, we compare the number of (non-terminal) vertices $|V'|$ in the BDD with the number of literals $|V|$ in the DNF, since we can define every rule as a separate path in a BDD.

The results are shown in Table 1. Both the ground truth and the learned rule set have a higher number of rules and concepts in the deep rule set and a higher number of vertices in the flat rule set. Thus, by converting the DNF into a deep rule set, we can compact the structure by finding intermediate concepts and merge vertices at the cost of more rules for defining these intermediate concepts. Thereby, we can also see that the average number of rules, concepts and vertices is almost identical for the ground truth and the learned rule set, even if individual values deviate from each other.

4.2   Mushroom Dataset

We also tried our approach on the *mushroom* dataset[2] from the UCI repository [10]. This dataset is known to be solvable with very simple rules, and, in fact,

---

[2] For all rule sets, the attributes have been one-hot-encoded to meet the requirements for BDD processing.

Table 1. Number of rules $|R|$, concepts $|C|$, and vertices $|V|$ in artificial datasets for both the ground truth and the rule set from our learner. The columns without prime denote the values for the rule set in DNF, the values with prime those for the rule set extracted from the BDD.

Seed	Ground truth						LORD					
	$|R|$	$|R'|$	$|C|$	$|C'|$	$|V|$	$|V'|$	$|R|$	$|R'|$	$|C|$	$|C'|$	$|V|$	$|V'|$
5	8	20	0	7	29	18	13	20	0	6	52	19
16	17	27	0	4	49	25	18	26	0	4	51	26
19	4	8	0	1	9	10	5	6	0	1	11	7
24	15	46	0	12	59	45	18	39	0	11	72	36
36	21	62	0	16	85	53	25	61	0	12	99	62
44	16	28	0	5	48	28	25	31	0	5	75	28
53	30	37	0	7	104	31	13	12	0	3	36	11
57	6	10	0	2	19	13	8	22	0	5	27	17
60	18	26	0	5	57	27	20	28	0	5	63	29
65	7	14	0	3	23	15	8	15	0	4	27	13
68	17	31	0	8	68	34	23	46	0	10	92	43
69	14	24	0	6	60	30	16	36	0	6	70	30
70	18	41	0	7	78	46	26	56	0	13	113	51
81	20	43	0	11	84	39	28	34	0	10	121	33
82	4	5	0	1	8	6	4	8	0	2	8	6
85	3	3	0	0	8	6	3	3	0	0	8	6
89	12	48	0	11	47	41	19	41	0	11	72	36
107	17	47	0	10	70	41	32	32	0	7	132	33
112	18	37	0	8	67	33	33	41	0	10	126	36
118	14	32	0	8	51	27	16	32	0	6	59	30
∅	14.0	29.5	0	6.6	51.2	28.4	17.7	29.5	0	6.6	65.7	27.6

even LORD, which aims for finding the best explanation for each individual example, produces a very small rules set consisting of only 8 rules with a total of 10 conditions. For these reason, we also tried two rule sets generated with a conventional separate-and-conquer rule learning algorithm using a regular and an inverted Laplace heuristic. Whereas the first heuristic prefers short rules, the second results in longer rules and literals with multiple occurrences in the rule set [31]. The goal of this experiment was to see whether BDDs can be used to successfully structure the complex rule sets learned by such inverted heuristics.

In Table 2 we can see that our approach cannot find interesting subconcepts in the two rule sets with short rules, because the learned rules often only consist of single conditions. The few found concepts typically only capture that a previous rule does not fire. Only for the more complex rule set of the inverted Laplace heuristic, our approach delivers new subconcepts. However, these increase the

Table 2. Number of rules, concepts and vertices for the mushroom dataset for three different rule learners. See Table 1 for the meaning of the variables.

Rule learner	$|R|$	$|R'|$	$|C|$	$|C'|$	$|V|$	$|V'|$
h_{Lap} learner	7	57	0	12	35	46
h_{Lap} learner	11	13	0	1	13	13
LORD	8	12	0	2	10	10

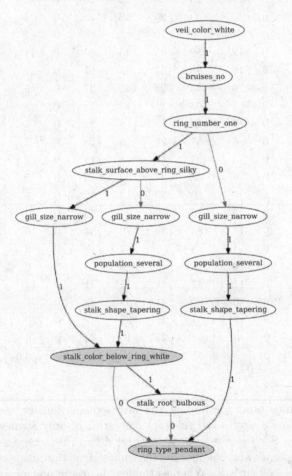

Fig. 5. Part of the BDD for the mushroom dataset

size of the found concept descriptions, not only in the number of rules but also in the number of vertices.

Figure 5 shows a part of the BDD resulting from the DNF learned from inverted Laplace heuristics. The whole BDD is too big and too complex to be shown in a figure and to be considered interpretable. We cannot reproduce all

$|R'| = 57$ rules and $|C'| = 12$ concepts that are formed from this BDD by our method, but we can take a closer look at the pink colored vertex, which joins two different green incoming paths. These correspond to the following two rules, defining an intermediate concept c1.

```
c1 :- veil_color_white, bruises_no, ring_number_one,
      stalk_surface_above_ring_silk,  gill_size_narrow.
c1 :- veil_color_white, bruises_no,  ring_number_one,
      \+ stalk_surface_above_ring_silky, gill_size_narrow,
      population_several, stalk_shape_tapering.
```

Obviously, these rules could be further simplified by extracting common rules conditions. We have not implemented this step yet, but it essentially corresponds to the *intra-construction* operator first proposed for propositional inverse resolution in the DUCE system [19,20]. An application of this rule results in the following, even more structured rule set:

```
c1 :- veil_color_white, bruises_no, ring_number_one,
      gill_size_narrow, c1a.

c1a :- stalk_surface_above_ring_silky.
c1a :- population_several, stalk_shape_tapering.
```

While this looks like a straight-forward step, which we could have easily implemented, it is actually more complex than it appears. This may be seen when we, based on the above definition, try to define the pink colored 'join' vertex with three incoming edges (two red and one green), which would, straight-forwardly, result in the following definition for a concept c2:

```
c2 :- veil_color_white, bruises_no, \+ ring_number_one,
      gill_size_narrow, population_several, stalk_shape_tapering.
c2 :- c1, stalk_color_below_ring_white, \+ stalk_root_bulbous.
c2 :- c1, \+ stalk_color_below_ring_white.
```

As can be seen, the concept c1 defined above is used in two of the above-mentioned rules. However, also the first rule, has a strong similarity to the parts of the definitions of c1, in that it only differs in whether ring_number_one is true or not. Based on this, one could further restructure these rules in the following way:

```
c1 :- c12, ring_number_one, c1a.

c1a :- stalk_surface_above_ring_silky.
c1a :- population_several, stalk_shape_tapering.

c12 :- veil_color_white, bruises_no, gill_size_narrow.
```

```
c2 :- c12, \+ ring_number_one, c1a.
c2 :- c1, \+ stalk_root_bulbous.
c2 :- c1, \+ stalk_color_below_ring_white.
```

Note that we additionally performed an algebraic optimization in the second rule of c2, which made use of the \+ stalk_color_below_ring_white-term in the third rule. The definition of c1 could even be removed altogether, and c2 could be defined on the basis of c12, c1a and c2a, emphasizing the similarity of the three rules defining c2 and extracting their differences to a subconcept c2a. After performing algebraic optimizations in the rules of c2, this leads to the following rule set:

```
c1a :- stalk_surface_above_ring_silky.
c1a :- population_several, stalk_shape_tapering.

c12 :- veil_color_white, bruises_no, gill_size_narrow.

c2a :- \+ ring_number_one.
c2a :- \+ stalk_root_bulbous.
c2a :- \+ stalk_color_below_ring_white.

c2 :- c12, c1a, c2a.
```

Obviously, finding a compressive and interpretable structured theory is a very hard problem, which requires a deeper investigation.

5   Conclusion and Future Work

Motivated by the unsolved problem of the invention of new intermediate concepts, we present a novel method which uses BDDs to extract hidden concepts in existing rule sets. We show in our experiments that this approach detects concepts reliably in artificial datasets and one real-world dataset. While for the artificial datasets the rule set structure could be compacted by the concepts found, the effectiveness of the method on one-hot-encoded nominal data is limited so far, which we plan to address in future work.

The proposed method has some substantial limitations so far. One main drawback is that BDDs are binary by definition and therefore both the input attributes and the class attribute are limited to two values. While we can easily convert nominal, numeric and multi-class datasets to fit this format by using discretization, one-hot-encoding and one-vs.-one or one-vs.-rest classification, the size of the corresponding BDD grows quickly which makes it both inefficient to compute and hard to interpret. A suitable extension could be the use of multi-valued decision diagrams (MDD) instead of BDDs [17], which can reduce the size of the diagram and the corresponding rule set drastically.

The practical utility of BDD-based compression is also limited by its lack of efficiency. The main problem is that the size of a BDD depends on the order in which the variables are processed. A good compression can only be obtained with a good variable reordering. The approach that we use essentially tries many different orderings in order to identify the one that results in the minimal graph [29]. However, if we are only looking for a restructuring and not a compression of the rule set, we are not necessarily interested in the minimal representation given by the best variable ordering. Whereas the default ordering can still be inappropriate for finding a compact structure, a good heuristic for finding not the best, but a good ordering might be a good compromise.

As already indicated in Sect. 4.2, we also intend to bring in ideas from compression-based systems such as DUCE [19,20], with its systematic refinement operators based on inverse resolution, or KRIMP [32], from which we hope to be able to adapt ideas from database compression to the problem of compressing predictive theories. We also intend to apply algebraic optimizations like shown in Sect. 4.2 more systematically to remove irrelevant conditions and rules for further compressing.

Finally, we noticed that 'join' vertices in the BDD are often just caused by rules that do not apply, which would only be relevant for rule lists, but not for rule sets. We think that an appropriate structure for rule sets would therefore need to process all rules at the same time in a non-deterministic way, very much in the same way as non-deterministic finite automata can have multiple transitions simultaneously as opposed to deterministic automata. This also comes closer to the representation in neural networks, where we can use activations of the previous layer in 0, 1 or multiple vertices just like we can follow 0, 1 or multiple paths in the decision graph. We plan to explore all these options in subsequent work.

References

1. Beck, F., Fürnkranz, J.: An empirical investigation into deep and shallow rule learning. Front. Artifi. Intell. **4**, 145 (2021). https://doi.org/10.3389/frai.2021.689398
2. Biere, A., Heljanko, K., Wieringa, S.: AIGER 1.9 and beyond. Technical report 11/2, Institute for Formal Models and Verification, Johannes Kepler University, Linz, Austria (2011)
3. Bohanec, M., Rajkovic, V.: Knowledge acquisition and explanation for multi-attribute decision making. In: 8th International Workshop on Expert Systems and Their Applications, pp. 59–78 (1988)
4. Brace, K.S., Rudell, R.L., Bryant, R.E.: Efficient implementation of a BDD package. In: 27th ACM/IEEE Design Automation Conference, pp. 40–45. IEEE (1990)
5. Brayton, R.K., Hachtel, G.D., McMullen, C.T., Sangiovanni-Vincentelli, A.L.: Logic Minimization Algorithms for VLSI Synthesis. Kluwer Academic Publishers (1984)
6. Brayton, R.K., Rudell, R., Sangiovanni-Vincentelli, A., Wang, A.R.: MIS: a multiple-level logic optimization system. IEEE Trans. Comput. Aided Des. Integr. Circ. Syst. **6**(6), 1062–1081 (1987)
7. Bryant, R.E.: Symbolic Boolean manipulation with ordered binary-decision diagrams. ACM Comput. Surv. **24**(3), 293–318 (1992)

8. Courbariaux, M., Bengio, Y., David, J.: BinaryConnect: training deep neural networks with binary weights during propagations. In: Cortes, C., Lawrence, N.D., Lee, D.D., Sugiyama, M., Garnett, R. (eds.) Advances in Neural Information Processing Systems (NeurIPS), vol. 28, Montreal, Quebec, Canada, pp. 3123–3131 (2015)

9. Deng, Z.H., Lv, S.L.: PrePost+: an efficient N-lists-based algorithm for mining frequent itemsets via children-parent equivalence pruning. Expert Syst. Appl. **42**(13), 5424–5432 (2015)

10. Dua, D., Graff, C.: UCI machine learning repository (2017). http://archive.ics.uci.edu/ml

11. Džeroski, S., Cestnik, B., Petrovski, I.: Using the m-estimate in rule induction. J. Comput. Inf. Technol. **1**, 37–46 (1993)

12. Karnaugh, M.: The map method for synthesis of combinational logic circuits. Trans. Am. Inst. Electr. Eng. Part I: Commun. Electron. **72**(5), 593–599 (1953)

13. Kohavi, R.: Bottom-up induction of oblivious read-once decision graphs. In: Bergadano, F., De Raedt, L. (eds.) ECML 1994. LNCS, vol. 784, pp. 154–169. Springer, Heidelberg (1994). https://doi.org/10.1007/3-540-57868-4_56

14. Kramer, S.: A brief history of learning symbolic higher-level representations from data (and a curious look forward). In: Proceedings of the 29th International Joint Conference on Artificial Intelligence (IJCAI), Survey Track, pp. 4868–4876 (2020)

15. Matheus, C.J.: A constructive induction framework. In: Proceedings of the 6th International Workshop on Machine Learning, pp. 474–475 (1989)

16. McCluskey, E.J.: Minimization of Boolean functions. Bell Syst. Tech. J. **35**(6), 1417–1444 (1956). https://doi.org/10.1002/j.1538-7305.1956.tb03835.x

17. Miller, D.M.: Multiple-valued logic design tools. In: Proceedings of the 23rd International Symposium on Multiple-Valued Logic, pp. 2–11. IEEE (1993)

18. Miltersen, P.B., Radhakrishnan, J., Wegener, I.: On converting CNF to DNF. Theoret. Comput. Sci. **347**(1–2), 325–335 (2005)

19. Muggleton, S.H.: Structuring knowledge by asking questions. In: Bratko, I., Lavrač, N. (eds.) Progress in Machine Learning, pp. 218–229. Sigma Press, Wilmslow (1987)

20. Muggleton, S.H.: Inverting the resolution principle. In: Hayes, J.E., Michie, D., Tyugu, E. (eds.) Machine Intelligence, vol. 12, chap. 7, pp. 93–103. Clarendon Press, Oxford (1991)

21. Muggleton, S.H., Lin, D., Tamaddoni-Nezhad, A.: Meta-interpretive learning of higher-order dyadic datalog: predicate invention revisited. Mach. Learn. **100**(1), 49–73 (2015)

22. Oliveira, A.L., Sangiovanni-Vincentelli, A.: Using the minimum description length principle to infer reduced ordered decision graphs. Mach. Learn. **25**(1), 23–50 (1996)

23. Oliver, J.J.: Decision graphs – an extension of decision trees. In: Proceedings of the 4th International Workshop on Artificial Intelligence and Statistics, pp. 343–350 (1993)

24. Pagallo, G., Haussler, D.: Boolean feature discovery in empirical learning. Mach. Learn. **5**, 71–99 (1990)

25. Pfahringer, B.: Controlling constructive induction in CIPF: an MDL approach. In: Bergadano, F., De Raedt, L. (eds.) ECML 1994. LNCS, vol. 784, pp. 242–256. Springer, Heidelberg (1994). https://doi.org/10.1007/3-540-57868-4_62

26. Poon, H., Domingos, P.: Sum-product networks: a new deep architecture. In: 2011 IEEE International Conference on Computer Vision Workshops (ICCV Workshops), pp. 689–690. IEEE (2011)

27. Quinlan, J.R.: Generating production rules from decision trees. In: Proceedings of the 10th International Joint Conference on Artificial Intelligence (IJCAI-87), pp. 304–307. Morgan Kaufmann (1987)

28. Rai, S., et al.: Logic synthesis meets machine learning: trading exactness for generalization. arXiV Preprint arXiV:2012.02530 (2020)

29. Rudell, R.: Dynamic variable ordering for ordered binary decision diagrams. In: Proceedings of 1993 International Conference on Computer Aided Design (ICCAD), pp. 42–47. IEEE (1993)

30. Stahl, I.: Predicate invention in inductive logic programming. In: De Raedt, L. (ed.) Advances in Inductive Logic Programming, Frontiers in Artificial Intelligence and Applications, vol. 32, pp. 34–47. IOS Press (1996)

31. Stecher, J., Janssen, F., Fürnkranz, J.: Separating rule refinement and rule selection heuristics in inductive rule learning. In: Calders, T., Esposito, F., Hüllermeier, E., Meo, R. (eds.) ECML PKDD 2014, Part III. LNCS (LNAI), vol. 8726, pp. 114–129. Springer, Heidelberg (2014). https://doi.org/10.1007/978-3-662-44845-8_8

32. Vreeken, J., van Leeuwen, M., Siebes, A.: KRIMP: mining itemsets that compress. Data Min. Knowl. Discov. **23**(1), 169–214 (2011). https://doi.org/10.1007/s10618-010-0202-x. http://dx.doi.org/10.1007/ s10618-010-0202-x

33. Wnek, J., Michalski, R.S.: Hypothesis-driven constructive induction in AQ17-HCI: a method and experiments. Mach. Learn. **14**(2), 139–168 (1994). Special Issue on Evaluating and Changing Representation

Link Traversal with Distributed Subweb Specifications

Bart Bogaerts[1]([✉]), Bas Ketsman[1], Younes Zeboudj[1], Heba Aamer[2], Ruben Taelman[3], and Ruben Verborgh[3]

[1] Vrije Universiteit Brussel, Brussels, Belgium
{bart.bogaerts,bas.ketsman,younes.zeboudj}@vub.be
[2] Universiteit Hasselt, Hasselt, Belgium
heba.mohamed@uhasselt.be
[3] Ghent University – imec – IDLab, Ghent, Belgium
{ruben.taelman,ruben.verborgh}@ugent.be

Abstract. Link Traversal–based Query Processing (LTQP), in which a SPARQL query is evaluated over a web of documents rather than a single dataset, is often seen as a theoretically interesting yet impractical technique. However, in a time where the hypercentralization of data has increasingly come under scrutiny, a decentralized Web of Data with a simple document-based interface is appealing, as it enables data publishers to control their data and access rights. While LTQP allows evaluating complex queries over such webs, it suffers from performance issues (due to the high number of documents containing data) as well as information quality concerns (due to the many sources providing such documents). In existing LTQP approaches, the burden of finding sources to query is entirely in the hands of the *data consumer*. In this paper, we argue that to solve these issues, *data publishers* should also be able to suggest sources of interest and *guide* the data consumer towards relevant and trustworthy data. We introduce a theoretical framework that enables such guided link traversal and study its properties. We illustrate with a theoretic example that this can improve query results and reduce the number of network requests.

Keywords: SPARQL · Link traversal–based query processing · Web of linked data

1 Introduction

The World-Wide Web provides a permissionless information space organized as interlinked documents. The Semantic Web builds on top of it by representing data in a machine-interpretable format, fueled by the Linked Data principles. In contrast to more complex data-driven APIS, the simplicity of document-based interfaces comes with multiple advantages. They scale easily, and can be hosted on many different kinds of hardware and software; we can realize the *"anyone can say anything about anything"* principle because every publisher has their

© Springer Nature Switzerland AG 2021
S. Moschoyiannis et al. (Eds.): RuleML+RR 2021, LNCS 12851, pp. 62–79, 2021.
https://doi.org/10.1007/978-3-030-91167-6_5

own domain in the Web, within which they can freely refer to concepts from other domains; and complex features such as access control or versioning are technically easy to achieve on a per-document basis.

However, decentralized interfaces are notoriously more difficult to query. As such, the past decade has instead been characterized by Big Data and hyper-centralization, in which data from multiple sources becomes aggregated in an increasingly smaller number of sources. While extremely powerful from a query and analytics perspective, such aggregation levels lead to a loss of control and freedom for individuals and small- to medium-scale data providers. This in turn has provoked some fundamental legal, societal, and economical questions regarding the desiredness of such hypercentral platforms. As such, there is again an increasing demand for more decentralized systems, where data is stored closer to its authentic source, in line with the original intentions of the Web [14].

As with Big Data, query processing on the Semantic Web has traditionally focused on *single* databases. The SPARQL query language allows querying such a single RDF store through the SPARQL protocol, which places significantly more constraints on the server than a document-based interface [15]. While *federated* query processing enables incorporating data from multiple SPARQL endpoints, federated queries have very limited link traversal capabilities and SPARQL endpoints easily experience performance degradation [2].

Fortunately, a technique was introduced to query webs of data: *Link Traversal–based Query Processing* (LTQP) [5,8], in which an agent evaluates a SPARQL query over a set of documents that is continuously expanded by selectively following hyperlinks inside of them. While LTQP demonstrates the independence of queries and selection of sources (on which these queries need to be executed), it has mostly remained a theoretical exercise, as its slow performance makes it unsuitable for practical purposes. The fact that LTQP can yield more results than single-source query evaluation, gave rise to different notions of *query semantics* and *completeness* [9]. While more data can be considered advantageous, it can also lead to doubts regarding *data quality, trustworthiness,* or *license compatibility*. Together with performance, these concerns seem to have pushed LTQP to the background.

In this article, we identify two limitations of existing LTQP approaches. Essentially, all existing LTQP approaches identify a *subweb* of the web of linked data on which a query needs to be executed. The first limitation is that *the responsibility for defining how to construct this subweb is entirely in the hands of the data consumer, from now on referred to as the **querying agent*** (which can be an end-user or machine client). In other words, existing approaches make the assumption that the querying agent can determine perfectly which links should be traversed. However, since every data publisher can freely choose how to organize their data, we cannot expect a single agent to possess complete knowledge of how such traversals should proceed. A second restriction is that current LTQP formalisms provide an all-or-nothing approach: a document is either included in the subweb of interest in its entirety, or not at all, while for data-quality reasons, it would be useful to only take parts of documents into account. For instance, an

```
<https://uma.ex/#me> foaf:knows
  <https://ann.ex/#me>, <https://bob.ex/#me>.
<https://bob.ex/#me> foaf:img <bob.jpg>.
```

Document 1: Contents of
https://uma.ex/

```
<https://ann.ex/#me> foaf:name "Ann";
  foaf:mbox <mailto:ann@corp.ex>;
  foaf:img <me.jpg>.
```

Document 4: Contents of
https://corp.ex/ann/

```
<https://ann.ex/#me> foaf:isPrimaryTopicOf <https://corp.ex/ann/>.
<https://ann.ex/#me> foaf:weblog <https://ann.ex/blog/>.
<https://ann.ex/#me> foaf:maker <https://photos.ex/ann/>.
```

Document 2: Contents of
https://ann.ex/

```
<https://bob.ex/#me> foaf:name "Bob";
  foaf:mbox <mailto:me@bob.ex>;
  foaf:img <funny-fish.jpg>.
<https://uma.ex/#me> foaf:knows
  <http://dbpedia.org/resource/Mickey_Mouse>.
<https://ann.ex/#me> foaf:name "Felix".
```

Document 3: Contents of *https://bob.ex/*

```
SELECT ?friend ?name ?email ?picture WHERE {
  <https://uma.ex/#me> foaf:knows ?friend.
  ?friend foaf:name ?name.
  OPTIONAL { ?friend foaf:mbox ?email.
             ?friend foaf:img  ?picture. }
}
```

Query 1: Application query in SPARQL

	?friend	?name	?email	?picture
1	`<https://ann.ex/#me>`	"Ann"	`<mailto:ann@corp.ex>`	`<https://corp.ex/ann/me.jpg>`
2	`<https://bob.ex/#me>`	"Bob"	`<mailto:me@bob.ex>`	`<https://uma.ex/bob.jpg>`
3	`<https://bob.ex/#me>`	"Bob"	`<mailto:me@bob.ex>`	`<https://bob.ex/funny-fish.jpg>`
4	`<https://ann.ex/#me>`	"Felix"	`<mailto:ann@corp.ex>`	`<https://corp.ex/ann/me.jpg>`
5	`dbr:Mickey_Mouse`	"Mickey Mouse"@en	*NULL*	*NULL*

Results 1: Possible results of LTQP of the query in Query 1 with *https://uma.ex/*
as seed

academic who has moved institutions might specify that the data provided by institution A is trustworthy up to a certain date and that for later information about them, institution B should be consulted. More radically, a certain end user might wish to specify that Facebook's data about who her friends are is correct, without thereby implying that any triple published by Facebook should be taken into account when performing a query.

In this paper, building on the use case of the next section, we propose an approach for *guided* link traversal that overcomes these two limitations. In our proposal, each data publisher has their own subweb of interest, and publishes a specification of how it can be constructed. They can use this for instance to describe the organization of their data, or to describe parties they trust (as well as for which data they trust them). The data consumer can then construct a subweb of interest *building on* the subwebs of the publishers, e.g., deciding to include parts of a subweb, or to omit it. As such, the data publishers *guide* the data consumer towards relevant data sources. We focus on the theoretical foundations and highlight opportunities for result quality and performance improvements.

2   Use Case

As a guiding example throughout this article, we introduce example data and queries for a use case that stems from the Solid ecosystem [14], where every person has their own *personal data vault*. Let us consider 3 people's profile documents, stored in their respective data vaults. Uma's profile (Document 1) lists her two friends Ann and Bob. Ann's profile (Document 2) contains links to her corporate page and various other pages. Bob, a self-professed jokester, lists his real name and email address in his profile (Document 3), in addition to a funny profile picture and a couple of factually incorrect statements (which he is able to publish given the open nature of the Web). Note how Ann provides additional facts about herself into the external document she links to (Document 4), and Uma's profile suggests a better profile picture for Bob (Document 1).

Next, we consider an *address book* application that displays the details of a user's contacts. At design-time, this application is unaware of the context and data distribution of the user and their friends. If we assume Uma to be the user, then the application's data need can be expressed as Query 1, which is a generic SPARQL template in which only the URL corresponding to Uma's identity (*https://uma.ex/#me*) has been filled out.

With traditional LTQP (under c_{All} semantics [9]), results include those in Results 1. However, the actually desired results are Rows 1 and 2, which contain Uma's two friends with relevant details. Rows 3–5 are formed using triples that occur in Bob's profile document but are not considered trustworthy by Uma (even though other triples in the same document are). To obtain these results, a query engine would need to fetch at least 7 documents: the profile documents of the 3 people (Uma, Ann, Bob), the 3 documents referred to by Ann's profile (Document 2), and the DBpedia page for Mickey Mouse.

3   Preliminaries

As a basis for our data model of a Web of Linked Data, we use the RDF data model [3]. That is, we assume three pairwise disjoint, infinite sets: $\mathcal{U}$ (for URIs), $\mathcal{B}$ (for blank nodes), $\mathcal{L}$ (for literals). An RDF *triple* is a tuple $(s, p, o) \in \mathcal{T}$, with $\mathcal{T}$ the set of all triples defined as $\mathcal{T} = (\mathcal{U} \cup \mathcal{B}) \times \mathcal{U} \times (\mathcal{U} \cup \mathcal{B} \cup \mathcal{L})$; if $t = (s, p, o) \in \mathcal{T}$, then $\mathrm{uris}(t) = \{s, p, o\} \cap \mathcal{U}$. A set of triples is called a *triple graph* or RDF *graph*. An RDF *dataset* is a set of tuples $\{\langle n_i, g_i \rangle\}$ where $n_i \in \mathcal{U}$ and g_i an RDF graph, where g_0 is referred to as the *default graph*.

We assume another set $\mathcal{D}$, disjoint from the aforementioned sets $\mathcal{U}$, $\mathcal{B}$ and $\mathcal{L}$, whose elements are referred to as *documents*. The RDF graph contained in each document is modeled by a function $data : \mathcal{D} \to 2^{\mathcal{T}}$ that maps each document to a finite set of triples.

Definition 1. *A* Web of Linked Data *(WOLD) W is a tuple $\langle D, data, adoc \rangle$ where D is a set of documents $D \subseteq \mathcal{D}$, data a function from D to $2^{\mathcal{T}}$ such that $data(d)$ is finite for each $d \in D$, and adoc a partial function from $\mathcal{U}$ to D. If W is a WOLD, we use D_W, $data_W$, and $adoc_W$ for its respective components. The set of all WOLDs is denoted $\mathcal{W}$.*

We aim to define parts of a web as subwebs. While existing definitions only consider the inclusion of documents in their entirety [9], we allow for *partial* documents to enable fine-grained control about which data is to be used for answering certain queries.

Definition 2. *Consider two* WOLDs $W = \langle D, data, adoc \rangle$ *and* $W' = \langle D', data', adoc' \rangle$. *We say that* W' *is a* subweb *of* W *if i)* $D' \subseteq D$ *ii)* $\forall d \in D'$: $data'(d) \subseteq data(d)$ *iii)* $adoc'(u) = adoc(u)$ *if* $adoc(u) \in D'$ *and* $adoc'(u)$ *is undefined otherwise*
We write subwebs(W) *for the set of subwebs of* W.

The simplest type of subwebs are those only consisting of a single document.

Definition 3. *Let* W *be a* WOLD *and* $d \in D$. *We use* singleton(d, W) *to denote the (unique) subweb* $\langle \{d\}, data', adoc' \rangle$ *of* W *with* $data'(d) = data(d)$.

Additionally, if two subwebs of a given WOLD are given, we can naturally define operators such as union and intersection on them; in this paper, we will only need the union.

Definition 4. *If* W_1 *and* W_2 *are subwebs of* W, *we define* $W_1 \cup W_2$ *to be the unique subweb* $\langle D', data', adoc' \rangle$ *of* W *with*

- $D' = D_{W_1} \cup D_{W_2}$, *and*
- $data'(d) = data_{W_1}(d) \cup data_{W_2}(d)$ *for each* $d \in D'$, *where, slightly abusing notation, we use* $data_{W_i}(d) = \emptyset$ *if* $d \notin D_{W_i}$.

4   Requirements

From the use case, we extracted four requirements that motivate our definitions.

A Declarative Language for Selecting Data Sources. Similar to existing LTQP approaches, we need a language to describe which data sources to select (possibly starting from a given seed). We want such a language to be declarative, i.e., focus on *which* sources to use, rather than *how* to obtain them. Formally, we expect a source selection expression to evaluate in a given WOLD to a set of URIs representing the documents to be included.

Independence of Query and Subweb Specification. Motivated by principles of reusability and separation of concerns, we want the *query* to be formulated independently from the *subweb over which the query is to be evaluated*. While it might—to a certain extent—be possible to encode traversal directions in (federated) SPARQL queries, *what do I want to know* and *where do I want to get my information* are two orthogonal concerns that we believe should be clearly separated, in order to improve readability, maintainability, and reusability. E.g., in the use case, the phone book application defines the *query*, while Uma defines her own *subweb of interest* (consisting of her own document, as well as parts of the documents of her friends). The application should be able to run with different subwebs (e.g., coming from other users), and Uma's subweb of interest should be reusable in other applications.

Scope Restriction of Sources. One phenomenon that showed up in the use case is that we want to trust a certain source, but only for specific data. We might for instance want to use all our friends' data sources, but only to provide information about themselves. This would avoid "faulty" data providers such as Bob to publish data that pollute up the entire application, and it would give a finer level of control over which data is to be used to answer queries. On the formal level, this requirement already manifests itself in the definition of *subweb* we chose: contrary to existing definitions [9], we allowed a document in a subweb to have only a subset of the data of the original document.

Distributed Subweb Specifications. Finally, we arrive at the notion of distribution. This is the feature in which our approach most strongly deviates from the state-of-the-art in link traversal. While the semantic web heavily builds on the assumption that *data* is decentralized and different agents have different pieces of data to contribute, existing link traversal–based approaches still assume that the *knowledge of where this data can be found* is completely in the hands of the querying agent at query time, or at least that the *principles by which the web has to be traversed* can be described by the querying agent. However, as our use case illustrates, this is not always the case: Ann decided to distribute her information over different pages; the agent developing the phone book application cannot possibly know that the triple `<https://ann.ex/#me> foaf:isPrimaryTopicOf <https://corp.ex/ann/>.` indicates that information from `<https://corp.ex/ann/>` is "equally good" as information from Ann's main document. Stated differently, only Ann knows how her own information is organized and hence if we want to get personal information from Ann, we would want her to be able to describe herself how or where to find this data. To summarize, we aim to allow *document publishers to publish specifications of subwebs in the same declarative language as used by query agents* and *query agents to decide whether or not to include the data from such subwebs.*

5   Related Work

Link Traversal-Based Query Processing. Over a decade ago, the paradigm of Link Traversal-based Query Processing was introduced [8], enabling queries over document-oriented interfaces. The main advantage of this approach is that queries can always be executed over live data, as opposed to querying over indexed data that may be stale. The main disadvantages of this approach are that query termination and result completeness are not guaranteed, and that query execution is typically significantly slower than database-centric approaches such as SPARQL endpoints. Several improvements have been suggested to cope with these problems [5]. For example, the processing order of documents can be changed so that certain documents are *prioritized* [10], which allows relevant results to be emitted earlier in an iterative manner [6], but does not reduce total execution time. In this work, we propose to tackle this problem by allowing publishers to specify their subweb of interest. These specifications are then used to *guide* the query engine towards relevant (according to the data publishers at hand) documents.

Reachability Semantics. The SPARQL query language was originally introduced for query processing over RDF databases. Since LTQP involves a substantially different kind of sources, a family of new semantics was introduced [9], involving the concept of a *reachable* subweb. When executing a query over a set of *seed documents*, the reachable Web is the set of documents that can be reached from these seeds using one of different *reachability criteria*. These criteria are functions that test each data triple within retrieved documents, indicating which (if any) of the URIs in the triple components should be dereferenced by interpreting them as the URI of a document that is subsequently retrieved over HTTP. The c_{All} reachability criterion involves following all encountered URIs, which is the strategy in the example of Results 1. A more elaborate criterion is c_{Match}, which involves following URIs from data triples that match at least one triple pattern from the query. c_{Match} can significantly reduce the number of traversals compared to c_{All}. However, evaluating Query 1 with c_{Match} semantics would not yield results for Ann (rows 1 and 4). Her details are only reachable via a triple with predicate `foaf:isPrimaryTopicOf`, which does not match any of the query's triple patterns; hence, the relevant document is never visited. So while c_{Match} can lead to better performance, it comes at the cost of fewer results, showing that none of these approaches are optimal.

Delegation. The concept of subwebs is somewhat related to the presence of active rules in rule-based languages for distributed data management. A particularly relevant project in this context is Webdamlog [1], a Datalog-based declarative language for managing knowledge on the web with support for rule-delegation. Here, delegation is achieved by allowing rules to get partially materialized by different peers.

6   A Formalism for Subweb Specifications

Inspired by the desired properties from Sect. 4, we now define a formalism to describe subwebs of interest. In our formalism, different agents will be able to provide a description of a *subweb of interest*; they will be able to specify declaratively in (which parts of) which documents they are interested. We do not make any assumption here about what the reason for this "interest" is; depending on the context at hand, different criteria such as relevance, trustworthiness, or license-compatibility can be used. Such a description of a subweb of interest can be given by the **querying agent** (an end-user or machine client) which provides it at runtime to the **query processor**. Additionally, every **data publisher** can use the same mechanism to make assertions about her beliefs, such that other data publishers or querying agents can reuse those instead of requiring explicit knowledge. For instance, a data publisher can express which sources they consider relevant or trustworthy for what kinds of data: a researcher might indicate that a certain source represents her publication record correctly, whereas another source captures her affiliation history. A certain agent *might* or *might not* choose to take the subweb of interest of a data publisher into consideration.

In the use case of Sect. 2, the application generates a query P as Query 1, and end-user Uma expresses she trusts her own profile for her list of contacts, and to trust those contacts for their own details. Furthermore, each of these friends can indicate which other documents they trust for which information. For instance, Ann could express that she trusts *corp.ex* for her personal details. Essentially, in this case Uma partially *delegates* responsibility of traversing the web to Ann, but only retains information about Ann from Ann's subweb of interest. This leads to the following definitions.

Definition 5. *A* source selector *is a function* $\sigma : \mathcal{W} \to 2^{\mathcal{U}}$. *A* filter *is a function* $f : 2^{\mathcal{T}} \times \mathcal{U} \to 2^{\mathcal{T}}$ *such that* $f(S, u) \subseteq S$ *for every* $S \subseteq \mathcal{T}$ *and* $u \in \mathcal{U}$. *For a* WOLD $W = \langle D, data, adoc \rangle$ *and* URI u; *we extend the notation and also write* $f(W, u)$ *to denote the subweb* $\langle D, data', adoc \rangle$ *of* W *with* $data'(d) := f(data(d), u)$ *for each* $d \in D$.

In our running example, if Uma wants for each of her friends to only include statements they make about themselves, she can use a source selector σ that extracts her friends, e.g., with $\sigma(W) = \{o \mid \langle s, \mathsf{foaf:knows}, o \rangle \in data(adoc(s))$ with $s = $ `<https://uma.ex/#me>`$\}$ and with a filter that maps (S, u) to $\{\langle s, p, o \rangle \in S \mid s = u\}$. If we assume that W is a WOLD in which only a particular friend u of Uma provides triples, then $f(W, u)$ is the subweb of W in which friend u has only the triples making statements about him or herself.

Definition 6. *A* subweb specification, *often denoted* Θ, *is a set of tuples of the form* (σ, b, f), *where* σ *is a source selector;* b *is a Boolean; and* f *is a filter.*

Intuitively, the Boolean b in (σ, b, f) indicates whether to include for each URI $u \in \sigma(W)$ (the filtered version of) the subweb of $adoc(u)$ or only u's document. Finally, this brings us to the definition of a specification-annotated WOLD (sa-WOLD in short): a WOLD extended with the construction rules of all data publishers.

Definition 7. *A* specification-annotated WOLD *is a tuple* $\mathbb{W} = \langle W, \Theta \rangle$ *consisting of a* WOLD $W = \langle D, data, adoc \rangle$ *and an associated family* $\Theta = (\Theta_d)_{d \in D}$ *of subweb specifications.*

In a sa-WOLD, each data publisher declares her subweb specification that can be used to construct her subweb of interest. The value of a subweb specification in a sa-WOLD is defined as follows:

Definition 8. *Let* $\mathbb{W} = \langle W, \Theta \rangle$ *be a sa-*WOLD *with* $W = \langle D, data, adoc \rangle$, *and* Θ *a subweb specification. Then,* $[\![\Theta]\!]^{\mathbb{W}}$ *denotes the subweb specified by* Θ *for* $\mathbb{W}$,

$$[\![\Theta]\!]^{\mathbb{W}} := \bigcup_{(\sigma, b, f) \in \Theta \wedge u \in \sigma(W)} f \left(singleton(adoc(u), W) \cup \left([\![(\Theta_{adoc(u)})]\!]^{\mathbb{W}} \; \textbf{if } b \right), u \right),$$

where $(S \textbf{ if } b)$ *equals* S *if* b *is true and the empty* WOLD *(the unique* WOLD *without documents) otherwise. The* subweb of interest *of a document* $d \in D$ *in* $\mathbb{W}$ *is defined as* $soi(d, \mathbb{W}) := singleton(d, W) \cup [\![\Theta_d]\!]^{\mathbb{W}}$.

Since not just the data publishers, but also the querying agents should be able to specify a subweb of interest, we naturally obtain the following definition.

Definition 9. *A specification-annotated query is a tuple* $\mathbb{P} = \langle P, \Theta \rangle$ *with P a* SPARQL *query and* Θ *a subweb specification. The evaluation of* $\mathbb{P}$ *in* $\mathbb{W}$*, denoted* $[\![\mathbb{P}]\!]^{\mathbb{W}}$*, is defined by* $[\![\mathbb{P}]\!]^{\mathbb{W}} := [P]^{[\Theta]^{\mathbb{W}}}$

Here, we use $[P]^{W'}$ to denote the evaluation of the SPARQL query in the dataset that is the union of all the documents in W' (to be precise, this is the RDF dataset with as default graph the union of all the data in all documents of the subweb, and for each URI u with $adoc(u) = d$ a named graph with name u and as triples the data of d). Of course, we need a mechanism to *find* all those documents, which is what Θ will provide.

In the next section, we propose a concrete SPARQL-based instantiation of the theoretical framework presented here and illustrate our use case in that setting. Afterwards, we will formally compare our proposal to existing LTQP approaches.

7   Expressing Subweb Specifications

In this section, we propose a syntax for subweb specifications (as formalized in Sect. 6), named the Subweb Specification Language (SWSL), inspired by LDQL and SPARQL. In order to lower the entry barrier of this syntax to existing SPARQL engine implementations, we deliberately base this syntax upon the SPARQL grammar. This enables implementations to reuse (parts of) existing SPARQL query parsers and evaluators.

The grammar below represents the SWSL syntax in Extended Backus–Naur form (EBNF) with start symbol $\langle start \rangle$. The specifications begin with the **FOLLOW** keyword, followed by a $\langle sources \rangle$ clause, an *optional* **WITH SUBWEBS** keyword, and an *optional* $\langle filter \rangle$ clause.

$$\langle start \rangle \models \textbf{FOLLOW } \langle sources \rangle \text{ [\textbf{WITH SUBWEBS}] } [\langle filter \rangle]$$
$$\langle sources \rangle \models \langle variables \rangle \text{ \{ } \langle GroupGraphPattern \rangle \text{ \} } [\langle recurse \rangle]$$
$$\langle variables \rangle \models \textbf{?}\langle VARNAME \rangle \text{ | } \textbf{?}\langle VARNAME \rangle \langle variables \rangle$$
$$\langle recurse \rangle \models \textbf{RECURSE } [\langle INTEGER \rangle]$$
$$\langle filter \rangle \models \textbf{INCLUDE } \langle ConstructTemplate \rangle \text{ [\textbf{WHERE} \{ } \langle GroupGraphPattern \rangle \text{ \}]}$$

Intuitively, a full SWSL expression corresponds to a single subweb specification tuple (σ, b, f) where the $\langle sources \rangle$ clause correspond to the source selection function σ, the keyword **WITH SUBWEBS** corresponds to the Boolean b, and the $\langle filter \rangle$ clause corresponds to the filter function f. We explain each of these parts in more detail hereafter.

Selection of Sources. The ⟨*sources*⟩ will be evaluated in the context of a set S of seed documents. For subweb specifications provided to the query processor, this set of seeds will be given explicitly, whereas for subweb specifications found in a document, the set S is the URI of that document . A ⟨*sources*⟩ clause begins with a list of SPARQL variables, followed by a source extraction expression defined as SPARQL's ⟨*GroupGraphPattern*⟩ clause. The output is a set of bindings of the given variables, indicating URIs whose documents are to be included. For instance, when evaluating the expression ?v_1 ... ?v_n { G } in a WOLD W with seed set S, the resulting source selection is

$$\sigma(W) = \bigcup_{u \in S} \{\mu(v_i) \in \mathcal{U} \mid 1 \leq i \leq n \wedge \mu \in [\![G]\!]^{data(adoc(u))}\},$$

where $[\![G]\!]^{DS}$ is the evaluation of the GroupGraphPattern G on a dataset DS.

Recurring Source Selection. A ⟨*sources*⟩ clause may have at the end an optional ⟨*recurse*⟩ clause. If **RECURSE** is not used in a specification, then this latter will only apply to the document in which it is defined; else, the specification will apply to that document, and all output URIs, taken as seed (recursively). In other words, the ⟨*sources*⟩ clause will be applied to all documents that are obtained when following a chain of one or more links using the specification. The ⟨*recurse*⟩ clause has an optional nonnegative integer parameter, which indicates the maximum recursion *depth*. A depth of 0 is equivalent to not defining the ⟨*recurse*⟩ clause. A depth of m means that all documents that are obtained when following a link path of length m from the seeds are considered. This recursion capability calls for the need to express *the current document's* URI. To achieve this, SWSL syntax reuses SPARQL's relative IRI capability. Concretely, every time an SWSL specification is applied on a document, the document's URI will be set as base IRI to the SWSL specification, so that relative IRIs can be resolved upon this IRI.

Inclusion of Subwebs of Selected Sources. This is determined by the optional keyword **WITH SUBWEBS**. Thus, if an SWSL specification has the **WITH SUBWEBS** option, this is equivalent to a subweb specification tuple with b is true. Otherwise, b is false.

Document Filtering. The ⟨*filter*⟩ clause is an optional clause indicating that only certain parts of the document are considered. Without this clause, the entire document is included. The ⟨*filter*⟩ clause is similar to SPARQL's ⟨*ContructQuery*⟩ clause. It exists in *compact* or *extended* forms; in the latter, filtering constraints can be added via **WHERE** keyword.

Concretely, the extended form is defined by the SPARQL's ⟨*Construct Template*⟩ and ⟨*GroupGraphPattern*⟩ productions. The ⟨*ConstructTemplate*⟩ acts as a template of triples to accept, while the ⟨*GroupGraphPattern*⟩ imposes conditions to do so. It is also possible that in the bodies of the ⟨*GroupGraphPattern*⟩ and ⟨*ConstructTemplate*⟩ there are variables

```
<https://uma.ex/#me> ex:hasSpecification <#spec1>.     <https://ann.ex/#me> ex:hasSpecification <#spec2>.
<#spec1> ex:appliesTo <https://uma.ex/>;               <#spec2> ex:appliesTo <https://ann.ex/>;
        ex:scope """                                            ex:scope """
        FOLLOW ?friend WITH SUBWEBS {                           FOLLOW ?page {
          <https://uma.ex/#me> foaf:knows ?friend.                ?topic foaf:isPrimaryTopicOf ?page.
        } INCLUDE { ?friend ?p ?o. }                           } INCLUDE { ?topic ?p ?o. }
        """^^ex:SWSL.                                          """^^ex:SWSL.
```

Listing 1. Subweb Specification of *https://uma.ex/*   **Listing 2.** Subweb Specification of *https://ann.ex/*

that are mentioned in the $\langle GroupGraphPattern \rangle$ of $\langle sources \rangle$ clause. This implies that they should be instantiated according to the result of the first $\langle GroupGraphPattern \rangle$.

The compact form is defined by $\langle ConstructTemplate \rangle$, which acts as syntactical sugar to the extended with an empty $\langle GroupGraphPattern \rangle$. Thus, to define $\langle filter \rangle$ clause's semantics, we only need the extended form. To illustrate this, consider an expression

$$\text{FOLLOW } ?v_1 \text{ \{ } G_1 \text{ \} INCLUDE } C \text{ WHERE \{ } G_2 \text{ \}}$$

We already saw that when evaluated in context u, this induces a source selector selecting those v such that $\mu_1(?v_1) = v$, for some $\mu_1 \in [\![G_1]\!]^{data(adoc(u))}$. The associated filter is

$$f(S, v) = \bigcup_{\mu_1 \in [\![G_1]\!]^{data(adoc(u))} | \mu_1(?v_1) = v} \{ t \in S \mid t \in [\![\mu_2(\mu_1(C))]\!]^S \text{ for some } \mu_2 \in [\![\mu_1(G_2)]\!]^S \}$$

Expressing Document Subwebs. In this work, we assume that each published document can link to its own context where they indicate the documents they consider relevant using an SWSL subweb specification. For illustration, we consider the predicate *ex:hasSpecification* that is attached to the current document. An *ex:Specification* is a resource that contains at least a value for *ex:scope*, pointing to one or more SWSL strings. This resource can also contain metadata about the subweb specification.

Application to the Use Case. Listing 1 shows a part of Uma's profile where she exposes an SWSL subweb specification to indicate that her friends can express information about themselves. This specification states that all *foaf:knows* links from Uma should be followed, and that from those followed documents, only information about that friend should be included. By **WITH SUBWEBS**, she indicates that her friends' subwebs must be included in her subweb. Then, Ann can express in her subweb specification (Listing 2) that she trusts documents pointed to by *foaf:isPrimaryTopicOf* links about triples about the topic she indicates. With these subweb specifications, Query 1 produces only Rows 1–3 of Results 1. However, we still include the non-desired profile picture from Bob in our results (Row 3). Extending the notion of filter to also allow this is left for future work.

8   Power and Limitations of Existing LTQP Approaches

Since LDQL is a powerful link traversal formalism that has been shown to subsume other approaches such as reachability-based querying [4], this raises the

Table 1. Value of link path expressions

lpe	$[\![lpe]\!]^u_W$
ϵ	$\{u\}$
lp	$\{u' \mid lp$ matches with $t)$ with result u' in context u for some $t \in$ $data(adoc(u))\}$
lpe_1/lpe_2	$\{v \mid v \in [\![lpe_2]\!]^{u'}_W$ and $u' \in [\![lpe_1]\!]^u_W\}$
$lpe_1 \vert lpe_2$	$[\![lpe_1]\!]^u_W \cup [\![lpe_2]\!]^u_W$
lpe^*	$\{u\} \cup [\![lpe]\!]^u_W \cup [\![lpe/lpe]\!]^u_W \cup [\![lpe/lpe/lpe]\!]^u_W \cup ...$
$[lpe]$	$\{u \mid [\![lpe]\!]^u_W \neq \emptyset\}$

question: to which extent can LDQL in itself achieve the requirements set out in Sect. 4? In the current section we formally investigate this, after introducing some preliminaries on LDQL.

8.1 Preliminaries: LDQL

LDQL is a querying language for linked data. Its most powerful aspect is the navigational language it uses for identifying a subweb of the given WOLD. The most basic block that constitutes LDQL's navigational language is a *link pattern* that is a tuple in $(\mathcal{U} \cup \{\_, +\}) \times (\mathcal{U} \cup \{\_, +\}) \times (\mathcal{U} \cup \mathcal{L} \cup \{\_, +\})$. Intuitively, a link pattern requires a context uri u_{ctx}, then evaluates to a set of URIs (the links to follow) by matching the link pattern against the triples in the document that u_{ctx} is authoritative for. Formally, we say that a link pattern $lp = \langle \ell_1, \ell_2, \ell_3 \rangle$ *matches* a triple $\langle x_1, x_2, x_3 \rangle$ with result u in the context of a URI u_{ctx} if the following two points hold: i) there exists $i \in \{1, 2, 3\}$ such that $\ell_i = \_$ and $x_i = u$, and ii) for every $i \in \{1, 2, 3\}$ either $\ell_i = x_i$, or $\ell_i = +$ and $x_i = u_{ctx}$, or $\ell_i = \_$.

Link patterns are used to build *link path expressions* (LPEs) with the following syntax:

$$lpe := \varepsilon \mid lp \mid lpe/lpe \mid lpe \vert lpe \mid lpe^* \mid [lpe]$$

where lp is a link pattern. In a given WOLD W, the value of a link path expression lpe in context URI u (denoted $[\![lpe]\!]^u_W$) is a set of URIs as given in Table 1.

An LDQL query is a tuple $q = \langle lpe, P \rangle$ with lpe a link path expression and P a SPARQL query. The value of such a query q in a WOLD W with a set of seed URIs S is

$$[\![q]\!]^S_W := [\![P]\!]^{W'} \text{ where } W' = \bigcup_{s \in S, u \in [\![lpe]\!]^s_W} singleton(adoc(u), W),$$

i.e., the query P is evaluated over the (RDF dataset constructed from the) data sources obtained by evaluating the link path expression starting in one of the seeds.

Remark 1. [11] allows one other form of link path expression, where an entire LDQL query is nested in in an LPE; for the purpose of this paper, we opt to use a strict separation between query and source selection and omit this last option[1]. Additionally, they consider (Boolean) combinations of queries, thereby allowing to use different LPEs for different parts of the expression; we briefly come back to this when discussing scope restriction.

8.2 LDQL and the Requirements

A Declarative Language for Selecting Data Sources. In LDQL, the link path expressions provide a rich and flexible declarative language for describing source selection. Here, paths through the linked web are described using a syntax similar to regular expressions. For instance, the LDQL expression $\langle +, \texttt{foaf:knows}, \_\rangle / \langle +, \texttt{foaf:knows}, \_\rangle$ when evaluated in a given URI u (the context) traverses to u's friends f (as explicated by triples of the form `<u,foaf:knows,f>` in $adoc(u)$) and subsequently to their friends f_2 (as indicated by triples `<f,foaf:knows,f2>` in $adoc(f)$). In other words, this example expression identifies the documents of friends of friends of a given person.

Independence of Query and Subweb Specification. The design philosophy behind LDQL does not start from an independence principle similar to the one proposed here. That is, in its most general form, LDQL allows intertwining the source selection and the query. For instance, the LDQL query $\langle lpe_1, P_1 \rangle \text{AND} \langle lpe_2, P_2 \rangle$ expresses the SPARQL query $P_1 \text{AND} P_2$, and on top of that specifies that different parts of the query should be evaluated with respect to different sources, and hence violating our principle of independence. However, independence can easily be achieved in LDQL by only considering LDQL queries of the form $\langle lpe, P \rangle$ with lpe a link path expression and P a SPARQL query.

Scope Restriction of Sources. The semantics of an LDQL query $\langle lpe, P \rangle$ is obtained by first evaluating lpe starting from a seed document s, resulting in a set of URIs $[\![lpe]\!]_W^s$; the SPARQL query P is then evaluated over the union of the associated documents. That is, to compute the result of $\langle lpe, P \rangle$, for each document $adoc(u)$ with $u \in [\![lpe]\!]_W^s$, its entire content is used. As such, LDQL provides no mechanism for partial inclusion of documents. However, while LDQL cannot select *parts of documents*, it *can* be used, as discussed above, to apply source selection strategies only to *parts of queries* and thereby to a certain extent achieve the desired behaviour. E.g., the query $\langle lpe_1, (?x, \texttt{foaf:knows}, ?y) \rangle \text{AND} \langle lpe_2, (?y, \texttt{foaf:mbox}, ?m) \rangle$ will only use triples with predicate `foaf:knows` from documents produced by lpe_1. However, this sacrifices the independence property, and for complex queries and filters, this is not easy to achieve.

---

[1] Notably, this option was also not present in the original work [7].

Distributed Subweb Specifications. This now brings us to the main topic of this section: studying to which extent it is possible in LDQL to distribute the knowledge of how to construct the subweb of interest and as such to *guide* the data consumer towards interesting/relevant documents. To answer this question, we will consider a slightly simplified setting, without filters (all filters equal the identity function *id* on their first argument) and where the Boolean b in (σ, b, f) is always true. I.e., each agent states that they wish to include the complete subweb of interest of all URIs identified by σ. In this setting, we wonder if data publishers can, instead of publishing their subweb specification *in addition to* their regular data, encode their subweb specification as triples *in* the document (as meta-information), and use *a single* "meta" link path expression that interprets these triples for the traversal. This is formalized as follows.

Definition 10. *Let S be a set of source selectors, $enc : S \to 2^T$ a function mapping source selectors σ onto a set of triples $enc(\sigma)$, and $\mathbb{W} = \langle\langle D, data, adoc\rangle, \Theta\rangle$ a sa-WOLD in which each subweb specification is of the form $(\sigma, \text{true}, id)$ with $\sigma \in S$. The encoding of $\mathbb{W}$ by enc is the WOLD $enc(\mathbb{W}) = \langle D, data', adoc \rangle$ with for each $d \in D$:*

$$data'(d) = data(d) \cup \bigcup_{\{\sigma | (\sigma, \text{true}, id) \in \Theta_d\}} enc(\sigma).$$

Definition 11. *Let S be a set of source selectors, enc a function $S \to 2^T$, and e_{meta} an LPE. We say that (enc, e_{meta}) captures S if for each sa-WOLD in which subweb specifications only use triples of the form $(\sigma, \text{true}, id)$ with $\sigma \in S$ and for each URI u,*

$$[\![e_{meta}]\!]^u_{enc(\mathbb{W})} = soi(adoc(u), \mathbb{W}).$$

We will say that LDQL can capture distribution of functions in S if there exist some enc and e_{meta} that capture S.

To define the encodings, we will make use of some "fresh" URIs we assume not to occur in any WOLD. In our theorems, we will make use of some specific sets of source selectors. A source selector σ is *constant* if it maps all WOLDs onto the same set of URIs, i.e., if $\sigma(W) = \sigma(W')$ for all WOLDs W, W'; the set of all constant source selectors is defined as S_{const}. If p and u are URIs, we define the source selector $all_{p^*, u}$ as follows:

$$all_{p^*, u} : W \mapsto [\![(+, p, \_)^*]\!]^u_W.$$

Intuitively, the function $all_{p^*, u}$ identifies the set of all ps of ps of .... of u. For instance, by taking $p = friend$, we include all direct or indirect friends of u. For a fixed p, we write S_{p^*} for the set of source selectors $all_{p^*, u}$. We write S_* for the set of all source selectors of the form $all_{p^*, u}$ for any p. The set S_* allows each data publisher to choose her own strategy for constructing the subweb, e.g., one data publisher might include all her $friend^*$s, another her $colleague^*$s and a third one only URIs explicitly trusted (i.e., their $trust^*$s). Our main expressivity results are then summarized as follows:

"include p^*s of u_1"

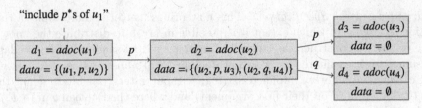

Fig. 1. Example WOLD used in LDQL inexpressivity proof.

Theorem 1. LDQL *captures distribution of* S_{const} *and* S_{p^*}, *but not of* S_*.

Proof (Sketch of the proof). For the positive results, we can provide an explicit encoding and meta-expression. For instance for showing that it captures S_{p^*} for a given p, we can take $enc(all_{p^*,u}) = \{(a, a, u)\}$ and $e_{meta} = ((a, a, \_)/(+, p, \_)^*)^*$ with a a fresh URI. In this expression e_{meta}, the link pattern $(a, a, \_)$ is used to navigate the u whose ps of ps of... we wish to include; the part $(+, p, \_)^*$ then navigates to all such p^*s. The outermost star ensures that for each u that is found, also their subweb of interest is included.

The proof of the negative result relies heavily on the fact that an LPE not mentioning p nor q, cannot distinguish the triples (x, p, z) and (x, q, z). If (e_{meta}, enc) were to capture S_*, we can construct a WOLD (see Fig. 1) using only URIs not occurring in e_{meta} in which only one document has a non-empty subweb specification. We then use the aforementioned fact to conclude that $d_3 \in [\![e_{meta}]\!]^{u_1}_{enc(\mathbb{W})}$ if and only if $d_4 \in [\![e_{meta}]\!]^{u_1}_{enc(\mathbb{W})}$.

9   Discussion

So far, we have studied LTQP from the perspective of data quality; namely, we allow querying agents and/or data publishers to capture a subweb of data that satisfies certain quality properties for them. In real-world applications, such quality properties could for example indicate different notions of trust, or something use-case-specific such as data sensitivity levels. While our formal framework only associates a single subweb specification to each agent, it is not hard to extend it to associate multiple subweb constructions with each agent and allow the querying agent to pick a suitable one.

The same mechanism can be used to improve *efficiency* in two ways: the data publishers can opt to *not* include certain documents in their subweb, and for the ones included, they can use a *filter* which indicates which data will be used from said document.

Most prominently, every publisher of Linked Data typically has their own way of organizing data across documents, and they could capture this structure in their subweb of interest. For example, in contrast to Bob (Document 3), Ann stores her profile information in multiple documents (Documents 2 and 4). If she were to declare this as a subweb specification, she can use filters to indicate which data can be found in which documents. A query processor can then exploit this information to only follow links to relevant documents (documents of Ann's subweb for which the filter *could* keep triples that contribute to the query result). For example, Uma's querying agent can use Ann's subweb construction of Listing 2 to prune the set of links to follow, and as such perform a guided navigation while maintaining completeness guarantees. Without even inspecting *https://photos.ex/ann/*, it knows Ann (and thus Uma) does not trust triples in this document for data about her, so fetching it will not change the final query result. Whereas LTQP under c_{All} semantics would require at least 7 HTTP requests, the filters allow us to derive which 4 requests are needed to return all 3 trusted results of the specification-annotated query. Analogous performance gains were observed in work on provenance-enabled queries [16]. In contrast, traditional LTQP cannot make any assumptions of what to encounter behind a link. The work on describing document structures using shapes [12] can be leveraged here.

As such, filters in subweb specifications serve two purposes: they define *semantics* by selecting only part of a data source, and give query processors *guidance* for saving bandwidth and thus processing time.

10 Conclusion

LTQP is generally not considered suitable for real-world applications because of its performance and data quality implications. However, if the current decentralization trend continues, we need to prepare for a future with multi-source query processing, since some data *cannot* be centralized for legal or other reasons.

Federated querying over expressive interfaces such as SPARQL endpoints only addresses part of the problem: empirical evidence suggests that, counterintuitively, less expressive interfaces can lead to faster processing times for several queries [15], while being less expensive to host. A document-based interface is about the simplest interface imaginable, and is thereby partly responsible for the Web's scalability. Hence the need to investigate how far we can push LTQP for internal and external integration of private and public data.

Our formalization for specification-annotated queries creates the theoretical foundations for a next generation of traversal-based (and perhaps *hybrid*) query processing, in which data quality can be controlled tightly, and network requests can be reduced significantly. Moreover, the efforts to realize these necessary improvements are distributed across the network, because every data publisher can describe their own subwebs. Importantly, the availability of such descriptions is also driven by other needs. For instance, initiatives such as Solid [14] store people's personal data as Linked Data, requiring every personal data space to describe their document organization such that applications can read and write data at the correct locations [12].

This article opens multiple avenues for future work. A crucial direction is the algorithmic handling of the theoretical framework, and its software implementation, for which we have ongoing work in the Comunica query engine [13]; an important open question here is how the expressed filters can be exploited for query optimization. Also on the implementation level, the creation and management of subweb specifications should be facilitated. Empirical evaluations will shed light on cases where subweb annotated WOLDs and queries result in a viable strategy.

Acknowledgements. This research received funding from the Flemish Government under the "Onderzoeksprogramma Artificiële Intelligentie (AI) Vlaanderen" programme. Ruben Taelman and Ruben Verborgh are postdoctoral fellows of the Research Foundation – Flanders (FWO) (1274521N). Heba Aamer is supported by the Special Research Fund (BOF) (BOF19OWB16).

References

1. Abiteboul, S., Bienvenu, M., Galland, A., Antoine, É.: A rule-based language for web data management. In: Proceedings of the 30th ACM SIGMOD-SIGACT-SIGART Symposium on Principles of Database Systems, PODS 2011, pp. 293–304. ACM (2011)
2. Buil-Aranda, C., Hogan, A., Umbrich, J., Vandenbussche, P.-Y., et al.: SPARQL web-querying infrastructure: ready for action? In: Alani, H. (ed.) ISWC 2013. LNCS, vol. 8219, pp. 277–293. Springer, Heidelberg (2013). https://doi.org/10. 1007/978-3-642-41338-4_18
3. Cyganiak, R., Wood, D., Lanthaler, M.: RDF 1.1: concepts and abstract syntax. Recommendation, W3C, February 2014. https://www.w3.org/TR/2014/REC-rdf11-concepts-20140225/
4. Hartig, O.: SPARQL for a web of linked data: semantics and computability. In: Simperl, E., Cimiano, P., Polleres, A., Corcho, O., Presutti, V. (eds.) ESWC 2012. LNCS, vol. 7295, pp. 8–23. Springer, Heidelberg (2012). https://doi.org/10.1007/978-3-642-30284-8_8
5. Hartig, O.: An overview on execution strategies for linked data queries. Datenbank-Spektrum **13**(2), 89–99 (2013)
6. Hartig, O.: SQUIN: a traversal based query execution system for the web of linked data. In: Proceedings of the ACM SIGMOD International Conference on Management of Data (2013)
7. Hartig, O.: LDQL: a language for linked data queries. In: Proceedings of the 9th Alberto Mendelzon International Workshop on Foundations of Data Management, Lima, Peru, 6–8 May 2015. CEUR Workshop Proceedings, vol. 1378. CEUR-WS.org (2015). http://ceur-ws.org/Vol-1378/AMW_2015_paper_34.pdf
8. Hartig, O., Bizer, C., Freytag, J.-C., et al.: Executing SPARQL queries over the web of linked data. In: Bernstein, A. (ed.) ISWC 2009. LNCS, vol. 5823, pp. 293–309. Springer, Heidelberg (2009). https://doi.org/10.1007/978-3-642-04930-9_19
9. Hartig, O., Freytag, J.C.: Foundations of traversal based query execution over linked data. In: Proceedings of the 23rd ACM Conference on Hypertext and Social Media (2012)
10. Hartig, O., Özsu, M.T., et al.: Walking without a map: ranking-based traversal for querying linked data. In: Groth, P. (ed.) ISWC 2016, Part I. LNCS, vol. 9981, pp. 305–324. Springer, Cham (2016). https://doi.org/10.1007/978-3-319-46523-4_19
11. Hartig, O., Pérez, J.: LDQL: a query language for the web of linked data. J. Web Semant. **41**, 9–29 (2016)

12. Prud'hommeaux, E., Bingham, J.: ShapeTrees specification. Editor's draft, May 2020. https://shapetrees.github.io/specification/spec

13. Taelman, R., Van Herwegen, J., Vander Sande, M., Verborgh, R.: Comunica: a modular SPARQL query engine for the web. In: Proceedings of the 17th International Semantic Web Conference, October 2018. https://comunica.github.io/Article-ISWC2018-Resource/

14. Verborgh, R.: Re-decentralizing the web, for good this time. In: Linking the World's Information. ACM (to appear)

15. Verborgh, R., et al.: Triple pattern fragments: a low-cost knowledge graph interface for the Web. J. Web Semant. **37–38**, 184–206 (2016)

16. Wylot, M., Cudré-Mauroux, P., Groth, P.: Executing provenance-enabled queries over web data. In: Proceedings of the 24th International Conference on World Wide Web (2015)

Event-Based Microcontroller Programming in Datalog

Stefan Brass[(⊠)]

Martin-Luther-Universität Halle-Wittenberg, Institut für Informatik,
Von-Seckendorff-Platz 1, 06099 Halle (Saale), Germany
brass@informatik.uni-halle.de

Abstract. We propose a declarative language for event-based microcontroller programming. The language uses rules and can be seen as a more convenient notation for a pure Datalog program (with a small external controller). In this way, it has a clear semantics and the large body of previous work on declarative programming in Datalog can be used.

We defined and implemented a Datalog-based language for microcontroller programming before [12,13]. It was based on ideas from Dedalus [1] and Statelog [6]. However, programming in that language needed polling, e.g., repeatedly querying system time until a certain time interval was over. For more complex programs, event-based programming is generally recommended. The language proposed in this paper is event-based and also contains a module concept in order to manage more complex tasks.

1 Introduction

A microcontroller is a small computer on a single chip. For instance, the Amtel ATmega328P contains an 8-bit CPU, 32 KByte flash memory for the program, 2 KByte static RAM, 1 KByte EEPROM for persistent data, 23 general purpose I/O pins, 3 timers (with pulse-width modulators), an analog/digital-converter with 6 inputs, and serial interfaces (UART, I^2C, SPI). It costs about 2 dollars and consumes little energy. Microcontrollers are used in many electronic devices.

For hobbyists, schools, and the simple development of prototypes, the Arduino platform is quite often used. It basically consists of a few variants of boards with a microcontroller (e.g., the ATmega328P), a preinstalled boot loader that permits programming via a USB interface, an IDE with a programming language based on C, and fitting hardware extension boards ("shields").

The software for microcontrollers is often developed in Assembler or C. However, declarative programming has advantages also for such small devices:

- Declarative programs are usually shorter than an equivalent program in a procedural language. This enhances the productivity of the programmers.
- There can be no problems with uninitialized variables or dangling pointers. While programs in general should be bug-free, the correctness requirements for embedded programs are usually higher than, e.g., for an office application:

S. Moschoyiannis et al. (Eds.): RuleML+RR 2021, LNCS 12851, pp. 80–94, 2021.
https://doi.org/10.1007/978-3-030-91167-6_6

Microcontrollers often directly control hardware devices, whereas for normal programs, there is a human user, who might detect and handle obvious errors.
- The language has a mathematically precise semantics based on logic, which makes programs easier to verify. For instance, in [2] we presented a method for proving integrity constraints (invariants).
- The simple semantics also permits powerful optimization, e.g. in [13], we translate a subclass of programs to a finite automaton extended with a fixed set of variables (i.e. we use "parameterized states").
- Many programs become easier to understand and more flexible by a data-driven architecture. E.g., the configuration data for a home-automation system used as an example in [13] is basically a small database.
- The language is relatively simple, therefore it can be used also by non-experts (e.g., Arduino boards are a nice device to be used in school).

One reason for the current revival of Datalog is that it is used also for applications that are not typical database applications, such as static analysis of program code [9], cloud computing [10], and semantic web applications [3].

In [12,13], we proposed a language "Microlog" for programming microcontrollers like on the Arduino. The language is based on Datalog (simple logical rules). More specifically, we were inspired by the language Dedalus [1]. We described the computation as a sequence of states, where interface functions (for input and output) are called during the state transition.

However, the language basically required polling, e.g., querying system time until a certain time interval was over. It is also not nice for simulation and debugging that there are long sequences of states where basically nothing happens.

The approach presented in this paper is event-based, and new states are created only when events occur. This allows to concentrate on the important state changes. It is also very natural to handle interrupts as special events. Our previous language had no specific support for interrupts.

Our new language permits to specify the system as a set of interconnected modules, whereas previously, we had a single set of rules. Modules are important, because they permit to concentrate on a subsequence of states for a component of the program.

Of course, there is a large body of previous work on microcontroller programming for embedded systems. Statecharts [4] were developed to specify such reactive systems, the textbook [8] uses them for event-driven programming of embedded systems. In the database area, there are several approaches to extend Datalog by updates and states, or to unify deductive and active rules, see, e.g., [1,6]. In logic programming and artificial intelligence, the specification of planning tasks or agents acting in some domain all require a formalization of a state that is changed by actions. A recent paper in this area is [5].

In Sect. 2, we review standard Datalog and approaches to handle time in Datalog. In Sect. 3, we define the proposed language for microcontroller programming. The semantics of the language is defined by a translation to standard Datalog (the translation of the event queue is a bit lengthy and postponed to Sect. 5). A few examples are presented in Sect. 4. In Sect. 6, we propose a simple module system. This is important because it allows to concentrate on a subsequence of the states. Conclusions are contained in Sect. 7.

2   Datalog and Time

Our proposed language uses logical rules similar to Datalog. Its semantics is defined by a translation to "standard" Datalog. In this section, we briefly review the Datalog version we are using, as well as some previous approaches to handle time in Datalog.

2.1   Standard Datalog

Let us first quickly repeat the definition of standard Datalog. A Datalog program is a finite set of rules of the form $A \leftarrow B_1 \wedge \cdots \wedge B_n \wedge \neg C_1 \wedge \cdots \wedge \neg C_m$, where the head literal A and the positive body literals B_i are atomic formulas of the form $p(t_1, \ldots, t_k)$ with a predicate p and terms $t_1, \ldots, t_k$. The negative body literals $\neg C_j$ are negations of such atomic formulas. Terms are constants or variables.

Rules must be range-restricted, i.e. all variables appearing in the head A or a negative body literal $\neg C_j$ must also appear in at least one positive body literal B_i. This ensures that all variables are bound to a value when the rule is applied. In addition, when built-in predicates (such as $<$) are used, variables appearing in input arguments (e.g., both arguments of $<$) must occur already in a body literal to the left of the literal with the built-in predicate (so that at least a left-to-right evaluation of the rule body is possible). Of course, built-in predicates cannot be used in rule heads because they have a fixed semantics built into the system.

A fact is a rule with an empty body, i.e. it has the form $p(c_1, \ldots, c_k)$ with constants c_i. A "rule about p" is a rule with predicate p in the head literal. The anonymous variable "_" can be used to mean a different variable for each occurrence (distinct from all other variables).

The semantics of a Datalog program is given by the well-founded model [7, 11]. As [1], we require a time-stratification (see below) which ensures that the well-founded model is actually two-valued.

2.2   Time

The program on a microcontroller must act in time. It basically runs forever (until the power is switched off), but the time-dependent inputs lead to some state change, and outputs depend on the state and also change over time. So it is quite clear that a programming language for microcontrollers must be able to define a sequence of states. We use natural numbers from $\mathbb{N}_0$ to identify time points (states). Note that this is logical time, the numbers have no specific meaning except being a linear order. We need the built-in predicate $\mathsf{succ}(\mathsf{T}, \mathsf{S})$ (with input argument T). This returns the next point in time (state number) S

for a given time point T, i.e. succ is interpreted as $\{(T,S) \in \mathbb{N}_0 \times \mathbb{N}_0 \mid S = T+1\}$. We also need two distinguished variables T and S that are not otherwise used in the program.

In our previous language Microlog [12,13], we borrowed from Dedalus [1] the idea to add a time (or state number) argument to every predicate. The current proposal permits both: Time-dependent predicates (with the extra argument) and time-independent predicates (without time argument). The time argument is added as "zeroth" argument in front of the other arguments.

As in Dedalus [1], we do not use arbitrary Datalog rules, but restrict the use of the time argument. There are the following types of rules:

1. Rules and facts with only time-independent predicates.
2. Rules for deriving facts within a state, i.e. rules where all time arguments are filled with the same variable T. The body might contain also time-independent literals, but there must be at least one positive literal with time-dependent predicate (so that the variable T is bound and does not violate the range-restriction condition).
3. Rules for deriving facts for the next state, i.e. rules where all time arguments in the body are filled with T, the body contains the literal succ(T,S), and the head literal has the time argument S. Again, time-independent literals are allowed in the body (with the same requirement to ensure that T is bound).
4. Facts filled with the constant 0 for the time argument (to define the initial state).

As in Dedalus [1], we require that the Datalog program without rules defining the next state (Type 3 above) are stratified, i.e. there is no recursion through negation. This avoids that a fact might depend on itself negatively, which might lead to the third "undefined" truth value in the well-founded model. Rules deriving facts for the next state can never lead to such negative cycles. Basically, the stratification order of facts is first by time, and then by the standard stratification order for the predicates derived from the state-local and time-independent rules.

3   A Datalog-Variant for Microcontroller Systems

In this section, we present a language "Microlog^e" for microcontroller programming (modules are deferred to Sect. 6). Its semantics is defined by a translation to an internal, "pure Datalog" version (plus a small interface to the environment, i.e. the actual hardware). It is important to distinguish these two levels:

– The language that is used by the programmer (Microlog^e), and
– the "pure Datalog" translation result.

The presentation of the language is structured by the different kinds of predicates that can be used.

In the following, we write $\bar{B}$ for mapping a literal B from Microlog^e to Datalog. The exact mapping depends on the type of predicate of B, but usually $p(t_1, \ldots, t_n)$ is mapped to $p(T, t_1, \ldots, t_n)$ with the special variable T for the current point in time.

3.1   Static Predicates (Time-Independent)

There are time-independent (static) predicates, used for configuration data and fixed data tables (e.g., for mapping digits to the inputs of a 7-segment display). Often static predicates are defined by a set of facts. But there can be also derived static predicates that are defined by rules. Of course, such rules can contain only static predicates in the body. Obviously, static predicates do not need the additional time argument. For them, the mapping from the user notation (Microlog^e) to the internal Datalog version is the identity, i.e. $\bar{B}$ is simply B. Since the entire approach is based on Datalog, it is good that one can have a part of the program that is just pure Datalog.

3.2   State Predicates (Updateable)

State predicates store persistent time-dependent information. Their extension can be changed by means of updates. For each state predicate p, there is an insertion predicate $+p$ and a deletion predicate $-p$ with the same arity.

All these predicates are time-dependent, so the internal Datalog version has the additional time argument at the beginning. For each state predicate p of arity n, the following rules are automatically added to the pure Datalog version:

- Facts persist over time unless they are deleted:
  $$p(\mathsf{S}, X_1, \ldots, X_n) \leftarrow p(\mathsf{T}, X_1, \ldots, X_n) \wedge \neg -p(\mathsf{T}, X_1, \ldots, X_n) \wedge \mathsf{succ}(\mathsf{T}, \mathsf{S}).$$
- Inserted facts are true in the next state:
  $$p(\mathsf{S}, X_1, \ldots, X_n) \leftarrow +p(\mathsf{T}, X_1, \ldots, X_n) \wedge \mathsf{succ}(\mathsf{T}, \mathsf{S}).$$

Updates become effective in the next state. If a fact is simultaneously inserted and deleted, the insertion "wins". One might consider this situation as an error and put the following integrity constraint (invariant) on the list of verification goals:

$$\leftarrow +p(\mathsf{T}, X_1, \ldots, X_n) \wedge -p(\mathsf{T}, X_1, \ldots, X_n).$$

(The empty rule head is considered as "false", i.e. this rule must never be applicable.) However, it simplifies programming in certain situations if one allows "deleting everything" and inserting the single fact that one wants in the next state.

For instance, in our previous proposal for Microlog [12], we used the syntax of Dedalus [1] for specifying predicate extensions in the next state:

$$p(t_1, \ldots, t_n)@\mathsf{next} \leftarrow B_1 \wedge \cdots \wedge B_m.$$

One must explicitly write rules to persist a predicate (Dedalus has a macro for this). In our current approach, the intention is that the programmer can concentrate on changes. Persistence is the default. However, if one wants to translate a program from Microlog or Dedalus to Microlog^e, this is possible by changing the above rule to an insertion and deleting everything by default:

$$+p(t_1,\ldots,t_n) \quad \leftarrow B_1 \wedge \cdots \wedge B_m.$$
$$-p(X_1,\ldots,X_n) \leftarrow p(X_1,\ldots,X_n).$$

In Microlog^e, a predicate p is classified as "state predicate" if $+p$ or $-p$ appears in the program. In that case, there can be no rules about p, i.e. p itself cannot appear in rule heads. The semantics of p is defined exclusively by updates. There is a "setup" event (see below) that is sent at the very beginning of program execution. It can be used in order to initialize p. It would have been an option to permit facts about p to define the initial extension of p. However, this looks quite similar to facts about a static predicate, which hold in all states. Therefore, it seemed better to clearly separate this.

The following abbreviation for updates is sometimes useful. We allow to write

$$\hat{}p(t_1,\ldots,t_k \to t_{k+1},\ldots,t_n) \leftarrow B_1 \wedge \cdots \wedge B_m.$$

This means that for given key values $t_1,\ldots,t_k$, the remaining arguments are set to $t_{k+1},\ldots,t_n$. This is treated as the following two rules:

$$-p(t_1,\ldots,t_k,X_{k+1},\ldots,X_n) \leftarrow p(t_1,\ldots,t_k,X_{k+1},\ldots,X_n) \wedge B_1 \wedge \cdots \wedge B_m.$$
$$+p(t_1,\ldots,t_k,t_{k+1},\ldots,t_n) \quad \leftarrow B_1 \wedge \cdots \wedge B_m.$$

If the arrow "$\to$" is missing, $k = 0$ is assumed, i.e. the extension of the predicate is overwritten with the result of the rule application. This can be used to set a kind of "global variable".

3.3   Interface Predicates

A Datalog program for a Microcontroller must interface with the libraries for querying input devices and performing actions on output devices. A few examples of interface functions (from the `Arduino.h` header file) are:

```
#define HIGH    0x1    void pinMode(uint8_t pin, uint8_t mode);
#define LOW     0x0    void digitalWrite(uint8_t pin, uint8_t val);
#define INPUT   0x00   int  digitalRead(uint8_t pin);
#define OUTPUT  0x01   unsigned long millis(void);
```

For each function f that can be called, there is a special predicate !f with the same arguments as the function to be called (on the Microlog^e level) and in addition the standard time argument (on the internal Datalog level). E.g. derived facts about the predicate !digitalWrite(T, Pin, Val) lead to the corresponding calls of the interface faction `digitalWrite` at time point T. The implementation ensures that duplicate calls are eliminated, i.e. even if there are different ways to deduce the fact, only one call is done.

The sequence of calls in the same state (time point) is undefined. If a specific sequence is required, one must use multiple states. Conflicts between functions (where a different order of calls has different effects) can be specified by means of constraints/invariants.

If an interface function f returns a value, there is a second predicate ?f that contains all parameters of the call and a parameter for the return value. For instance, for the function `digitalRead`, there are two predicates:

- !digitalRead(T, Pin), and
- ?digitalRead(T, Pin, Val).

When a !digitalRead-fact is derived, the call is done, and the corresponding result fact with the predicate ?digitalRead is added to the same state, i.e. can be used for further derivations. Of course, the result predicates ?f cannot be used in rule heads. Basically, ?f can be seen as defined by an (internal) system rule like

$$?digitalRead(T, Pin, Val) \leftarrow \ !digitalRead(T, Pin) \wedge Val = digitalRead(Pin).$$

The body of this special rule is evaluated from left to right, i.e. the call is only done when the !digitalRead is derived. In contrast, the evaluation sequence of literals in a normal rule body can be chosen by the optimizer. In our previous language, the results of interface function calls were available only in the next state. The present solution helps to reduce the number of states.

In Microlog^e, actions (such as calling a function) are defined by the rule heads. If actions were done in the body (as, e.g., in Prolog), the language would be less declarative, because we would need a prescribed evaluation order. The return predicates can appear in the rule body, but there can be facts about them only when a call was previously derived. That the calls are done during the derivation in a state also explains why we cannot guarantee a specific order.

Finally, we need also constants from the interface definition. If our Datalog program contains e.g. $HIGH, this corresponds to the constant HIGH in the generated C-code. We assume that different symbolic constants denote different values (unification will fail for them). Thus, the programmer may not use synonyms.

3.4 Event Predicates and the Event Queue

Programs for microcontrollers can often be viewed as reactive systems which are driven by events. An event can be an interrupt caused by a change on an input pin, or a timer that has reached its goal value. The program specifies the reaction on the event. This is dependent on the current state of the system and can cause a state-change (update of a predicate), as well as the execution of actions, such as calling an interface function. Events can also cause other internal events. Usually part of the program would abstract from the pure hardware-oriented event to a higher level application-oriented event. When modules are introduced in Sect. 6, events will be heavily used for communication between the modules.

A fact that describes an event exists only in one state, i.e. it is transient in contrast to facts with static or state predicates. However, events are queued, so that in each state, there is only one active event. It simplifies programming if one does not have to handle simultaneous events, and microcontrollers like the one in the Arduino have only a single core. Thus, we anyway have to handle one event after the other. Furthermore, our goal is that each single event can be processed quickly, so that the processing of interrupts is not delayed.

In Microlog^e, event predicates are marked as @p. They are time-dependent, i.e. they have the additional argument for the time point (state number) in the pure Datalog version. It is guaranteed that the special event @setup occurs in the very first state 0, i.e. the internal Datalog program contains @setup(0).

All actions that are caused by an event @p (such as updates of state predicates or calls to interface functions) appear in heads of rules that contain @p in the body, or another (transient) predicate that depends on @p. In this way, "something happens" only when an event occurs.

There is an event queue (the details are given in Sect. 5). All derived events are put into the queue, and at each time point (i.e., in each state), one event is taken out of the queue. For instance, if one needs to call interface functions at setup in a certain order, one could create another event:

$$@setup2[] \leftarrow @setup.$$

Rules with an event in the head will put this event into the queue in the next time point. If there is no other event, it will leave the queue immediately in that time point (i.e., @setup2 will occur immediately after @setup). In general, it is at least guaranteed that @setup2 will occur sometime after @setup. The meaning of the [] will become clearer when we look at real time delays in Subsect. 3.6 (one can specify a time in [. . .]).

A rule to define an event that immediately repeats itself (so that one gets an infinite sequence of events) is written as

$$@e[] \leftarrow @e.$$

Without the marker [], this rule would look like a tautology: @e ← @e. However, since there can be only one event in each state, rules that derive different events in the same state are anyway impossible. One can derive events only for a future state (via the queue). Transient predicates (see Subsect. 3.5) are a kind of "auxiliary synchronous events": They are derived within a state and can be used like an event in rules that specify actions in their head literal.

If one needs to perform polling, an event like @e can be used to ensure that the processor keeps working at maximal speed. Otherwise, when the event queue is empty, it might wait for an interrupt or a timed event (see Subsect. 3.6).

We permit that the user defines a priority of events from 0 (lowest) to 9 (highest). If no priority is specified, we use 5 as a default. Hardware interrupts are treated as having priority 10. In the Microlog^e syntax, priorities can be specified by attaching #0 to #9 to the derived event predicate (it is illegal to use different priorities with the same event predicate). In the internal Datalog version, priorities are given by a predicate prio with the event predicate name and the priority as arguments. For simplicity we assume that this contains priorities for all event predicates, including the default priority.

Besides the @setup event at time 0, the queue contains also the event @start of priority 1 from the beginning. The @start event has a very low priority so that the setup can finish, even if it requires several states. When @start is processed, the system should begin with its normal function.

There are further special events for different kinds of hardware interrupts. If the interrupts need to be configured, this can be done by calling interface functions.

It would have been also possible to treat interface function calls as events. However, our definition guarantees that function calls to handle an event are finished before the next event is processed. This seems to simplify programming. Our solution also corresponds to updates of state predicates that will certainly be done in the next state. Furthermore, interface function calls can be seen as the output of the reactive system, whereas events are the input.

3.5 Transient Predicates (Synchronous Events)

If the computation of the actions for an event becomes more complicated, one of course wants to use derived predicates. We call such predicates transient, because all facts about such a predicate exist only in a single state when the event is handled. They do not carry over to the next state.

One can also view these predicates as a kind of synchronous derived events. Normally, when an event is derived, it is entered into the queue and is executed in the next state or a later state. It does not influence the current state. But normal predicates can be derived from events, and they are available in the same state. These predicates can then be used for deriving actions, i.e. calls of interface functions or the generation of events.

A predicate p is called transient if each rule about p contains at least one body literal with an event predicate or a transient predicate. (The definition is slightly cyclic: We use the maximal set of predicates that satisfies this condition, i.e. we start with all predicates and successively eliminate predicates not satisfying the condition. The reason for this is that if we worked "bottom-up", recursive rules about transient predicates would block the classification as transient, because *all* rules about a transient predicate must contain an event or a transient predicate in the body.)

In order to clearly separate the persistent state and the definition of reactions on events, we expect that a rule containing an action predicate in its head (i.e., an event predicate $@p$, a function call predicate $!f$ or an update predicate $+p$ or $-p$), has at least one body literal with an event predicate or transient predicate. (Actually, everything would still defined if this style rule were violated: The events define a state sequence, and the corresponding action would be done in every state in which the body is true. But it seems better to explicitly define a transient predicate that is implied by each event, if one really should want such a behaviour.)

3.6 Real Time

In many programs for microcontrollers, something has to be done periodically, but only every n milliseconds (not at maximal speed). In other cases, something has to be done once after a certain time. For instance, to de-bounce an input key, one can check its value several times over a period of 20–50 ms (e.g. five times every 10 ms).

For this, we need the additional construct that one can derive an event delayed by a certain time:

$$@\mathsf{p}(t_1, \ldots, t_n)[n \; \mathsf{ms}] \leftarrow B_1 \wedge \cdots \wedge B_m.$$

After n milliseconds, the event is entered into the standard event queue. If the queue is then otherwise empty (or the event has high priority), it is immediately taken out of the queue and processed. In this construct, the time unit ms (milliseconds) is the default and can be left out. We now also see that the previous case [] simply means "delayed by 0 ms": The event is entered immediately into the standard queue.

Of course, events can reproduce themselves. In this way, a periodic event is created:

$$@\mathsf{tick}[10 \; \mathsf{ms}] \leftarrow @\mathsf{tick}.$$

In order to avoid that any additional delays in the event queue or the time for processing the event add up over many executions of such periodic events, the implementation can remember the originally scheduled time of the event, and use that time instead of the current time if it derives another timed event.

Internally, when a delayed event $@p$ is derived, the current system time is queried (on the Arduino with the function millis()), the scheduled time is computed, and the event is inserted into a queue prioritized by time. In each state, the scheduled time t of the first event in the queue is compared with the system time s, and if $t \le s$, the event is moved to the standard event queue. Of course, this works only as long as the standard event queue is not empty, so that the processor is busy generating new states. When there are no more events to be processed immediately, we must compute the remaining waiting time for the first event in the time queue and delay execution for that time. Microcontrollers (including the one on the Arduino) have various sleep modes in order to save energy while they are more or less idle. One can set a timer interrupt and enter a sleep mode where the CPU wakes up again when the timer reaches its goal.

4 Examples

Example 1. Most Arduino boards have an LED already connected to Pin 13. With the following program we can let this LED blink with 1000 ms on, then 1000 ms off, and so on. The similar program BlinkWithoutDelay from the Arduino tutorial has 16 lines of code.

$$
\begin{aligned}
!\,\mathsf{pinMode}(13, \$\mathtt{OUTPUT}) &\leftarrow @\mathsf{setup}. \\
@\mathsf{turn\_on}\,[] &\leftarrow @\mathsf{start}. \\
@\mathsf{turn\_off}\,[1000 \; \mathsf{ms}] &\leftarrow @\mathsf{turn\_on}. \\
@\mathsf{turn\_on}\,[1000 \; \mathsf{ms}] &\leftarrow @\mathsf{turn\_off}. \\
!\,\mathsf{digitalWrite}(13, \$\mathtt{HIGH}) &\leftarrow @\mathsf{turn\_on}. \\
!\,\mathsf{digitalWrite}(13, \$\mathtt{LOW}) &\leftarrow @\mathsf{turn\_off}.
\end{aligned}
$$

This program has the same number of rules as in our previous proposal, but now there is a state change only when something happens. The single state change from @start to @turn_on in the beginning could be avoided if we derive @turn_on immediately from @setup.   □

Example 2. If one does not like the repeated constants for the LED port and the on and off time, one can use static predicates with the configuration data:

```
led_pin(13).
on_time(1000).
off_time(1000).
!pinMode(P, $OUTPUT)  ← @setup ∧ led_pin(P).
@turn_on []           ← @start.

@turn_off[D ms]       ← @turn_on ∧ on_time(D).
@turn_on[D ms]        ← @turn_off ∧ off_time(D).

!digitalWrite(P, $HIGH) ← @turn_on ∧ led_pin(P).
!digitalWrite(P, $LOW)  ← @turn_off ∧ led_pin(P).
```

                                                                                                □

5   A Queue-Implementation in Datalog

In this section, we show how the event queue can be implemented in Datalog. Of course, the real implementation is in C. So this could be seen as only an academic exercise. However, since the semantics of Microlog^e is defined by its translation to Datalog, this is needed. It also gives the yardstick to measure the correctness of the C implementation. For space reasons, we handle only the case without real time delays.

For every event predicate @p, there is a queue predicate queue_p with one additional argument for the logical time (state number) when the event was queued. By including the time when the event was generated, it is also clearly defined that events are not lost even if they are generated later again before the first event was processed. The queue predicate is used only in the internal Datalog version, it cannot appear in Microlog^e programs. If the Microlog^e programmer puts an event in the head, e.g.,

$$@p(t_1, \ldots, t_n)\,[] \leftarrow B_1 \wedge \cdots \wedge B_m$$

this really means (in the internal Datalog version) that the corresponding event is put into the queue in the next state:

$$\text{queue\_}p(S, S, t_1, \ldots, t_n) \leftarrow \bar{B}_1 \wedge \cdots \wedge \bar{B}_m \wedge \text{succ}(T, S).$$

The second argument is the time when the event entered the queue. Queued events persist until they are selected for execution. Therefore, the internal Datalog program contains these rules for each event predicate of arity n:

$$\text{queue\_}p(S, Q, X_1, \ldots, X_n) \leftarrow \text{queue\_}p(T, Q, X_1, \ldots, X_n) \wedge$$
$$\neg\text{selected\_}p(T, Q, X_1, \ldots, X_n) \wedge \text{succ}(T, S).$$
$$@p(T, X_1, \ldots, X_n) \leftarrow \text{selected\_}p(T, Q, X_1, \ldots, X_n).$$

The indirection via selected_p is necessary so that one selected @p event does not delete other @p-events that were later queued. To define the queue, we need for each queue predicate queue_p a predicate wait_p formalizing that the event has to wait because there is another event in front. The predicate wait_p has the same arguments as queue_p. Then an event is selected if it does not have to wait:

$$\text{selected\_}p(\mathsf{T}, \mathsf{Q}, X_1, \ldots, X_n) \leftarrow \text{queue\_}p(\mathsf{T}, \mathsf{Q}, X_1, \ldots, X_n) \wedge$$
$$\neg \, \text{wait\_}p(\mathsf{T}, \mathsf{Q}, X_1, \ldots, X_n).$$

Now formalizing the wait predicate is a bit technical work. Because all events have predicates of their own, we define a single predicate queued that states which type of event with which priority waits since what time. For every queue predicate queue_p, the following rule is added to the Datalog program:

$$\text{queued}(\mathsf{T}, \mathsf{P}, \mathsf{Q}, p) \leftarrow \text{queue\_}p(\mathsf{T}, \mathsf{Q}, X_1, \ldots, X_n) \wedge \text{prio}(p, \mathsf{P}).$$

Here the predicate name is used as a data value in the head and in the lookup of the priority. If different events of the same priority wait for the same time, we use the alphabetic order to select one. However, the order of events of the same priority that entered the queue at the same time is "implementation defined". The first rule about wait_p states that an event has to wait when there is another event of higher priority:

$$\text{wait\_}p(\mathsf{T}, \mathsf{Q}, X_1, \ldots, X_n) \leftarrow \text{queue\_}p(\mathsf{T}, \mathsf{Q}, X_1, \ldots, X_n) \wedge \text{prio}(p, \mathsf{P}) \wedge$$
$$\text{queued}(\mathsf{T}, \mathsf{P}', \mathsf{Q}', p') \wedge \mathsf{P}' > \mathsf{P}.$$

The second rule states that an event has to wait if there is an event of the same priority that already waits already longer:

$$\text{wait\_}p(\mathsf{T}, \mathsf{Q}, X_1, \ldots, X_n) \leftarrow \text{queue\_}p(\mathsf{T}, \mathsf{Q}, X_1, \ldots, X_n) \wedge \text{prio}(p, \mathsf{P}) \wedge$$
$$\text{queued}(\mathsf{T}, \mathsf{P}, \mathsf{Q}', p') \wedge \mathsf{Q}' < \mathsf{Q}.$$

The third selection criterion is the event name:

$$\text{wait\_}p(\mathsf{T}, \mathsf{Q}, X_1, \ldots, X_n) \leftarrow \text{queue\_}p(\mathsf{T}, \mathsf{Q}, X_1, \ldots, X_n) \wedge \text{prio}(p, \mathsf{P}) \wedge$$
$$\text{queued}(\mathsf{T}, \mathsf{P}, \mathsf{Q}, p') \wedge p' < p.$$

Now we only have to define the sequence for the same type of event waiting for the same time. This is done by the argument values. The first rule of this type is:

$$\text{wait\_}p(\mathsf{T}, \mathsf{Q}, X_1, \ldots, X_n) \leftarrow \text{queue\_}p(\mathsf{T}, \mathsf{Q}, X_1, \ldots, X_n) \wedge$$
$$\text{queue\_}p(\mathsf{T}, \mathsf{Q}, Y_1, \ldots, Y_n) \wedge Y_1 < X_1.$$

This continues until the last argument defines the order if all previous arguments are the same.

Please note that all these rules to specify the event queue are contained only in the internal Datalog version. The Microlog^e programmer does not have to write them, and the implementor is free to use any prioritized queue implementation that conforms to this specification.

6 Modular Specifications

Larger programs should be separated into components that can be understood independently and help to avoid name clashes. When specifying a system based on a sequence of states, it is also helpful if one can consider only a subsequence of the states for each component.

We use a simple module system: Modules have the form

$$\langle \text{module-name} \rangle \ \{ \ \langle \text{rules} \rangle \ \}$$

Similar to the module systems of Prolog, the module name μ becomes a prefix of the predicate name, i.e. all predicate names internally have the form $\mu : p$. If a predicate p is used in module μ without prefix, this implicitly means $\mu : p$.

Now there should of course be restrictions in the rules so that modules can be understood separately as far as possible. With exception of events, the predicate in the head of a rule in module μ must have prefix μ (explicitly or implicitly). I.e., all predicates of a module are defined by the rules within that module. Only events of a module can come from the outside—they are the means of communication between the modules.

In order to give the module control over the events and their priority that can be expected from the outside, we optionally permit to specify this information:

$$\langle \text{module-name} \rangle \ [\langle \text{event} \rangle \# \langle \text{priority} \rangle, \dots \ ] \ \{$$
$$\langle \text{rules} \rangle$$
$$\}$$

If this is specified, only the given events of this module can be generated in other modules. This permits to have also internal events, presumably with higher priority, so that a sequence of states can be finished before the next event is handled.

Example 3. In the following example, there is a separate module for controlling the LED:

```
led {
      led_pin(13).
      !pinMode(P, $OUTPUT)    ← @setup ∧ led_pin(P).
      !digitalWrite(P, $HIGH) ← @turn_on ∧ led_pin(P).
      !digitalWrite(P, $LOW)  ← @turn_off ∧ led_pin(P).
}

blink {
      on_off_time(1000).
      @tick[]             ← @start.
      @tick[D ms]         ← @tick ∧ on_off_time(D).
      led : @turn_on      ← @tick ∧ ¬is_on.
      +is_on              ← @tick ∧ ¬is_on.
      led : @turn_off     ← @tick ∧ is_on.
      -is_on              ← @tick ∧ is_on.
}
```

□

In rule bodies, events and transient predicates from other modules are forbidden. The main motivation is that something changes in a module only if an event of that module occurs.

It is possible that one wants to access other predicates from a different module. E.g., in Example 3, it would make sense that the led module does the bookkeeping of the status of the LED. As explained above, only static predicates and state predicates can be accessed from the outside. Furthermore, we require in this case that they are explicitly listed in the export list (while events can be expected to come from the outside, the default for other predicates is that they are local).

It is important to understand that although used state predicates from other modules might change, own predicates change only at the next event. This is no problem when state predicates from other modules are used in action rules that contain an event or transient predicate in the body. This would cover, e.g., accessing the current LED state maintained by the led module in the blink module. Other usages of foreign state predicates are forbidden.

There is no restriction to use exported static predicates from other modules.

7   Conclusions

In this paper, we presented a rule-based language for programming microcontrollers. In our personal view, after experimenting with different language proposals, the language looks quite nice and useable. The language can be translated to Datalog with a state argument and with calls to external functions. This gives it a clearly defined semantics and makes the large body of work about Datalog applicable.

Of course, program verification is important for embedded systems, and such logic based languages should have an advantage in this aspect. In [2], we defined a class of integrity constraints called "generalized exclusion constraints" and presented a method for proving that they are always satisfied. In particular, this kind constraints can be used to ensure that each state does not contain "too many" facts, e.g. more than what fits in the restricted memory of a microcontroller. But they also can express conflicts between different interface functions that cannot be called in the same state. For the event queue, we certainly have to prove that it is always quite small. In the general case, this would need also time bounds for processing events.

We are working on a prototype implementation of the language. The current state of the project is described at:

https://users.informatik.uni-halle.de/~brass/micrologE/.

Acknowledgement. I would like to thank Mario Wenzel for the inspiration, helpful questions and important suggestions.

References

1. Alvaro, P., Marczak, W.R., Conway, N., Hellerstein, J.M., Maier, D., Sears, R.: DEDALUS: Datalog in time and space. In: de Moor, O., Gottlob, G., Furche, T., Sellers, A. (eds.) Datalog 2.0 2010. LNCS, vol. 6702, pp. 262–281. Springer, Heidelberg (2011). https://doi.org/10.1007/978-3-642-24206-9_16. http://www.neilconway.org/docs/dedalus_dl2.pdf

2. Brass, S., Wenzel, M.: Integrity constraints for microcontroller programming in Datalog. In: Bellatreche, L., Dumas, M., Karras, P., Matulevičius, R. (eds.) ADBIS 2021. LNCS, vol. 12843, pp. 152–166. Springer, Cham (2021). https://doi.org/10.1007/978-3-030-82472-3_12

3. Chabin, J., Halfeld-Ferrari, M., Markhoff, B., Nguyen, T.B.: Validating data from semantic web providers. In: Tjoa, A.M., Bellatreche, L., Biffl, S., van Leeuwen, J., Wiedermann, J. (eds.) SOFSEM 2018. LNCS, vol. 10706, pp. 682–695. Springer, Cham (2018). https://doi.org/10.1007/978-3-319-73117-9_48

4. Harel, D.: Statecharts: a visual formalism for complex systems. Sci. Comput. Program. **8**, 231–274 (1987)

5. Kowalski, R., Sadri, F.: Reactive computing as model generation. New Gener. Comput. **33**, 33–67 (2015). https://doi.org/10.1007/s00354-015-0103-z

6. Lausen, G., Ludäscher, B., May, W.: On active deductive databases: the statelog approach. In: Freitag, B., Decker, H., Kifer, M., Voronkov, A. (eds.) DYNAMICS 1997. LNCS, vol. 1472, pp. 69–106. Springer, Heidelberg (1998). https://doi.org/10.1007/BFb0055496

7. Przymusinski, T.C.: Every logic program has a natural stratification and an iterated least fixed point model. In: Proceedings of the Eighth ACM SIGACT-SIGMOD-SIGART Symposium on Principles of Database Systems, (PODS 1989), pp. 11–21. ACM (1989)

8. Samek, M.: Practical UML Statecharts in C/C++: Event-Driven Programming for Embedded Systems, 2nd edn. CRC Press, Boca Raton (2009)

9. Scholz, B., Jordan, H., Subotić, P., Westmann, T.: On fast large-scale program analysis in Datalog. In: Proceedings of the 25th International Conference on Compiler Construction (CC 2016), pp. 196–206. ACM (2016)

10. Shkapsky, A., Yang, M., Interlandi, M., Chiu, H., Condie, T., Zaniolo, C.: Big data analytics with Datalog queries on Spark. In: Proceedings of the 2016 International Conference on Management of Data (SIGMOD 2016), pp. 1135–1149. ACM (2016). http://yellowstone.cs.ucla.edu/~yang/paper/sigmod2016-p958.pdf

11. Van Gelder, A., Ross, K., Schlipf, J.S.: Unfounded sets and well-founded semantics for general logic programs. In: Proceedings of the Seventh ACM SIGACT-SIGMOD-SIGART Symposium on Principles of Database Systems (PODS 1988), pp. 221–230 (1988)

12. Wenzel, M., Brass, S.: Declarative programming for microcontrollers - Datalog on Arduino. In: Hofstedt, P., Abreu, S., John, U., Kuchen, H., Seipel, D. (eds.) INAP/WLP/WFLP 2019. LNCS (LNAI), vol. 12057, pp. 119–138. Springer, Cham (2020). https://doi.org/10.1007/978-3-030-46714-2_9. https://arxiv.org/abs/1909.00043

13. Wenzel, M., Brass, S.: Translation of interactive Datalog programs for microcontrollers to finite state machines. In: Fernández, M. (ed.) LOPSTR 2020. LNCS, vol. 12561, pp. 210–227. Springer, Cham (2021). https://doi.org/10.1007/978-3-030-68446-4_11

Combining Deep Learning and ASP-Based Models for the Semantic Segmentation of Medical Images

Pierangela Bruno(✉) , Francesco Calimeri(✉) , Cinzia Marte(✉) ,
and Marco Manna(✉)

Department of Mathematics and Computer Science, University of Calabria,
Rende, Italy
{bruno,calimeri,marte,manna}@mat.unical.it

Abstract. Automatic segmentation represents a huge breakthrough in computer-aided diagnosis and medicine, as it allows to provide clinicians important with information for interventional and diagnostic tasks. Recent advancements in Deep Learning (DL), such as Convolutional Neural Networks (CNNs), have proved to be greatly promising in identifying anatomical and pathological structures, and in extracting meaningful patterns from huge amounts of data. However, such approaches suffer from the lack of proper means for interpreting the choices made by the models, and it is not easy to drive the decisions according to prior knowledge. In this context, deductive rule-based approaches, such as Answer Set Programming (ASP), can allow to effectively encode problems or specific features via logic programs in a declarative fashion, while possibly also helping at improving performance.

In this seminal work, we propose the use of ASP to drive DL approaches in performing semantic segmentation of medical images. Specifically, we encoded prior medical knowledge via ASP, thus defining a rule-based model for deducting all admitted combinations of classes and right locations in medical images. The results of an experimental analysis are reported with the aim to assess the viability of the proposed approach.

Keywords: Answer set programming · Knowledge representation and reasoning · Deep learning · Semantic segmentation · Inductive-deductive coupling

1 Introduction

Semantic image segmentation, also defined as pixel-level classification, refers to the task of segmenting an image into regions corresponding to meaningful objects and then assigning them an object category label [22,30]. Notably, in medical contexts, semantic segmentation of images can be extremely useful to support clinicians in providing proper diagnosis, identifying pathological conditions, and

© Springer Nature Switzerland AG 2021
S. Moschoyiannis et al. (Eds.): RuleML+RR 2021, LNCS 12851, pp. 95–110, 2021.
https://doi.org/10.1007/978-3-030-91167-6_7

highlighting image regions related to a specific disease. In the last decades, Deep Learning (DL)-based approaches have shown a great deal of potential in extracting meaningful information from different types of images (e.g., computed tomography (CT), magnetic resonance imaging (MRI), endoscopic imaging), being particularly suitable for semantic segmentation and, in general, for supporting automated diagnosis, surgical scene understanding and computer-assisted interventions [32]. For instance, thanks to DL-based approaches, clinicians can confirm the size of tumors, identify lesion sites and quantitatively evaluate the effect before and after treatment [23].

However, DL-based approaches suffer from some limitations, for instance in (i) providing clear interpretations and explanations of the decisions made by the network, or (ii) driving the decisions according to prior knowledge, thus affecting successful deployment in real-life experiments.

To overcome such limitations, we propose the use of Answer Set Programming (ASP) to steer neural networks decisions and refine the predicted output. Specifically, we create a rule-based model by encoding prior medical knowledge to compute all the admitted combinations of classes and, for each class, identify the wrong pixel location in medical images.

We make use of this ASP-based model to: (i) define a novel loss function which includes a penalty for each misclassified element detected by the network, and (ii) perform post-processing to discard small islands of noise and predicted classes which do not comply with prior medical knowledge. We also re-assign misclassified elements to the more frequent class in the neighborhood. We tested our approach using different artificial neural networks (i.e., DeepLab-v3, SegNet, U-Net) for performing semantic segmentation of Laryngeal Endoscopic Images [21].

The remainder of the paper is structured as follows. We first briefly report on related work in Sect. 2; in Sect. 3 we present preliminaries on ASP and deep learning; in Sect. 4 we provide a detailed description of our approach, that has been assessed via a careful experimental activity, which is in turn discussed in Sect. 5; we analyze and discuss results in Sect. 6, eventually drawing our conclusions in Sect. 7.

2   Related Work

In this section we report some related works regarding ASP, DL and their combination.

Deep Learning in Image Analysis. In the literature, several works have been proposed to perform the segmentation of medical images [7,14,31]. In the context of semantic segmentation, Laves et al. [21] used different CNN-based methods (i.e., SegNet, U-Net, ENet and ErfNet) to perform semantic segmentation of Laryngeal Endoscopic Images. Rezaie et al. [28] proposed a recurrent generative adversarial architecture to perform semantic segmentation on small lesions and anatomical regions. This approach aims to mitigate imbalanced data problems in medical images (i.e., the number of pixels belongs the background are significantly higher than those belonging to the desired object). Similarly,

Kim et al. [20] used a cascaded 3D U-Net, trained with active learning, to both reduce labeling efforts through CNN-corrected segmentation and increase training efficiency with limited data. The approach was tested in performing semantic segmentation of renal cell carcinoma and fine substructures of the kidney, showing promising results. Finally, Ni et al. [26] proposed a Residual Attention U-Net to perform semantic segmentation of cataract surgical instruments. Specifically, this approach was designed to learn discriminative features and address the specular reflection issue, outperforming the state-of-the-art methods.

Answer Set Programming. To the best of our knowledge, there are no works for employing Answer set programming (ASP) in segmenting medical images; however, it has been applied in several areas of AI, like planning, probabilistic reasoning, data integration, query answering, computational biology, bioinformatics, etc. (see, e.g., [11,17]). Among the huge literature, Adrian et al. [1] relied on ASP to provide a declarative characterization of the basic geometric properties of PDF documents, by combining geometrical, structural, and semantic analysis, to obtain a more precise representation of complex documents; Costabile et al. [16] defined a novel decision support system via ASP to perform a diagnosis of headache disorders (HEAD-ASP); Alviano et al. [4] present an ASP encoding to solve a variant of the Nurse Scheduling problem (NSP), which is a combinatorial problem that consists of assigning nurses to shifts according to given practical constraints.

Combination of Deep Learning with ASP. Very recently, ways for combining deductive and inductive approaches have raised a lot of interest in the scientific community. Maratea et al. [24] proposed machine learning techniques to ASP solving, aiming at developing a fast and robust multi-engine ASP solver. Similarly, Young et al. [34] presented an extension of ASP by embracing neural networks (NeurASP). This approach showed promising results in improving the training of a neural network, by exploiting ASP rules. Mastria et al. [25] presented a combined approach based on Machine Learning and ASP to automatically decide whether to rewrite an input encoding for producing alternative ASP programs that are semantically equivalent to the input ones, yet more efficiently processed by actual ASP systems. Calimeri et al. [8] combine the use of ML and ASP to propose a framework for supporting the analysis and the understanding of the evolution of neurological disorders.

It is worth noting that methodologies for connecting automated reasoning with existing deep learning architectures have already been proposed in the literature (e.g., [33]); however, they rely on propositional logic and, to the best of our knowledge, our approach is one of the first attempts to combine DL and ASP through the use of both rule-based loss function and post-processing phase.

3   Methodology: Preliminaries and Background

In this section, we briefly introduce the basic notations, terminologies, and preliminaries on ASP and DL which will be used throughout this paper.

3.1 Answer Set Programming

We report next some basics on Answer Set Programming; for further details and advanced ASP features we refer the reader to [6,10,13] and the huge literature. A *term* is either a *simple term* or a *functional term*. A simple term is either a constant or a variable. If $t_1, \ldots, t_n$ are terms and f is a function symbol of arity n, then $f(t_1, \ldots, t_n)$ is a *functional term*. If $t_1, \ldots, t_k$ are terms and p is a predicate symbol of arity k, then $p(t_1, \ldots, t_k)$ is an *atom*. A *literal* l is of the form a or *not* a, where a is an atom; in the former case l is *positive*, otherwise negative. A *rule* r is of the form $\alpha_1 | \cdots | \alpha_k : -\beta_1, \ldots, \beta_n,\ not\ \beta_{n+1}, \ldots,\ not\ \beta_m$. where $m \geq 0, k \geq 0$; $\alpha_1 | \cdots | \alpha_k$ and $\beta_1, \ldots, \beta_m$ are atoms. We define $H(r) = \{\alpha_1 | \cdot | \alpha_k\}$ (the *head* of r) and $B(r) = B^+(r) \cup B^-(r)$ (the *body* of r), where $B^+(r) = \{\beta_1, \ldots, \beta_n\}$ (the *positive body*) and $B^-(r) = \{not\ \beta_{n+1}, \ldots,\ not\ \beta_m\}$ (the *negative body*). If $H(r) = \emptyset$, then r is a *(strong) constraint*; if $B(r) = \emptyset$ and $|H(r)| = 1$, then r is a *fact*. A rule r is safe if each variable of r has an occurrence in $B^+(r)$. For a rule r, we denote as $headvar(r)$, $bodyvar(r)$ and $var(r)$ the set of variables occurring in $H(r)$, $B(r)$ and r, respectively. An ASP program is a finite set P of safe rules. A program (a rule, a literal) is *ground* if it contains no variables. A predicate is defined by a rule r if it occurs in $H(r)$. A predicate defined only by facts is an *EDB* predicate, the remaining are *IDB* predicates. The set of all facts in P is denoted by $Facts(P)$; the set of instances of all *EDB* predicates in P is denoted by $EDB(P)$. Given a program P, the *Herbrand universe* of P, denoted by U_P, consists of all ground terms that can be built combining constants and function symbols appearing in P. The *Herbrand base* of P, denoted by B_P, is the set of all ground atoms obtainable from the atoms of P by replacing variables with elements from U_P. A *substitution* for a rule $r \in P$ is a mapping from the set of variables of r to the set U_P of ground terms. A *ground instance* of a rule r is obtained applying a substitution to r. The *full instantiation $Ground(P)$* of P is defined as the set of all ground instances of its rules over U_P. An *interpretation* I for P is a subset of B_P. A positive literal a (resp., a negative literal *nota*) is true with respect to I if $a \in I$ (resp., $a \notin I$); it is false otherwise. Given a ground rule r, we say that r is satisfied with respect to I if some atom appearing in $H(r)$ is true with respect to I or some literal appearing in $B(r)$ is false with respect to I. Given a program P, we say that I is a *model* of P, iff all rules in $Ground(P)$ are satisfied with respect to I. A model M is *minimal* if there is no model N for P such that $N \subset M$. The *Gelfond-Lifschitz reduct* (Gelfond and Lifschitz 1991) of P, with respect to an interpretation I, is the positive ground program P^I obtained from $Ground(P)$ by: (i) deleting all rules having a negative literal false with respect to I; (ii) deleting all negative literals from the remaining rules. $I \subseteq B_P$ is an answer set for a program P iff I is a minimal model for P^I. The set of all answer sets for P is denoted by $AS(P)$.

During the years, the language of ASP has been enriched to several extents with different constructs, even beyond the language standard [10]. In this work, we make use of the *aggregate atoms*, that are expression of the form $\#aggr\{t_1, \ldots, t_m : l_1, \ldots, l_n\} \circledast u$ where $aggr \in \{count, sum, max, min\}$, $\circledast \in \{<, \leq, =, \neq, >, \geq\}$, $t_1, \ldots, t_m$ are terms, $l_1, \ldots, l_n$ are literals and u is a variable or a number.

3.2   Deep Learning

Loss Function is an important component of Neural Networks able to ensure that the model is working properly. It is used to evaluate how well the algorithm manages to fit the training data [18] by comparing predicted images to ground truth segmentation. The aim of the training is to minimize the loss function, which computes a dissimilarity measure between a prediction p obtained by the model on an input image x, and a corresponding ground truth segmentation y. To this aim, we choose the pixel-wise cross-entropy loss function, defined as $\mathscr{L}_{CE} = - \sum y_i \log(p_i)$, where y_i is the ground truth segmentation and p_i is the prediction value for a given pixel i.

DeepLab-V3 is a semantic segmentation architecture that uses Atrous Spatial Pyramid Pooling (ASPP) with the aim of extracting dense features [15]. The authors proposed the use of several parallel atrus convolution with different rates, with the image-level features [27]. To do this, they applied a global average pooling on the last feature map and, then, they upsample the feature to the desired spatial dimension [15].

SegNet has an encoder network and a corresponding decoder network. The first one consists of 13 convolutional layers, corresponding to the first 13 convolutional layers in the VGG16 network [5]. Each layer is followed by batch-normalization, ReLu, and maxpooling with a 2×2 window and stride 2.

Similarly, each decoder contains 13 layers. The decoder upsamples input feature maps through the max-pooling indices previously memorized in the corresponding encoder feature maps [5]. The final decoder output uses soft-max to produce class probabilities for each pixel independently.

U-Net is a symmetric encoder/decoder structure composed of a contracting and an upsampling path [29]. The contracting path is composed of the repeated 3×3 convolutions and a 2×2 maxpooling operation with stride 2 for downsampling. In the expansive path feature and spatial information are combined through a sequence of 3×3 up-convolutions and concatenations with high-resolution features from the contracting path [29].

In the final layer, a 1×1 convolution is used to map all 64 component feature vectors to the 7 classes. All layers use ReLU, except for the last layer which uses soft-max.

4   ASP-Enhanced Semantic Segmentation

The herein proposed approach relies on the use of ASP for facilitating the task of semantic segmentation. Such an approach requires to face three main challenges: (*i*) the design of a model based on knowledge representation for describing domain medical knowledge, (*ii*) the design of a standard methodology to convert

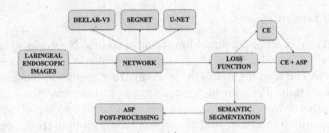

Fig. 1. Workflow of the proposed framework. Laryngeal endoscopic images are used to train three different neural networks. The training phase is supported by ASP-based model through loss function and the predicted output is refined by rule-based post processing.

network prediction into logical rules over the data model mentioned above, (*iii*) a proper interpretation of the output of ASP computation and its conversion into values understandable by the network, to determine the loss function in real-time. To date, there's no well-established methodology for combining DL and ASP-based models in performing semantic segmentation; hence, the contribution of this paper is two-fold (see Fig. 1):

- To drive the network's learning and penalize the misclassification, we quantify a penalty value using an ASP-based model that compares the network's prediction to medical knowledge and ground truth segmentation; this value, which expresses "how wrong" the classification is, takes part in defining the loss function. Specifically, we introduce the penalty value in the last 250 epochs of the training to refine the network decisions.
- To improve the quality of the results, we define an ASP-based post-processing to remove noise (i.e., small "islands" of misclassified pixels) and wrong predicted classes (i.e., classes which do not respect medical requirements). Specifically, we first translate the network's prediction into logical rules, and then define an ASP-based model to identify pixels that need to be removed; eventually, we rely on such model to re-assign misclassified pixels/elements to the more frequent class in the neighborhood.

In the following we illustrate the proposed approach in detail: we first describe rule-based loss function and then the post-processing phase.

ASP-Based Loss Function. We encode an ASP program $\mathcal{P}_L$ that defines a declarative loss function for driving the neural network's decisions, discarding the non-eligible ones according to prior medical knowledge. The idea is to apply a penalty to the network, combining the $\mathcal{L}_{CE}$ function and our parameter Λ, which depends on the number of wrong objects identified by the network. To this aim, we compare the ground truth segmentation with respect to the predicted one and, to compute Λ, we discern three main scenarios in which the network can recognize wrong objects. Specifically, the schema of $\mathcal{P}_L$ consists of 18 predicates.

We use four extensional predicates to model the information about the ground truth segmentation (for simplicity of exposition, we will refer to it as "original image") and the predicted image. In particular, with

$$original(I, Class, Seq), \ predicted(I, Class, Seq),$$

we represent the classes contained in the original (resp., predicted) image I, for each possible sequence. Since we are interested in understanding how wrong the network's prediction is, in our analysis, we consider the identified objects, and especially the positions in which they appear.

In particular, we use facts of the form

$$position\_original(I, Class, Seq, Pos_1, Pos_2),$$

$$position\_predicted(I, Class, Seq, Pos_1, Pos_2),$$

where variables Pos_1 and Pos_2 can be mapped to the sets of constants $\{up, center, bottom\}$ and $\{left, center, right\}$, respectively.

On the basis of this definition of the input information, we define the three main scenarios in which the network makes mistakes more often.

1. *Incorrect number of object occurrences in the image.* The first scenario refers to all cases in which the network recognizes non-existent objects or misses something else according to the original image. We use the following rules to count the number of objects both in the original and in the predicted image.

$$totalOriginal(I, N, S) : - \ original(I, \_, S),$$
$$N = \#count\{I, C, S : original(ID, C, S)\}.$$
$$totalPredicted(I, N, S) : - \ predicted(I, \_, S),$$
$$N = \#count\{I, C, S : predicted(ID, C, S)\}.$$

After that, we are able to deduce if the network recognizes something more (resp., less) via instances of the predicate $penality\_occ\_more(I, Seq)$ (resp., $penality\_occ\_less(I, Seq)$) obtained by comparing the second term of predicates $totalOriginal$ and $totalPredicted$. Please note that to each atom of the form $penality\_occ\_less(I, Seq)$ we assign a penalty which is directly proportional to the number of undetected object.

2. *Wrong object detection, according to medical knowledge.* In this scenario we consider all cases in which the network recognizes an object which do not comply to the prior medical knowledge. The dataset that we used is composed of different sequences from two patients, each featuring constraints like "in Sequence 1 the tumor is clearly visible", or "in Sequence 1 there are not instruments visible" (see Sect. 5.1 for more details). We use the following rules to count the number of images in which this problem shows:

$$penality\_scen(I, sequence_1) : -predicted(I, intubation, sequence_1).$$

$$penality\_scen(I, Seq) : -predicted(I, pathology, Seq).$$

where $Seq \in \{sequence_3, \ldots, sequence_8\}$.

3. *Wrong positions of objects detection.* In the last scenario, we collect all the cases in which the network predicts objects in wrong positions. In particular, we count how many images are such that the predicted position of a given class C for an image I and a sequence S is different from the original position, and vice-versa, via the following rules:

$$penality\_pos\_less(I, C, S) : - \; position\_original(I, C, S, Pos_1, Pos_2),$$
$$not \; position\_predicted(I, C, S, Pos_1, Pos_2).$$
$$penality\_pos\_more(I, C, S) : - \; position\_predicted(I, C, S, Pos_1, Pos_2),$$
$$not \; position\_original(I, C, S, Pos_1, Pos_2).$$

For each scenario described above, we obtain the number λ_i of images that are affected by these possible wrong detections. Exploiting the result of $\mathcal{P}_L$, we associate to it a penalty in the range $(0, 1)$, and a weighting factor, obtaining the following parameter Λ, that we will combine with the loss function $\mathcal{L}_{CE}$ (see Sect. 5.4), $\Lambda = \sum_{i=1}^{3} \tilde{\lambda}_i \cdot p_i$, where each p_i is a weighting factor that depends on the severity of the mistake, and $\tilde{\lambda}_i$ is obtained by the product of λ_i and the penalty associated to it. In particular, we set the weighting factors as follow: $p_1 = 0.30$, $p_2 = 0.15$, $p_3 = 0.55$. These values have been chosen empirically. Finally, we need to scale the value of Λ to ensure comparability with the $\mathcal{L}_{CE}$ value; to this aim, after an empirical analysis, we have chosen to compute $\log_{100}(\Lambda)$.

ASP-Based Post Processing. The second program $\mathcal{P}_P$ is aimed at improving the quality of the prediction via a post processing phase. The purpose is to clean the image from noise (i.e. small island of pixels), which under a certain size, can be considered as wrongly detected areas. These islands are afterwards colored by selecting the most frequent color (i.e., classes) in the neighborhood. Specifically, the program takes in input two types of predicates: *cell_island* used to represent the island, and *cell_neighbor* used to represent adjacent island's cells (i.e., its neighborhood). Exploiting the latter, fixed the island, denoted by its identifier ID, we count the number of its adjacent cells and its relative color, via the rule

$$adj\_group(N, Col, ID) : - \; cell\_island(\_, \_, \_, ID), cell\_neighbor(\_, \_, Col, ID),$$
$$N = \#count\{X, Y, Col : cell\_neighbor(X, Y, Col, ID)\}.$$

After that, we compute the biggest group of adjacent cells, in order to identify the color C to re-assign to the island. We observe that, in the selection of C, we exclude all the assignments that would not comply the prior medical knowledge (see Sect. 5.1). Whit the following rule, we show an example of how we encode the fact that we don't want to assign color 4 (representing the pathology) to the island in the sequence 6.

$$max\_adj\_group(M, ID) : - \; sequence(6), cell\_neighbor(\_, \_, ID),$$
$$M = \#max\{N : adj\_group(N, C, ID), C \neq 4\}.$$

Finally, we assign the color to the island as follows:

$$color\_island(ID, C) : - \; max\_adj\_group(M, ID), adj\_group(N, C, ID).$$

We remark that we also remove all the areas that, according to the prior medical knowledge, are wrongly detected (for example, the network cannot detect pathology class in images referring to sequence i, with $i > 2$). To re-assign the color to these wrong detected areas, we argue as above.

5   Experimental Activity

We illustrate next the experimental settings, then discuss the results.

5.1   Dataset Description

For the experimental analysis, we used the Laryngeal Endoscopic Images dataset [21]. It consists of 536 manually segmented in vivo color images (512 × 512 pixels) of the larynx captured during two different resection surgeries. The images are categorized in 7 classes: *void, vocal folds, other tissue, glottal space, pathology, surgical tool and intubation*, corresponding to index 0, 1, 2, 3, 4, 5, 6, respectively.

The dataset features 8 sequences from two patients, collected in 5 different groups. The sequences have the following characteristics, as described in [21]:

1. Sequence 1: pre-operative with clearly visible tumor on vocal fold, changes in scale, translation, rotation, without intubation, no instruments visible;
2. Sequence 2: pre-operative with clearly visible tumor, changes in scale and translation, visible instruments, with intubation;
3. Sequence 3–4: post-operative with removed tumor, changes in scale and translation, damaged tissue, with intubation;
4. Sequence 5–7: pre-operative with instruments manipulating and grasping the vocal folds, changes in scale and translation, with intubation;
5. Sequence 8: post-operative with blood on vocal folds, instruments and surgical dressing, with intubation.

5.2   Training Phase

The dataset was split into training (80%) and testing (20%) sets; specifically, the 10% of the training set is used as validation set.

Each networks was implemented in Pytorch and trained for 1000 epochs, using the SGD [19] optimizer, cross-entropy (CE) as loss function for the first 750 epochs and a combination of CE and ASP-based loss function (see Sect. 4) for the remaining 250, learning rate 0.01 and batch size 32. All experiments have been performed on a GNU/Linux machine equipped with a NVIDIA Quadro P6000 GPU. All the networks have been trained using a pre-trained weight and with the same set of hyperparameters, in order to maintain comparability between different experiments. As already mentioned, we implemented our deductive approach into ASP; for the sake of experiments, we used one of the most widespread ASP system, namely DLV2 [2], that combines the fully-compliant ASP-Core-2 grounder $\mathcal{I}$-DLV [9, 12] with the solver WASP [3].

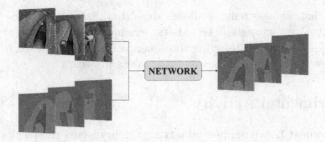

Fig. 2. Workflow of the architecture, which takes in input raw images and corresponding ground truth segmentations and returns the predicted semantic segmentantions.

5.3   Performance Metrics

We assessed the effectiveness of our approach by measuring the Intersection-over-Union (IoU) evaluation metric, given by $IoU = \frac{TP}{TP+FP+FN}$, where TP is the number of true positive, FP false positive and FN false negative pixels, respectively. The IoU metric was computed independently for each class.

The proposed architecture for semantic segmentation is illustrated in Fig. 2. Specifically, each tested network (i.e., DeepLab-v3, SegNet and U-Net) takes in input raw images and corresponding ground truth segmentations and outputs semantic segmentantions. In the following, we first discuss the consequence of including ASP-based model in the training phase, and then the effect of performing a post-processing phase via ASP.

5.4   Effects of Including ASP in Loss Function

Table 1 reports the performance of the 3 tested neural networks in terms of IoU. Specifically, for each network we compare the results achieved using (i) $\mathscr{L}_{CE}$ and (ii) a combination of $\mathscr{L}_{CE}$ and Λ (i.e., ASP-based) as loss function defined as $\Upsilon = \mathscr{L}_{CE} + \Lambda$ (see Sect. 3.2 and 4). The results of the two experiments are obtained according to the number of epochs described in Sect. 5.2. We report per-class IoU value but we have excluded the class "void" (i.e., 0) from accuracy assessment due to lower occurrence in the whole dataset (see, e.g., [21]). Results show that the most efficient architectures were the DeepLab-v3 and SegNet. The first network obtained the highest mean value in experiment (i) (IoU mean value of 0.744) and the second one achieved the best IoU value in experiment (ii) (IoU mean value of 0.738). Generally, the penalty computed by ASP and included in the loss function involves an improvement in the IoU mean value. The herein proposed approach achieves promisingly results also on class *pathology* (i.e., 4), which is considered as the most difficult since the lower occurrence in the dataset [21], achieving an IoU value of 0.701 and 0.659 using, respectively, DeepLab-v3 and SegNet. On the contrary, U-Net achieved the worst results on class *pathology*, not reaching a value higher than 0.28 in both experiments. Even with a promising performance, we outline that in some

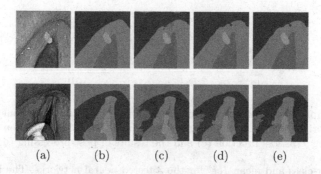

(a)   (b)   (c)   (d)   (e)

Fig. 3. Example results obtained using 2 different patients. From left to right: raw image (a), ground truth segmentation (b), semantic segmentation obtained using only $\mathscr{L}_{CE}$ as loss function (c), semantic segmentation obtained using Υ as loss function (d), post-processing applied on the results obtained using Υ (e).

classes our approach achieved better improvement; for instance, DeepLab-v3 and SegNet trained with our approach reached relevant results for classes vocal folds (i.e., $\mathscr{L}_{CE}$ 0.788 vs. Υ 0.803, $\mathscr{L}_{CE}$ 0.848 vs. Υ 0.851). Also, SegNet trained with our approach outperformed the other networks on the glottal space classes (i.e., $\mathscr{L}_{CE}$ 0.740 vs. Υ 0.764). In general, U-Net achieves the worst performance in both experiments which probably depends on the hyperparameters setting (i.e., learning rate, optimizer) that were the same for all the networks, even if IoU showed an improvement using ASP-based loss function. Figures 3 (c) and (d) present an example of the results that we obtained using $\mathscr{L}_{CE}$ and Υ as loss function. The results, which is graphically compared with raw images and ground truth segmentation, show the capability of our approach in removing misclassification errors.

5.5 Effect of Using ASP as Post Processing

Table 2 reports performance of the 3 tested neural networks in terms of IoU. Specifically, for each network, we compare the results achieved before (i) and after post-processing (ii) applied on images obtained using Υ. The post-processing, which is able to remove small island of noise and re-assign class label according to the more frequent class in the neighborhood and medical knowledge, shows promising results. Indeed, the mean IoU value is higher after post-processing phase for all networks (i.e., DeepLab-v3 (ii) 0.755 vs (ii) 0.768, SegNet (ii) 0.738 vs (ii) 0.794, U-Net (i) 0.629 vs (ii) 0.702). Figures 3 (e) present an example of the results obtained using post processing applied on Figures (d).

6   Results and Discussion

The experiments in our setting showed that the use of ASP requires a relevant effort in terms of computational time; however, they also showed that it leads

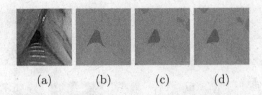

(a)   (b)   (c)   (d)

Fig. 4. Example of results obtained by U-Net on a patient selected from sequence 8. From left to right, we show: raw image (a), ground truth segmentation (b), results achieved using Υ as loss function (c) and the results of post-processing (d).

Table 1. Per-class and mean IoU for the 3 tested neural networks. The first column reports the results obtained using $\mathscr{L}_{CE}$ and the second using Υ. Most significant results are highlighted.

DeepLab-v3			SegNet			U-Net		
CLASS	$\mathscr{L}_{CE}$	Υ	CLASS	$\mathscr{L}_{CE}$	Υ	CLASS	$\mathscr{L}_{CE}$	Υ
1	0.788	0.803	1	0.848	**0.851**	1	0.774	0.776
2	0.706	0.715	2	0.761	**0.765**	2	0.672	0.684
3	0.714	0.716	3	0.740	**0.764**	3	0.641	0.667
4	0.658	0.701	4	0.623	**0.659**	4	0.267	0.275
5	**0.787**	0.782	5	0.710	0.685	5	0.554	0.579
6	0.808	0.811	6	0.816	**0.819**	6	0.728	0.791
Mean	0.744	0.755	Mean	0.730	**0.738**	Mean	0.606	0.629

Table 2. Per-class and mean IoU for the 3 tested neural networks. The first column reports the results obtained using Υ without post-processing (no p.p.) and the second using ASP-based post processing (p.p.). Most significant results are highlighted.

DeepLab-v3			SegNet			U-Net		
CLASS	IoU		CLASS	IoU		CLASS	IoU	
	no p.p.	p.p.		no p.p.	p.p.		no p.p.	p.p.
1	0.803	0.805	1	0.851	**0.853**	1	0.776	0.779
2	0.715	0.717	2	0.765	**0.776**	2	0.684	0.687
3	0.716	0.720	3	0.764	**0.769**	3	0.667	0.675
4	0.701	0.701	4	0.659	**0.761**	4	0.275	0.638
5	0.782	**0.851**	5	0.685	0.817	5	0.579	0.604
6	0.811	0.813	6	0.819	**0.856**	6	0.791	0.830
Mean	0.755	0.768	Mean	0.738	0.794	Mean	0.629	0.702

to better performance: even if the improvements do not look too dramatic, yet they are systematic, proving that the approach is viable and encouraging at further exploring the field. Furthermore, the additional computational time can be reduced by optimizing the rule-based model.

In particular, U-Net achieved a relevant improvement on class pathology (i.e., (i) 0.275 vs (ii) 0.638) which is considered one of the most difficult class to be recognized [21], due to its low occurrence in the dataset and the small size of the corresponding object. This is not surprising, given the limited ability of U-Net in properly identifying this class, and, in particular in respecting medical knowledge (i.e., it is not possible that pathology class is detected in some Sequence i, with $i > 2$). A visual example is shown in Fig. 4 which represents a result achieved by U-Net on a specific image selected from sequence 8. A more thorough analysis reveals that, without post-processing, our approach based only on the function Υ identifies a pathology class (i.e., the violet island) on the lower right (see Fig. 4(c)), which does not comply with medical requirements. However, the post-processing phase proved to be able to solve this problem, removing the wrongly detected classes, resulting in a relevant improvement (see Fig. 4(d)).

Results suggest that there is room for improving performance; in addition, it is worth noting that including a deductive, rule-based approach in our workflow not only can improve the quality of the results, but, more interestingly, enhances the interpretability of the resulting AI model.

7 Conclusion

In this work we explored a way for combining inductive and deductive approaches to Artificial Intelligence; in particular, we used Answer Set Programming to drive approaches based on Deep Learning in performing semantic segmentation of Laryngeal Endoscopic Images. We defined a novel loss function Υ as a combination of the cross-entropy loss function $\mathscr{L}_{CE}$ with the parameter Λ that is derived from a ASP-based model and indicates the number of objects wrongly identified by the network. Moreover, we took advantage of the potential coming from the declarative nature of ASP to improve the quality of results via a proper post-processing phase. Hence, we defined an ASP-based model to identify (i) small islands of noise, which, under a certain size, can be considered as wrongly detected areas, and (ii) classes which do not comply with requirements defined by the medical knowledge; then, we re-assigned misclassified elements to the more frequent class in the neighborhood. We performed a thorough experimental analysis; our proposal achieved promising results, proving to be able to improve the quality of semantic segmentation according to IoU metric. Furthermore, it is worth noting that, besides performance, the presented approach is very flexible, easing the "incorporation" of explicit additional domain knowledge into the model by extending and refining declarative ASP programs. As future work is concerned, we aim to investigate misclassification errors and improve the generalization capability of the model, as well as the overall performance. With this respect, we plan to investigate the best bound for island size to distinguish between noise and small object and, consequently, to maximize the number of wrongly detected elements removed. Our efforts will also focus on better "tailoring" program $\mathcal{P}_L$ in order to improve the function Υ; at the same time, another purpose is to evaluate our approach including Υ at the beginning of the training and analyze the effects of working with Λ only as loss function.

Acknowledgements. The authors gratefully acknowledge the following projects:

- PRIN PE6, Title: "Declarative Reasoning over Streams", funded by the Italian Ministero dell'Università, dell'Istruzione e della Ricerca (MIUR), CUP: H24I17000080001;
- PON-MISE MAP4ID, Title: "Multipurpose Analytics Platform 4 Industrial Data", funded by the Italian Ministero dello Sviluppo Economico (MISE), CUP: B21B19000650008;
- PON-MISE S2BDW, Title: "Smarter Solution in the Big Data World", funded by the Italian Ministero dello Sviluppo Economico (MISE), CUP: B28I17000250008.

References

1. Adrian, W.T., Leone, N., Manna, M., Marte, C.: Document layout analysis for semantic information extraction. In: Esposito, F., Basili, R., Ferilli, S., Lisi, F. (eds.) AI*IA 2017. LNCS, vol. 10640, pp. 269–281. Springer, Heidelberg (2017). https://doi.org/10.1007/978-3-319-70169-1_20
2. Alviano, M., et al.: The ASP system DLV2. In: Balduccini, M., Janhunen, T. (eds.) LPNMR 2017. LNCS (LNAI), vol. 10377, pp. 215–221. Springer, Cham (2017). https://doi.org/10.1007/978-3-319-61660-5_19
3. Alviano, M., Dodaro, C., Leone, N., Ricca, F.: Advances in WASP. In: Calimeri, F., Ianni, G., Truszczynski, M. (eds.) LPNMR 2015. LNCS (LNAI), vol. 9345, pp. 40–54. Springer, Cham (2015). https://doi.org/10.1007/978-3-319-23264-5_5
4. Alviano, M., Dodaro, C., Maratea, M.: Nurse (re) scheduling via answer set programming. Intelligenza Artificiale **12**(2), 109–124 (2018)
5. Badrinarayanan, V., Kendall, A., Cipolla, R.: SegNet: a deep convolutional encoder-decoder architecture for image segmentation. IEEE Trans. Pattern Anal. Mach. Intell. **39**(12), 2481–2495 (2017)
6. Brewka, G., Eiter, T., Truszczynski, M.: Answer set programming at a glance. Commun. ACM **54**(12), 92–103 (2011)
7. Bruno, P., et al.: Using CNNs for designing and implementing an automatic vascular segmentation method of biomedical images. In: Ghidini, C., Magnini, B., Passerini, A., Traverso, P. (eds.) AI*IA 2018. LNCS (LNAI), vol. 11298, pp. 60–70. Springer, Cham (2018). https://doi.org/10.1007/978-3-030-03840-3_5
8. Calimeri, F., et al.: A logic-based framework leveraging neural networks for studying the evolution of neurological disorders. Theory Pract. Logic Program. **21**(1), 80–124 (2021)
9. Calimeri, F., Dodaro, C., Fuscà, D., Perri, S., Zangari, J.: Efficiently coupling the I-DLV grounder with ASP solvers. Theory Pract. Log. Program. **20**(2), 205–224 (2020)
10. Calimeri, F., Faber, W., Gebser, M., Ianni, G., Kaminski, R., Krennwallner, T., Leone, N., Maratea, M., Ricca, F., Schaub, T.: Asp-core-2 input language format. Theory Pract. Log. Program. **20**(2), 294–309 (2020)
11. Calimeri, F., Fuscà, D., Germano, S., Perri, S., Zangari, J.: Fostering the use of declarative formalisms for real-world applications: the embasp framework. New Gener. Comput. **37**(1), 29–65 (2019). https://doi.org/10.1007/s00354-018-0046-2
12. Calimeri, F., Fuscà, D., Perri, S., Zangari, J.: I-dlv: the new intelligent grounder of dlv. Intelligenza Artificiale **11**(1), 5–20 (2017)
13. Calimeri, F., Perri, S., Zangari, J.: Optimizing answer set computation via heuristic-based decomposition. Theory Pract. Logic Program. **19**(4), 603–628 (2019)

14. Casella, A., Moccia, S., Paladini, D., Frontoni, E., De Momi, E., Mattos, L.S.: A shape-constraint adversarial framework with instance-normalized spatio-temporal features for inter-fetal membrane segmentation. Med. Image Anal. **70**, 102008 (2021)

15. Chen, L.C., Papandreou, G., Schroff, F., Adam, H.: Rethinking atrous convolution for semantic image segmentation. arXiv preprint arXiv:1706.05587 (2017)

16. Costabile, R., Catalano, G., Cuteri, B., Morelli, M.C., Leone, N., Manna, M.: A logic-based decision support system for the diagnosis of headache disorders according to the ICHD-3 international classification. Theory Pract. Logic Program. **20**(6), 864–879 (2020)

17. Erdem, E., Gelfond, M., Leone, N.: Applications of answer set programming. AI Mag. **37**(3), 53–68 (2016)

18. Janocha, K., Czarnecki, W.M.: On loss functions for deep neural networks in classification. arXiv preprint arXiv:1702.05659 (2017)

19. Kiefer, J., Wolfowitz, J., et al.: Stochastic estimation of the maximum of a regression function. Ann. Math. Stat. **23**(3), 462–466 (1952)

20. Kim, T., et al.: Active learning for accuracy enhancement of semantic segmentation with CNN-corrected label curations: evaluation on kidney segmentation in abdominal CT. Sci. Rep. **10**(1), 1–7 (2020)

21. Laves, M.-H., Bicker, J., Kahrs, L.A., Ortmaier, T.: A dataset of laryngeal endoscopic images with comparative study on convolution neural network-based semantic segmentation. Int. J. Comput. Assist. Radiol. Surg. **14**(3), 483–492 (2019). https://doi.org/10.1007/s11548-018-01910-0

22. Li, H., Cai, J., Nguyen, T.N.A., Zheng, J.: A benchmark for semantic image segmentation. In: 2013 IEEE International Conference on Multimedia and Expo (ICME), pp. 1–6. IEEE (2013)

23. Liu, X., Song, L., Liu, S., Zhang, Y.: A review of deep-learning-based medical image segmentation methods. Sustainability **13**(3), 1224 (2021)

24. Maratea, M., Pulina, L., Ricca, F.: A multi-engine approach to answer-set programming. Theory Pract. Logic Program. **14**(6), 841–868 (2014)

25. Mastria, E., Zangari, J., Perri, S., Calimeri, F.: A machine learning guided rewriting approach for asp logic programs. arXiv preprint arXiv:2009.10252 (2020)

26. Ni, Z.-L., et al.: RAUNet: residual attention U-Net for semantic segmentation of cataract surgical instruments. In: Gedeon, T., Wong, K.W., Lee, M. (eds.) ICONIP 2019. LNCS, vol. 11954, pp. 139–149. Springer, Cham (2019). https://doi.org/10.1007/978-3-030-36711-4_13

27. Pashaei, M., Kamangir, H., Starek, M.J., Tissot, P.: Review and evaluation of deep learning architectures for efficient land cover mapping with UAS hyper-spatial imagery: a case study over a wetland. Remote Sens. **12**(6), 959 (2020)

28. Rezaei, M., Yang, H., Meinel, C.: Recurrent generative adversarial network for learning imbalanced medical image semantic segmentation. Multimed. Tools Appl. **79**(21), 15329–15348 (2020). https://doi.org/10.1007/s11042-019-7305-1

29. Ronneberger, O., Fischer, P., Brox, T.: U-Net: convolutional networks for biomedical image segmentation. In: Navab, N., Hornegger, J., Wells, W.M., Frangi, A.F. (eds.) MICCAI 2015. LNCS, vol. 9351, pp. 234–241. Springer, Cham (2015). https://doi.org/10.1007/978-3-319-24574-4_28

30. Shotton, J., Kohli, P., Ikeuchi, K.: Semantic image segmentation (2014)

31. Spadea, M.F., et al.: Contrast-enhanced proton radiography for patient set-up by using x-ray CT prior knowledge. Int. J. Radiat. Oncol.* Biol.* Phys. **90**(3), 628–636 (2014)

32. Asgari Taghanaki, S., Abhishek, K., Cohen, J.P., Cohen-Adad, J., Hamarneh, G.: Deep semantic segmentation of natural and medical images: a review. Artif. Intell. Rev. **54**(1), 137–178 (2020). https://doi.org/10.1007/s10462-020-09854-1

33. Xu, J., Zhang, Z., Friedman, T., Liang, Y., Broeck, G.: A semantic loss function for deep learning with symbolic knowledge. In: International Conference on Machine Learning, pp. 5502–5511. PMLR (2018)

34. Yang, Z., Ishay, A., Lee, J.: NeurASP: embracing neural networks into answer set programming. In: Proceedings of the Twenty-Ninth International Joint Conference on Artificial Intelligence, IJCAI, pp. 1755–1762 (2020)

A Two-Phase ASP Encoding for Solving Rehabilitation Scheduling

Matteo Cardellini[1,4] , Paolo De Nardi[2], Carmine Dodaro[3] ,
Giuseppe Galatà[1] , Anna Giardini[2], Marco Maratea[4(✉)] , and Ivan Porro[1]

[1] SurgiQ srl, Genova, Italy
{matteo.cardellini,giuseppe.galata,ivan.porro}@surgiq.com
[2] ICS Maugeri, Pavia, Italy
{paolo.nardi,anna.giardini}@icsmaugeri.it
[3] DeMaCS, University of Calabria, Rende, Italy
dodaro@mat.unical.it
[4] DIBRIS, University of Genova, Genova, Italy
marco.maratea@unige.it

Abstract. The rehabilitation scheduling process consists of planning rehabilitation physiotherapy sessions for patients, by assigning proper operators to them in a certain time slot of a given day, taking into account several requirements and optimizations, e.g., patient's preferences and operator's work balancing. Being able to efficiently solve such problem is of upmost importance, in particular after the COVID-19 pandemic that significantly increased rehabilitation's needs.

In this paper, we present a solution to rehabilitation scheduling based on Answer Set Programming (ASP), which proved to be an effective tool for solving practical scheduling problems. Results of experiments performed on both synthetic and real benchmarks, the latter provided by ICS Maugeri, show the effectiveness of our solution.

1 Introduction

The rehabilitation scheduling process [17–19,24] (RSP) consists of planning patients' physiotherapy sessions inside a rehabilitation institute. Hospitals that may profitably make a practical use of such scheduling, including those managed by ICS Maugeri[1] that will provide benchmarks in this paper, deal with up to hundreds of patients with a team of just few tens of physiotherapists; so, it is of paramount importance to be able to assign patients to operators efficiently. A recent article [9] found that 2.41 billion people could benefit from rehabilitation services. This finding means that almost one third of the people in the world needs rehabilitation at some point during the course of their disease or injury; further, this number is predicted to trend upward given the current demographic and health shifts. In addition, there is emerging evidence that many of the people affected by the COVID-19 pandemic have long-term consequences regardless

---

[1] https://www.icsmaugeri.it/.

© Springer Nature Switzerland AG 2021
S. Moschoyiannis et al. (Eds.): RuleML+RR 2021, LNCS 12851, pp. 111–125, 2021.
https://doi.org/10.1007/978-3-030-91167-6_8

of the disease severity or length of hospitalisation, thus further increasing the demand for rehabilitation services globally.

The RSP is subject to several constraints, i.e., legal, medical and ethical, that need to be taken into consideration in order to find a viable schedule. For example, the main constraints that have to be dealt with are the maximum capacity of rehabilitation gyms, the legal working time and rest periods for operators, and the minimum durations of physiotherapy sessions. Moreover, several preferences shall be considered, e.g., due to clinical and organizational reasons it is often best for the patient to be treated as often as possible by the same operator and defined slots for the rehabilitation sessions are to be preferred; also rehabilitation professionals' work balancing needs to be taken into proper account.

In this paper, we present a solution to the RSP based on Answer Set Programming (ASP) [6,7,16,20], which proved to be an effective tool for solving practical scheduling problems [4,10,15,22], thanks to efficient solvers (such as CLINGO [13] and WASP [1]; see, e.g., [14] for an overview). The solution is designed as a two-phase encoding (Sect. 3): The first phase, called *board*, deals with the problem of assigning a physiotherapist to every patient considering the total working time of the physiotherapist and the minimum mandatory time of rehabilitation sessions. In the second phase, called *agenda*, a start and end time of every rehabilitation session is defined given the assignments between patients and physiotherapists found in the first phase. Our two-phase solution is not guaranteed to find the best possible overall solution, but has been designed in this way because: (*i*) it simplifies the overall encoding and its practical use, and (*ii*) it mimics how schedules have been computed so far (in a non-automatic way) in ICS Maugeri and gives freedom to physiotherapists' coordinators to perform any desired manual change to the board, before planning the agenda. We first tested our encoding (Sect. 4) on real benchmarks from ICS Maugeri related to the daily scheduling of neurological patients from two of their rehabilitation institutes in the North of Italy, namely Genova Nervi and Castel Goffredo: Results using the ASP solver CLINGO [13], focused on understanding the percentage of the real benchmarks in which no solution can be found in very short time, i.e., much shorter than in production, show that this happens approximately for only less than one third of the instances. Then, given that ICS Maugeri is planning to instrument with automated techniques other, possibly larger, institutes in addition to Genova Nervi and Castel Goffredo, we generated a wide set of synthetic benchmarks, whose parameters are inspired by the real data. We made a wide experimental evaluation, and statistically confronted these results with those with real data using classification decision tree methods [21], with the aim of predicting the behavior of our solution on such larger institutes. Results show that the accuracy is high, so our synthetic benchmarks look significant to indicate a possible behavior on real data coming from other institutes with other parameters. Moreover, our analysis also outlined what are the features of the problems that affect the results mostly. The paper is then completed by problem description in Sect. 2, and related work discussion and conclusions in Sect. 5.

2   Problem Description

The delivery of rehabilitation services is a complex task that involves many healthcare professions such as physicians, physiotherapists, speech therapists, psychologists and so on. In particular, physiotherapists spend most of their time with the patients and their sessions constitute the core of the daily agenda of the patient, around which all other commitments revolve. For this reason, this article is focused on scheduling the physiotherapy sessions in the most efficient way, optimising the overall time spent with the patient.

The agenda for the physiotherapy sessions is computed by the coordinator of the physiotherapists. This process is repeated on a daily basis in order to take into account any change in the number and type of patients to be treated, the number of operators available, and, until recently, it has been performed manually, without any automation. In the following, the main elements and constraints of the problems are described.

The usual scheduling practice, entails two subsequent phases resulting in the computation of a board and an agenda, that we herewith describe. In short, the first phase, called board, deals with the problem of assigning a physiotherapist to every patient, keeping track of the total working time of the operator and the minimum mandatory time of rehabilitation sessions. In the second, consequential phase, called agenda, a start and end time of every rehabilitation session is searched given the assignments between patients and operators found in the first phase.

Going more in details, in the board phase, the working hours of operators are simplified by counting their total working time, in minutes, and assigning patients to each operator in order to keep the cumulative time of all the sessions in which the operators are involved underneath their total working time. In this phase, patient-operator assignment preferences, expressed by the coordinator before the start of the scheduling procedure, are taken into account and respected as far as possible. In the agenda phase, given an assignment found by the board, every patient-operator session is assigned a starting and ending time, respecting the more granular working hours of the operators and the times in which the patients are unavailable. At this stage, the location in which the rehabilitation session is performed, is also considered: a gym is assigned to every session, keeping into consideration the maximum number of simultaneous sessions allowed inside the gym. The choice of the gym has also to be made between a subset of gyms that are located at the same floor of the room of the patient in order to avoid elevators and stairs that can result in discomfort to patients and can quickly congest the hospital. In this phase, time preferences for each patient are also considered: in fact, plans in which the sessions are performed nearer the desired time of the patients are preferred to the others.

In the next paragraphs, we describe more in details the main elements of our encoding, namely patients, operators and sessions, as well as the constraints and preferences entailed by the board and agenda phases.

Patients. Patients are characterized by their:

- type (Neurological, Orthopaedic, Alcoholic, COVID-19 Positive, COVID-19 Negative, Outpatient),
- aid needs, i.e., if they need specific care or not,
- payment status (full payer or in charge of the National Healthcare Service),
- forbidden times, i.e., the time intervals when the patient cannot be scheduled,
- ideal time, i.e., the preferred scheduled time expressed by the coordinator,
- preferred operators, i.e., the list of physiotherapists, ordered by priority, the patient can be assigned to,
- overall minimum length, i.e., the minimum amount of care time that the patient is guaranteed to be scheduled,
- sessions, i.e., the list of sessions to be scheduled.

Operators. Physiotherapists, that will be called operator from now on, are characterized by their:

- qualifications, i.e., patient's types which the operator can treat,
- operating times, i.e., the part of the operator's working times dedicated to the direct care of the patients. The operating times are usually split in morning and afternoon shifts.

Sessions. The coordinator, in accordance with the rehabilitation program set by the physician, determines the daily activities of the patient. These activities can be performed in one or two therapy sessions, in the latter case one session will be scheduled in the morning and the other in the afternoon shift.

Each session can be delivered to patients either by individualized ("one-on-one" sessions) or supervised (one therapist supervising more patients at the same time, each patient carrying out their personal activity independently). It must be noted that, while operators are delivering one-on-one therapy to patients, they can supervise other patients but cannot deliver one-to-one therapy to another patient. When the operators are particularly overbooked, their one-to-one sessions can be partially converted to supervised ones. These mixed sessions can either start with a supervised part and then continue with the one-on-one part, or vice-versa, or even start and end with a supervised part with a middle one-on-one session. Obviously, an operator can supervise different patients only if their sessions are located at the same place. The characteristics are:

- delivery mode (one-on-one, supervised),
- minimum one-on-one length, i.e., the minimum length of the session guaranteed to be delivered one-on-one,
- ideal overall length, i.e., the overall length of the session including the one-on-one and supervised parts,
- optional status, i.e., if the session can be left out of the schedule in case of overbooked operators,
- forced time, i.e., the time when the session must be scheduled; if empty, the session is placed as close as possible to the patient's preferred time,
- location, i.e. the place where the session must be delivered.

Board. In the board phase all patients are assigned to an available operator, according to the following criteria:

- compatibility between patient and operator, depending on the patient's type and operator qualifications, the patient's forced time, if any, and the operator working times, by also checking if the operator has enough time to provide the guaranteed overall minimum length and minimum one-to-one length to each patient and session,
- forced assignments of a patient to an operator: In special cases, the coordinator can override the preferred operators list and force an assignment regardless of all other considerations,
- the patients should be fairly distributed among all available operators, taking into account their type, aid needs and payment status,
- the patients should be assigned to the operators respecting as much as possible their preferred operators list, which considers primarily the choices of the coordinator and secondarily the history of the past assignments.

Agenda. The results of the board phase can be revised and, if necessary, manually modified by the coordinator. Once the coordinator is satisfied with the board, it is possible to proceed to the agenda scheduling, using the approved board as input data. The criteria for the agenda phase are:

- compliance with the forced time of the session, if specified,
- two sessions of the same patient must be assigned in different shifts,
- compliance with the minimum one-on-one length of the session,
- no overlap between two one-on-one sessions (or their one-on-one sections if the sessions are mixed) assigned to the same operator,
- observance of the maximum capacity of the locations (1 for each room, varying for the gyms),
- respect of the overall minimum length of the patient,
- respect of the one-on-one minimum session length,
- compliance with the forbidden times of the patient,
- sessions can only be scheduled within the working times of the operator,
- the start time of each session should be as close as possible to the preferred time, either specified by the coordinator or inferred from previous schedules,
- for mixed sessions, the one-on-one part should be maximized,
- the largest possible number of optional sessions should be included,
- the overall length, including the one-on-one and supervised parts in case of mixed sessions, should be as close as possible to the ideal overall length specified by the coordinator.

3   A Two-Phase ASP Encoding

In the following, we assume the reader is familiar with syntax and semantics of ASP. Starting from the specifications in the previous section, here we present the ASP encoding, based on the input language of CLINGO [11]. For details about syntax and semantics of ASP programs, we refer the reader to [8].

3.1   Board Encoding

Data Model. The input data is specified by means of the following atoms:

- Instances of `patient(P)`, `operators(O)`, and `type(T)` represent the identifiers of patients, operators, and the different types of patients that can be visited, respectively, where P and O are numbers, whereas T can be: *neurologic*, *neurologic-lifter*, *orthopaedic*, *orthopaedic-lifter*, *covid-19-positive*, *covid-19-negative*, or *outpatient*. Moreover, a fictitious operator with ID equals to -1 is included in the list of all the operators, and it is needed to intercept all patients that cannot be assigned to other operators.
- Instances of `operator_contract(ID,TIME,MAX)` represent the contract of the operator with the identifier ID, and include the quantity of time (in time units) the operator works in a day (TIME), and the maximum number of patients the operator can visit during the day (MAX).
- Instances of `operator_limit(ID,T,VALUE)` represent the maximum number of patients (VALUE) of type T the operator with identifier ID can visit. The operator with ID equals to -1 has no patients limits.
- Instances of `patient_data(ID,T,MIN)` represent the data associated to the patient with the identifier ID, and include the type of the patient (T), and the minimum cumulative time of all sessions of the patient during the day (MIN).
- Instances of `patient_session(ID,MIN,LOC)` represent a rehabilitation session that the patient with identifier ID needs to perform during the day. The session is characterized by a minimum length for the session in time units (MIN), and the location of the session (LOC).
- Instances of `patient_preference(ID,OP,W)` represent the preference of the patient with identifier ID to be treated by the operator with identifier OP, where W specifies the weight of the preference.
- Similarly, instances of `history_preference(ID,OP,W)` represent the preference of the patient based on the history of previous sessions.

The output is an assignment represented by atoms of the form `assignment(OP, PAT)` stating that the patient PAT will be treated by the operator OP.

Encoding. The related encoding is shown in Fig. 1, and is described in the following. To simplify the description, the rule appearing at line i in Fig. 1 is denoted with r_i. Rule r_1 ensures that each patient is assigned to exactly one operator. Rules r_2 and r_3 are used to define if the session between a patient and an operator will be performed individually in a single location (r_2), or it will be executed in the same location of another session (r_3). Rule r_4 ensures that the time required by the patients assigned to an operator does not exceed the maximum time of her/his contract. Rule r_5 ensures that each operator does not exceed the maximum number of patients to visit during the day. Rule r_6 is similar to the previous one, but in this case the limits are imposed according to the type of the patient.

Weak constraints from r_7 to r_9 are then used to provide preferences among different assignments. In particular, r_7 is used to maximize the assignments that fulfil the preferences of each patient. Then, r_8 is used to minimize the number

```
1 {assignment(OP, PAT) : operator(OP)} = 1 :- patient(PAT).
2 uniqueLocationLength(OP,PAT,DUR) :- assignment(OP,PAT), patient_session(PAT,_,LOC),
       patient_data(PAT,_,DUR), #count{ID:patient_session(ID,_,LOC), assignment(OP,ID)} < 2.
3 sameLocationLength(OP,PAT,DUR) :- assignment(OP,PAT), patient_session(PAT,DUR,LOC),
       #count{ID:patient_session(ID,_,LOC), assignment(OP,ID)} > 1.
4 :- operator_contract(OP,TIME,_), #sum{U,PAT:uniqueLocationLength(OP,PAT,U); S,
       PAT:sameLocationLength(OP,PAT,S)} > TIME.
5 :- operator_contract(OP,_,N), #count{PAT:assignment(OP,PAT)} > N.
6 :- operator_limit(OP,T,N), #count{PAT:assignment(OP,PAT), patient_data(PAT,T,_} > N.
7 :~ #sum{W, PAT:assignment(OP,PAT), patient_preference(PAT,OP,W)} = N. [N@3]
8 :~ #count{PAT: assignment(-1, PAT)} = N. [N@2]
9 :~ #sum{W, PAT:assignment(OP,PAT), history_preference(PAT,OP,W)} = N. [N@1]
```

Fig. 1. ASP Encoding for the allocation problem.

of patients that are assigned to the fictitious operator. Finally, r_9 is used to maximize the solutions that preserve assignments dictated by the history of previous sessions.

3.2 Agenda Encoding

Data Model. The following atoms constitute the input data:

- Instances of patient(ID,MIN) represent a patient identified by ID, and a minimum rehabilitation session of MIN length in time units that the patient has to undertake during the day.
- Instances of period(PER,OP,STA,END) define the start (STA) and end (END) time in the period PER (which can be *morning* or *afternoon*), which corresponds to the shift, of the operator with identifier OP.
- Instances of time(PER,OP,T) define the time slots (T) during the period PER where the operator OP works. In particular, T ranges from STA to END defined for instances of period(PER,OP,STA,END).
- Instances of location(ID,CAP,PER,STA,END) represent a location, with an identifier ID, a maximum capacity of CAP, and during the period PER is open from the time unit STA until END.
- Instances of macro_location(MLOC,LOC) define that the location LOC is inside the macro-location MLOC.
- Instances of session(ID,PAT,OP) represent a session between the patient PAT and the operator OP, coming from the assignment(OP,PAT) output of the board phase to which a unique ID is added (to discriminate between *morning* and *afternoon* shifts).
- Instances of session_type(ID,OP,TYPE) represent that the session with identifier ID assigned to operator OP is of type TYPE (which can be *individual* or *supervised*).
- Instances of session_macro_location(ID,MLOC) represent that the session with identifier ID has to be held in the macro-location MLOC.
- Instances of session_length(ID,MIN,IDEAL) represent that the session ID has a minimum length (MIN) that has to be performed in individual, and an

ideal length (IDEAL) that would be beneficial to the patient, but it is not mandatory to perform.

- Instances of mandatory_session(ID) and optional_session(ID) identify sessions that are mandatory and optional, respectively.
- Instances of forbidden(PAT,PER,STA,END) represent an unavailability of the patient PAT in the period PER from the time unit STA to END.
- Instances of session_preference(ID,PER,START,TYPE) represent the preference of the patient, stating that session should be held during the period PER and it must start at the time unit START, where TYPE indicates if the preference is *high* or *low*.

The output is represented by atoms start(ID,PER,T), length(ID,PER,L), and session_location(SES,LOC), which indicate the start, length and location of each session, respectively.

Encoding. In Fig. 2 the encoding for the agenda is presented.

Rules r_1 and r_2 assign a start time to every session; for the optional session, the start atom can be unassigned. Rule r_3 defines a length for all the sessions: the session length cannot be lower than the minimum time of the session and cannot be greater than the ideal time the session should take. Rule r_4 assigns a location for each session. Rules r_5 and r_6 reserve to each session slots of time before it starts and after it ends, in which the session can be performed in a supervised fashion. These extensions cannot be longer than the difference between the maximum and the minimum length of the session.

Then, rules r_7 and r_8 define auxiliary atoms ext_start and ext_length using the slots of times reserved for the extensions. Rule r_9 defines an auxiliary atom of the form individual_session_location(ID,LOC,OP,MIN,IDEAL) which represents that an individual session ID is in the location LOC, is assigned to the operator OP, and its minimum and ideal lengths are equal to MIN and IDEAL, respectively. Rule r_{10} defines session_time(ID,OP,PL,PER,T) which states that during time T of period PER the session ID is being performed by operator OP.

Rule r_{11} states that two individual assignments shall not overlap. Rule r_{12} imposes that each patient is assigned to at most one session per period. Rules r_{13} trough r_{15} impose that the optional individual time (i.e., the difference between the minimum length of the session and the planned length) is added fairly to all individual sessions, starting with shorter ones. Rule r_{16} imposes that for each time slot, the operator is not in two different places. Rule r_{17} states that patients must have their minimum time reserved. Rule r_{18} imposes a limit on the concurrent use of locations with limited capacity. Rules r_{19} trough r_{21} impose that a session cannot happen during a forbidden time. Rule r_{22} avoids that, during a time slot, the distribution of sessions between each pair of locations inside the same macro location is unfair (i.e., a location is at its full capacity while another is empty).

The weak constraint r_{23} states that each session duration should be as close as possible to the ideal duration. Rules r_{24} and r_{25} minimize the distance between the actual and the preferred starting time for the *high* session priority preferences. Rule r_{26} maximizes the number of optional sessions included in the

```
1   {start(ID,PER,TS) : time(PER,OP,TS)} = 1 :- session(ID,_,OP), mandatory_session(ID).
2   {start(ID,PER,TS) : time(PER,OP,TS)} <= 1 :- session(ID,_,OP), optional_session(ID).
3   {length(ID,PER,NL) : time(PER,OP,L), NL=L-ST, TS+NL <= END, NL>= MIN, NL<= IDEAL} = 1 :-
        start(ID,PER,TS), period(PER,OP,ST,END), session(ID,_,OP),
        session_length(ID,MIN,IDEAL).
4   {session_location(ID,LOC): macro_location(MAC,LOC)} = 1 :- session_macro_location(ID,MAC).
5   {before(ID,NL): time(PER,OP,L), NL=L-ST, NL<=TS-ST} = 1 :- start(ID,PER,TS),
        period(PER,OP,ST,_), session(ID,_,OP).
6   {after(ID,NL): time(PER,OP,L), NL=L-ST, NL<=END-TS-LEN} = 1 :- start(ID,PER,TS),
        period(PER,OP,ST,END), length(ID,PER,LEN), session(ID,_,OP).
7   ext_start(ID,PER,TS-LB) :- start(ID,PER,TS), before(ID,LB).
8   ext_length(ID,PER,L+LA+LB) :- length(ID,PER,L), after(ID,LA), before(ID,LB).
9   individual_session_location(ID,LOC,OP,MIN,IDEAL) :- session_type(ID,OP,individual),
        session_location(ID,LOC), session_length(ID,MIN,IDEAL).
10  session_time(ID,OP,PL,PER,TS..TS+L-1) :- session(ID,_,OP), session_location(ID,PL),
        ext_start(ID,PER,TS), ext_length(ID,PER,L).
11  :- start(ID,PER,TS), length(ID,PER,L), session_type(ID,OP,individual), start(ID2,PER,TS2),
        session_type(ID2,OP,individual), ID!=ID2, TS2>=TS, TS2<TS+L.
12  :- session(ID1,PAT,_), session(ID2,PAT,_), start(ID1,PER,_), start(ID2,PER,_), ID1!=ID2.
13  :- individual_session_location(ID1,LOC,OP,MIN1,OPT1), length(ID1,PER,L1),
        individual_session_location(ID2,LOC,OP,MIN2,OPT2), length(ID2,PER,L2), OPT1-L1 <=
        OPT2-MIN2, OPT2-L2 <= OPT1-MIN1 , |OPT1 -L1 - OPT2 + L2| > 1.
14  :- individual_session_location(ID1,LOC,OP,MIN1,OPT1), length(ID1,PER,L1),
        individual_session_location(ID2,LOC,OP,MIN2,OPT2), length(ID2,PER,L2), OPT1-L1 >
        OPT2-MIN2, L2 > MIN2.
15  :- individual_session_location(ID1,LOC,OP,MIN1,OPT1), length(ID1,PER,L1),
        individual_session_location(ID2,LOC,OP,MIN2,OPT2), length(ID2,PER,L2), OPT1-L1 <=
        OPT2-MIN2, OPT2-L2 <= OPT1-MIN1, OPT2 < OPT1, OPT1-L1 < OPT2-L2.
16  :- session_time(ID,OP,PL,PER,T), session_time(ID2,OP,PL2,PER,T), ID != ID2, PL != PL2.
17  :- patient(PAT,MIN), #sum{LEN, ID: session(ID,PAT,_), ext_length(ID,_,LEN)} < MIN.
18  :- location(LOC,LIM,PER,ST,END), LIM>0, time(PER,_,T), T>=ST, T<END, #count{ID:
        session_time(ID,_,LOC,PER,T)} > LIM.
19  :- forbidden(PAT,PER,ST,_), session(ID,PAT,_), ext_start(ID,PER,TS), ext_length(ID,PER,L),
        ST>=TS, ST<TS+L.
20  :- forbidden(PAT,PER,_,END), session(ID,PAT,_), ext_start(ID,PER,TS), ext_length(ID,PER,L),
        END>TS, END<=TS+L.
21  :- forbidden(PAT,PER,ST,END), session(ID,PAT,_), ext_start(ID,PER,TS),
        ext_length(ID,PER,L), ST<=TS,END>TS.
22  :- time(PER,_,T), macro_location(MAC,LOC1), macro_location(MAC,LOC2),
        #sum{1,ID1:session_time(ID1,_,LOC1,PER,T); -1,ID2:session_time(ID2,_,LOC2,PER,T)} > 2.
23  :~ length(ID,_, L), session_length(ID,MIN,IDEAL), D=|L-IDEAL|. [D@6, ID]
24  :~ start(ID,PER,_), session_type(ID,_,individual), session_preference(ID,PER2,_,high),
        D=|PER-PER2|. [D@5, ID]
25  :~ start(ID,PER,TS), session_type(ID,_,individual), session_preference(ID,PER,TS2,high),
        D=|TS-TS2|. [D@4, ID]
26  :~ optional_session(ID), time(PER,_,TS), not start(ID,PER,TS). [1@3,ID]
27  :~ start(ID,PER,_), session_preference(ID,PER2,_,low), session_type(ID,_,individual),
        optional_session(ID), D=|PER-PER2|. [D@2, ID]
28  :~ start(ID,PER,TS), session_preference(ID,PER,TS2,low), session_type(ID,_,individual),
        optional_session(ID), D=|TS-TS2|. [D@1, ID]
```

Fig. 2. ASP Encoding for the timetable problem.

scheduling. Rules r_{27} and r_{28} are similar to r_{24} and r_{25}, respectively, but for the *low* session priority preferences.

4   Experimental Analysis

In this section, analyses performed on the two encodings are presented. The first part of our analysis is performed on real data (that of course can encapsulate also forced assignments and timings, and revisions between phases, if any) coming from the institutes of Genova Nervi and Castel Goffredo; then, in order to

Table 1. Dimensions of the ICS Maugeri's institutes.

Institute	# Operators	# Patients	Density	# Floors	# Gyms
Genova Nervi	[9,18]	[37,67]	[2.4,5.2]	1	1
Castel Goffredo	[11,17]	[51,78]	[3.5, 6.4]	2	3

Table 2. Results on ICS Maugeri institutes.

	Branch & Bound + RoM				Unsatisfiable Core			
	Genova Nervi		Castel Goffredo		Genova Nervi		Castel Goffredo	
	Board	Agenda	Board	Agenda	Board	Agenda	Board	Agenda
% Optimum	35%	0%	0%	0%	22%	45%	0%	0%
% Satisfiable	65%	100%	100%	67%	78%	55%	100%	70%
% Unknown	0%	0%	0%	33%	0%	0%	0%	30%
Avg Time for opt	1.1 s	–	–	–	10 s	0.01 s	–	–
Avg Time Last SM	1.3 s	30 s	5.2 s	30 s	12.1 s	21.3 s	10.4 s	30 s

evaluate the scalability of the approach and to analyse how our solution would behave in larger institutes, an analysis is performed on synthetic instances with increasing dimensions, but considering real parameters. A comparison between the real and synthetic instances validates the approach and demonstrates that synthetic instances can reasonably model the problem at hand. Encodings and benchmarks used in the experiments can be found at: http://www.star.dist.unige.it/~marco/RuleMLRR2021/material.zip.

Real Data. ICS Maugeri utilizes, in its daily activity of scheduling the rehabilitation session of its patients, a web-based software called QRehab [23], developed by SurgiQ, which is built on top of the specified encoding; thus, analysis can be performed on real data coming from the institutes of Genova Nervi and Castel Goffredo which tested and used this software since mid 2020 for Genova Nervi and the beginning of 2021 for Castel Goffredo. This allowed us to access 290 instances for Genova Nervi and 100 for Castel Goffredo. Table 1 provides an overview of the dimension of the instances in the two institutes in terms of number of physiotherapists, number of daily patients, density of patients per operator, number of floors (i.e., macro-locations) and number of total gyms (i.e., locations). In Table 2, the results obtained by the two encodings are presented in terms of percentage of instances for which an optimal/satisfiable/no solution is computed. Last two rows report the mean time of instances solved optimally and of the last computed solution for all satisfiable instances, respectively. The scheduling was performed using the ASP solver CLINGO [13] with a cut-off of 30 s using two different optimization methods: the first is the default Branch&Bound (BB) optimization method [12] with the option --restart-on-model enabled; the second instead leverages the Unsatisfiable Core (USC) algorithm [3,5] with the clingo options --opt-strategy=usc,k,0,4 and --opt-usc-shrink=bin

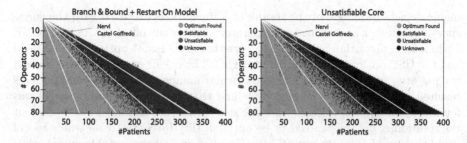

Fig. 3. Results of CLINGO using the BB optimization algorithm (left) and the USC optimization algorithm (right) on synthetic benchmarks of the board.

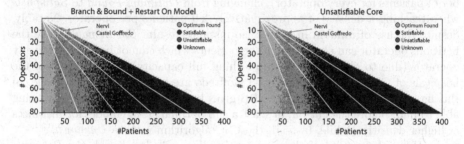

Fig. 4. Results of the synthetic benchmarks of the agenda produced by CLINGO with the BB optimization algorithm and the option `--restart-on-model` enabled (left) and the USC optimization algorithm (right).

enabled. As it can be seen in Table 2, results are mixed: the USC algorithm performs better in the agenda encoding while BB algorithm is better on the board scheduling: moreover, 100% of the board instances are solved, while for approximately one third of the agenda instances a solution can not be found. Considering these are hard real instances, results are positive and highly appreciated by ICS Maugeri members.

Synthetic Data. In order to understand how the system scales to larger institutes, that ICS Maugeri plans to instrument soon with such solution, a simulated approach is needed. For this reason, a generator able to produce random instances with features as close as possible to the ones of real hospitals was developed. Some examples of real data utilized are: the percentage of individual and supervised sessions, the medium length of operator's shifts, the occurrence of forbidden time slots for patients, and the ideal length of sessions. For every new instance created, each feature was extracted from a random distribution which was modelled from the real data coming from the hospitals or from the knowledge of institute administrators and managers. In Fig. 3 results of the scheduling of the board encoding, computed from the synthetic data, are presented. The x-axis defines the number of patients and the y-axis the number of operators; white lines represent points in which the density is an integer. Every pixel of the image depicts the mode of the results of 5 simulations executed with the corresponding number of patients and operators with a cut-off of 30s using the BB optimization algorithm and with the `--restart-on-model` option enabled (left) and the USC optimization algorithm (right). The colour of a pixel thus signals if the majority of instances with that particular number of operators and patients resulted in: (i) *Optimum Found*, signalling that the optimal stable model was found, (ii) *Satisfiable*, when at least one sub-optimal stable model was found, but the solution is not guaranteed to be optimal, (iii) *Unknown*, if no stable model could be found before the cut-off, (iv) *Unsatisfiable*, when no stable model exists which can satisfy all the constraints. As it can be seen from the figure, the results of the scheduling are directly proportional to the density (i.e., the average number of patients for every operator), changing from *Optimum Found* to *Satisfiable* when reaching a density of approximatively 2.9 patients per operator. Notably, despite the use of random instances, no instance results *Unsatisfiable* since the fictitious operator can always catch the patients which cannot be assigned to any operator (due to all the operators reaching full capacity). The position of the hospitals of Genova Nervi and Castel Goffredo are highlighted with a circle. In this figure it can be noted how the BB gives better results than USC, by being able to find, before the cut-off, at least a sub-optimal stable model for instances of higher densities, while, instead, the USC algorithm returns *Unknown*.

In Fig. 4 the results of the agenda encoding, scheduled with the BB optimization algorithm (left) and USC algorithm (right), are presented in the same format as the previous experiment. The instances for this experiment are the same as the previous one, but are augmented with the assignments between patients and operators found by CLINGO with the board encoding and other needed parameters. As previously stated, each pixel represent 5 instances and its color represents the mode of the CLINGO results. Here two things can be noted: (i) unlike the board results, which showed a proportionality with the density, these results show a correlation only with the number of patients, and (ii) some red dots scattered in the image indicate that some instances result *Unsatisfiable*; this can happen since the random data could create some instances with features that cause an impossibility to plan. With the BB optimization algorithm, the transition between the *Optimum Found* results and *Satisfiability* is located near 40 patients and near 120 patients for the transition between *Satisfiability* and *Unknown*. As it can be seen in Fig. 4 (right), the USC algorithm, instead, performs better and moves the transition between the *Optimum found* results and *Satisfiable* from 40 to 60 patients but, on the other hand, the transition between *Satisfiable* and *Unknown* slightly decreases from 120 patients to 110. The improvements on the transition between the *Optimum found* results and *Satisfiable* is very important in our setting, since Genova Nervi and Castel Goffredo fall into this area, confirming the improvements obtained in Table 2. The loss with USC could be resolved by launching the two algorithms in two different threads, so the USC algorithm will perform better on instances with fewer patients while the BB algorithm will at least return a sub-optimal stable model for instances with more patients.

Validation of Synthetic Instances. In order to understand if the simulated instances correctly represent the real data and can be therefore used to predict the behavior of the system in larger institutes, a validation is needed to compare the results on real and synthetic instances. Intuitively, we have considered the data presented in Table 2 and compared it to the result of the instances within the circles around Genova Nervi and Castel Goffredo in Figs. 3 and 4, to check if they "coincide". For doing so, a decision tree was trained, taking as dataset all the features of the simulated instances, some of them listed in the previous paragraph. Then, a test dataset with features extracted from the real instances was produced and given as an input to the decision tree, and the predicted result was then compared to the result given by CLINGO on the real instances. This test showed that for the board encoding, all the results on real instances were equal to the predicted ones for both institutes; the agenda encoding produced the same results in 93% of the cases for Genova Nervi and in 67% of the cases for Castel Goffredo, thus showing that overall the synthetic data behaves similarly as the real one and can be used for predicting the behavior of instances in larger institutes. Finally, the computed decision trees also confirm what are the most relevant features outlined above by inspecting the graphs in the figures.

5 Related Work and Conclusions

There have been few attempts to solve rehabilitation scheduling, since most hospitals are still doing it in a manual way. Among the automated solutions, often they are applied to real world data. However, their results are not directly comparable to ours, since their constraints and objective functions are different from the ones that emerged from our meetings with the physiotherapists and management at ICS Maugeri. In particular, to our knowledge, no other solution takes into account several aspects like the preferred time for the session scheduling and the preferences in the assignment of the patient to the operator. Huang, Zheng and Chien [17] developed a system, equipped with a Graphical User Interface, which can generate the optimal schedules for rehabilitation patients to minimize waiting time and thus enhance service quality and overall resource effectiveness of rehabilitation facilities. More recently, Huyinh, Huang and Chien [18] further refined the algorithm in order to develop a hybrid genetic algorithm (GASA) that integrates genetic algorithm (GA) and simulated annealing (SA). Recently, Li and Chen [19] designed a genetic algorithm based on Waiting Time Priority Algorithm (WTPA) which was tested on a rehabilitation department. Schimmelpfeng, Helber and Kasper [24] developed a decision support system for the scheduling process based on mixed-integer linear programs (MILPs) to determine appointments for patients of rehabilitation hospitals, subject to numerous constraints that are often found in practice. We already mentioned in the introduction that ASP has been already successfully used for solving application problems in several research areas (see, e.g., [11,22]), including the Healthcare domain (see, e.g., [2] for an overview). Differently from this set of papers in the same domain, the current work designs a two-phase encoding rather than a direct encoding, and evaluates the solution on real benchmarks.

In this paper, we have presented a two-phase ASP encoding for solving rehabilitation scheduling. Our solution has been tested with CLINGO and both real
and synthetic benchmarks, the former provided by ICS Maugeri while the latter
created with real parameters and employed to understand a possible behavior
of the solution on upcoming institutes where the solution will be employed.
Results are positive for the institutes employed at the moment and give some
indications on the upcoming, e.g., there are few institutes that may fall close
to the transition between satisfiable and unknown instances. Thus, despite the
current positive results, a possible topic for future research is to improve the current encoding, as well as combining the strengths of the optimizations algorithms
employed. Another interesting direction is to design also rescheduling solutions,
to be applied in case of unavailability of operators and/or patients.

References

1. Alviano, M., Amendola, G., Dodaro, C., Leone, N., Maratea, M., Ricca, F.: Evaluation of disjunctive programs in WASP. In: Balduccini, M., Lierler, Y., Woltran, S.
(eds.) LPNMR 2019. LNCS, vol. 11481, pp. 241–255. Springer, Heidelberg (2019).
https://doi.org/10.1007/978-3-030-20528-7_18
2. Alviano, M., et al.: Answer set programming in healthcare: Extended overview. In:
Joint Proceedings of the 8th IPS Workshop and the 27th RCRA Workshop Co-
located with AIxIA 2020. CEUR Workshop Proceedings, vol. 2745. CEUR-WS.org
(2020)
3. Alviano, M., Dodaro, C.: Unsatisfiable core analysis and aggregates for optimum
stable model search. Fund. Inform. **176**(3–4), 271–297 (2020)
4. Alviano, M., Dodaro, C., Maratea, M.: An advanced answer set programming
encoding for nurse scheduling. In: Esposito, F., Basili, R., Ferilli, S., Lisi, F.A.
(eds.) AI*IA 2017. LNCS, vol. 10640, pp. 468–482. Springer, Heidelberg (2017).
https://doi.org/10.1007/978-3-319-70169-1_35
5. Alviano, M., Dodaro, C., Marques-Silva, J., Ricca, F.: Optimum stable model
search: algorithms and implementation. J. Log. Comput. **30**(4), 863–897 (2020)
6. Baral, C.: Knowledge Representation, Reasoning and Declarative Problem Solving. Cambridge University Press, Cambridge (2003). https://doi.org/10.1017/
CBO9780511543357
7. Brewka, G., Eiter, T., Truszczynski, M.: Answer set programming at a glance.
Commun. ACM **54**(12), 92–103 (2011)
8. Calimeri, F., et al.: ASP-Core-2 input language format. Theory Pract. Logic Program. **20**(2), 294–309 (2020)
9. Cieza, A., Causey, K., Kamenov, K., Hanson, S.W., Chatterji, S., Vos, T.: Global
estimates of the need for rehabilitation based on the global burden of disease study
2019: a systematic analysis for the global burden of disease study 2019. Lancet
396(10267), 2006–2017 (2020)
10. Dodaro, C., Maratea, M.: Nurse scheduling via answer set programming. In: Balduccini, M., Janhunen, T. (eds.) LPNMR 2017. LNCS (LNAI), vol. 10377, pp.
301–307. Springer, Cham (2017). https://doi.org/10.1007/978-3-319-61660-5_27
11. Gebser, M., Kaminski, R., Kaufmann, B., Ostrowski, M., Schaub, T., Wanko, P.:
Theory solving made easy with clingo 5. In: Carro, M., King, A., Saeedloei, N.,
Vos, M.D. (eds.) Proceedings of ICLP (Technical Communications). OASICS, vol.
52, pp. 2:1–2:15. Schloss Dagstuhl - Leibniz-Zentrum fuer Informatik (2016)

12. Gebser, M., Kaminski, R., Kaufmann, B., Romero, J., Schaub, T.: Progress in *clasp* Series 3. In: Calimeri, F., Ianni, G., Truszczynski, M. (eds.) LPNMR 2015. LNCS (LNAI), vol. 9345, pp. 368–383. Springer, Cham (2015). https://doi.org/10.1007/978-3-319-23264-5_31

13. Gebser, M., Kaufmann, B., Schaub, T.: Conflict-driven answer set solving: from theory to practice. Artif. Intell. **187**, 52–89 (2012)

14. Gebser, M., Maratea, M., Ricca, F.: The design of the seventh answer set programming competition. In: Balduccini, M., Janhunen, T. (eds.) LPNMR 2017. LNCS (LNAI), vol. 10377, pp. 3–9. Springer, Cham (2017). https://doi.org/10.1007/978-3-319-61660-5_1

15. Gebser, M., Obermeier, P., Schaub, T., Ratsch-Heitmann, M., Runge, M.: Routing driverless transport vehicles in car assembly with answer set programming. Theory Pract. Logic Program. **18**(3–4), 520–534 (2018)

16. Gelfond, M., Lifschitz, V.: Classical negation in logic programs and disjunctive databases. New. Gener. Comput. **9**(3/4), 365–386 (1991). https://doi.org/10.1007/BF03037169

17. Huang, Y.C., Zheng, J.N., Chien, C.F.: Decision support system for rehabilitation scheduling to enhance the service quality and the effectiveness of hospital resource management. J. Chin. Inst. Ind. Eng. **29**, 348–363 (2012)

18. Huynh, N.T., Huang, Y.C., Chien, C.F.: A hybrid genetic algorithm with 2D encoding for the scheduling of rehabilitation patients. Comput. Ind. Eng. **125**, 221–231 (2018)

19. Li, X., Chen, H.: Physical therapy scheduling of inpatients based on improved genetic algorithm. J. Phys.: Conf. Ser. **1848**(1), 012009 (2021)

20. Niemelä, I.: Logic programs with stable model semantics as a constraint programming paradigm. AMAI **25**(3–4), 241–273 (1999). https://doi.org/10.1023/A:1018930122475

21. Quinlan, J.R.: Induction of decision trees. Mach. Learn. **1**(1), 81–106 (1986). https://doi.org/10.1007/BF00116251

22. Ricca, F., et al.: Team-building with answer set programming in the Gioia-Tauro seaport. Theory Pract. Logic Program. **12**(3), 361–381 (2012)

23. Saverino, A., Baiardi, P., Galata, G., Pedemonte, G., Vassallo, C., Pistarini, C.: The challenge of reorganizing rehabilitation services at the time of Covid-19 pandemic: a new digital and artificial intelligence platform to support team work in planning and delivering safe and high quality care. Front. Neurol. **12**, 501 (2021)

24. Schimmelpfeng, K., Helber, S., Kasper, S.: Decision support for rehabilitation hospital scheduling. OR Spectr. **34**(2), 461–489 (2012). https://doi.org/10.1007/s00291-011-0273-0

An Answer Set Programming Based Framework for High-Utility Pattern Mining Extended with Facets and Advanced Utility Functions

Francesco Cauteruccio[(✉)] [iD] and Giorgio Terracina [iD]

DEMACS, University of Calabria, Rende, Italy
{cauteruccio,terracina}@mat.unical.it

Abstract. In the context of pattern mining, the utility of a pattern can be described as a preference ordering over a choice set; it can be actually assessed from very different perspectives and at different abstraction levels. However, while the topic of High-Utility Pattern Mining (HUPM) has been widely studied, the basic assumption is that each item in a knowledge base is associated with *one, static* utility. In this paper we introduce, among others, the notion of *facets* for items, which allows to cope with this limitation and, moreover, we show how a more structured representation of available information, coupled with facets defined also for higher abstraction levels, paves the way to new opportunities for HUPM. In particular, the proposed framework allows to introduce some new advanced classes of utility functions in the detection process, whose relevance is also experimentally evaluated. A real use case on paper reviews is exploited to analyze the potentiality of the proposed framework in knowledge creation and discovery. Given the wide variety of analytical scenarios that can be envisioned in this new setting, we take full advantage of the capabilities of Answer Set Programming and its extensions for a fast encoding and testing of the framework.

Keywords: High-utility pattern mining · Answer set programming · Facets · Advanced utility functions

1 Introduction

Pattern mining is one of the data mining branches that attracted vast attention in the literature. Pattern mining algorithms extract knowledge from databases that can be understood by humans and several types of patterns have been studied, all of them having different and peculiar properties. These approaches are basically designed to derive interesting and/or unexpected information from databases of transactions, and their derivation rely on the concept of *pattern frequency*.

Frequent patterns are useful in many domains; however, the fundamental assumption that pattern frequency is the most interesting factor may not hold in

© Springer Nature Switzerland AG 2021
S. Moschoyiannis et al. (Eds.): RuleML+RR 2021, LNCS 12851, pp. 126–141, 2021.
https://doi.org/10.1007/978-3-030-91167-6_9

several contexts. As an example, consider a purchase transaction database; here, the pattern {*flour, yeast*} might be frequent but uninteresting, since it is fairly obvious that those who buy flour also buy yeast. In light of such consideration, the academic community started pointing out that a wide variety of patterns may be characterized by a low frequency but a high *utility*, where the utility of a pattern is given by a *utility function*. For example, in a sales database, a pattern may have a low co-occurrence frequency but may provide a higher profit than more frequent patterns (think, for instance, of the pattern {*car, car alarm*} against the pattern {*windshield washer fluid, new windshield wipers*}). The introduction of the notion of pattern utility, besides the one of pattern frequency, shifts the focus from frequent pattern mining to high-utility pattern mining (hereafter, HUPM) [5, 6].

Academic research have been very active in this context, focusing, e.g. on efficiency issues, extensions of the basic HUPM setting to different kind of patterns [6], and representation of concise/correlated patterns [5, 7]. The mostly correlated area to the present paper regards the introduction of variants for utility functions, such as average utility [12], expected/potential utility [15], affinitive utility [14], and utility occupancy [8].

However, the basic assumption of all these approaches is that each item is associated with *one, static*, external utility. As a matter of fact, in the economics domain a utility function "represents a consumer's preference ordering over a choice set" and, consequently, it is a subjective measure . Then, it is fair to assume that the utility of an item can be defined from very different points of view (we refer to them as *facets* in the following) depending on the preference ordering. In current approaches, switching the facet actually means to completely change the computation scenario or, at least, the dataset; moreover, different facets of item utilities cannot be combined to detect the utility of a pattern, unless a new definition of item utility is introduced as a derived measure. This also implies that the notion of utility is intended as local and computed for each pattern occurrence; having more facets at disposal, it is possible to compute transverse utilities across pattern occurrences, such as the correlation degree among (groups of) facets across pattern occurrences.

Another basic assumption of current approaches is based on a *flat* notion of transactions, whereas different levels of abstraction, coupled with utility facets defined also for these levels, can boost the semantics of derived patterns. As an example, consider the classical sales context; transactions can be grouped by customer and customers can be grouped by store. Both customers and stores can be associated with some utility facets and contribute to the computation of the overall pattern utility, such as the correlation between a purchase, customer properties and store type, given that pattern occurrences can be associated with different customers and stores.

The present paper aims at providing a contribution in this setting, with the definition of a more general framework for HUPM which extends basic notions along the following directions:

- *Transaction set representation.* In particular, for each transaction, an Object, a Container and a Database level of aggregation can be defined.

- *Facets.* We introduce the notion of facet, which can be associated with an item, a transaction, an object or a container; each of these elements may be characterized by more than one facet.
- *Utility functions.* In order to make the most of facets and database structure, we introduce a taxonomy of utility functions classes; moreover, we show how functions in different classes can be combined in several ways in order to fit different notions of utility over the same data set.

Extensions above pave the way to brand new opportunities for HUPM where new methods for pattern analysis can be envisioned; patterns extracted by the proposed framework can be exploited to identify and manage information that characterize the way people engage in knowledge centered activities. The focus of the present paper is to show the versatility of these extensions and, consequently, we do not currently deal with computational issues. In particular, we take full advantage of the expressiveness of declarative programming, focusing on Answer Set Programming (ASP) and its recent extensions, and we show how a simple ASP encoding of the problem can be set up in a modular way such that, given a pool of alternative encodings for each module, even non ASP practitioners can set up their own variant for the analysis, and the same dataset can be analyzed from different points of view by just switching the modules. The application of our framework to a real use case scenario is also presented. Experimental results on this use case show both the applicability and versatility of the approach.

It is worth pointing out that some approaches based on ASP for pattern mining have been proposed in the past [9,11,13,18]. The general aim of such approaches is to blend together the expressiveness and readiness to use of a declarative system within the problem of pattern mining. However, to the best of our knowledge, none of them considered HUPM and, consequently, the extensions we introduce in the present work.

The remainder of the paper is organized as follows. In Sect. 2 the general framework is proposed, along with all of its components and the problem definition. Section 3 is devoted to the design of the ASP solution. The experimental evaluation, along with the use case scenario, is presented in Sect. 4. Finally, in Sect. 5 we draw our conclusions and highlight future directions.

2   A General Framework for Extended High-Utility Pattern Mining (e-HUPM)

In this section we present our framework in detail. First, we briefly recall the classical background definitions related to the HUPM problem. Then, we show how we extend the classical problem in several ways.

Given a quantitative transaction database D composed of a set of transactions, the objective of classical HUPM is the identification of sets of items (also called patterns) that present a high utility, i.e. a utility higher than a certain threshold th_u. The utility of an item i in a transaction T_p is obtained as $eu(i) \times iu(i, T_p)$, where $eu(i)$ represents the *external utility* of i and $iu(i, T_p)$ its *internal utility* which generally represents the quantity of i in T_p. Given a pattern P appearing in a transaction T_p, the utility of P in T_p is denoted as $tu(P, T_p)$ and is computed as $\sum_{i \in P} eu(i) \times iu(i, T_p)$. Now, given the set T_P of transactions containing occurrences of the pattern P, the utility of P in the database D is denoted by $u(P)$ and computed as $u(P) = \sum_{T_p \in T_P} tu(P, T_p)$.

Having stated the classical HUPM background, we are now able to introduce the proposed framework. The first presented extension is needed to define advanced utility functions and is about the database representation. In particular, instead of a flat set of transactions, we assume that the knowledge base is organized with the following general hierarchy:

$$Database \;\rightarrow\; Container \;\rightarrow\; Object \;\rightarrow\; Transaction$$

In particular, given a database D and a set of transactions $\{T_1, T_2, \ldots, T_n\}$, D is organized as a set of *containers* $C = \{C_1, C_2, \ldots, C_r\}$ where each container C_s can be associated with a set of *objects* $O = \{O_1, O_2, \ldots, O_t\}$ and each object O_u contains a set of transactions $\{T_1, T_2, \ldots, T_v\}$. Clearly each transaction is composed of a (possibly ordered) set of items. Each transaction belongs to precisely one object and each object is associated with precisely one container. Observe that this representation allows to cover several interesting application scenarios. As it will be clear in the following, being able to group transactions at different abstraction levels allows for a more advanced evaluation of pattern utilities.

The second main generalization deals with utility representation. As a matter of fact, a great limit of the classical definition of HUPM, and its variants, is that each item is associated with a unique, external, and fixed value of utility. We next extend the notion of utility with the concept of *facets*. In fact, in several contexts, the utility of an item may be defined from different perspectives, which we call facets. Then, each item can be associated with a list of values defining its utility from different perspectives. Moreover, given the new organization of the database, facets can be defined also for transactions, objects, and containers. Formally:

Item Utility Vector: Given an item i, the utility of i is defined by an *item utility vector* $IU_i = [iu_1, iu_2, \ldots, iu_l]$, where each iu_k describes a certain facet of i.

Transaction Utility Vector: Given a transaction T_p, the utility of T_p is defined by a *transaction utility vector* $TU_{T_p} = [tu_1, tu_2, \ldots, tu_m]$, where each tu_k describes a facet of T_p. Observe that these facets for the transaction describe properties of the transaction as a whole and represent a different information than the standard internal utility of an item i in the transaction T_p. In order to keep the compatibility with the classical problem, we assume that the internal utility of i in T_p is available and represented as $q(i, T_p)$.

Object Utility Vector: Given an object O_u, the utility of O_u is defined by an *object utility vector* $OU_{O_u} = [ou_1, ou_2, \ldots, ou_n]$, where each ou_k describes a facet of O_u.

Container Utility Vector: Given a container C_s, the utility of C_s is defined by a vector $CU_{C_s} = [cu_1, cu_2, \ldots, cu_o]$, where each cu_k describes a facet of C_s.

It is worth observing that the length of any of the utility vectors above might be 0 if no interesting facet can be defined for it. The list of facets is fixed at problem modelling stage; however, we assume that all utility vectors of a certain type have the same number of facets. All utilities introduced above are not constrained to be numeric values. The interpretation and combination of utilities is left to the pattern utility computation function.

Now, recall that a pattern is a (possibly ordered) set of items and it may occur in a certain number of transactions. We next introduce the novel and advanced ways in which utility functions can be defined, based on the extensions introduced above.

Intra-pattern Utility: First of all, given a pattern P, composed of a set of r items and occurring in a transaction T_p, all the item utility vectors of items $i \in P$ must be merged into a unique item utility vector IU. In this process, internal utilities of items for T_p can be taken into account. Formally, given the set $IUS = \{IU_1, \ldots IU_r\}$ of item utility vectors associated with each item $i \in P$, let define the *intra-pattern* utility function ip which takes as input the pattern P, the transaction T_p and the associated set of item utility vectors IUS, and generates a unique item utility vector for the pattern occurrence: $IU_{T_p} = ip(P, T_p, IUS)$. An example of *intra-pattern* utility function is the following:

$$IU_{T_p} = ip(P, T_p, \{IU_1, \ldots IU_r\}) =$$

$$\left[\sum_{i\in[1..r]} (IU_i[1] \times q(i, T_p)), \sum_{i\in[1..r]} (IU_i[2] \times q(i, T_p)), \ldots, \sum_{i\in[1..r]} (IU_i[l] \times q(i, T_p)) \right]$$

Depending on the context of interest, the combination of the utilities across the single facets can be carried out with functions different from the SUM. As an example, MAX, MIN, or AVG operators can be applied across the same facet of the different items in the pattern.

Pattern Utility Functions: Now, given a pattern P occurring in a transaction T_p, the corresponding *occurrence utility vector* $OccU_{T_p}$ is obtained by juxtaposing the item, transaction, object and container utility vectors:

$$OccU_{T_p} = [IU_{T_p}, TU_{T_p}, OU_{T_p}, CU_{T_p}] = [iu_1, .., iu_l, tu_1, .., tu_m, ou_1, .., ou_n, cu_1, .., cu_o]$$

Here, for the sake of simplicity, we refer to OU_{T_p} (resp., CU_{T_p}) as the object (resp., container) utility vector of the object (resp., container) containing transaction T_p.

Given the set T_P of transactions containing occurrences of the pattern P, the *pattern utility vector* U_P is obtained as the collection of all the occurrence utility vectors of P:

$$U_P = \bigcup_{T_p \in T_P} OccU_{T_p}$$

Now, from U_P we can virtually build a matrix where each row represents a utility vector associated with an occurrence of P and each column represents a facet of P. The utility u of P can be then obtained as an arbitrary combination of the values in U_P, using a function $u(P)$.

In order to formalize $u(P)$ we distinguish between formulas that operate *by row* (we call them *horizontal first* and we refer them as f_h), formulas that operate *by column* (we call them *vertical first* and we refer them as f_v), and formulas that operate on the whole data at once (we call them *mixed* and we refer them as f) . Formally, utility of P can be classified in:

- *Horizontal first*; it first combines utilities of the various facets in each occurrence (by row) and then combines the values across all occurrences (by column): $u(P) = f_v(f_h(U_P))$
- *Vertical first*; it first evaluates utilities on a facet basis across the occurrences (by column) and then combines the obtained values across the facets (by row): $u(P) = f_h(f_v(U_P))$
- *Mixed*; it combines the values in U_P at once: $u(P) = f(U_P)$

Observe that $u(P)$ is a single number, whereas intermediate computations may provide sets of values.

Both *Horizontal first*, *Vertical first*, and *Mixed* utility functions may be further classified in:

- *inter-transaction* utility: these are functions that combine item and transaction utilities;
- *pattern-vs-object* utility: these are functions that compute the utility of the pattern by correlating one or more item or transaction utility facets with one or more object utility facets;
- *pattern-vs-container* utility: these are functions that compute the utility of the pattern by correlating one or more item or transaction utility facets with one or more container utility facets.

It is worth pointing out that, beside classical utility functions, the setting defined above can be exploited to define advanced utility measures such as: *(i)* coherence degree, i.e. the percentage of pattern occurrences in which values of two or more facets agree/disagree; *(ii)* Pearson correlation between one of the item/transaction facets and one of the object/container facets; *(iii)* Multiple correlation among sets of facets. The interested reader can find in online Appendix[1] a complete example showing the application of some of these utility functions.

We are now ready to formally introduce the definition of the problem addressed in this paper.

Problem Definition. Given a pattern P containing a set of items, P is an extended high-utility pattern if its utility $u(P)$ is greater than a utility threshold th_u, and it occurs in at least th_f transactions. The problem of extended high-utility pattern mining is to discover all extended high-utility patterns in a database D.

---

[1] The online Appendix is available at https://www.mat.unical.it/~cauteruccio/rulemlrr21.

Listing 1.1. A general ASP encoding for the e-HUPM problem

```
1   %%% Input schema:
2   %container(ContainerId)
3   %object(ObjectId,ContainerId)
4   %transaction(Tid, ObjectId)
5   %item(Item, Tid, Position, Q)
6   %itemUtilityVector(Item, I1, ..., Il)
7   %transactionUtilityVector(Tid, T1, ..., Tm)
8   %objectUtilityVector(ObjectId, O1, ..., On)
9   %containerUtilityVector(ContainerId, C1, ..., Co)
10
11  %%% Parameters
12  occurrencesThreshold(...). utilityTreshold(...).
13
14  %%% Item pre-filtering
15  usefulItem(I):- item(I,_,_,_),....any condition on the items.
16
17  %%% Candidate pattern generation
18  {inCandidatePattern(I)}:- usefulItem(I).
19
20  %%% Occurrences computation and check
21  inTransaction(Tid):- transaction(Tid,_), not incomplete(Tid).
22  incomplete(TiD):- transaction(Tid,_), inCandidatePattern(I), not contains(I,Tid).
23  contains(I,Tid):- item(I,Tid,_,_).
24  :- #count{ Tid : inTransaction(Tid)}=N, N < Tho, occurrencesThreshold(Tho).
25
26  %%% Utility computation
27  patternItemUtilityVectors(Tid,Item,I1,...,Il,Q):- inCandidatePattern(Item), itemUtilityVector(Item,
        I1, ..., Il), inTransaction(Tid), item(Item, Tid, Position, Q).
28  intraPatternUtilityVector(Tid,I1,...,Il):- &computeIntraPatternUtility[patternItemUtilityVectors](Tid
        ,I1,...,Il).
29  occurrenceUtilityVector(Tid,I1,...,Il,T1,...Tm,O1,...On,C1,...,Co):- inTransaction(Tid),
        intraPatternUtilityVector(Tid,I1,...,Il), transactionUtilityVector(Tid, T1, ..., Tm),
        transaction(Tid, ObjectId), objectUtilityVector(ObjectId, O1, ..., On), object(ObjectId,
        ContainerId), containerUtilityVector(ContainerId, C1, ..., Co).
30  :- &computeUtility[occurrenceUtilityVector](U), U < Thu, utilityTreshold(Thu).
```

3   Design of the ASP Approach

As previously pointed out, one of the main objectives of this work is to provide as much flexibility as possible in the definition of what is a useful pattern. In what follows, we provide a general encoding for the problem at hand. In the online appendix we provide some specializations of the encoding on the use case exploited for the experiments, in order to show how different code portions can be composed in order to cope with different scenarios of interest.

It is important to point out that the implementation of complex formulas for pattern utility, outlined in Sect. 2, can be in general not easy (and even inefficient) to be carried out using only rules in an ASP program. However, we may resort to recent extensions of ASP systems, such as DLVHEX [3], WASP [2], clingo [10], etc., which allow the integration of external computation sources, usually written in Python, within the ASP program. In particular, the problem at hand requires to send a set of utility vectors to an external source of computation, functionality which is not straightforward even in some of these systems. The ASP standardization group has not released standard language directives yet for such features; in order to present our ASP formalization, we make use of syntax and semantics of DLVHEX [3], while slightly different formulations and mechanisms must be used to exploit clingo [10] or WASP [2].

The general encoding is presented in Listing 1.1; it is structured in separate parts, in such a way that the various aspects of the problem can be modelled, and changed, with localized choices.

The first part defines the expected schema for input facts (lines 1–9). This models the general setting introduced in Sect. 2. Moreover, since the approach is based on some thresholds for pattern frequency and utility, these must be provided as input as well (line 12). In order to keep the formalization as general as possible, there can be contexts in which some items should be pre-filtered; these are items that we want to discard from any pattern (e.g., items with a price lower than a certain threshold). Filters can be set up with rules like the one in line 15.

In order to generate all valid patterns, we generate one answer set for each pattern; this simplifies both pattern representation and the computation of utilities (see line 18). After the candidate pattern is built, its number of occurrences is computed by rules in lines 21–23. A first pattern validity criterion is applied here, in order to check whether the frequency of the pattern is higher than the given threshold or not (line 24).

Finally, in order to compute pattern utility, the occurrence utility vectors must be derived first (see lines 28 and 29). Here, a generic external function *computeIntraPatternUtility* builds the intra-pattern utility vector first. The generic external function *computeUtility* takes as input all occurrence utility vectors and derives the utility of the pattern; only patterns with a utility greater than the given threshold are kept (lines 29 and 30).

4   Experimental Evaluation

In this section we show and discuss the results of some experiments we carried out in order to assess the appropriateness of the proposed approach. In particular, we first provide some details on the use case adopted for the experiments and the corresponding dataset; then, we consider two kind of analyses: a *quantitative* analysis aiming to characterize the applicability of our approach in terms of performances, and a *qualitative* analysis aiming to assess the effectiveness of the proposed approach, in terms of potential and quality of results.

4.1   Use Case and Dataset Details

The use case of interest is built upon the work presented in [1], in which aspect-based sentiment analysis of scientific reviews is exploited to correlate reviews with the accept/reject decision. It is well known that reviews largely follow a well-defined structure, identifying the pros and cons of a paper. We exploit an important feature from the results in [1], that is the automatic annotation of review sentences around eight different aspects: *appropriateness, clarity,*

Table 1. Terminology and facets for the paper reviews use case

e-HUPM	Use Case	Facets	Domain of the facet
Database	Set of reviews	–	
Container	Paper	(Decision)	({0 (Reject), 1 (Accept)})
Object	Review	(Rating, Confidence)	({1-10}, {1-5})
Transaction	Sentence	(Appropriateness, Clarity, Originality,	
		Soundness, Comparison, Substance,	{−1 (Negative), 1 (Positive),
		Impact, Recommendation)	0 (Neutral or Absent) }
Item	Word	–	

originality, empirical/theoretical soundness, meaningful comparison, substance, impact of dataset/software/ideas and recommendation. For each of these aspects one out of four possible sentiments is assigned: *positive, negative, neutral, absent.* The Authors of [1] show that a correlation exists between sentiments associated with review sentences and accept/reject decisions.

In this paper, we move a step forward showing that sentiment polarities may be exploited to find high utility patterns in reviews. In this context, the database D is composed of a set of *reviews*. Each review is relative to a *paper* and provides a *rating* and a *confidence* for it; the paper is associated with a final *Accept/Reject* decision. Each review contains a set of *sentences*; each sentence can be associate with sentiment annotations on *appropriateness, clarity, originality, empirical/theoretical soundness, meaningful comparison, substance, impact of dataset/software/ideas and recommendation.* Finally, each sentence is composed of a set of *words.* Table 1 illustrates the correspondence between the terms adopted in our framework and the use case, along with the facets available for each aspect.

The dataset provided by [1] contains ICLR open reviews from 2017, 2018 and 2019, from which different sentences have been extrapolated and annotated by means of eight different facets. For each facet, a sentiment label is provided in the form of an integer number in $[-1, 0, 1]$, corresponding to negative, absent or neutral, and positive sentiment respectively. Furthermore, each review consists of a list of sentences and is annotated with the confidence of the reviewer (an integer number in $[1, 5]$) and the rating (an integer number in $[1, 10]$). The dataset features 814 papers with a total of 1148 reviews. There are 2230 annotated lines, and the number of distinct words in these lines is 15214.

4.2 Quantitative Analysis

All of the experiments have been performed on a 2.3GHz MacBook computer (Intel Core i9) with 16 GB of memory. The data preprocessing pipeline was implemented in Python 3.8 and exploited the spàCy[2] library. The experiments

---

[2] https://spacy.io/.

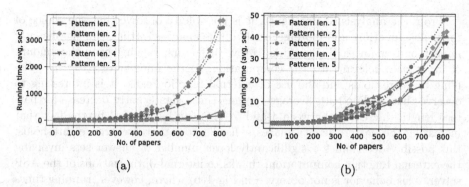

Fig. 1. Average running time for utility functions SUM (a) and disagreement degree (b)

employing the HUPM classic systems, namely Two-Phase [17], UPGrowth [19], HUI-Miner [16] and EFIM [20], were performed using their implementation provided in the SPMF data mining library [4].

In a first series of experiments, we computed the average running times for two different settings. The first one is a sort of a stress test: it involves all the facets provided by the use case and computes their sum via an external function call; thus, all input items and values are relevant for the computation and, consequently, a large number of patterns are expected. The second one is more realistic and computes the disagreement degree between one of the annotated sentiments and the decision about the corresponding paper, namely the percentage of pattern occurrences showing a positive sentiment on originality and a reject decision; in this case the utility function is directly encoded with ASP rules. Results are shown in Fig. 1 for increasing number of papers in the data set and different pattern lengths; each data point represents the average running time computed for occurrence thresholds equal to $[4, 6, 8, 10]$ and utility thresholds equal to $[1, 5, 10, 15, 20, 25, 30]$ for the sum and $[15, 50, 75, 100]$ for the disagreement degree.

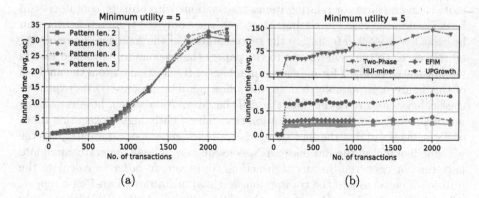

Fig. 2. Comparison of our ASP-based solution (a) and state-of-the-art HUPM systems (b)

From the analysis of this figure, it is possible to observe that the choice of the utility function, and more generally of the analysis setting, can significantly impact performances. This is due to several factors, ranging from the amount of input data relevant for the computation, to the number of patterns satisfying the thresholds and the use of external function calls. It is interesting to observe that, in Fig. 1(a), average running times significantly decrease for pattern lengths increasing between 4 and 5. This can be justified by the fact that increasing the pattern length makes it harder to satisfy occurrence thresholds; this possibly determines a significantly lower number of answer sets involving the external function computation, thanks to internal optimizations of the ASP solver. This behavior is not observed in Fig. 1(b) where, however, running times are significantly lower in general.

In order to assess how our ASP-based approach relates to dedicated systems for the classical version of the HUPM problem, we compared the performance of our ASP-based solution with four famous and well known HUPM systems, namely Two-Phase, UPGrowth, HUI-Miner and EFIM. To provide an overall comparison that takes into account different aspects, we selected these systems according to three axes: different search strategies, number of phases and underlying basic algorithms. It is worth pointing out that the objective of this analysis is not to "find a winner", since our ASP-based approach could never compete, in terms of performances, with dedicated tools. The goal of this analysis is twofold: (i) we want to show that the analytical context must be significantly downsized in order to be able to apply classical tools on the paper reviews use case, and (ii) we want to show that our ASP-based solution provides its results in a reasonable amount of time for a well-studied context.

Before showing the details of this experiment, we specify the adopted setting; recall that classical HUPM systems allow for one single (positive) external utility for each item and one internal utility for each transaction. In order to fit our use case with these requirements, we set the external utility of each word to 1 and we exploit the sentiment provided for each sentence on the first facet as internal utility; specifically, we set the internal utility of an item as the absolute value of Appropriateness in the sentence it appears in. Observe that no analysis involving more than one facet, or relating items/transactions with objects/containers can be devised in the classical setting. Moreover, since only the transaction layer can be considered, we had to flatten the representation of the sentences by removing all references to the reviews and to the papers they belong to. Obtained results are illustrated in Fig. 2 for increasing numbers of transactions. From the analysis of this figure it is possible to draw the following observations: (i) As expected, classical systems are faster than the ASP-based solution which, however, shows reasonable behavior for the application case. The slightly higher execution times of Two-Phase are due the fact that this approach generates candidate patterns without looking at the database; as a consequence, it may generate candidate patterns not occurring in any transaction. Moreover, in order to calculate the utilities of patterns and the transaction-weighted utilization, Two-Phase repeatedly scans the database, thus representing a significant cost [5]. (ii) With the only exception of Two-Phase, classical systems are marginally affected by the number of transactions, whereas our ASP-based solution presents increasing running times. *(iii)* Classical systems are able to mine patterns of any length, whereas, in order to make our approach applicable, we need to fix a range for pattern lengths. This last is the main limitation of our approach; in fact, without a threshold on pattern length, the ASP generation process would consider all possible combinations of items. However, in many application contexts, fixing a range for the length of patterns of interest is reasonable.

4.3   Qualitative Analysis

In this section we describe the results of some experiments carried out to show if, and how much, facets and utility functions introduced in Sect. 2 can help users in analyzing input data from different points of view. Due to space constraints only a small subset of interesting analyses is presented.

Before going into the details of the analysis, in order to better show the properties of our approach, consider that the paper review dataset contains 686 words with contrasting values between a "sentiment" (on one of the aspects reported in Sect. 4.1) and the decision. Among them, 481 different words are in sentences with an "Originality" sentiment; this situation leads to 929 patterns of length between 2 and 4 with at least 4 occurrences just related to "Originality". As a consequence, any classical approach would be overwhelmed by a huge amount of patterns.

In our series of experiments, we computed patterns where the utility function is the Pearson correlation between the sentiment on a sentence aspect X and the final decision on the corresponding paper. In particular, given a certain aspect, let say $X = Clarity$, a pattern P showing a high utility should be read as follows: the set of review sentences containing P are characterized by a direct correlation between the sentiment on Clarity and the final decision on the corresponding paper; consequently, a positive sentiment on Clarity in sentences containing P (approximately) implies an Accept decision, whereas a negative sentiment on Clarity in sentences containing P (approximately) implies a Reject decision. In order to provide a more comprehensive analysis, we extracted both patterns showing a very high (≥ 0.7) Pearson correlation and patterns showing a very low (≤ -0.7) Pearson correlation. In both cases the minimum frequency has been set to 4. Results are shown in Table 2 for Clarity, Empirical/Theoretical Soundness (Soundness for short), and Impact of Dataset/Software/Ideas (Impact for short). In a similar way, we computed also patterns where the utility function is the Multiple correlation.

From the analysis of Table 2 we can draw the following observations: *(i)* The number of valid patterns is very low, thus simplifying a manual inspection of obtained results. *(ii)* An overlap between patterns found in different settings is not necessarily a negative point; indeed, it could strengthen the quality of obtained results. As an example, we found that the pattern [paper, technical, contribution] appears both with a Pearson correlation equal to 1 between Soundness and Decision and a Multiple correlation equal to 1 between (Clarity,

Table 2. Qualitative analysis on Pearson and Multiple Correlations

Pearson Correlation

Setting	# positive/ # negative	Sample patterns	Correlation
Clarity → Decision	27/32	think paper overall current	1
		paper iclr current	1
		think paper ready	0.80
		think paper iclr interesting	−1
		paper iclr relevant	−1
		think paper overall relevant	−1
Soundness → Decision	25/14	paper technical contribution	1
		interesting approach pros	1
		results convincing	0.81
		interesting results	0.72
		think claim	−0.73
		understand difficult	−1
		paper problems	−1
		paper clearly presented	−1
Impact → Decision	50/16	paper clear contribution	1
		good state art	1
		work significant	0.77
		paper like short	−0.77
		interesting problem	−0.81
		experimental evaluation	−1

Multiple Correlation

Setting	# tot	Sample patterns	Correlation
(Clarity, Soundness) → Decision	74	paper technical contribution	1
		paper nice idea	1
		good approach results	1
		paper interesting idea	0.79
		paper related convinced kind	0.71
(Clarity, Impact) → Decision	132	think paper overall relevant	1
		paper iclr interesting overall	1
		good state art	1
		think paper ready	0.83
		paper technical contribution	0.81
		datasets	0.76
(Originality, Impact) → Decision	106	paper iclr novel	1
		paper clear contribution	1
		works cited	1
		idea contribution	0.94
		main contribution	0.88
		paper work related novelty	0.70

Soundness) and Decision; this can be interpreted as a strong characterization of sentences containing the words [paper, technical, contribution]. *(iii)* In few cases, a small variation in the pattern may reverse the correlation; as an example consider the pattern [think, paper, overall, current], showing a Pearson correlation equal to 1 between Clarity and Decision and the pattern [think, paper, overall, relevant] showing a Pearson correlation equal to -1 between Clarity and Decision; this and similar situations should be carefully analyzed looking at the underlying data.

Note that, in the analysis conducted in [1] on the entire set of sentences studying the correlation between sentiments and the final recommendation, the Authors found the following values for Pearson correlation: Clarity = 0.212, Empirical/Theoretical Soundness = 0.267, and Impact of Dataset/Software/Ideas = 0.273. These were the aspects showing the higher correlation values. Our approach allows to go deeper in the analysis and to single out subsets of sentences, characterized by common patterns, showing very high correlations.

It is finally interesting to observe that the derivation of a knowledge base of such kind of patterns in historical data may help chairs in identifying and characterizing some portions of new reviews to focus on, in order to help them decide whether they have to intervene or not during the decision process, and in order to improve fairness of reviews.

5   Conclusion

In this paper we introduced a general framework for HUPM with several extensions allowing to significantly widen the applicability of HUPM even in non classical contexts. We provided an ASP based computation method, which exploits the most recent extensions of ASP, and we have shown that this solution allows for a reasonable and versatile implementation, which provides a fast way to analyze the data from different perspectives and different abstraction levels.

A real use case on paper reviews has been employed to analyze the different aspects of the proposed framework. We have shown that the introduction of facets and suitable advanced utility functions can both reduce the amount of relevant patterns and provide deep insights on the data, thus advancing the state-of-the-art on the interesting topic of HUPM.

The presented work is just a first step in this new direction of utility-based analyses and several future research directions are now open. First of all, it will be interesting to apply the framework to new contexts, such as biomedical data analysis and IoT data analysis. A classification of computational properties for the extended utility functions is necessary to devise ad-hoc algorithms. In particular, we plan to develop dedicated and efficient algorithms for computing high-utility patterns using the Pearson or the Multiple correlation.

References

1. Chakraborty, S., Goyal, P., Mukherjee, A.: Aspect-based sentiment analysis of scientific reviews. In: JCDL 2020: Proceedings of the ACM/IEEE Joint Conference on Digital Libraries in 2020, Virtual Event, China, 1–5 August 2020, pp. 207–216. ACM (2020)
2. Dodaro, C., Ricca, F.: The external interface for extending wasp. Theor. Pract. Log. Program. **20**(2), 225–248 (2020)
3. Eiter, T., et al.: The DLVHEX system. KI - Künstliche Intelligenz **32**(2–3), 187–189 (2018)
4. Fournier-Viger, P., et al.: The SPMF open-source data mining library version 2. In: Berendt, B. (ed.) ECML PKDD 2016. LNCS (LNAI), vol. 9853, pp. 36–40. Springer, Cham (2016). https://doi.org/10.1007/978-3-319-46131-1_8
5. Fournier-Viger, P., Lin, J.W., Nkambou, R., Vo, B., Tseng, V.: High-Utility Pattern Mining. Springer, Heidelberg (2019)
6. Gan, W., Lin, C., Fournier-Viger, P., Chao, H., Tseng, V., Yu, P.: A survey of utility-oriented pattern mining. IEEE Trans. Knowl. Data Eng. **33**(4), 1306–1327 (2021)
7. Gan, W., Lin, J.C.W., Chao, H.C., Fujita, H., Yu, P.: Correlated utility-based pattern mining. Inf. Sci. **504**, 470–486 (2019)
8. Gan, W., Lin, J.C., Fournier-Viger, P., Chao, H., Yu, P.S.: HUOPM: high-utility occupancy pattern mining. IEEE Trans. Cybern. **50**(3), 1195–1208 (2020)
9. Gebser, M., Guyet, T., Quiniou, R., Romero, J., Schaub, T.: Knowledge-based sequence mining with ASP. In: Proceedings of the Twenty-Fifth International Joint Conference on Artificial Intelligence, IJCAI 2016, New York, NY, USA, 9–15 July 2016, pp. 1497–1504. IJCAI/AAAI Press (2016)
10. Gebser, M., Kaminski, R., Kaufmann, B., Schaub, T.: Multi-shot ASP solving with clingo. Theor. Pract. Log. Program. **19**(1), 27–82 (2019)
11. Guyet, T., Moinard, Y., Quiniou, R., Schaub, T.: Efficiency analysis of ASP encodings for sequential pattern mining tasks. In: Pinaud, B., Guillet, F., Cremilleux, B., de Runz, C. (eds.) Advances in Knowledge Discovery and Management. SCI, vol. 732, pp. 41–81. Springer, Cham (2018). https://doi.org/10.1007/978-3-319-65406-5_3
12. Hong, T.P., Lee, C.H., Wang, S.L.: Effective utility mining with the measure of average utility. Expert Syst. Appl. **38**(7), 8259–8265 (2011)
13. Järvisalo, M.: Itemset mining as a challenge application for answer set enumeration. In: Delgrande, J.P., Faber, W. (eds.) LPNMR 2011. LNCS (LNAI), vol. 6645, pp. 304–310. Springer, Heidelberg (2011). https://doi.org/10.1007/978-3-642-20895-9_35
14. Lin, J.C., Gan, W., Fournier-Viger, P., Hong, T., Chao, H.: FDHUP: fast algorithm for mining discriminative high utility patterns. Knowl. Inf. Syst. **51**(3), 873–909 (2017)
15. Lin, J.C.W., Gan, W., Fournier-Viger, P., Hong, T.P., Tseng, V.S.: Efficient algorithms for mining high-utility itemsets in uncertain databases. Knowl. Based Syst. **96**, 171–187 (2016)
16. Liu, M., Qu, J.: Mining high utility itemsets without candidate generation. In: 21st ACM International Conference on Information and Knowledge Management, CIKM 2012, Maui, HI, USA, 29 October–02 November 2012, pp. 55–64. ACM (2012)

17. Liu, Y., Liao, W., Choudhary, A.: A two-phase algorithm for fast discovery of high utility itemsets. In: Ho, T.B., Cheung, D., Liu, H. (eds.) PAKDD 2005. LNCS (LNAI), vol. 3518, pp. 689–695. Springer, Heidelberg (2005). https://doi.org/10.1007/11430919_79

18. Paramonov, S., Stepanova, D., Miettinen, P.: Hybrid asp-based approach to pattern mining. Theor. Pract. Log. Program. **19**(4), 505–535 (2019)

19. Tseng, V.S., Shie, B., Wu, C., Yu, P.S.: Efficient algorithms for mining high utility itemsets from transactional databases. IEEE Trans. Knowl. Data Eng. **25**(8), 1772–1786 (2013)

20. Zida, S., Fournier-Viger, P., Lin, J.C.-W., Wu, C.-W., Tseng, V.S.: EFIM: a highly efficient algorithm for high-utility itemset mining. In: Sidorov, G., Galicia-Haro, S.N. (eds.) MICAI 2015. LNCS (LNAI), vol. 9413, pp. 530–546. Springer, Cham (2015). https://doi.org/10.1007/978-3-319-27060-9_44

Automatic Generation of Intelligent Chatbots from DMN Decision Models

Vedavyas Etikala$^{(\boxtimes)}$ ⓘ, Alexandre Goossens ⓘ, Ziboud Van Veldhoven ⓘ,
and Jan Vanthienen ⓘ

Department of Decision Sciences and Information Management (LIRIS),
KU Leuven, Leuven, Belgium
vedavyas.etikala@kuleuven.be

Abstract. Decision models are the consolidated knowledge representation of the requirements and the logic of operational decisions in business organizations. Decision models defined in the Decision Model and Notation (DMN) standard can contribute significantly to the automation of business decision management. However, the current scope of decision support is quite limited in presenting the decision-making process to an end-user in a reliable, user-friendly way. This paper provides a framework for automatically generating chatbots from DMN models that can handle numerous user scenarios for effective and explainable decision-making during customer support inquiries. The method can improve the digitalization of customer services and give customers more transparency and trust in the decision-making through user-friendly chatbots.

Keywords: Decision model and notation (DMN) · Chatbots · Knowledge reasoning

1 Introduction

With the increased digital transformation of our society [15], customers have become increasingly more demanding as they expect immediate and personalized assistance when interacting with companies [13]. More than 80% of businesses are investigating chatbots to deal with the increasing expectations and customer inquiries [4]. This increased attention for chatbots is evident from both an academic perspective [3] and commercial perspectives such as the customer help chatbot you can find on almost all commercial websites nowadays.

There are, however, several issues with chatbots. First, chatbots typically give general answers or refer to FAQs while customers increasingly demand personalized and instant answers [13]. Secondly, the construction and maintenance of chatbots are both time and resource-intensive. This is more prevalent for knowledge-intensive domains where both domain experts and IT experts have to work together. Third, current chatbots cannot deal well with more advanced reasoning such as explaining the user why certain outputs were achieved. They lack processable knowledge and reasoning mechanisms to answer more specific

S. Moschoyiannis et al. (Eds.): RuleML+RR 2021, LNCS 12851, pp. 142–157, 2021.
https://doi.org/10.1007/978-3-030-91167-6_10

questions about the business decisions and logic [3]. This is especially important for handling operational decisions that are characterized by their high frequency, repetitiveness, and need for knowledge such as loan calculators [16]. This knowledge deals with the day-to-day procedures and is often stored in manuals or ideally in decision model and notation (DMN) models.

In this paper, a novel approach to generate chatbots from DMN models is proposed. As explained in Sect. 2, declarative decision models hold both the structure and logic of operational decisions, which can be automatically converted into fully functioning chatbots with the framework in Sect. 3. In addition, the decision knowledge from the models supports numerous user scenarios, such as answering why the user received a particular outcome, detailed in Sect. 4. In Sect. 5, the user interaction methods are elaborated on and in Sect. 6 we showcase our prototype interface. The technical implementation is explained in Sect. 7. The discussion and conclusion are found in Sect. 8 and 9.

2   Background

Decision Modeling: Operational decisions have a strong impact on businesses due to their high volume and importance. To manage these decisions and represent their knowledge, decision models such as DMN introduced by the Object Management Group (OMG)[1] can be used. DMN is useful for companies as it serves as a bridge between business decision design and decision implementation.

A DMN model consists of two parts. The decisions and decision dependencies are visualized in the Decision Requirements Diagrams (DRD). For each decision, DMN also provides a specification of the decision logic usually in the form of decision tables. Decision tables easily enforce completeness and consistency, are evaluated in a straightforward manner, and are easy to automate thanks to their tabular input-output format [9,18]. For more complex cases, DMN also provides an expression language called Friendly-Enough Expression Language (FEEL) that supports complex expressions or in [1] an extension was developed for reasoning with constraints. The two levels, DRD and decision logic, together form a DMN model that is intuitive enough for the communication between stakeholders and powerful enough for automated reasoning [7,17].

Chatbots: Chatbots are computer-human dialog systems that mimic natural conversations [11]. This way users can interact with the underlying software through conversational questions and answers via text or voice. With the increased processing power, data availability and novel artificial intelligence methods, chatbots have seen a surge in research in recent years [19].

Many types of chatbots exist that differ in both the area of application, such as aftersales chatbots or lead generation chatbots [10], and in the technical implementations. Typical chatbots are based on one or a combination of the following techniques: parsing, pattern matching, AIML, chatscript, ontologies, markov chain models, and artificial neural networks [8]. In this paper, we focus

---

[1] https://www.omg.org/spec/DMN/1.0.

on customer support chatbots using ontology-based techniques meaning the use of knowledge graphs to store facts about a domain and reason with them [2].

3   Overview of the Chatbot Framework

Intelligent conversational agents have the potential to offer personalized decision-making support to the user. We propose a framework for chatbots generated from DMN to facilitate the communication between knowledge (in DMN models) and users with interactive input gathering, friendly output presentation, and decision making and explanation. This permits companies to move away from building problem specific chatbots towards using a generic chatbot that is automatically complemented with knowledge from DMN models.

3.1   Solution Components

The proposed approach is visualized in Fig. 1 and consists of three main components: the user interface (UI), Dialog Engine and Knowledge Reasoner. This framework follows the general structure for chatbots as described in [14].

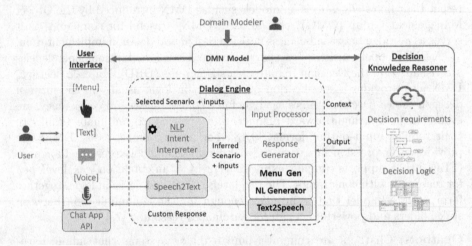

Fig. 1. Framework for automatic chatbot generation from DMN decision models

First, the UI collects the user scenarios (explained in Sect. 4) and inputs via menu buttons, text, or voice. Second, these inputs are sent to the dialog engine that consists of speech and natural language processing modules and are then used to build context for the DMN reasoner. This context is sent to the reasoner and the DMN model is executed with the corresponding reasoning mechanism. Finally, the derived outcome or additional information requirement is communicated to the user through the response generator and UI.

3.2 Running Example

A Corona vaccination example based on the Belgian situation in spring 2021 will be used as running example. A DRD is shown in Fig. 2 describing that the type of Corona vaccine depends on age and on the month of vaccination. It is possible to get either Pfizer, Moderna, Johnson & Johnson or AstraZeneca depending on the month of vaccination, phase, age, employment, and place of stay. The corresponding decision tables for each decision are shown in Fig. 3.

Fig. 2. DRD vaccine strategy

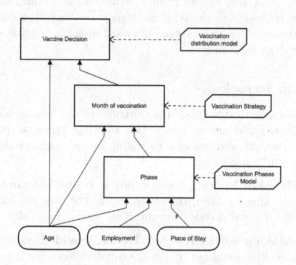

Vaccine Decision

U	Age	Month of Vaccination	Vaccine	Number of doses
1	[0..16]	-	No vaccination	0
2	]16..18[	-	Pfizer	2
3	[18..100]	January	Pfizer	2
4		February or March	Moderna	2
5		April	AstraZeneca	2
6		May	Johnson & Johnson	1
7		June	AstraZeneca	2
8		July	Moderna	2

Phase

U	Place of Stay	Employment	Age	Phase
1	"Hospital" or "Residential care center"	-	-	Phase 1
2	"At home"	Healthcare	-	Phase 1
3		Police	-	Phase 2
4		Retired or Other	[0..65[	Phase 3
5			[65..100]	Phase 2

Month of Vaccination

U	Phase	Age	Month of Vaccination
1	Phase 1	[49..100]	January
2		[0..49[	February
3	Phase 2	[49..100]	March
4		[0..49[	April
5	Phase 3	[49..100]	May
6		[28..49[	June
7		[0..28[	July

Fig. 3. Decision tables vaccine strategy

4   Decision and Explanation Scenarios

A first challenge for a good chatbot is to find out what the user wants to do or know, certainly when using natural language (and a limited screen surface). Because decision models and tables can be executed in multiple ways, various use cases of interaction with the chatbot and the underlying decision models are possible, such as making a decision or explaining outcomes. We define these user interaction options as user scenarios. It was opted to suggest the user the scenarios via the UI to help the user find the different scenarios (more advanced intent detection is present in the NLP interface). In this way, a complete DMN model with decision tables and a straightforward reasoning engine already offers an advanced chatbot solution.

4.1   Execution Scenarios

A conventional use is to determine the outcome of the top decision given the values of the input information items. But multiple types of queries can be answered with a simple and efficient reasoning procedure since decision tables can be examined in many ways.

Scenario 1: Decision-Making from Known Input Information. In this classic decision-making scenario, the chatbot asks the user the required inputs and then returns the final decision output. Two forms are possible:•

1a: Decision-Making with All Input Items Provided. Once all the input items are provided, the matching rule in the top decision table is searched based on the given value of the required information items for unique hit tables. In the running example, *A 27-year-old healthcare worker living at home*, the reasoner will derive "Phase 1" as the value for Phase, and "February" as the Month of Vaccination, so the result will be 2 doses of the Moderna vaccine.

1b: Decision-Making with Only Relevant Input Items Provided. To make a decision, only relevant information items are necessary. When irrelevant ('-') entries in the chosen rules are identified, the reasoner ignores these input questions. In the running example, giving the input *Age is 17*, is sufficient to derive the corresponding decision outcome for the age group between 16 and 18, the result is always 2 doses of Pfizer. 'Employment status' and 'Place of Stay' are irrelevant and thus not asked from the user.

Scenario 2: Decision Support With Unknown Information. This scenario is similar to the previous one in terms of reasoning. It allows the chatbot to work with 'unknown' inputs from the user (who is either not willing or not able to answer the question). The reasoner takes ('?') as an extra input for unknown values and applies the reasoning procedure and returns a list of conditional expressions for each possible outcome where some inputs values are now assumed. In the running example, consider *a 65-year-old healthcare worker, living at home*. Normally the age of retirement in Belgium is 65 but due to the high demand for healthcare workers, the user is unsure of their retirement. When the user mentions 'unknown' for Employment, the response is in this case:

> **Q: What is my vaccine decision?(unknown values)**
>
> - scenario: make decision
> - inputs : [age = 65, employment = '?', place = 'at home']
>
> -
>
> -[Doses = 2, Vaccine = 'Pfizer'] IF [Employment = 'Healthcare']
> -[Doses = 2, Vaccine = 'Moderna'] IF [Employment = 'Retired']

Scenario 3: Partial Decision Making with Incomplete Information. The user can stop the question-answering dialogue early after which the reasoning system returns a list of all rules that match based on the current inputs and their corresponding outcomes. When the following input is provided in the running example: *Age is 27 and Place is At home*, the intermediate result can be either of Phase 1, 2 or 3, in February, April or July, respectively. From the top decision table, it is evident that the Vaccine will be 2 doses of Moderna (for February), AstraZeneca (for April), or Moderna (for July). In many existing decision support applications, the decision process stops when the user fails to provide an input. If that input is not crucial, however, our chatbot can return the possible outcomes to give the user an idea of the available possibilities.

Scenario 4a: Reasoning Towards a Known Outcome. A decision model with decision tables can be traversed easily in both directions: from inputs to an outcome or outcome to inputs. The latter can be used to answer questions such as "What do I need as input values to get this desired outcome?". Of course, there are inputs that can (or should) not be manipulated (e.g., Age) but there might be a degree of freedom in other information items. In the running example, a person might ask *How to obtain Moderna?*. The result will be a list of valid input combinations from the knowledge in requirements and logic levels to reach the desired goal. Notice that Age is identified as a common precondition but with varied conditional values. The intersection of values of these common preconditions is done to have logical consistency. In the example, the updated Age requirement would be [18..49[to get the vaccine in the month of February.

> **Q: How to obtain Moderna?**
>
> **Context**
> - scenario: seek goal
> - goal : [vaccine = moderna]
> **Output**
> -[place, employment, *(phase)*, age, *(month)*]
>
> -[hospital, - , 1, [18..49[, 'february']
> -[hospital, healthcare, - , [18..49[, 'february']
> -[at home, police , 2, [49..100] , 'april']
> -[at home, retired or other, 2, [65..100] , 'april']
> -[at home, retired or other, 3, [18..49[, 'july']]

Scenario 4b: Optimization. Sometimes a user is disappointed with the outcome and wants to know which inputs could be altered to reach the desired outcome. To facilitate this scenario, the reasoner needs additional domain knowledge to differentiate between fixed inputs, such as age and height, and inputs that can be changed. With these additional constraints, the reasoner could turn this case into a constraint satisfaction problem to determine the best possible conditions to achieve the desired goal. In the running example: A 28-year-old, after receiving Moderna as a suggested vaccine, wants to know *What do I have to change to switch from Moderna to Johnsen&Johnsen?*, The result will be a list of conditions that considers same age and checks the feasible conditions for employment and place of stay.

4.2   Explanation Scenarios for the User

The explanation scenarios allow users to seek clarification or an explanation after the outcome was obtained. Better explainability capabilities enhance the chatbot's transparency and improve the user's trust and satisfaction.

Scenario 5: Why Did I Receive This Output. If the users want to know why they received their particular output, the reasoning mechanism will return the (set of) rule(s) used in the reasoning of that output.

Scenario 6: What-If Scenario. Users can ask what outcome they would receive if they changed one input value or want to update a wrong input. To answer such questions, the reasoner saves the context with inputs of the previous inquiry and allows for modifying the desired input alone and rerun the decision process. Notice that previous unchanged inputs in the context are used once again. In some situations, previously irrelevant inputs could become relevant in the follow-up decisions.

Q: What if age is 49 instead of 27?

- scenario: what if
- old inputs: [age = 27, employment = healthcare, place = at home]
- outcome: [vaccine = moderna]
- inputs: [age = 49]

- [vaccine = 'pfizer']

Scenario 7: Most Important Information Items. A user might also be interested in knowing what inputs are the most important to determine a particular outcome, e.g. *"Which factors mainly influence the type of vaccine?"*. In this case, the output would be: "Employment has the most determining impact on the type of vaccine". The processing of the models is done in a top-down manner. The reasoning engine searches through all the input columns in the selected rows that lead to the required output and calculates the proportion of unique values to the number of rows, giving the variability rate of input values. It returns the ordered list of input values and removes the values with the least variability (usually those with the same values in all the rows). If the input condition is the output from an intermediate decision, the same steps are recursively applied on the sub-decision table.

Scenario 8: Sensitivity. After knowing the outcome of a decision, a user might be interested in knowing which inputs can be changed without changing the output. In running example, a 65 year old healthcare worker might be favoring Pfizer and wants to know if they can retire and still get the Pfizer vaccine. The decision tables hold the required information for the reasoner to determine the factors that are more sensitive or least sensitive to the desired goal.

4.3   Information Scenarios for the Designer

Scenario 9: Decision Model Information. Modelers and practitioners of the DMN models can ask the chatbot about the specifics of the models found in the DMN files. Possible questions are, among others:

1. What is the size of the model?
2. How many execution paths are there?
3. How many outputs/inputs are there in total?
4. Which values can output X or input X have?
5. What is the shortest/longest path to a decision?
6. Is the model semantically and syntactically correct? (Debugging)

These answers can be useful for validation and optimization. It is also beneficial for quality checking of the DMN model and the applications developed using that model.

5   Scenario Selection and User Interaction Methods

To guide the user through the different scenarios, the UI suggests the scenarios to the user via buttons, or dynamic menu options. These can be tapped, or the user can type (or say) the name of the scenario. In this way, the knowledge reasoner knows exactly which scenario to execute and the user is aware of the different options. The available options depend on the status of the conversation.

5.1   Scenario Selection

The chatbot follows the structure summarized in Table 1 when suggesting scenarios. The different options are presented to the user in a logical order (e.g. no explaining scenarios before reaching a decision).

When the user starts a conversation with the chatbot, the chatbot introduces itself and suggests the basic decision making (scenario 1a or 1b) and goal seeking (scenario 4a) with menu options. For internal use, such as testing and developing, the chatbot also suggests scenario 9. The suggestions are button-based but can also be responded to in text or voice as explained in more detail in the next section.

Table 1. User interactions

Menu option\When	Scenario (s)	At start	During decision	After decision
Make decision	1a, 1b, 2, 3	X		X (restart)
Seek goal	4a, 4b	X		X (restart)
Ask info (internal)	9	X		X (restart)
Inputs dialogue	All		X	
Stop input	All		X	
Explain why	5			X
What if	6			X
Major items	7			X
Sensitivity	8			X

When menu option **make decision** is chosen, the chatbot will ask the user for the needed inputs (both scenarios 1a and 1b are supported). During this process, the user can prematurely stop the question-answering by giving 'stop' as input (activating scenario 3) to receive the output based on the current inputs. In this process, the chatbot can also handle 'unknown' inputs from the user (scenario 2). In case mistakes are made, an error message is returned and the input question is repeated to the user. When all the questions are answered, the chatbot gives the final decision and suggests several options to the user: Why did I receive this output? (scenario 5), what if I change some of the inputs (scenario 6), what are the most important information items (scenario 7), which inputs can change while keeping the same output (scenario 8), and repeat scenario 1.

When **explain why** is chosen, the chatbot returns the fired rules to explain the end result to the user (scenario 5). When **what if** is chosen, the user is asked which input should to change together with a list of the inputs. The user can then select the wanted input and give the new value. The new outcome is returned together with the previous outcome to showcase the difference. Similar processes are carried out for **major items** and **sensitivity**. After each scenario, the chatbot suggests the other scenarios the user can choose or repeat from the start. If the user first chose **seek goal**, the chatbot lists the possible outcomes of the top decision (scenario 4a) and asks the user which output they would like to obtain. A list of the valid input combinations for that output is returned and the chatbot suggests the other scenarios to the user in a similar vein as above.

5.2   Three Interaction Levels

The menu options and scenarios discussed in Sect. 5.1 can be made available to the user in three manners. Each level is built on top of the previous level adding additional ways of interacting with the chatbot.

Menu: The basic level of communication is to use buttons and formatted text (numbers, dates, formats, strings). When the chatbot proposes which scenarios to run, the user can tap the corresponding button to start that scenario. Here,

Fig. 4. Chatbot concept interface with menus and text

the chatbot can give an example so the user knows the correct format, e.g. "please insert date as DDMMYY". For categorical variables, a list is provided of possible values and the user can tap or type the right value.

Text: The second level allows for the user to interact with the chatbot using written natural language. The user can initiate the desired scenarios with sentences such as 'I would like to run scenario X' or give inputs such as 'my age is 28'. This requires that the chatbot understands the intent of the user. Intent detection solutions are available, e.g. LUIS[2], or Facebook AI. This is discussed in more detail in Sect. 7. After the user gives a textual input, the chatbot returns what intent or input it understood and reasons further with it to the next step. A button is added to repeat the previous input in case the chatbot misunderstood the intent or textual input.

Voice: A final way for the user to interact with the chatbot is through voice by connecting the chatbot to a voice-to-text and text-to-speech service such as IBM Watson[3]. This way the user can communicate in spoken natural language with the chatbot and receives an answer with voice. This method is useful for integrating the chatbot with smart home devices such as Google Home. Here as well a repeat option is added in case the chatbot misunderstood the user.

---

[2] https://www.luis.ai/.
[3] https://www.ibm.com/cloud/watson-assistant.

6   User Interface

Level 1: In Fig. 4, a sample conversation is shown. All the scenarios provided in Sect. 4 are enabled with dynamic menu options and/or textual inputs. The conversation is initiated by offering two possible execution scenarios: execute a decision or determine how a certain vaccine is obtained. The user states they want to execute a scenario and all relevant inputs are asked until an output can be derived. After the outcome, the other five scenarios are proposed to the user. The user ask why they received the outcome and chatbot replies with the answer and again proposes the other unchosen options. The third part showcases scenario 6. *Level 1 extended with level 2 and 3:* Fig. 5 shows an early prototype with the third and second interaction levels, intent detection and voice messages. The intent detection implementation is explained in detail in Sect. 7.

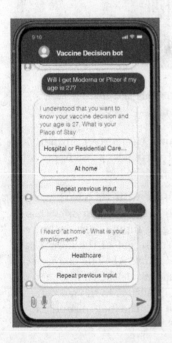

```
1   "query": "Will I get Moderna or
          Pfizer?, my age is 27",
2   "prediction": {
3       "topIntent": "MakeDecision",
4       "intents": {
5           "MakeDecision": {
6               "score": 0.98
7           },
8           "GiveInput": {
9               "score": 0.70
10          },
11          "None": {
12              "score": 0.04
13          },
14          ...
15      },
16      "entities": {
17          "Decision":[ "vaccine"]
18          "Age": [ "27" ]
19      ...
```

Fig. 5. Chatbot interface showcasing intent detection and voice. Corresponding Intents detected by LUIS

7   Technical Implementation

The implementation of the prototype chatbot consists of three main components: UI, Dialog Engine, and Knowledge reasoner.

UI: A custom chat app API is used to create the look-and-feel of the chatbot. Once a DMN model is loaded, the initial menu items are generated by our framework and rendered by the chat API. Additionally, buttons for voice or text are enabled. Our approach can be easily integrated with messaging apps that offer the required capabilities.

Dialog Engine: It is used to understand and process inputs, to pass the right context onto the reasoning mechanism, and to generate the right response that the chat app API must render to the user. It exists of several components:

Input Processor: Once the scenario has been decided explicitly by the user through the menu or inferred from the intent interpreter, the corresponding entities are mapped to the inputs of the user. The scenario, relevant input values, and chat history (old inputs and previous outcomes) are compiled as context and then sent to the knowledge reasoner. After a preliminary check for missing inputs, the user is prompted to give the required inputs via the response generator.

Response Generator: This component converts the input requirements or decision outcomes into user friendly responses. For each decision making scenario, the input requirements are gathered from the user in the form of a question-answer. The order of questions is based on the order of inputs mentioned in the decision tables and the DRD, but that could be sub-optimal if a user has to answer irrelevant questions. Hence, the order of inputs is dynamically optimized after each input based on the significance of the input to reach a conclusion. When an input is required, the response generator automatically creates the relevant question in the 'what is your *input*?' format. The menu items or natural language statements are generated depending on the user input format (menu, speech, or text) and the reasoner's output.

Speech2text: The IBM Watson API is used to transform audio data into text data. Because voice recognition is prone to errors, the chatbot returns to the user what it 'heard' and the user is prompted with a 'repeat previous input' button in case there was a mistake. The text2speech component from the API is also used in the prototype bot to convert texts into voice responses. This component can be replaced with a different speech2text API.

Intent Interpreter: A possible extension to our framework is the use of an intent interpreter to allow natural language interaction instead of buttons or exact words. For example, "Will I get Moderna or Pfizer?", "I want to know my vaccine", and "which vaccine will I receive?" are possible user inquiries to start the first scenario. Here, the AI-based LUIS[4] model was used and trained to recognize the intents and detect the entities. First, a dictionary of keywords and matching intents is defined following the DMN standards. For instance, "make decision" intent is set to ("what is", "decide", "decision", "calculate", "determine", "to know"). Then, using this dictionary, a set of phrases is created to use as the base-training set. For example, a phrase such as "what is my eligibility decision?" with the keyword "decision" is added to the training set of the "make decision" intent. This LUIS model is trained to detect the nine

---

[4] www.luis.ai/home.

scenario intents and four other static intents give_input, end, go_back, and reset. For each subsequent DMN model, the entity extraction training is improved with a phrase list of noun concepts that are automatically extracted from the example DMN models such as "eligibility", "loan", and "credit score". Hence, this method avoids manual retraining for each DMN model and is sufficient for the intent detection of basic questions. The LUIS model returns the probabilities for detected intents and entities for each given input (text or voice). These probabilities are used with a threshold (75%) to infer the appropriate scenario or input. A sample intent response can be seen in Fig. 5.

Knowledge Reasoner: A knowledge reasoner was built that can automatically handle the scenarios explained in Sect. 4. This reasoner is simple yet powerful, assuming that the logic in the DMN models is in a complete and consistent decision table format. For each scenario, an appropriate reasoning mechanism was constructed to query the decision tables. The context from the input processor is passed to the reasoner, and a list of rules is fired to execute the decision. When there is any missing information identified by the reasoner, it is passed to the dialog engine, which converts that into queries for the user to acquire that information to continue decision making. The resulting output is returned to the dialog engine with the fired rules and decision path for the explanation scenarios. Our reasoner can be extended with third-party reasoning mechanisms through RESTFul services API providers such as Camunda[5] and Signavio[6], but they currently do not facilitate all the user scenarios. Future extensions could use declarative knowledge-based AI reasoners such as IDP [5].

8   Discussion

8.1   Evaluation

We evaluated our approach of automatic generation of fully functioning chatbots from decision models with the following five dimensions and found several advantages. These dimensions reflect more of the framework capabilities than the generated chatbot alone.

- *Comprehension*: of the chatbots usually depends on the efficiency of the speech recognizer and language understanding components. By including menu-based interaction, the comprehension is more efficient, and the errors of misunderstanding of user intents are reduced.
- *User engagement:* is built over various user-centric scenarios. This way, DMN chatbots are able to provide advice, explanations and handle incomplete and unknown values.
- *Maintenance and Speed*: One major advantage is the automatic chatbot generation from DMN models. By updating the decision models, the behavior of the chatbot can be changed instantly. This approach does not demand special

---

[5] https://camunda.com/products/camunda-platform/dmn-engine/.
[6] https://www.signavio.com/.

IT skills as domain experts can build the chatbot through modeling itself. In addition to the flexible usage of APIs, the maintenance and flexibility are much improved.

- *Functionality:* Another major advantage is that DMN-based chatbots have advanced reasoning and explainability capabilities as explained in Sect. 4.
- *Scalability and Interoperability:* We kept the chatbot creation generic, scalable, and domain-independent. Moreover, the chatbot API is platform-independent and can be adapted to work on platforms such as Telegram or Messenger.

8.2   Limitations and Future Work

The approach discussed in this paper has some limitations. First, it is dependent on the quality of the decision model itself. Secondly, the reasoning mechanism currently only supports decision tables as decision logic representation in the DMN models. However, as is elaborated extensively in this paper, decision tables are powerful tools for capturing knowledge and reasoning with logic. Another limitation is related to errors in the NLP for intent detection and translation into natural language, which is a known problem widely studied [12]. Lastly, the chatbot only deals with the domain knowledge that is integrated into the DMN models. It could benefit from linking to specific external domain vocabularies.

In future work, further integration between the different components and the NLP for intent detection of the framework is planned. While the level 1 interface is entirely functional, levels 2 and 3 are not fully integrated yet for all scenarios. Another point of improvement is the inclusion of external domain knowledge together with NLP or extracting entities from textual domain knowledge [6]. This would imply a separate module within the chatbot so that the domain modeler can provide more background knowledge. Next, a thorough quantitative and qualitative evaluation on dimensions will be conducted to see how the chatbot can be improved. Lastly, more research must be conducted to investigate and compare the usage of different declarative knowledge formats (FEEL or boxed expressions) for automatic chatbot construction. Supporting other formats might offer different features than discussed here and could improve the overall feasibility of automatic chatbot generation.

9   Conclusion

In this paper, a novel approach to automatically generate chatbots from DMN models is proposed. This method allows for rapid development and maintainability of decision support chatbots, e.g., for online businesses. A general chatbot framework is built over user-centric reasoning scenarios that facilitate decision and explainability features to the end-user. This work contributes both to the DMN and chatbot research areas. In addition, we believe generating chatbots from knowledge representations merits more academic attention.

References

1. Aerts, B., Vandevelde, S., Vennekens, J.: Tackling the DMN challenges with cDMN: a tight integration of DMN and constraint reasoning. In: Gutiérrez-Basulto, V., Kliegr, T., Soylu, A., Giese, M., Roman, D. (eds.) RuleML+RR 2020. LNCS, vol. 12173, pp. 23–38. Springer, Cham (2020). https://doi.org/10.1007/978-3-030-57977-7_2

2. Al-Zubaide, H., Issa, A.A.: OntBot: ontology based ChatBot. In: 2011 4th International Symposium on Innovation in Information and Communication Technology, ISIICT 2011, pp. 7–12 (2011). https://doi.org/10.1109/ISIICT.2011.6149594

3. Androutsopoulou, A., Karacapilidis, N., Loukis, E., Charalabidis, Y.: Transforming the communication between citizens and government through AI-guided chatbots. Gov. Inf. Q. 36(2), 358–367 (2019)

4. Dale, R.: The return of the chatbots. Nat. Lang. Eng. 22(5), 811–817 (2016). https://doi.org/10.1017/S1351324916000243

5. Dasseville, I., Janssens, L., Janssens, G., Vanthienen, J., Denecker, M.: Combining DMN and the knowledge base paradigm for flexible decision enactment. In: Supplementary Proceedings of the RuleML 2016 Challenge, vol. 1620 (2016)

6. Etikala, V., Van Veldhoven, Z., Vanthienen, J.: Text2Dec: extracting decision dependencies from natural language text for automated DMN decision modelling. In: Del Río Ortega, A., Leopold, H., Santoro, F.M. (eds.) BPM 2020. LNBIP, vol. 397, pp. 367–379. Springer, Cham (2020). https://doi.org/10.1007/978-3-030-66498-5_27

7. Figl, K., Mendling, J., Tokdemir, G., Vanthienen, J.: What we know and what we do not know about DMN. Enterp. Model. Inf. Syst. Archit. Int. J. Concept. Model. 13(2), 1–16 (2018)

8. Hussain, S., Ameri Sianaki, O., Ababneh, N.: A survey on conversational agents/chatbots classification and design techniques. In: Barolli, L., Takizawa, M., Xhafa, F., Enokido, T. (eds.) WAINA 2019. AISC, vol. 927, pp. 946–956. Springer, Cham (2019). https://doi.org/10.1007/978-3-030-15035-8_93

9. Huysmans, J., Dejaeger, K., Mues, C., Vanthienen, J., Baesens, B.: An empirical evaluation of the comprehensibility of decision table, tree and rule based predictive models. Decis. Support Syst. 51(1), 141–154 (2011)

10. Janssen, A., Rodríguez Cardona, D., Breitner, M.H., et al.: More than FAQ! Chatbot taxonomy for business-to-business customer services. In: Følstad, A. (ed.) CONVERSATIONS 2020. LNCS, vol. 12604, pp. 175–189. Springer, Cham (2021). https://doi.org/10.1007/978-3-030-68288-0_12

11. Jia, J.: The study of the application of a keywords-based chatbot system on the teaching of foreign languages, pp. 1–11 (2003)

12. Kang, Y., Cai, Z., Tan, C.W., Huang, Q., Liu, H.: Natural language processing (NLP) in management research: a literature review. J. Manag. Anal. 7(2), 139–172 (2020)

13. von Leipzig, T., et al.: Initialising customer-orientated digital transformation in enterprises. Proc. Manuf. 8, 517–524 (2017). https://doi.org/10.1016/j.promfg.2017.02.066

14. López, A., Sànchez-Ferreres, J., Carmona, J., Padró, L.: From process models to chatbots. In: Giorgini, P., Weber, B. (eds.) CAiSE 2019. LNCS, vol. 11483, pp. 383–398. Springer, Cham (2019). https://doi.org/10.1007/978-3-030-21290-2_24

15. Van Veldhoven, Z., Vanthienen, J.: Digital transformation as an interaction-driven perspective between business, society, and technology. Electron. Mark. 16 (2021). https://doi.org/10.1007/s12525-021-00464-5

16. Vanthienen, J.: On smart data, decisions and processes. In: 2015 7th International Joint Conference on Knowledge Discovery, Knowledge Engineering and Knowledge Management (IC3K), vol. 1, p. 5. IEEE (2015)
17. Vanthienen, J.: Decisions, advice and explanation: an overview and research agenda. In: A Research Agenda for Knowledge Management and Analytics (2021)
18. Vanthienen, J., Mues, C., Aerts, A.: An illustration of verification and validation in the modelling phase of KBS development. Data Knowl. Eng. **27**(3), 337–352 (1998)
19. Zierau, N., Elshan, E., Visini, C., Janson, A.: A review of the empirical literature on conversational agents and future research directions. In: International Conference on Information Systems (ICIS) (2020)

Deep Learning for the Identification of Decision Modelling Components from Text

Alexandre Goossens$^{(\boxtimes)}$ ⓘ, Michelle Claessens, Charlotte Parthoens, and Jan Vanthienen ⓘ

Leuven Institute for Research on Information Systems (LIRIS), KU Leuven, Leuven, Belgium
`alexandre.goossens@kuleuven.be`

Abstract. Decision and process descriptions often find themselves encapsulated in long descriptions such as regulations or guidelines. Decision modelling aims at modelling the structure and logic of a decision. For decision modellers, analysing textual documents in search for relevant sentences is a time consuming activity. A promising research topic is to build decision models from text. In this paper, an automatic decision modelling component classifier using deep learning is proposed. Using a large dataset consisting of labeled sentences, the usability of deep learning techniques is investigated. In total three deep learning techniques are evaluated and compared to non-deep learning techniques using both Bag of Words and Term Frequency-Inverse Document Frequency. We conclude that classifying decision modelling components is possible and report that BERT for sequence classification is the best performing technique.

Keywords: Deep learning · Decision Model and Notation (DMN) · Decision model extraction

1 Introduction

Most organizations take repetitive decisions in high volumes every day, with the logic of these operational decisions originating from text formats such as guidelines or manuals [33]. Moreover, these textual descriptions often combine both decision and process descriptions. Decision and process modelling aims at modelling a decision and a process and building these models manually is a time consuming task. To alleviate this task, research has been conducted to extract decision models from logs [2,5] or from process models [6]. Another promising research topic is to build decision models directly from text. Some research already exists in extracting dependencies [12] or logic [4].

This paper tries to bring the latter two research directions together by classifying parts of texts into the right decision modelling components and currently

S. Moschoyiannis et al. (Eds.): RuleML+RR 2021, LNCS 12851, pp. 158–171, 2021.
https://doi.org/10.1007/978-3-030-91167-6_11

only deals with the identification of decision modelling components (dependency rules, logic rules). The scope can be broadened to also identify process modelling components. More precisely, this paper will investigate if deep learning techniques can be used for classifying sentences into irrelevant for decision modelling, decision logic or decision dependency. Deep learning is able to abstract from the need of predetermined patterns, meaning that it does not need a predefined pattern to understand the meaning of a sentence. Several deep learning techniques will be compared, such as Bidirectional Encoder Representations from Transformers (BERT) [9], GloVe [24] with Convolutional Neural Networks (CNN) or with Multilayer Perceptron (MLP). A comparison with non-deep learning techniques will also be provided. A labeled dataset consisting of approximately 550 sentences will be used for the construction of the classifiers. To the best of our knowledge, no research has been conducted yet in this regard.

The paper is structured as follows: Sect. 2 will introduce the problem with an example; Sect. 3 will look into related work and Sect. 4 will describe the methodology; Sect. 5 will discuss the experiments and the results; Sect. 6 deals with discussion, limitations and future work and finally Sect. 8 will conclude this paper.

2   Problem Statement

Decision and process descriptions are often intertwined, long and unstructured, and not all sentences are relevant for a decision or process model. These relevant sentences are manually discovered by modelling experts, but currently there is no automatic way of identifying them. Hence the requirement of first separating sentences into: **irrelevant for the decision model**; **dependency** when the sentence is relevant to build the DRD (the decision structure); **logic** when the sentence contains decision logic for the construction of a decision table (containing the decision logic rules). Note that currently all sentences irrelevant for decision modeling are labelled as such, but it would be perfectly possible to identify sentences relevant for process modelling. This paper investigates whether deep learning techniques can be used for the classification of sentences into **irrelevant**, **dependency** and **logic**. The textual description below is based on the corona vaccination strategy of Belgium. On this example, the classification has been performed with the labels put between brackets.

Example. *In order to expand the immunity of the population and protect the most vulnerable people against the Covid-19 virus, the vaccination must take place over different periods (**irrelevant**). The period in which a person will get vaccinated depends on the number of available doses and the person's assigned group (**dependency**). The person's assigned group is divided into three groups depending on their vulnerability, exposure, medical risks and age (**dependency**). If you are a resident or employee in a residential care centre or if you work in a first line care occupation then you belong to the most vulnerable and exposed people and you will be vaccinated first (**logic**). Moving on to the second group, if you are older than 65, or if you are between 45 and 65 with an increased* medical risk due to healthcare issues, you will get vaccinated next (**logic**). Lastly, the third group consists of the broader population of people above the age of 18 (**logic**). Invitations will be sent via text message, letter or email (**irrelevant**). After receiving a personal vaccine invitation, you need to register in order to confirm or move the appointment (**irrelevant**).

From this text, a decision model can be used to represent the decision. The Decision Model and Notation (DMN) is a recent decision modelling standard introduced by the Object Management Group (OMG) in 2015 [23] and can be used next to the Business Process Model and Notation (BPMN [22]) to model the decisions of a process [33]. In Fig. 1, a DMN model has been created based on the previous example. A DMN model consists of two parts. A first part, called the decision requirements level, will visualize the structure of the decision in so called Decision Requirements Diagrams (DRD). These DRDs capture the dependencies and requirements between decisions. A rectangle represents a decision. In this case vaccination priority is the final decision but it also needs the output of decision Person's assigned group and the input Available dosis. A rectangle with round borders represents the input necessary for a decision. All required inputs for a decision are linked to the decision with solid arrows called information requirements. The second part of a DMN model is called the decision logic level. In this part, the exact logic of a decision is often written down in a decision table format. The decision table for Person's assigned group is visualized in Fig. 1. Note that in this case, the First hit policy is applied. This means that the first rule applicable is the rule that will be fired.

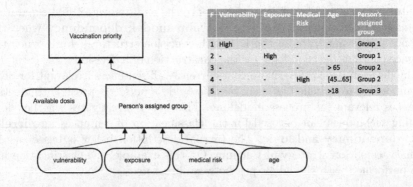

F	Vulnerability	Exposure	Medical Risk	Age	Person's assigned group
1	High	-	-	-	Group 1
2	-	High	-	-	Group 1
3	-	-	-	> 65	Group 2
4	-	-	High	[45...65]	Group 2
5	-	-	-	>18	Group 3

Fig. 1. DMN model of the example

3   Related Work

Decision model extraction has been studied in the past from process models [6] and from process execution logs [8]. The extraction of business rules and Semantics Of Business Vocabulary And Business Rules (SBVR) vocabularies from Unified Modeling Language (UML) use case diagrams was studied in [7]. Extracting decision models from text however has not been widely studied yet. In [4], decision rules and a decision table are automatically generated from a single sentence following the principles of DMN and in [10] extraction of rules from legal documents is investigated. Automatically extracting decision dependencies from paragraphs using pattern recognition is discussed in [12].

The field of process modelling is somewhat related to decision modelling and extracting process models from text has been studied more widely. In [14] a method to extract small parts of a BPMN model is proposed and in [3] BPMN models are generated from group stories. In [34] a method is proposed to extract a BPMN model given that it follows their definition of a business policy which requires the identification of several BPMN elements. Given that the text is in a sequential format and no irrelevant sentences or questions are present, the authors of [13] can extract a BPMN model from a text and in [1] the extraction of declarative process models from text was studied. By making use of textual annotations, the authors of [27] are able to structure an unstructured text and thereby propose a method to reason formally with text. Some other works investigating the extraction of process models from texts are [11,17,31].

Although text classification has been widely studied in the past and still is today, this has not been done yet in the context of DMN. Several text classification techniques exist, in [21,32] an overview of these techniques is provided. Classifying texts has also seen a wide array of application such as in the finance industry [18] or oil industry [28]. Text classification can also be used to perform sentiment analysis [20] or to detect spam and fake news [16].

4   Methodology

The construction of a decision model from text requires a sequence of steps, each with their own challenges, regardless of whether a human or a machine is performing it (Fig. 2): coreference resolution (where all expressions that refer to the same entity are resolved); preprocessing (preparing the data for analysis); text classification (identifying the relevant sentences for a modelling problem) and decision dependency and logic extraction (identifying the relevant elements needed for the construction of the model). This paper will mainly focus on the text classification part and the use of deep learning techniques within that context.

4.1   Specific Steps of the Methodology

Step 1: Coreference Resolution. It is common within text to use different words to refer to the same concept. Coreference resolution deals with identifying these words and making these words unambiguous, e.g.: *"If your employee experiences symptoms of COVID-19, she should not go to the office."* becomes *"If your employee experiences symptoms of COVID-19, your employee*

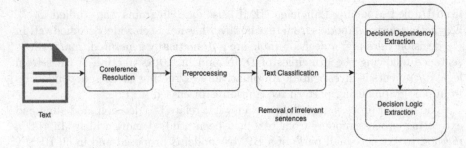

Fig. 2. From text to decision model

should not go to the office.". The open-source NeuralCoref4 package[1] was used for the coreference resolution.

Step 2: Preprocessing. First all the words are lowercased and lemmatized, meaning that a word is replaced by a simpler common form e.g. eligibility becomes eligible. Next, stopwords and punctuation are removed. The text is also split into distinct 'words' or tokens (a word, a part of a word or a punctuation symbol). Finally the tokens are converted into a number and together create a feature vector. Each number in the vector corresponds with the tokenID of the glossary used for the pre-trained deep learning model. Therefore, it is important to use the tokenizer function of each pre-trained deep learning model. For non-deep learning models, feature vectors are created by using BoW or TF-IDF.

Step 3: Text Classification. Once preprocessed, a classifier will classify the sentences into their respective classes. As this paper deals with the construction of such a classifier, more information about the classifiers considered for this problem is provided in Sect. 4.2. In total 9 experiments were performed and the best performing classifier is used for the text classification task. In order to not only rely on a labeled dataset, the deep learning models will make use of transfer learning. This will allow the model to re-use the insights obtained from larger pre-trained models and it reduces the need of having a large dataset [9]. The sentences that have been labeled as **dependency** or **logic** are kept for step 4. If a sentence is classified as irrelevant for the decision model, that sentence might still contain other useful information (e.g. process descriptions).

Step 4: Decision Model Creation. After step 3, the modeller can proceed with the (semi-automatic) creation of the decision model. When constructing a decision model, expert modellers often identify decision dependencies in conjunction with decision logic. This is why step 4a and 4b can also be seen as parallel steps. On an analogical manner, we are currently investigating whether this step can be done with deep learning [15].

---

[1] https://github.com/huggingface/neuralcoref.

a: Decision Dependency Extraction: At the end of this step, the modeller identifies a list of concepts and dependencies relevant for the DRD.

b: Decision Logic Extraction: Once the dependencies have been (partially) identified, the logic rules behind each decision can be formalized resulting in decision tables.

The final goal is the creation of a DMN model by using the decision logic and dependencies extracted in step 4.

4.2   Techniques Considered for Text Classification

In order to perform text classification, it is possible to use deep learning or traditional machine learning techniques.

Deep Learning Classifiers. It has been decided to compare the performance of feature-based transfer learning with GloVe and model-based transfer learning with BERT. The feature-based transfer learning will provide us with the features (the dictionary) whilst the model-based transfer learning will also provide us with a pretrained model which will be further finetuned.

1. **BERT for Sequence Classification:** With [35], it is possible to perform sequence classification with BERT. For that, a pre-trained BERT model is fine-tuned using DistilBERT [29] which consists out of 6 layers and 12 attention heads to perform sequence classification. As BERT is not a multinomial classifier but a binary classifier, the approach for classifying the sentences was adapted. Firstly, a BERT model will classify sentences into irrelevant for decision models or relevant for decision models. A second BERT classifier will classify the relevant sentences further into decision logic and decision dependency. To dive into the specifics, when instantiating a BERT model, it comes with pretrained encoder weights and a single linear layer is added that will be used as a sequence classifier. Afterwards, the transformed dataset is fed to the BERT model and to the classification layer, updating the pre-trained weights by backpropagating the error.

2. **Neural Network with GloVe as an Embedding Layer:** It has been decided to work with GloVe [24] as GloVe is able to capture global statistics on top of local statistics of a corpus. As MLPs tend to include too many parameters due to its connectivity, it has been decided to also use CNNs which allow for more finetuning.

   (a) For the MLP model the simplest form consisting of three layers is used. The first layer consists of the pretrained GloVe embedding, followed by a feedforward neural network of one hidden layer with 150 nodes. The final layer is the classification layer where a softmax function will predict the three class probabilities.

   (b) Regarding the CNN layer, the first layer also consists of the pre-trained GloVe embeddings, followed by a 1D-convolutional layer (as the vector is 1D) with 200 output filters and convolution window of 4. To reduce the dimension, a max pooling layer is applied. To finally classify the sentences, a MLP of 100 nodes with a softmax layer is applied.

Non-Deep Learning Models: As deep learning models require more computing power and are more complex, the performance of non-deep learning models is also analyzed on our classification problem. Regarding the feature vectors it is possible to use:

1. **Bag of Words (BoW):** BoW will count the number of unique words present in a document without taking into account the context meaning that BoW will give a higher weight to more common words. For this research, BoW with 2-grams was used.
2. **Term Frequence-Inverse Document Frequency (TF-IDF):** TF-IDF also takes into account the rarity of a word and not only looks at word frequence within the dataset. This means that TF-IDF will give more weight to rare but relevant words.

Three non deep learning models have been implemented: multinomial logistic regression, naive bayes and support vector machines. In total, this amounts to 6 combinations between the feature vectors and the non deep learning models.

5   Experiments

In total 9 classifiers have been trained and tested on a labeled dataset for the text classification step of the methodology (step 3).

5.1   Collected Data

A hybrid dataset consisting of sentences has been constructed from various sources originating from the academic world, business world or medical world. All sentences describing decisions or logic were included in the dataset regardless of their grammatical structure. Furthermore, irrelevant sentences containing process descriptions were also added to further diversify the dataset as decision and process descriptions are often mixed together in the same descriptions. To further increase the robustness of our classifiers, variants of the sentences were constructed using synonyms or by changing the structure of a sentence. All these different sentences in the dataset cover most of the average description sentence structures of an operational decision description. Hence, we estimate this dataset to be varied enough to test a proof of concept.

The training set consists of 398 sentences and the test set contains 148 sentences. For the creation of the test set, the model did not get a variant of a sentence on which the classifier was trained on. Each individual sentence was manually labeled into **irrelevant, dependency or logic**.

Based on the data source, this dataset has 3 broad categories.

– **Web Search**: By entering search terms such as 'eligibility criteria internship', "selection procedure MBA" or "diagnostic criteria for diabetes", 16 real-life textual examples were gathered. A fragment of the search terms and their corresponding data sources can be found in Table 1.

- **GitHub Sources**: More textual decision descriptions were gathered from [12] and process descriptions were gathered from the github page[2].
- **DMN Descriptions**: More textual descriptions of decision models were collected from course material. Moreover if only a DMN model was available then a textual description was derived from the DMN model.

Table 1. Fragment of data sources of the web search.

Domain	Search term	Source
Medical	Assessing health status	https://www.healthknowledge.org.uk/public-health-textbook
	Obesity risk assessment	https://www.nhlbi.nih.gov/files/docs/guidelines/prctgdc.pdf
	Diagnostic criteria for autism	https://www.cdc.gov/ncbddd/autism/hcp-dsm.htm
	Diagnostic criteria for diabetes	https://www.diabetes.org/a1c/diagnosis
Eligibility criteria	Selection procedure HEC MBA	https://www.hec.edu/en/mba-programs/mba/admissions
	Trainee eligibility european commission	https://ec.europa.eu/stages/information/applicationen
	Winter fuel payment eligibility	https://www.gov.uk/winter-fuel-payment/eligibility
	Bank credit analysis	https://corporatefinanceinstitute.com/resources/knowledge/credit/bank-credit-analysis/
Requirements & Criteria	Requirements for passing a course	https://www.kuleuven.be/english/education/student/examinations/grading-system
	Amazon shipping policy	https://www.amazon.com/gp/help/customer/display.html
Other	DRD examples	https://camunda.com/dmn/
	How is your car insurance premium determined	https://www.iii.org/article/what-determines-price-my-auto-insurance-policy
Processes & Procedures	Claims tribunal process of callovers	https://www.justice.govt.nz/about/lawyers-and-service-providers/criminal-procedure-act/
	Billing process model exercise	https://www.chegg.com/homework-help/questions-and-answers/
	BPMN examples	https://camunda.com/bpmn/examples/
	Election process for chairman	https://democracy.kent.gov.uk/documents/s77889/Item%201%20-%20Election%20of%20Chairman.pdf

5.2 Results

In Table 2, an overview of the results is provided for both the deep learning and non deep learning models. For each label, precision, recall and F1-score are reported and also the overall accuracy for each model is reported. The F1-score is considered as it is an indicator of how well a classifier performs on both precision and recall. From the results, it can be concluded that BERT for sequence classification outperforms the other deep learning models in terms of

---

[2] https://github.com/NielsRogge/Description2Process.

Table 2. Overview of results

Deep learning models					
Model	Label	Precision	Recall	F1-score	Accuracy
GloVe+MLP	Dependency	0.61	0.59	0.60	0.58
	Logic	0.56	0.63	0.59	
	Irrelevant	0.60	0.54	0.57	
GloVe + CNN	Dependency	0.74	0.50	0.60	0.65
	Logic	0.71	0.57	0.63	
	Irrelevant	0.60	0.82	0.70	
BERT for sequence classification	Dependency	0.72	1.00	0.84	**0.83**
	Logic	0.86	0.86	0.86	
	Irrelevant	0.91	0.70	0.79	
Non-deep learning models					
BoW + Logistic Regression	Dependency	0.70	0.62	0.66	0.69
	Logic	0.81	0.57	0.67	
	Irrelevant	0.63	0.84	0.72	
BoW + Naïve Bayes	Dependency	0.66	0.85	0.74	**0.72**
	Logic	0.80	0.63	0.70	
	Irrelevant	0.71	0.72	0.71	
BoW + SVM	Dependency	0.67	0.59	0.62	0.66
	Logic	0.81	0.51	0.63	
	Irrelevant	0.60	0.84	0.70	
TF-IDF + Logistic Regression	Dependency	0.68	0.74	0.70	0.70
	Logic	0.93	0.53	0.67	
	Irrelevant	0.62	0.82	0.71	
TF-IDF + Naïve Bayes	Dependency	0.75	0.62	0.68	0.64
	Logic	0.70	0.45	0.55	
	Irrelevant	0.58	0.82	0.68	
TF-IDF + SVM	Dependency	0.65	0.82	0.73	0.71
	Logic	0.86	0.63	0.73	
	Irrelevant	0.66	0.72	0.69	

accuracy (0.83) and F1-score (above 0.8 for labels Dependency and Logic, 0.79 for label Irrelevant). More importantly, BERT is able to retrieve all sentences labeled as dependency (Recall = 1.00), is good at identifying sentences labeled as logic (Recall = 0.86) and precise in labelling sentences as Irrelevant (Precision = 0.91).

6   Discussion

In the following section, the insights of Table 2 are discussed and compared in Sect. 6.1. Next in Sect. 6.2, a human intuition is provided to when BERT classifies a sentence into irrelevant, dependency or logic, also the relevant words for classification are identified. Finally in Sect. 6.3, the results are applied to a full decision model.

6.1   Comparison of the Results

It is good to see that BERT achieves a higher recall for relevant sentences than for irrelevant sentences as this means that most relevant sentences are identified but also that irrelevant sentences are sooner classified as relevant. This is not a big issue as this implies removing a few irrelevant sentences from relevant sentences instead of the contrary.

Interestingly GloVe does not perform better compared to traditional machine learning models. The poor performance of GloVe-based classifiers compared to bag-of-word classifiers may be due to the capability of the latter to "see" and specifically handle specific terms (e.g. "determining", "depend", "if", "from",...) that may not be easily identifiable through their GloVe embeddings. GloVe + MLP performs less well than GloVe + CNN, as was expected. When comparing the other deep learning models with traditional machine learning models, no performance improvement can be noticed. Also interesting to notice is that using BoW or TF-IDF yields comparable results.

6.2   Understanding How BERT Classifies

Since deep learning models are functioning as black boxes, the following section will dive into which words determine the classification of a sentence into a category. This analysis will be performed on the BERT model as it is the best performing model in this case.

Using the Local Interpretable Model Agnostic Explanations or LIME [26], it is possible to determine how much each word contributes to the classification of a sentence. In Fig. 3 and Fig. 4, two sentences of the running example are analysed. From this it can be concluded that words describing actions contribute to being classified as Irrelevant for the first sentence. For the second sentence it seems that words describing dependencies such as "divided" or "depending" contribute to being classified as Dependency.

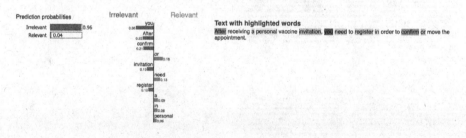

Fig. 3. Explaining irrelevant vs relevant

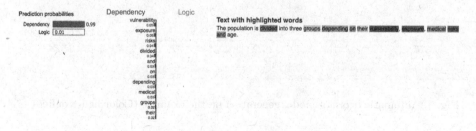

Fig. 4. Explaining dependency vs logic

With the knowledge acquired from the whole dataset, BERT uses a human-like intuition for the classification of sentences. Words such as 'determining', 'depend', 'assess' make BERT label a sentence as dependency whilst words such as 'if', 'from', 'when', 'account' make BERT label a sentence as logic. Finally, action verbs and sequence indicators make BERT label a sentence as irrelevant (for decision modeling) as these are often used in process descriptions. These results are similar to how sentences containing logic are identified in [12] which uses a pattern-based approach.

6.3   Applying the Results to the Full Decision Model

With this classifier a decision description can now be split into three parts: decision dependency, decision logic and irrelevant. These sentences (containing dependency rules and logic rules) can be used for the construction of DRDs and decision logic. This in itself is a valuable contribution for automated decision modelling from text as now the text classification step of decision modelling from text can be done (semi-)automatically.

Since the classifier works well on individual sentences, experiments on complete decision descriptions will probably yield similar results. Nevertheless, a more thorough evaluation is ongoing. In Fig. 5, the running example is applied to the classifier. In the left part, the sentences are automatically classified into the three labels (red = irrelevant, blue = dependency, green = logic). In the right part of the screen, preliminary results show that by only providing the relevant sentences to a prototype it is possible to automatically construct a DRD and extract certain logic clauses using the deep learning classifiers described in [15]. The latter however is still preliminary and beyond the scope of this paper.

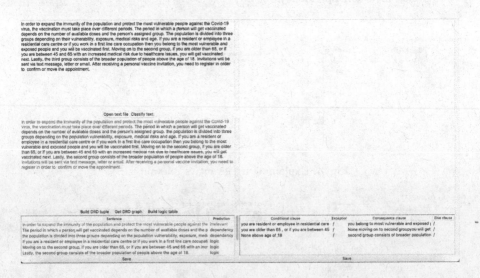

Fig. 5. Automatic decision model generation on the example (Color figure online)

7 Limitations and Future Work

Some limitations have to be pointed out. This classification problem was tackled with 2 distinct BERT classifiers and BERT was confirmed to be best performing classifier. Further research will investigate whether the other deep learning models could also benefit from this approach of using two separate classifiers. Next, some very ambiguous sentences mixing dependencies and logic are more difficult to label and thus more difficult to teach BERT to identify. For these cases, a more finetuned BERT model or manual intervention can be considered. We also believe the dataset is diverse enough to show a proof of a concept, even though it does not contain all the subtleties of the English language. More interestingly, this approach is also language independent. If another dataset in another language is provided, pretrained BERT models are available such as CamemBERT [19] for French, GottBERT for German [30] or AlBERTo for Italian [25].

Currently, coreference resolution is currently not able deal with vocabulary, concepts or synonyms. An interesting research direction therefore would be to deal with these issues for coreference resolution. Other future work will be to increase the robustness of the sentence classifier by extending the dataset with more real-life textual descriptions with the idea of also making the dataset publicly available later on. Another step is to identify process sentences from texts and classify these accordingly. A formal evaluation on different texts is also planned.

8 Conclusion

In this paper, a proof of concept for the extraction of decision modelling components using deep learning is developed. A black-box deep learning BERT classifier has been developed and compared to other statistical methods. We conclude that the classification of sentences is performing well with BERT for sequence classification being the best performing classifier. Moreover, when investigating how BERT classifies sentences it can be concluded that BERT uses a human-like intuition to classify sentences into a certain class. With this classifier, it is possible for decision modellers to (semi)-automatically extract relevant pieces of text for decision modelling hence providing the first step for the automatic decision model construction from text. The extracted relevant pieces can then be provided as input to automatically construct decision models using deep learning [15] or using patterns [12].

References

1. van der Aa, H., Di Ciccio, C., Leopold, H., Reijers, H.A.: Extracting declarative process models from natural language. In: Giorgini, P., Weber, B. (eds.) CAiSE 2019. LNCS, vol. 11483, pp. 365–382. Springer, Cham (2019). https://doi.org/10. 1007/978-3-030-21290-2_23
2. van der Aalst, W., Weijters, T., Maruster, L.: Workflow mining: discovering process models from event logs. IEEE Trans. Knowl. Data Eng. 16(9), 1128–1142 (2004)

3. de AR Goncalves, J.C., Santoro, F.M., Baiao, F.A.: Business process mining from group stories. In: 2009 13th International Conference on Computer Supported Cooperative Work in Design, pp. 161–166. IEEE (2009)
4. Arco, L., Nápoles, G., Vanhoenshoven, F., Lara, A.L., Casas, G., Vanhoof, K.: Natural language techniques supporting decision modelers. Data Min. Knowl. Disc. **35**(1), 290–320 (2020). https://doi.org/10.1007/s10618-020-00718-4
5. Bazhenova, E., Buelow, S., Weske, M.: Discovering decision models from event logs. In: Abramowicz, W., Alt, R., Franczyk, B. (eds.) BIS 2016. LNBIP, vol. 255, pp. 237–251. Springer, Cham (2016). https://doi.org/10.1007/978-3-319-39426-8_19
6. Bazhenova, E., Weske, M.: Deriving decision models from process models by enhanced decision mining. In: Reichert, M., Reijers, H.A. (eds.) BPM 2015. LNBIP, vol. 256, pp. 444–457. Springer, Cham (2016). https://doi.org/10.1007/978-3-319-42887-1_36
7. Danenas, P., Skersys, T., Butleris, R.: Natural language processing-enhanced extraction of SBVR business vocabularies and business rules from UML use case diagrams. Data Knowl. Eng. **128**, 101822 (2020)
8. De Smedt, J., Hasić, F., vanden Broucke, S.K., Vanthienen, J.: Holistic discovery of decision models from process execution data. Knowl.-Based Syst. **183**, 104866 (2019)
9. Devlin, J., Chang, M.W., Lee, K., Toutanova, K.: BERT: pre-training of deep bidirectional transformers for language understanding. arXiv preprint arXiv:1810.04805 (2018)
10. Dragoni, M., Villata, S., Rizzi, W., Governatori, G.: Combining NLP approaches for rule extraction from legal documents. In: 1st Workshop on MIning and REasoning with Legal texts (MIREL 2016) (2016)
11. Epure, E.V., Martín-Rodilla, P., Hug, C., Deneckère, R., Salinesi, C.: Automatic process model discovery from textual methodologies. In: 2015 IEEE 9th International Conference on Research Challenges in Information Science (RCIS), pp. 19–30. IEEE (2015)
12. Etikala, V., Van Veldhoven, Z., Vanthienen, J.: Text2Dec: extracting decision dependencies from natural language text for automated DMN decision modelling. In: Del Río Ortega, A., Leopold, H., Santoro, F.M. (eds.) BPM 2020. LNBIP, vol. 397, pp. 367–379. Springer, Cham (2020). https://doi.org/10.1007/978-3-030-66498-5_27
13. Friedrich, F., Mendling, J., Puhlmann, F.: Process model generation from natural language text. In: Mouratidis, H., Rolland, C. (eds.) CAiSE 2011. LNCS, vol. 6741, pp. 482–496. Springer, Heidelberg (2011). https://doi.org/10.1007/978-3-642-21640-4_36
14. Ghose, A., Koliadis, G., Chueng, A.: Process discovery from model and text artefacts. In: 2007 IEEE Congress on Services (Services 2007), pp. 167–174. IEEE (2007)
15. Goossens, A., Claessens, M., Parthoens, C., Vanthienen, J.: Extracting decision dependencies and decision logic using deep learning techniques, BPM 2021 DEC2H Workshop (2021)
16. Hadeer, A., Issa, T., Sherif, S.: Detecting opinion spams and fake news using text classification. Secur. Priv. **1**(1), e9 (2018)
17. Honkisz, K., Kluza, K., Wiśniewski, P.: A concept for generating business process models from natural language description. In: Liu, W., Giunchiglia, F., Yang, B. (eds.) KSEM 2018. LNCS (LNAI), vol. 11061, pp. 91–103. Springer, Cham (2018). https://doi.org/10.1007/978-3-319-99365-2_8

18. Luss, R., d'Aspremont, A.: Predicting abnormal returns from news using text classification. Quantit. Finan. **15**(6), 999–1012 (2015)
19. Martin, L., et al.: CamemBERT: a tasty French language model. arXiv preprint arXiv:1911.03894 (2019)
20. Melville, P., Gryc, W., Lawrence, R.D.: Sentiment analysis of blogs by combining lexical knowledge with text classification. In: Proceedings of the 15th ACM SIGKDD International Conference on Knowledge Discovery and Data Mining, pp. 1275–1284 (2009)
21. Mirończuk, M.M., Protasiewicz, J.: A recent overview of the state-of-the-art elements of text classification. Expert Syst. Appl. **106**, 36–54 (2018)
22. OMG: Business process model and notation 1.0 (2010). https://www.omg.org/spec/BPMN/1.0
23. OMG: Decision model and notation 1.0 (2015). https://www.omg.org/spec/DMN/1.0/
24. Pennington, J., Socher, R., Manning, C.D.: Glove: global vectors for word representation. In: Proceedings of the 2014 Conference on Empirical Methods in Natural Language Processing (EMNLP), pp. 1532–1543 (2014)
25. Polignano, M., Basile, P., de Gemmis, M., Semeraro, G., Basile, V.: AlBERTo: Italian BERT language understanding model for NLP challenging tasks based on Tweets. In: Proceedings of the Sixth Italian Conference on Computational Linguistics (CLiC-it 2019), vol. 2481. CEUR (2019). https://www.scopus.com/inward/record.uri?eid=2-s2.0-85074851349&partnerID=40&md5=7abed946e06f76b3825ae5e294ffac14
26. Ribeiro, M.T., Singh, S., Guestrin, C.: "Why should I trust you?" explaining the predictions of any classifier. In: Proceedings of the 22nd ACM SIGKDD International Conference on Knowledge Discovery and Data Mining, pp. 1135–1144 (2016)
27. Sànchez-Ferreres, J., Burattin, A., Carmona, J., Montali, M., Padró, L.: Formal reasoning on natural language descriptions of processes. In: Hildebrandt, T., van Dongen, B.F., Röglinger, M., Mendling, J. (eds.) BPM 2019. LNCS, vol. 11675, pp. 86–101. Springer, Cham (2019). https://doi.org/10.1007/978-3-030-26619-6_8
28. Sanchez-Pi, N., Martí, L., Garcia, A.C.B., et al.: Text classification techniques in oil industry applications. In: Herrero, Á. (ed.) International Joint Conference SOCO'13-CISIS'13-ICEUTE'13. AISC, pp. 211–220. Springer, Heidelberg (2014). https://doi.org/10.1007/978-3-319-01854-6_22
29. Sanh, V., Debut, L., Chaumond, J., Wolf, T.: DistilBERT, a distilled version of BERT: smaller, faster, cheaper and lighter. arXiv preprint arXiv:1910.01108 (2019)
30. Scheible, R., Thomczyk, F., Tippmann, P., Jaravine, V., Boeker, M.: GottBERT: a pure German language model. arXiv preprint arXiv:2012.02110 (2020)
31. Sinha, A., Paradkar, A.: Use cases to process specifications in business process modeling notation. In: 2010 IEEE International Conference on Web Services, pp. 473–480. IEEE (2010)
32. Thangaraj, M., Sivakami, M.: Text classification techniques: a literature review. Interdisc. J. Inf. Knowl. Manag. **13** (2018)
33. Vanthienen, J.: Decisions, advice and explanation: an overview and research agenda. A Research Agenda for Knowledge Management and Analytics (2021)
34. Wang, H.J., Zhao, J.L., Zhang, L.J.: Policy-driven process mapping (PDPM): discovering process models from business policies. Decis. Support Syst. **48**(1), 267–281 (2009)
35. Wolf, T., et al.: HuggingFace's transformers: state-of-the-art natural language processing. arXiv preprint arXiv:1910.03771 (2019)

Combining Sub-symbolic and Symbolic Methods for Explainability

Anna Himmelhuber[1,2]([✉]), Stephan Grimm[1], Sonja Zillner[1], Mitchell Joblin[1], Martin Ringsquandl[1], and Thomas Runkler[1,2]

[1] Siemens AG, Munich, Germany
{anna.himmelhuber,stephan.grimm,sonja.zillner,mitchell.joblin,
martin.ringsquandl,thomas.runkler}@siemens.com
[2] Technical University of Munich, Munich, Germany

Abstract. Similarly to other connectionist models, Graph Neural Networks (GNNs) lack transparency in their decision-making. A number of sub-symbolic approaches have been developed to provide insights into the GNN decision making process. These are first important steps on the way to explainability, but the generated explanations are often hard to understand for users that are not AI experts. To overcome this problem, we introduce a conceptual approach combining sub-symbolic and symbolic methods for human-centric explanations, that incorporate domain knowledge and causality. We furthermore introduce the notion of fidelity as a metric for evaluating how close the explanation is to the GNN's internal decision making process. The evaluation with a chemical dataset and ontology shows the explanatory value and reliability of our method.

Keywords: Graph neural networks · XAI · Symbolic methods · Inductive logic learning

1 Introduction

Many important real-world data sets come in the form of graphs or networks, including social networks, knowledge graphs, protein-interaction networks, the World Wide Web and many more. Graph neural networks are connectionist models that capture the dependence structure induced by links via message passing between the nodes of graphs. Unlike standard neural networks, GNNs retain a state that can represent information from its neighborhood with arbitrary depth as well as incorporate node feature information [10]. Similarly to other connectionist models, GNNs lack transparency in their decision-making. Since the unprecedented levels of performance of such AI methods lead to increasing use in the daily life of humans, there is an emerging need to understand the decision-making process of such systems [1]. While symbolic methods such as inductive logic learning come with explainability, they perform best when dealing with relatively small and precise data. Sub-symbolic methods such as graph neural networks are able to handle large datasets, have a higher tolerance to noise in

© Springer Nature Switzerland AG 2021
S. Moschoyiannis et al. (Eds.): RuleML+RR 2021, LNCS 12851, pp. 172–187, 2021.
https://doi.org/10.1007/978-3-030-91167-6_12

real world data, generally have high computing performance and are easier to scale up [4].

Through the increasing popularity and need for explainability in AI, a variety of explainable models for neural networks are being developed [18]. These include surrogate models which are interpretable models that are trained to approximate the predictions of a black box model [8]. Other approaches include the identification of the most relevant features [11,18]. The explainer methods named above, allow the user to relate properties of the inputs to their output. However, the user is responsible for compiling and comprehending the explanations, relying on their own implicit form of knowledge and reasoning about them. Since humans are depending on their background knowledge and therefore also their biases about the data and its domain, different explanations about why a model makes a decision may be deduced. Since such sub-symbolic models are often built for AI researchers, it can make them hard to understand for non-experts. We strive to go beyond that by justifying predictions with background or common sense knowledge in a human understandable way [3]. This is of increased importance, as explainable AI and with it the widespread application of AI models are more likely to succeed if the evaluation of these explainer models is focused more on the user's needs [17].

We aim to develop a hybrid method by combining GNNs, sub-symbolic explainer methods and inductive logic learning. This enables human-centric and causal explanations through extracting symbolic explanations from identified decision drivers and enriching them with available background knowledge. These are generated for individual predictions, and are therefore instance-level explanations. With this method, high-accuracy sub-symbolic predictions come with symbolic-level explanations, and provide an effective solution for the performance vs. explainability trade-off.

As far as we know, this is the first work to study integrating a sub-symbolic explainer with symbolic methods for more human-centric instance-level explanations. Our fidelity metric indicates how close an explanation is to the GNN's internal decision making process. Additionally, the employment of justifications in our method provides causality that makes use of the background knowledge.

2 Background and Problem Definition

For incorporating explicit domain knowledge into our explanation method on the side of symbolic representation, we use ontologies expressed in the W3C OWL 2 standard[1] [6] based on the description logic formalism. In this section we first introduce semantic web ontology, then revisit the notions of entailment, inductive logic learning and justifications, followed by graph neural networks and a sub-symbolic explainer method. Eventually, we define the problem of learning explainer classes by combining a GNN's output with inductive logic learning[2].

---

[1] https://www.w3.org/TR/owl2-overview/.

[2] For better readability we will denominate variables represented in ontology form in greek letters and sub-symbolic graph representations in latin letters.

Semantic Web Ontology. The basic constituents for representing knowledge in OWL are individuals, classes and properties. They are used to form axioms, i.e. statements within the target domain, and an ontology $\mathcal{O}$ is a set of axioms to describe what holds true in this domain. The most relevant axioms for our work are class assertions $\tau(\sigma)$ assigning an individual σ to a class τ, property assertions $\rho(\sigma_1, \sigma_2)$ connecting two individuals σ_1, σ_2 by property ρ, and subclass axioms $\tau_1 \sqsubseteq \tau_2$ expressing that class τ_1 is a subclass of class τ_2. Classes can be either atomic class names, such as 'Compound' or 'Bond', or they can be composed by means of complex class expressions. An example for a complex class expression noted in Manchester syntax is 'Compound and hasStructure some Nitrogen_Dioxide', which refers to all molecule compounds having some nitrogen dioxide compound in their structure. For details about all types of axioms and the way complex concepts are constructed we refer to [6].

Table 1. Example excerpt of δ^{Mutag}.

(1)	Carbon $\sqsubseteq$ Atom	carbons are atoms
(2)	Hetero_aromatic_5_ring Ring_Size_5 $\sqsubseteq$ RingStructure $\sqsubseteq$	hetero-aromatic rings of size 5 are rings of size 5, which are ring structures
(3)	Nitrogen(feature_100_5)	feature_100_5 is a nitrogen
(4)	Compound(graph_100)	graph_100 is a compound
(5)	hasAtom(graph_100, feature_100_5)	graph_100 has atom feature_100_5

Example 1 (Mutagenesis Ontology)

As we are combining GNNs and ontologies, graph data has to be available as triples as well as background knowledge. We chose a chemical domain to test our method, as it comes with structured background knowledge. The domain knowledge used in our approach is given by the Mutagenesis ontology δ^{Mutag}[3], which is exemplified in Table 1.

Definition 1 (Entailment)

Given ontology $\mathcal{O}$, if axiom α logically follows from $\mathcal{O}$, as can be derived by a standard OWL reasoner, then we call α an entailment of $\mathcal{O}$ and write $\mathcal{O} \models \alpha$[4].

Definition 2 (Inductive Logic Learning (ILL)):

Given an ontology $\mathcal{O}$, a set of positive instances E^+ and a set of negative instances E^-, a resulting target predicate class expression ε is constructed such that $\mathcal{O} \models \varepsilon(\sigma)$ holds for all individuals $\sigma \in E^+$ and does not hold for individuals $\sigma \in E^-$[5].

In the context of OWL ontologies, ILL attempts to construct class expressions from an ontology $\mathcal{O}$ and two sets E^+, E^- of individuals that act as positive and

---

[3] https://github.com/SmartDataAnalytics/DL-Learner/tree/develop/examples/mutagenesis.

[4] As defined in [13].

[5] As defined in [16].

negative examples for being instances of the target class, respectively. Concretely, we use DL-Learner [16] as the key tool to derive OWL class expressions to be used for our explanations.

Definition 3 (Justification)
Given an ontology $\mathcal{O}$ and an entailment α, the justification $\mathcal{J}(\mathcal{O}, \alpha)$ for α in $\mathcal{O}$ is a set $\mathcal{J} \subseteq \mathcal{O}$, such that $\mathcal{J} \models \alpha$ and $\mathcal{J}' \not\models \alpha$ for all proper subsets $\mathcal{J}' \subset \mathcal{J}$ (See footnote 4).

Graph Neural Network (GNN)
For a GNN, the goal is to learn a function of features on a graph $G = (V, E)$ with edges E and nodes V. The input is comprised of a feature vector x_i for every node i, summarized in a feature matrix $X \in \mathbb{R}^{n \times d_{in}}$ and a representative description of the link structure in the form of an adjacency matrix A. The output of one layer is a node-level latent representation matrix $Z \in \mathbb{R}^{n \times d_{out}}$, where d_{out} is the number of output latent dimensions per node. Therefore, every layer can be written as a non-linear function: $H^{(l+1)} = f(H^{(l)}, A)$, with $H^{(0)} = X$ and $H^{(L)} = Z$, L being the number of stacked layers. The vanilla GNN model employed in our framework, uses the propagation rule [9]:

$$f(H^{(l)}, A) = \hat{s}(\hat{D}^{-\frac{1}{2}} \hat{A} \hat{D}^{-\frac{1}{2}} H^{(l)} W^{(l)}),$$

with $\hat{A} = A + I$, I being the identity matrix. $\hat{D}$ is the diagonal node degree matrix of $\hat{A}$, $W^{(l)}$ is a weight matrix for the $l - th$ neural network layer and $\hat{s}$ is a non-linear activation function. Taking the latent node representations Z of the last layer we define the logits of node v_i for classification task as $\hat{y}_i = \text{softmax}(z_i W_c^\top)$, where $W_c \in \mathbb{R}^{d_{out} \times k}$ projects the node representations into the k dimensional classification space.

Example 2 (GNN Classifications for Mutag Dataset)
For GNN predictions, the dataset Mutag is utilized, which is from a different source and therefore independent of the Mutagenesis ontology. It contains molecule graphs and is classified through a 3-layer vanilla Graph Convolutional Network with 85% accuracy [11]. The molecule graphs $G_i = (A_i, X_i)$, which are compounds existing out of atoms and bonds, with certain structures such as carbon rings, can be classified as mutagenic (m) or nonmutagenic (n) depending on their mutagenic effect on the Gram-negative bacterium S. typhimurium [12].

Sub-symbolic Explainer Method
The sub-symbolic explainer method takes a trained GNN and its prediction(s), and it returns an explanation in the form of a small subgraph of the input graph together with a small subset of node features that are most influential for the prediction. For their selection, the mutual information between the GNN prediction and the distribution of possible subgraph structures is maximized through optimizing the conditional entropy. The explainer method output is comprised of edge masks $M_{Ei} \in \{0, 1\}^{n \times n} \subset A_i$ and node feature masks $M_{Xi} \in \{0, 1\}^{n \times d} \subset X_i$, which is used as input to our framework.

Since it is the state-of-the-art method, which outperforms alternative baseline approaches by 43.0% in explanation accuracy [11], we chose the GNNExplainer for our framework, but our approach will work with any other explainer subgraph generation method.

Example 3 (GNNExplainer Output for Mutag Dataset Classifications)
The GNNExplainer is applied to identify the most influential parts of the respective graph for the classification decision. Figure 1 shows the original graph, its edge mask M_E as identified by the GNNExplainer and the ground truth for a mutagenic (left) and nonmutagenic (middle) molecule as well as the identified node feature mask M_X (right). It can be seen that the identified important graph motifs and node features align with some of ground truth mutagenic properties, as given by [12]. These include ring structures and the node features C, O, N and H. However, the fact that these results represent a carbon ring as well as the chemical group NO_2 (Nitrogen dioxide) is left up to the user for interpretation.

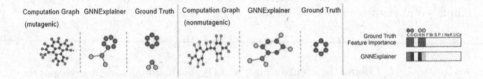

Fig. 1. GNNExplainer results for Mutag dataset classifications. Figure adapted from Fig. 4 and Fig. 5 in [11].

Definition 4 (Explainer Class Learning)
Given ontology $\mathcal{O}$ and a set of graph individuals $\{\eta_i\} \in \mathcal{O}^6$ with their respective classifications $\{y_1, y_2, ...y_i\}$ provided by a GNN for a certain category, we define explainer class learning as inductive logic learning such that $\eta_j|y_j = category \in E^+$ and $\eta_k|y_k \neq category \in E^-$.

$\mathcal{O}$ provides the background knowledge for inductive logic learning, and the classification decision by the GNN provides the positive and negative examples in order to learn explainer classes. We also define a metric called fidelity metric (to be specified in Sect. 3) for quantitative measurement. The higher the fidelity metric, the higher the reliability of the entailed explainer class.

3   Combining Sub-symbolic and Symbolic Methods

3.1   Explainer Class Learning

We are proposing a hybrid method, within which the coupling of the sub-symbolic explainer method GNNExplainer with the symbolic DL-Learner is used

---

[6] Mapping sub-symbolic graph representations $(X_i, A_i) \mapsto \mathcal{O}$, resulting in individuals η_i is specified in Sect. 3.1.

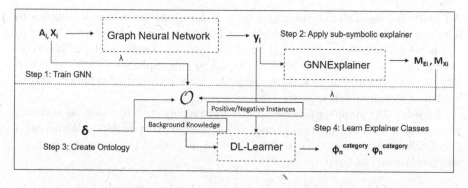

Fig. 2. Learning explainer classes process flow.

to explain GNN instance-level predictions. Our approach is shown for a graph classification task, but would equally apply to node classification or link prediction. The process flow of learning explainer classes can be seen in Fig. 2. Firstly, a GNN is trained on and applied to training and testing data and subsequently the sub-symbolic explainer method GNNExplainer is applied to all generated predictions, as can be seen in Fig. 2 (Step 1 and Step 2). Secondly, to create explainer classes for the GNN decision making process, DL-Learner is applied for a specific predicted category, with positive and negative examples labelled accordingly through y_i (Step 4). The background knowledge used by the DL-Learner to learn explainer classes is comprised of the adjacency matrices A_i and node feature matrices X_i, edge masks M_{Ei} and node feature masks M_{Xi} and domain knowledge δ. As the DL-Learner can only process ontologies, the matrices are mapped to an ontology (Step 3) through λ as detailed below:

Extraction and Mapping Step

A set of graphs detailed in their associated matrices A_i and X_i[7] are modelled as set of individuals $\{\eta_i\}$. Their edges and node features are extracted from $A_i's$ and $X_i's$ edge and feature lists and modelled as set of individuals $\{v_j\}$ and $\{\chi_k\}$. If there are graph-specific structures common in the respective domain, such as certain motifs, e.g. a ring structure, the set of possible structures $\{structure_z\}$ along with their extraction functions $\{\gamma_z(A_i, X_i)\}$ is defined and mapped through mapping function $S : \{structure_z\} \mapsto \{\gamma_z(A_i, X_i)\}$.

If $structure_1$ is contained in (A_i, X_i), extraction function $\gamma_1(A_i, X_i)$ returns all individuals contained in the structure. The found structures are modelled as a set of individuals $\{\psi_g\}$. To assign all individuals their type declarations and roles, a set of roles $\{\rho_v\}$ and type declarations $\{\tau_w\}$ as well as further mapping functions based on domain knowledge δ are needed. Defining these sets and mapping functions has been done as a one-time manual step, with their complexity depending on the domain.

$P : \{\eta_i\} \times (\{v_j\} \cup \{\chi_k\} \cup \{\psi_g\}) \mapsto \{\rho_v\}$, maps a pair of individuals to their role. $T : (\{\eta_i\} \cup \{v_j\} \cup \{\chi_k\} \cup \{\psi_g\} \mapsto \{\tau_w\}$ maps individuals to their types.

---

[7] Their size is dependent on the number of layers used by the GNN, to keep the consistency in coupling the sub-symbolic with the symbolic method.

All extracted individuals, roles and type declarations are added as axioms to ontology $\mathcal{O}$ through function $AddAxiom(\mathcal{O}, axiom)$ as is shown in Algorithm 1. Therefore, λ is defined as $\lambda(A_i, X_i, T, P, S) \mapsto \mathcal{O}$. Equivalently, λ is carried out for all corresponding sub-symbolic explainer subgraphs with their associated edge masks M_{Ei} and node feature masks M_{Xi}, with the set of explainer graphs modelled as individuals η_sub_i.

Additionally, mapping function μ is defined as bijective function, as is shown in Algorithm 1. This function is needed for the fidelity calculation. Function μ is defined in such a way, that if the input, e.g. σ_1, doesn't map to anything, σ_1 will be returned as output.

Example 4 (Mapping Mutag Dataset with Mutagenesis Ontology)
The mapping functions $S^{Mutag} = \{Azanide : \gamma_{Azanide}, Methyl : \gamma_{Methyl}, ...\}$, $R^{Mutag} = \{(\eta_i, \upsilon_j) : hasBond, (\eta_i, \chi_k) : hasAtom, ...\}$ and $T^{Mutag} = \{\eta_i : Compound, \upsilon_j : Bond, \chi_k : Carbon, ...\}$ are defined based on domain terminology δ^{Mutag}. For example, from molecule graph G_1 with associated matrices X_1 and A_1, the edge individuals edge_1_2, edge_1_3, etc., are modelled. For extracting structure Methyl (CH_3), which is defined as containing one carbon atom bonded to three hydrogen atom, function $\gamma_{Methyl}(A_1, X_1)$ is employed. All accruing axioms are added to the ontology $\mathcal{O}^{Mutag}$. Through μ, the set of edges forming the identified structure, e.g. {edge_1_2, edge_1_3, edge_1_4} is mapped to the individual structure_1_1_1.

Algorithm 1: Graph Structure Extraction λ

Data: Set of graphs with adjacency matrices A_i, feature matrices X_i, mapping functions for type declarations $T(\sigma)$, roles $P(\sigma_1, \sigma_2)$ and structures $S(x)$

Result: $\mathcal{O}, \mu$

$\mathcal{O} : \{\}$

foreach *graph in range(i)* **do**

    $AddAxiom(\mathcal{O}, T(graph)(\eta_{graph}))$

    foreach *edge in Edgelist(A_{graph})* **do**

        $AddAxiom(\mathcal{O}, T(edge)(\upsilon_{edge\_graph}))$

        $AddAxiom(\mathcal{O}, P(graph, edge)(\eta_{graph}, \upsilon_{edge\_graph}))$

    foreach *feature in Featurelist(X_{graph})* **do**

        $AddAxiom(\mathcal{O}, T(feature)(\chi_{feature\_graph}))$

        $AddAxiom(\mathcal{O}, P(graph, feature)(\eta_{graph}, \chi_{feature\_graph}))$

    foreach *structure in $\{structure_z\}$* **do**

        if $S(structure)(A_{graph}, X_{graph})$ *not* **None** **then**

            foreach *number in range(count($S(structure)(A_{graph}, X_{graph})$))* **do**

                $AddAxiom(\mathcal{O}, T(structure)(\psi_{graph\_structure\_number}))$

                $AddAxiom(\mathcal{O}, P(graph, structure)(\eta_{graph}, \psi_{graph\_structure\_number}))$

                $\mu : S(structure)(A_{graph}, X_{graph}) \mapsto \psi_{graph\_structure\_number}$

According to the GNN's classifications positive and negative examples of graphs are distinguished and explainer classes are learned. The background knowledge is the ontology $\mathcal{O} = \delta \cup \lambda(A_i, X_i, T, P, S) \cup \lambda(M_{Ei}, M_{Xi}, T, P, S)$. We differentiate between two types of explainer classes:

Input-Output Explainer Classes
Given Definition 4, background knowledge $\delta \cup \lambda(A_i, X_i, T, P, S)$, $\eta_i | y_i = category$ $\in E^+$ and $\eta_i | y_i \neq category \in E^-$, a set of Input-Output Explainer Classes $\{\phi_n^{category}\}$ are learned. Input-output explainer classes are candidate explanations, that capture the global behavior of a GNN through investigating what input patterns can lead to a specific class prediction, comparable to the input-output mapping approach in [15].

Importance Explainer Classes
Given Definition 4, background knowledge $\delta \cup \lambda(M_{Ei}, M_{Xi}, T, P, S)$, $\eta\_sub_i |$ $y_i = category \in E^+$ and $\eta\_sub_i | y_i \neq category \in E^-$, a set of Importance Explainer Classes $\{\varphi_m^{category}\}$ are learned. Importance Explainer classes show which edges, nodes, features and motifs are important for the GNN to predict a certain class. These class expressions represent the inner workings of a GNN, by incorporating the output of the sub-symbolic explainer.

3.2 Explainer Class Application for Instance-Level Explanations

The pool of possible explainer classes for all categories as learned in Sect. 3.1, consisting of $\{\phi_n\}$ and $\{\varphi_n\}$, are used in the application step to generate instance-level explanations through explainer class entailment and justification steps.

Explainer Class Entailment
Given Definition 1, a set of explainer classes $\{\phi_n^{category}\}$ and $\{\varphi^{category}\}$, ontology $\mathcal{O}$ and individual η_j classified as category, entailments for η_j are generated. By doing so, we check if the learned overall decision-making pattern of the GNN applies to a specific instance. For all available explainer classes, entailments for a specific individual η_j are generated. It is possible, that several entailments hold, just as it is possible that a classification decision of G_j is based on several different factors. The set of entailments for η_j is given by $C_{Exp}(\eta_j) = \{\phi \mid \mathcal{O} \models \phi^{category}(\eta_j)\} \cup \{\varphi \mid \mathcal{O} \models \varphi^{category}(\eta_j)\}$.

Definition 5 (Entailment Frequency)
Given an ontology $\mathcal{O}$, explainer class $\phi_i^{category}$ and a set of indivdiuals $\{\eta_i\}$, we define the entailment frequency as the number of entailments for $|\{\eta \in \{\eta_i\} : \mathcal{O} \models \phi_i^{category}(\eta)\}|$ over the number of instances $|\{\eta_i\}|$.

The entailment frequency gives insight over the generality or specificity of explainer classes and representing the average frequency with which a certain explainer class is entailed.

Explainer Class Entailment Justification
Given $\mathcal{O}$ and entailment $\mathcal{O} \models \phi_i^{category}(\eta_j)$, justification $\mathcal{J}(\mathcal{O}, \phi_i^{category}(\eta_j))$ is generated. The number of generated axioms gives some insight about the level of

domain knowledge employed. As there can be several justifications for an entailment, we limit them to only one. It is not in the scope of this paper to determine which justification would provide the best explanation, but since a shorter justification tends to be more efficient, the justification with the minimum number of axioms is chosen.

Example 5 (Justification for Mutag Explainer Class)
Table 2 shows an example justification for the entailment $\mathcal{O}^{Mutag} \models \phi_8^m(\eta_1)$, which contributes to a meaningful explanation, as it carries causal information present in expert knowledge about the conclusion.

Table 2. Example justification $\mathcal{J}(\mathcal{O}^{Mutag}, \phi_8^m(\eta_1))$.

(1)	η_1 hasStructure structure_1_1_1
(2)	structure_1_1_1 Type Hetero_aromatic_5_ring
(3)	Hetero_aromatic_5_ring SubClassOf Ring_size_5
(4)	ϕ_8^m EquivalentTo hasStructure some Ring_size_5

Fidelity Calculation
Fidelity is defined as the measure of the accuracy of the student model (DL-Learner) with respect to the teacher model (GNN). High fidelity is therefore fundamental, whenever a student model is to be claimed to offer a good explanation for a teacher model. Without high fidelity, an apparently perfectly good explanation produced by an explainable system is likely not to be an explanation of the underlying sub-symbolic system which it is expected to explain [21]. We calculate Fidelity as follows:

$$Fidelity(\phi_i, \eta_j) = \frac{|\mu^{-1}(ind(\mathcal{J}(\mathcal{O}, \phi_i(\eta_j)))) \cap \eta\_sub_j|}{|\mu^{-1}(ind(\mathcal{J}(\mathcal{O}, \phi_i(\eta_j))))|},$$

where $ind()$ is a function that collects all individuals that are provable instances of a set of axioms. The denominator equals the count of the set of edges or node features that have to be part of η_i, for the entailment of explainer class ϕ_i to hold. The fidelity metric is defined as the overlap of the sub-symbolic explainer output with the entailed explainer classes, as can be seen in Fig. 3, which means that the effectiveness of the sub-symbolic explainer method in representing the GNN decision making is therefore assumed.

Example 6 (Fidelity for Explainer Class *hasStructure some Methyl*)
As the explainer classes are represented through axioms, e.g. ϕ_2^n = hasStructure some Methyl, we apply the justification mechanism to arrive at the axioms containing the corresponding individual(s) for the specific example η_1, such as η_1 hasStructure structure_1_2_1 $\in \mathcal{J}(\phi_2^n, \eta_1)$. Since there might be a multiplicity of individuals, function $ind(\mathcal{J}(\mathcal{O}, \phi_2(\eta_1))$ is applied, which

collects all individuals that are provable instances of the justification. These individuals are then inversely mapped (μ^{-1}) to their corresponding set of individuals, in this example {edge_1_2, edge_1_3, edge_1_4}. In case there is no corresponding set of individuals, the inverse mapping simply returns the given individual. For the numerator, we count the overlap of the identified set of individuals with the individuals in η_sub_i, the subgraph identified by the GNNExplainer.

Definition 6 (Final Explanation)
Given the set of entailments, that hold for η_j, we define the final explanation $E(\eta_j)$ as the set of the respective justifications $E(\eta_j) = \{\mathcal{J}(\mathcal{O}, C(\eta_j))\} \mid C \in C_{Exp(\eta_j)}$.

Example 7 (Molecule Graph G_1)
In Fig. 3, the final explanation for the classification of molecule graph G_1 as mutagenic can be seen, complete with justifications and fidelity score.

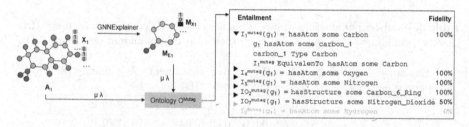

Fig. 3. Final explanation for molecule graph G_1, which has been classified as mutagenic.

4   Evaluation

Experiment Setting. We used a subset of 530 molecule graphs as training data to learn explainer classes, and 800 molecule graphs as testing data. The graphs have been classified by a 3-layer vanilla Graph Convolutional Network. All molecule graphs come with adjacency matrices A_i^{Mutag}, and feature matrices X_i^{Mutag} and their corresponding GNNExplainer importance masks (M_{Ei}^{Mutag} and X_{Ei}^{Mutag}), equally split between mutagenic and nonmutagenic classifications. The DL-Learner can create arbitrarily many class expressions, functioning as explainer classes, which are ordered by predictive accuracy (number of correctly classified examples divided by the number of all examples). We are taking a cut-off point of > 50% predictive accuracy, as an explainer class with less than 50% predictive accuracy, wouldn't represent a pattern for mutagenic classification decisions but rather the opposite, and v.v. for nonmutagenic classification decisions[8].

---

[8] All experimental data, code and results are available from https://github.com/XAI-sub-symbolic/Combining-Sub-Symbolic-Explainer-Methods-with-SWT.

Explainer Classes

The generated pool of explainer classes provides a total of 14 explainer classes for mutagenic and 12 explainer classes for nonmutagenic classifications. All the comprehensible explanation for mutagenic classification decisions that can be identified and interpreted from the GNNExplainer output (see Sect. 2), have been learnt by the DL-Learner. These include ϕ_2^m = hasStructure some Carbon_6_ring, ϕ_7^m = hasStructure some Nitrogen_dioxide, φ_1^m = hasAtom some Carbon, φ_2^m = hasAtom some Hydrogen, φ_3^m = hasAtom some Nitrogen, and φ_4^m = hasAtom some Oxygen, along with several others, which have not been identified by the GNNExplainer. The explainer class ϕ_6^m = hasStructure some Phenanthrene is a compelling example for the effectiveness of our hybrid approach, as Phenanthrene is a strong indicator for mutagenic potency [12], but isn't identifiable in the GNNExplainer output. This shows that our hybrid method can identify and verbalize decision-making processes of the GNN, which a comprehensible sub-symbolic explainer system, whose output might not be easily understood and interpreted by a user, is missing.

Table 3. Input-output and importance explainer classes with avg. pred. accuracy (DL-Learner), entailment rate and fidelity with their respective standard deviations (SD).

Explainer class type	Number	Avg. Pred. Acc. (SD)	Avg. entailment rate (SD)	Avg. fidelity (SD)
ϕ_n^m	1, ..., 10	0.56 (0.04)	0.64 (0.3)	0.88 (0.12)
ϕ_n^n	1, ..., 5	0.59 (0.03)	0.09 (0.04)	0.82 (0.12)
φ_n^m	1, ..., 4	0.77 (0.06)	0.86 (0.15)	0.99 (0.01)
φ_n^n	1, ..., 7	0.56 (0.01)	0.41 (0.25)	0.81 (0.05)

Entailment Frequency

The entailment frequency gives us insight over the generality or specificity of explainer classes. As can be seen in Table 3 (Avg. Entailment Rate), there is a wide range of entailment rates. Some explainer classes, e.g. ϕ_4^m = hasAtom some Carbon always apply, while others are quite rare, such as ϕ_4^n = hasAtom some Phosphorus, that comes with only a 4% entailment rate. As expected, we have an overall lower entailment rate for nonmutagenic explainer classes, as the there are also less distinct factors indicating nonmutagenicity [12]. Most nonmutagenic classifications come with about 3 entailments, while mutagenic classifications come with more than 5 entailments on average. This is due to a lower generality of the explainer classes, which implies that such an explainer class only applies to specific instances. This notion is also confirmed by the lower average predictive accuracy of the DL-Learner results for nonmutagenic (57%) as opposed to mutagenic (63%) explainer classes, as can be seen in Table 3 (Avg. Pred. Acc). The predictive accuracy of the DL-Learner is defined as the number of correctly classified examples divided by the number of all examples [14].

Explanation Fidelity

Fidelity gives the user a measure of reliability of the explanation, with the average fidelity ranging from 64% for ϕ_5^n = hasStructure some Carbon_5_ring to 100% for e.g. φ_2^m = hasAtom some Hydrogen. While an explainer class with an average fidelity of 64% might still give the user some insight, its explanatory value cannot be considered as reliable as for an explainer class with a higher fidelity. An explainer class, that has a low generality, meaning it is rarely applied to explain a classification, can nonetheless come with a high fidelity such as ϕ_4^n (100%). This suggests that also low generality explainer classes can be valuable for specific instances.

We can observe a positive correlation of 88% between the average fidelity and predictive accuracy for $\{\varphi_n\}$ and of 50% between the average fidelity and $\{\varphi_n\}$ $\cup$ $\{\phi_n\}$, signalising the effectiveness of representing the sub-symbolic decision-making process with the DL-Learner. As the predictive accuracy of the output given by the DL-Learner is the metric on which we base our choice of explainer classes included in the pool, the correlation with the fidelity indicates that this approach leads to reliable explanations.

Explainability of sub-symbolic methods is desirable not only to justify actions taken based on the predictions made by the system, but also to identify false predictions. Therefore, it is also important to evaluate our method based on its ability to not generate explanation for wrong predictions and therefore validating them. Table 4 shows the difference in entailments for the correctly classified (true positives TP) and incorrectly classified graphs (false positives FP). We can see, that the average fidelity for entailments is 30% points lower for mutagenic FP than mutagenic TP, and 38% points for nonmutagenic FP. While this might not be sufficient to clearly identify a wrong classification, it indicates the validity of the fidelity metric, as it is significantly lower for explainer classes applied to incorrect classification.

Table 4. Average fidelity for true positives and false positives.

	TP^m	FP^m	TP^n	FP^n
Number of instances	371	29	374	26
Average fidelity	0.96	0.66	0.82	0.44

Justification Axioms

Through justifications we provide causality for explanations, based on domain knowledge. The ontology δ^{Mutag} utilized has little structural depth as can be seen in the example excerpt in Table 1. Nonetheless, there is a minimum of 3 axioms for all entailments. For 20% of explainer classes, 4 axiom justifications and for 8% of explainer classes, 5 axiom justifications are generated. This means, that for all explanations generated, the explanations carry some causal information about the conclusion, supported by expert knowledge.

4.1 Comparison of Our Hybrid Method with DL-Learner Explanations and Input-Output Explanations

DL-Learner: Classifications along with corresponding explanations can be generated by only using a symbolic classifier such as the DL-Learner. When comparing this purely symbolic approach with our hybrid method, we find that using only the DL-Learner comes with significantly lower prediction accuracy and also explanatory value. The predictive accuracy of the GNN using the same subset of training data is 78%, so considerably above the DL-Learner result, as shown below. When applying the DL-Learner to carry out classifications, we are restricted to only one classifier. This means, even if we allow more complex class expressions, we only have one explanation for the target predicate mutagenic:

    hasStructure some Nitrogen dioxide or hasThreeOrMoreFusedRings
    value true (pred. acc.: 65.76%)

GNN with Input-Output Explanations: We want to look at the benefits of integrating a sub-symbolic explainer into our framework, as opposed to explaining GNN predictions with only the input-output matching method as done in e.g. [15]. We can see, that for some explainer classes such as $\phi_3^m = \varphi_3^m =$ hasAtom some Nitrogen, we have overlap of the importance explainer classes with the input-output explainer classes. However, the importance explainer classes come with a significantly higher predictive accuracy of 77% as can be seen in Table 3, indicating their significance for the classification decision. For the nonmutagenic classifications, explainer class $\varphi_2^n =$ hasStructure some Carbon_6_ring, which is equivalent with the ground truth as shown in Fig. 1, wouldn't have been included in ϕ_n^n. Here, we can clearly see the added benefit of generating explainer classes from the GNNExplainer as opposed to only observing the input-output behaviour of a GNN. The main benefit of including such a sub-symbolic explainer, however, is the provision of the fidelity metric. Without such a metric there is no means to quantify the reliability of the explanation. These results justify the strategy of using a hybrid method.

4.2 Deeper Integration of GNNs with Domain Knowledge

We carried out an initial integration of sub-symbolic and symbolic methods, by mapping and integrating the GNN input and GNNExplainer output to and with the available domain knowledge. A deeper integration could be reached through integrating available domain knowledge δ into the GNN before training. As the domain knowledge δ and the input graphs G_i are from different sources, they are independent. It was therefore not known if their integration could significantly worsen the GNN classification results. Initial results, where we included common molecule structure from domain knowledge δ^{Mutag} as a simple binary vector into the feature matrices X_i^{Mutag}, show that the overall prediction accuracy of the GNN only decreases insignificantly by 2% points, which is a promising first result. It indicates that the domain knowledge, and the explanations generated with it, don't contradict the decision making process of the GNN.

5   Related Work

Explainable AI including model-level interpretation and instance-level explanations have been the focus of research for years [3]. In this section we first give an overview for explainable AI for Graph Neural Networks and then for using symbolic methods to explain sub-symbolic models.

Sub-symbolic Explainer Methods. Current work towards explainable GNNs attempts to convert approaches initially designed for Convolutional Neural Networks (CNNs) into graph domain [18]. The drawback of reusing explanation methods previously applied to CNNs are their inability to incorporate graph-specific data such as the edge structure. Another method, a graph attention model, augments interpretability via an attention mechanism by indicating influential graph structures through learned edge attention weights [7]. It cannot, however, take node feature information into account and is limited to a specific GNN architecture. To overcome these problems, [11] created the model-agnostic approach GNNExplainer, that finds a subgraph of input data which influence GNNs predictions in the most significant way by maximizing the subgraph's mutual information with the model's prediction.

Explanations with Symbolic Methods. A different type of explainability method tries to integrate ML with symbolic methods. The symbolic methods utilized alongside Neural Networks are quite agnostic of the underlying algorithms and mainly harness ontologies and knowledge graphs [19]. One approach is to map network inputs or neurons to classes of an ontology or entities of a knowledge graph. For example, [15] map scene objects within images to classes of an ontology. Based on the image classification outputted by the Neural Network, the authors run ILP on the ontology to create class expressions that act as model-level explanations. Furthermore, [20] learn a mapping between individual neurons and domain knowledge. This enables the linking of a neuron's weight to semantically grounded domain knowledge. A ontology-based approach for human-centric explanation of transfer learning is proposed by [2]. While there is some explanatory value to these input-output methods, they fail to give insights into the inner workings of a graph neural network and cannot identify which type of information was influential in making a prediction. This work bridges this gap by combining the advantages of both approaches is among the first to study the coupling of a sub-symbolic explanation method with symbolic methods.

6   Conclusion

In this paper, we addressed the problem of grounding explanations in domain knowledge while keeping them close to the decision making process of a GNN. We showed that combining sub-symbolic with symbolic methods can generate reliable instance-level explanations, that don't rely on the user for correct interpretation. We tested our hybrid framework on the Mutag dataset mapped to the Mutagenesis ontology, to evaluate its explanatory value, its practicability and the validity of the idea. We used data from a chemical domain, as it comes with complex domain knowledge that is universally accepted and can therefore be considered as ground truth when evaluating explanations. Our results show, that there are significant advantages of our hybrid framework over only using the sub-symbolic explainer, where the output is susceptible to biased or faulty interpretations by the user. Equally, there are advantages of our hybrid method over a purely symbolic method such as ILL, as it comes with significantly higher accuracy, while for an input-output method, the decision-making process of the neural network isn't considered and there are no means to validate the reliability of the explanations. In future, we will evaluate how our hybrid framework compares for different datasets. Furthermore, we will analyze the effect on explanations when the coupling of available domain knowledge with GNNs is deepened before training.

References

1. Arrieta, A.B., et al.: Explainable artificial intelligence (XAI): concepts, taxonomies, opportunities and challenges toward responsible AI. Inf. Fusion **58**, 82–115 (2020)
2. Chen, J., et al.: Knowledge-based transfer learning explanation. In: Sixteenth International Conference on Principles of Knowledge Representation and Reasoning (2018)
3. Biran, O., Cotton, C.: Explanation and justification in machine learning: a survey. In: IJCAI-17 Workshop on Explainable AI (XAI), vol. 8, no. 1 (2017)
4. Ilkou, E., Koutraki, M.: Symbolic vs sub-symbolic ai methods: friends or enemies? In: CIKM (Workshops) (2020)
5. Tiddi, I.: Foundations of explainable knowledge-enabled systems. Knowl. Graph. eXplainable Artif. Intell.: Found. Appl. Challenges **47**, 23 (2020)
6. McGuinness, D.L., Van Harmelen, F.: OWL web ontology language overview. W3C Recommendation **10**(10), 2004 (2004)
7. Veličković, P., et al.: Graph attention networks. In: ICLR (2018)
8. Ribeiro, M.T., Singh, S., Guestrin, C.: Why should i trust you? Explaining the predictions of any classifier. In: Proceedings of the 22nd ACM SIGKDD International Conference on Knowledge Discovery and Data Mining (2016)
9. Kipf, T.N., Welling, M: Semi-supervised classification with graph convolutional networks. In: ICLR (2017)
10. Zhou, J., et al.: Graph neural networks: a review of methods and applications. AI Open **1**, 57–81 (2020)
11. Ying, R., et al.: GNNExplainer: generating explanations for graph neural networks. In: Advances in Neural Information Processing Systems, vol. 32, p. 9240 (2019)
12. Debnath, A.K., et al.: Structure-activity relationship of mutagenic aromatic and heteroaromatic nitro compounds. Correlation with molecular orbital energies and hydrophobicity. J. Med. Chem. **34**(2), 786–797 (1991)
13. Horridge, M., et al.: Understanding entailments in OWL. In: OWLED (2008)
14. Lehmann, J., et al.: Class expression learning for ontology engineering. J. Web Semant. **9**(1), 71–81 (2011)
15. Sarker, M.K., et al.: Explaining trained neural networks with semantic web technologies: first steps. arXiv preprint arXiv:1710.04324 (2017)

16. Lehmann, J.: DL-learner: learning concepts in description logics. J. Mach. Learn. Res. **10**, 2639–2642 (2009)
17. Miller, T., Howe, P., Sonenberg, L.: Explainable AI: beware of inmates running the asylum or: how I learnt to stop worrying and love the social and behavioural sciences. In: IJCAI Workshop on Explainable Artificial Intelligence (XAI) (2017)
18. Pope, P.E., et al.: Explainability methods for graph convolutional neural networks. In: Proceedings of the IEEE/CVF Conference on Computer Vision and Pattern Recognition (2019)
19. Seeliger, A., Pfaff, M., Krcmar, H.: Semantic web technologies for explainable machine learning models: a literature review. In: PROFILES/SEMEX@ ISWC, vol. 2465, pp. 1–16 (2019)
20. Selvaraju, R.R., et al.: Choose your neuron: incorporating domain knowledge through neuron-importance. In: Proceedings of the European Conference on Computer Vision (ECCV) (2018)
21. Garcez, A.A., Lamb, L.C.: Neurosymbolic AI: the 3rd wave. arXiv preprint arXiv:2012.05876 (2020)

Practical Rule-Based Qualitative Temporal Reasoning for the Semantic Web

Guilherme Lima[1]([⊠]), Marcelo Machado[1], Rosario Uceda-Sosa[2],
and Marcio Moreno[1]

[1] IBM Research Brazil, Rio de Janeiro, Brazil
{guilherme.lima,marcelo.machado}@ibm.com, mmoreno@br.ibm.com
[2] IBM T.J. Watson Research Center, Yorktown Heights, NY, USA
rosariou@us.ibm.com

Abstract. We present an approach for practical rule-based temporal reasoning over RDF/OWL using Allen's Interval Algebra (IA). Reasoning in Allen's IA is only tractable for certain subalgebras and is done through path-consistency, a constraint propagation algorithm whose rule-based implementation requires $O(n^2)$ rules for a subalgebra with n relations. Our approach uses custom built-ins to implement path-consistency using a constant number of rules (just 6) and in a way that is subalgebra-agnostic. In the paper, we present the approach, its implementation in Apache Jena, and an experimental evaluation against traditional rule-based implementations. The evaluation shows a considerable speed-up when backward-chaining is used. A further contribution of the paper is the problem set used in the evaluations.

Keywords: Temporal reasoning · Allen's interval algebra · Rule-based reasoning · Apache Jena · SWRL · HermiT · Pellet

1 Introduction

Many applications require reasoning about time using qualitative rather than quantitative descriptions. Temporal question-answering over text is a typical example [22]. Its goal is to extract events and temporal relations from text data and then answer queries about implicit temporal relations. For instance, if event A occurred before B and B occurred before C then, under the usual meaning of "before", we can conclude that A occurred before C. This type of reasoning is called qualitative because it only considers temporal relations such as before, after, during, etc., as opposed to quantitative notions, such as dates and durations, which occur less frequently in text data.[1]

The paradigmatic calculus for reasoning with qualitative temporal relations was introduced by James F. Allen in 1983 [2]. Allen's calculus, the Interval

---

[1] When dates and durations do occur they can be used to infer further qualitative relations: If A occurred in 2020 and B in 2021, then A occurred *before* B.

© Springer Nature Switzerland AG 2021
S. Moschoyiannis et al. (Eds.): RuleML+RR 2021, LNCS 12851, pp. 188–202, 2021.
https://doi.org/10.1007/978-3-030-91167-6_13

Algebra (IA), defines a notion of time interval and 13 basic, but exhaustive, interval relations. More importantly, by considering sets of basic relations, Allen's IA can deal with uncertainty. For instance, using Allen's IA we can say that A occurred either before B *or* during B, that is, we can state "A {*before, during*} B", and draw consequences from such a statement.

The advantages of combining a qualitative temporal reasoning calculus, like Allen's IA, with Semantic Web technologies, such as RDF or OWL, are evident. On the one hand, the type of ontological inference supported by RDFS or OWL can be used to further enrich or restrict the facts derived from the temporal relations. On the other hand, large databases of publicly available linked data, such as WikiData and DBpedia, can be used to bring previously missing facts and temporal relations into the system.

To combine Allen's IA with RDF/OWL a few challenges must be overcome. First, one needs a vocabulary for representing time and the 13 basic interval relations. One popular alternative for this is W3C's OWL-Time [8]; another alternative is tOWL [24]. The second difficulty is the definition of general interval relations, that is, sets of basic interval relations which are used to represent uncertainty; neither OWL-Time nor tOWL support these. The third and more significant difficulty lies in reasoning itself. Reasoning in Allen's IA requires constraint propagation algorithms which cannot be implemented in OWL alone; but can be implemented (though not necessarily efficiently) using rules.

This third difficulty, the efficient implementation of Allen's IA reasoning algorithms using Semantic Web-compatible technologies (specifically, rules), is the focus of this paper. The fundamental reasoning problem of Allen's IA is known to be intractable for the full algebra [31]. But there are subalgebras with fewer relations which are tractable [9,18]. Reasoning with the tractable subalgebras is usually done through a constraint propagation algorithm called *path-consistency* [20,21]. This algorithm can be naturally formulated using Horn clauses, which are directly translatable to a rule language such as SWRL [17]. However, using this approach, it takes $O(n^2)$ rules to implement path-consistency for a subalgebra with n relations, which is not feasible for subalgebras with more than a couple hundred of relations.[2]

In this paper, we present an alternative implementation of the Horn-clause formulation of path-consistency for temporal reasoning over RDF/OWL data. Our implementation uses Apache Jena [30] rules. It circumvents the $O(n^2)$ rule-set growth problem by moving the Allen's IA composition table, which is at the heart of the path-consistency algorithm, from the rules to custom built-ins. Our experimental evaluation shows that, when combined with backward-chaining, our approach not only scales better than traditional implementations but also provides a significant speed-up in the question-answering task. A further advantage of our approach is that it's completely agnostic to the subalgebra used.

To the best of our knowledge, there are no datasets to adequately evaluate a proposal such as ours. So, as an additional contribution of this paper,

---

[2] The direct translation of the Horn-clause formulation of path-consistency to SWRL was proposed by Batsakis et al. in [4,5]. To make the translation practical they adopted a subalgebra with just 29 relations.

we generated a problem set with about 12K problems together with questions and expected answers for two tractable subalgebras of Allen's IA: the Batsakis et al.'s [4,5] 29-relation subalgebra and the pointisable [7,19] subalgebra with 187 relations. The dataset is available under an open-source license.[3] We used this dataset in the evaluation and compared our approach against a vanilla implementation of path-consistency using Jena rules and against Batsakis et al.'s SWRL rules.

The rest of the paper is organized as follows. Section 2 describes Allen's IA, the path-consistency algorithm, and its Horn-clause formulation. Section 3 details our proposal and its implementation. Section 4 presents our experimental setup and results. Section 5 discusses some related work. Section 6 summarizes our contribution and discusses next steps.

2   Background

2.1   Allen's Interval Algebra

The Interval Algebra (IA) is a formalism for representing and reasoning qualitatively about time [2]. The basic entity of Allen's IA is the time interval. An *interval* is an ordered pair of points (x^-, x^+) such that $x^- < x^+$. Given two intervals x and y, their relative position can be described by one of the 13 *basic interval relations* listed in Table 1. It follows from the definition of the 13 basic relations that they are JEPD (jointly exhaustive, pairwise disjoint); that is, given any two intervals, exactly one of the basic relations must hold.

In Allen's IA, uncertainty is represented by sets of basic relations. For instance, the statement $x\{eq, d\}y$ means that interval x coincides (is equal to) *or* occurs during y; that is, $x\{eq, d\}y$ iff $x\,eq\,y$ or $x\,d\,y$. Each such set of basic relations, denotes a *(general) interval relation*. The set $\mathcal{A}$ of all possible interval relations contains $2^{13} = 8192$ members, including the *empty relation* $\varnothing$, which holds for no two intervals, and the *full relation* $\mathbf{A} = \{eq, b, bi, m, mi, o, oi, d, di, s, si, f, fi\}$, which holds for any two intervals.

The following operations are defined on $\mathcal{A}$:

$$x\,(R^-)\,y \quad \text{iff} \quad y\,R\,x \qquad\qquad \text{(converse)}$$
$$x\,(R \cap S)\,y \quad \text{iff} \quad x\,R\,y \text{ and } x\,S\,y \qquad\qquad \text{(intersection)}$$
$$x\,(R \circ S)\,y \quad \text{iff} \quad \exists z\colon x\,R\,z \text{ and } z\,S\,y \qquad\qquad \text{(composition)}$$

for all interval relations $R, S \in \mathcal{A}$ and intervals x, y, and z. The set $\mathcal{A}$ is closed under the three operations and together with them it constitutes an algebra (hence the name "Interval Algebra").

A few remarks about the operations are in order:

1. The converse of R is the relation denoted by the union of the converses of the basic relations in R. E.g., $\{b, mi, o\}^- = \{bi, m, oi\}$.

---

[3] https://github.com/ibm-hyperknowledge/IAPL.

Table 1. The 13 basic interval relations of Allen's IA. (Adapted from [25].)

Basic relation	Symbol	Example	Endpoint relations
x before y	b	xxx	$x^- < y^-$, $x^- < y^+$,
y after x	bi	yyy	$x^+ < y^-$, $x^+ < y^+$
x meets y	m	xxxx	$x^- < y^-$, $x^- < y^+$,
y met-by x	mi	yyyy	$x^+ = y^-$, $x^+ < y^+$
x overlaps y	o	xxxx	$x^- < y^-$, $x^- < y^+$,
y overlapped by x	oi	yyyy	$x^+ > y^-$, $x^+ < y^+$
x during y	d	xxx	$x^- > y^-$, $x^- < y^+$,
y includes x	di	yyyyyyy	$x^+ > y^-$, $x^+ < y^+$
x starts y	s	xxx	$x^- = y^-$, $x^- < y^+$,
y started by x	si	yyyyyyy	$x^+ > y^-$, $x^+ < y^+$
x finishes y	f	xxx	$x^- > y^-$, $x^- < y^+$,
y finished by x	fi	yyyyyyy	$x^+ > y^-$, $x^+ = y^+$
x equals y	eq	xxxx	$x^- = y^-$, $x^- < y^+$,
		yyyy	$x^+ > y^-$, $x^+ = y^+$

2. The intersection of R and S is the relation denoted by the intersection of the corresponding sets. E.g., $\{b, m, o\} \cap \{o, f\} = \{o\}$.
3. The composition of R and S is the relation denoted by the union of the compositions of the pairs of basic relations in the corresponding sets. So, if $R = \{r_1, \ldots, r_n\}$ and $S = \{s_1, \ldots, s_m\}$ then $R \circ S$ is the relation denoted by the union of all $r_i \circ s_j$ for $r_i \in R$ and $r_j \in S$. The composition of basic relations is computed from the definitions in Table 1 and the result is usually arranged in a 13×13 *basic composition table* [2].

A problem in Allen's IA can be given as an *interval graph* where nodes stand for intervals and edges stand for the known relations between intervals. Given an interval graph such as the one in Fig. 1, the fundamental reasoning task of Allen's IA is to determine whether the graph is *consistent* (or *satisfiable*). That is, whether it is possible to assign pairs of points to the nodes

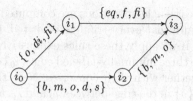

Fig. 1. An interval graph.

such that the restrictions given by the edges are fulfilled.[4] This is the satisfiability problem, ISAT, which is NP-complete [14,31] for the full algebra.

---

[4] Inconsistent graphs are those that contain contradictory statements, such as "$x \{b\} y$ and $y \{b\} x$" (x and y cannot be both, at the same time, "before" each other).

But there is a shortcut. The relations that occur in the above graph are all members of the 29-relation subalgebra defined by Batsakis et al. in [4,5]. This subalgebra is known to be tractable, which means that there are polynomial algorithms to decide ISAT in it—in particular, path-consistency.

2.2 Path-Consistency

Given three edges $x R_1 y$, $y R_2 z$, and $x S z$ in an interval graph, a *triangle operation* consists in replacing S by the relation $S \cap (R_1 \circ R_2)$. A triangle operation is said to *stabilize* if $S = S \cap (R_1 \circ R_2)$. So, after each triangle operation the label of the updated edge is either the same S or a smaller relation. The path-consistency algorithm consists in repeating triangle operations until every such operation stabilizes. At this point, two outcomes are possible:

1. If some edge is labeled by the empty relation $\varnothing$, then the original graph is *inconsistent*.
2. Otherwise, the original graph is said to be *path-consistent* and the resulting graph is equivalent and possibly less redundant than original one.[5]

Also, in case (2), if the set of relations occurring in the resulting graph is contained in some tractable subalgebra [9,18], then the original graph is *consistent* and, depending on the particular subalgebra, the resulting graph is minimal [6,10] (or the strongest implied graph [26]) in the sense that its edges contain no redundant basic relations. (Even if path-consistency does not guarantee minimality for a given subalgebra, it does provide a good approximation, and if the graph is consistent, it is usually this approximation that matters to users.)

The path-consistency algorithm can be formulated axiomatically as follows:

$$\bot \leftarrow x \varnothing y \tag{1}$$

$$x \, \mathbf{A} \, y \leftarrow \top \tag{2}$$

$$y \, R^- \, x \leftarrow x \, R \, y \tag{3}$$

$$x \, (R \cap S) \, y \leftarrow x \, R \, y, \, x \, S \, y \tag{4}$$

$$x \, (R \circ S) \, z \leftarrow x \, R \, y, \, y \, S \, z \tag{5}$$

The triangle operations are computed by rules (4) and (5), while rules (2) and (3) ensure that every triangle is visited. Rule (1) is the inconsistency check.

If we apply these rules exhaustively to the graph of Fig. 1, we eventually get the three minimally-labeled edges $i_0 \{o\} i_1$, $i_0 \{b, m, o, d, s\} i_3$, and $i_1 \{di, si, oi\} i_2$, together with their converses. Note the reduction in uncertainty from $\{o, di, fi\}$ to $\{o\}$ in the edge between i_0 and i_1, and from $\mathbf{A}$ to $\{b, m, o, d, s\}$ and $\{di, si, oi\}$ in the edges between i_0 and i_3 and i_1 and i_2.

In practice, rules (3)–(5) can be seen as schemas. Their implementation in a rule language like SWRL or Jena's requires a rule instance for each choice of R

---

[5] Strictly speaking this is the algorithm for 3-consistency, a notion which is equivalent to the more general notion of path-consistency. It has become standard practice to conflate the two notions [20].

and S in the given subalgebra. So, using this approach, it takes $O(n^2)$ rules to implement path-consistency in a subalgebra with n relations.

3   Proposal and Implementation

Our goal is to eliminate the quadratic growth in the number of rules required to implement path-consistency in rule languages like SWRL and Jena's. We do so by moving the converse, intersection, and composition operations from rules to custom built-ins which operate on a binary representation of the general interval relations. More specifically, we encode each general relation as a 13-bit number which stands for a set of basic relations. For example,

$$0\ \ 0\ \ 0\ \ 1\ \ 0\ \ 1\ \ 0\ \ 1\ \ 0\ \ 1\ \ 0\ \ 1\ \ 0 \quad\text{stands for}\quad \{b, m, o, d, s\},$$
$$\text{\scriptsize fi \quad f \quad si \quad s \quad di \quad d \quad oi \quad o \quad mi \quad m \quad bi \quad b \quad eq}$$

0 stands for the empty relation $\varnothing$, and 8191 stands for the full relation **A**. Using this encoding, the intersection operation can be computed by a simple bitwise "and", and converse and composition can be computed using lookup tables with about 8K and 67M entries each. In our case, we pre-computed these tables using our (still unpublished) qualitative temporal reasoning framework and checked them independently using GQR [12].

To expose the three operations to the rules, we extended Jena's rule system with the five built-ins listed in Table 2.[6] The first two, `allenId` and `allenURI`, convert to and from the 13-bit relation ids and their corresponding URIs. The URIs have the prefix `http://www.ibm.com/timex#` followed by the name of the relation, which is `empty` for $\varnothing$ and `full` for **A**. The remaining relations are named according to the bits set in their numeric ids. For instance, $\{b\}$ is `b`, $\{eq, f, fi\}$ is `eq_f_fi`, and so on. Back in Table 2, the last three built-ins take one or two URIs, apply the corresponding operation, and store the resulting URI on the last variable received as argument.

Table 2. Built-ins for reasoning with Allen's IA.

`allenId(r,i)`	Binds i to the numeric id of the relation with URI r
`allenURI(i,r)`	Binds r to the URI of the relation with numeric id i
`allenConv(r,s)`	Binds s to the converse of r
`allenCap(r,s,t)`	Binds t to the intersection of r and s
`allenComp(r,s,t)`	Binds t to the composition of r and s

With these custom built-ins, path-consistency can be implemented using six Jena rules, as shown in Fig. 2. The first rule (line 2) tells Jena's backward-chaining engine to table all goals. This is necessary to avoid infinite loops. (Most of the rules in Fig. 2 are written in backward style; we will discuss the

---

[6] Before deciding to extend Jena with custom built-ins, we tried to use its math and string manipulation built-ins to implement these operations. But that was really cumbersome, especially due to the lack of built-ins for integer division and modulus.

implications of this in Sect. 4.) The second and third rules (line 4; each -> or <-
introduces one rule) comprise the inconsistency check. They trigger a validation
error whenever an edge with the empty relation is derived. The fourth, fifth,
and sixth rules (lines 6–7, 9–13, and 15–19) derive, respectively, the converse of
an edge, the intersection of two edges, and the composition of two edges. The
reason for requiring that intervals ?x, ?y, and ?z be distinct in these rules is to
avoid self-loops. Also, we require that ?r and ?s be different from $\mathbf{A}$ and $\varnothing$ to
prevent vacuous inferences (e.g., for any r, $\mathbf{A} \cap r = r \cap \mathbf{A} = r$, $\mathbf{A} \circ r = r \circ \mathbf{A} = \mathbf{A}$,
$\varnothing \cap r = r \cap \varnothing = \varnothing$, and $\varnothing \circ r = r \circ \varnothing = \varnothing$).

```
1   @prefix : <http://www.ibm.com/timex#>
2   -> tableAll().
3
4   [(?_ rb:validation on()) -> [(?x rb:violation error('empty relation' ?y)) <- (?x :empty ?y)]]
5
6   [(?y ?ri ?x)
7     <- notEqual(?x ?y), (?x ?r ?y), allenConv(?r ?ri)]
8
9   [(?x ?t ?y)
10    <- notEqual(?x ?y),
11       (?x ?r ?y), notEqual(?r :full), notEqual(?r :empty),
12       (?x ?s ?y), notEqual(?s :full), notEqual(?s :empty),
13       allenCap(?r ?s ?t)]
14
15  [(?x ?t ?z)
16    <- notEqual(?x ?z), notEqual(?y ?z), notEqual(?x ?y),
17       (?x ?r ?y), notEqual(?r :full), notEqual(?r :empty),
18       (?y ?s ?z), notEqual(?s :full), notEqual(?s :empty),
19       allenComp(?r ?s ?t)]
```

Fig. 2. Jena ruleset using the custom built-ins. (For the sake of brevity, the rules listed
here are a simplified version of the rules we actually use in the experiments. The latter
have extra checks to prevent redundant inferences. For example, since intersection is
commutative, to avoid triggering the intersection rule twice, for $r \cap s$ and $s \cap r$, we add
a premise that restricts the comparison to the cases where the id of r is less than the
id of s.)

The ruleset of Fig. 2 is minimalist by design. It does not try to provide an
ontology of time intervals or interval relations. It concerns itself only with the
8192 relations in the "timex" namespace and it assumes nothing about the subjects and objects of these relations. Because of this, it is relatively straightforward to combine this ruleset with different time ontologies, such as OWL-
Time [8] or tOWL [24]. Also, the ruleset is subalgebra-agnostic. It will work for
any subalgebra—the built-ins can operate any of the 8192 relations in $\mathcal{A}$.

To illustrate how these rules are used in practice, consider the RDF document
(in Turtle syntax) of Fig. 3a. This document corresponds to the interval graph of
Fig. 1. With the rules loaded, if we ask Jena to list all relations from i_0 to i_1, we
get the list depicted in Fig. 3b. This list contains the initial relation, :o_di_fi,
but also other relations which were inferred by the rules. The strongest among
these is equal to the intersection of them all, which in this case is :o (overlaps).
So, the strongest thing we can say about the relation between i_0 and i_1 is that
i_0 overlaps i_1.

```
@prefix : <http://www.ibm.com/timex#> .
@prefix i: <http://ex.org/variable#> .

i:0 :o_di_fi i:1.

i:0 :b_m_o_d_s i:2 .

i:1 :eq_f_fi i:3 .

i:2 :b_m_o i:3 .
```

```
> select ?r where {i:0 ?r i:1.}

------------------------------
| r                          |
==============================
| :o_di_fi                   |
| :b_m_o_d_s                 |
| :o                         |
| :eq_b_m_o_oi_d_di_s_si_f_fi |
------------------------------
```

(a)   (b)

Fig. 3. (a) RDF document corresponding to the graph of Fig. 1. (b) Sample SPARQL query and its result.

4 Evaluation

We compared two variations of the ruleset presented of Sect. 3 against (i) corresponding vanilla implementations of path-consistency using Jena rules and (ii) the SWRL ruleset used by Batsakis et al. in [4,5] (available here[7]). We considered two tractable subalgebras: the minimal 29-relation subalgebra introduced by Batsakis et al. and the pointisable subalgebra [7,19] containing 187 relations. To execute the Jena rulesets we used the latest version of Jena extended with our five custom built-ins. The SWRL ruleset was executed on HermiT [13] and Openllet [27] using OWL API [16], and also on Openllet using Jena. (See Sect. 4.4 for the precise versions.)

4.1 Rulesets

Table 3 summarizes the rulesets we used. The Jena rulesets with `builtin` in the name are the ones that use our built-ins. Those with `fw` and `bw` in the name adopt, respectively, forward and backward rule styles. The difference between these two styles is significant, as Jena evaluates them using different rule engines.

Forward rules are evaluated by Jena's RETE-based [11] forward engine, which computes the complete deductive closure at once, as soon as the graph is loaded. This means that, when using forward rules, every consequence is computed even before the first query. So, no reasoning happens during the queries.

When using backward rules, in contrast, reasoning only happens during queries. The backward rules are evaluated by a logic programming (LP) tabled Datalog engine. Given a query, the LP engine translates it into a goal and attempts to solve it using a resolution-style algorithm. The LP engine stops as soon as the goal is solved. So, only the consequences required to solve the goal are computed.

Jena also supports hybrid rules mixing the forward and backward styles. In the rulesets of Table 3, the only place where mixed rules are used is in the rule for validation (e.g., Fig. 2, line 4).

---

[7] https://github.com/sbatsakis/TemporalRepresentations/blob/master/intervals/qualitative-Allen.owl (commit 3656fa5 on Jun 13, 2015).

Table 3. The rulesets used in the experiments.

Ruleset name	Subalgebra	Executor	Style	Num. rules
jena-bw-builtin	any	Jena	backward w. built-ins	6
jena-fw-builtin	any	Jena	forward w. built-ins	4
jena-bw-29	Batsakis et al.'s	Jena	backward	982
jena-fw-29	Batsakis et al.'s	Jena	forward	980
hermit-swrl-29	Batsakis et al.'s	HermiT (via OWL API)	SWRL	982
jena+openllet-swrl-29	Batsakis et al.'s	Openllet (via Jena)	SWRL	982
openllet-swrl-29	Batsakis et al.'s	Openllet (via OWL API)	SWRL	982
jena-bw-187	pointisable	Jena	backward	32511
jena-fw-187	pointisable	Jena	forward	32509

4.2 Problems

To evaluate the rulesets, we generated a set of problems (interval graphs) using our qualitative reasoning framework, which implements the $\mathcal{H}$-model method for generating random interval graphs [25].[8] Since our main interest was in evaluating query performance in Batsakis et al.'s 29-relation subalgebra and in the pointisable subalgebra, we generated only consistent graphs in these two subalgebras. The full problem set (available here[9]) contains about 12K problems, each in three different formats (GQR's format [12], RDF using Batsakis et al.'s vocabulary, and RDF using our "timex" vocabulary).

Most works that present performance evaluations of Allen's IA reasoners use randomly generated interval graphs [3–5,12,23,25]. To the best of our knowledge, there is no comprehensive dataset of real-world problems for the Allen's IA; let alone datasets targeting particular tractable subalgebras of the IA.

In our case, for each subalgebra, we generated consistent problems with sizes ranging from 10 to 200 intervals. Besides the size (number of intervals), in the $\mathcal{H}$-model two other important parameters of a problem are its average degree and its average relation size. The *average degree* is a measure of the average number of non-full edges leaving a node of the graph. The *average relation size* is the average number of basic relations occurring in an edge of the graph. Together with the size, degree and relation size can greatly influence the performance of the reasoner. This is especially true for the degree, which is directly related to the number of non-full edges in the graph.

---

[8] Our qualitative reasoning framework, called QReason, is a generic framework written in Python which adopts an architecture similar to that of GQR [12]. The user specifies a calculus by giving its basic relations and the framework derives the general relations and the calculus properties. Currently, QReason implements two problem generation algorithms. The first, adapted from [25], is a brute-force algorithm. Starting with an empty graph, we add one random edge at a time and check whether the graph is consistent at each step. If the graph becomes inconsistent, we backtrack the last edge choice and try again. The second algorithm, adapted from [20], consists in first generating a random initial solution (set of intervals) and then adding redundant edges until the required parameters of the $\mathcal{H}$-model are met. We used both algorithms to generate the problem set of this paper.

[9] https://github.com/ibm-hyperknowledge/IAPL.

Table 4. Average, minimum, and maximum values of average degree in the different problem groups. (Values rounded to the nearest integer.)

Batsakis et al.'s subalgebra (29 relations)																				
Degree Size	10	20	30	40	50	60	70	80	90	100	110	120	130	140	150	160	170	180	190	200
Avg	6	8	13	25	26	31	37	28	61	36	66	62	58	75	82	78	65	78	98	66
Min	2	1	1	7	9	10	10	4	13	1	14	17	3	2	10	26	5	8	48	4
Max	9	16	28	37	47	58	68	58	89	85	104	106	123	134	144	145	134	160	189	154
Pointisable subalgebra (187 relations)																				
Degree Size	10	20	30	40	50	60	70	80	90	100	110	120	130	140	150	160	170	180	190	200
Avg	6	12	20	16	27	34	34	35	44	49	50	57	62	83	68	73	76	79	139	112
Min	3	5	2	5	3	10	2	5	3	8	21	12	19	14	4	4	10	18	41	8
Max	8	18	28	27	42	59	68	74	82	96	92	117	121	137	148	156	142	129	187	195

For each subalgebra, we selected groups of 10 problems of the same size, with sizes starting at 10 and ending at 200 intervals with increments of 10. This gives a total of 200 problems per subalgebra. To ensure variety in degree and relation size, in each of the groups, the 10 problems were selected with uniform distribution among the available problems. Table 4 lists the average degree of the selected problems. (For instance, the 10 problems of size 20 of the pointisable subalgebra have, on average, an average degree of 12.) The average relation size for these problems fluctuates around 6 basic relations per general relation.

4.3 Queries

Each problem in our problem set is accompanied by a TSV file containing a list of queries which test the edges of the corresponding path-consistent graph. These queries were generated as follows. Immediately after generating each problem, we used our qualitative reasoning framework to compute the corresponding path-consistent graph and then generated a query for each of the edges in this graph (which was also checked using GQR). For instance, here is a line (query) in one of the TSV files:

```
http://ex.org/variable#0 http://www.ibm.com/timex#o http://ex.org/variable#1    1
```

This line states that the reasoner should be able to infer from the associated problem graph that interval 0 overlaps interval 1. (The 1 on the right-hand side means that the query is expected to succeed.)

For each problem, we selected 100 queries from the associated TSV with uniform distribution. This gives a total of 1000 queries for each of the sizes shown in Table 4, or 20K queries in total.

4.4 Environment

The experiments were run on an IBM Cloud's IaaS virtual-machine with 8 CPUs (Intel Xeon Gold 6140 2.30 GHz), 32G RAM, and 25G persistent storage running RedHat Enterprise Linux 8.0 64bit. We used the OpenJDK 11.0.11 with a stack size of 1G, initial heap size of 1G, and maximum heap size of 8G. We used the latest snapshots of Apache Jena 3.18.0[10] (February 8, 2021) and Openllet 2.6.6[11] (May 5, 2021), and the releases 1.4.5.519 of HermiT and 5.1.17 of OWL API.

4.5   Experiments and Results

We run two experiments, one for each subalgebra. Each experiment consisted of 10 runs of 100 queries over the 10 problems in each of the 10–200 groups shown in Table 4. This gives a total of 100 runs per group. Within a same group (e.g., problems of size 10) exactly the same problems and queries were fed to the various rulesets. Figure 4 depicts the average times of the 10 runs. (Note that we adopted a threshold of 900 s, or 15 min, for the runs. That is, if the average time of all runs for a given ruleset gets above 900s, we stop considering it in subsequent size increments.)

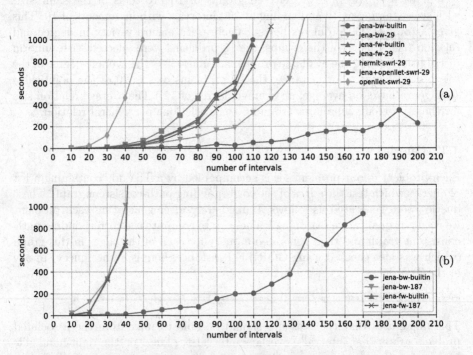

Fig. 4. Average time of 10 runs of 100 queries. (a) Batsakis et al.'s subalgebra (29 relations). (b) Pointisable subalgebra (187 relations).

We also measured the overall accuracy (percentage of correct answers) of each of the rulesets. The results are the following: `openllet-swrl-29` got 96.8%; `hermit-swrl-29` got 97.9%; `jena+openllet-swrl-29` got 98.1%; `jena-bw-29` got 99.6%. The remaining rulesets obtained an accuracy of 100%. We are currently investigating the causes of the incorrect answers given by the `jena-bw-29`

---

[10] https://github.com/apache/jena/tree/jena3.
[11] https://github.com/Galigator/openllet.

ruleset and the SWRL rulesets (which give incomplete answers even for small graphs).

4.6 Discussion

29-relation Subalgebra. In the experiment with the 29-relation subalgebra (Fig. 4a), Openllet and HermiT had the worst performance. Openllet hit the 900s threshold after 50 intervals, while it took 100 intervals to make HermiT hit the same threshold. This is consistent with the results reported in [4].[12]

Overall the Jena rules performed better than the SWRL rules. The SWRL rules running on Openllet via Jena had a similar performance to the forward rules using the custom built-ins (`jena-fw-builtin`). The latter ruleset performed slightly worse than its counterpart without the built-ins (`jena-fw-29`). The explanation for this is in the way forward rules are implemented by the RETE engine, which is similar to the way the lookup tables of the built-ins work, but without the extra overhead of built-in calls and id to URI translations.

The clear winner in Fig. 4a was the backward ruleset using the custom built-ins (`jena-bw-builtin`). Recall that backward rules are evaluated by the logic programming (LP) engine. The LP engine is query-driven and it only infers what is necessary to answer the query. Since the number of queries (100) is small compared to the of number of edges in the problems, the LP engine has to do less work than the forward engine (which always computes everything). This explains the difference between the backward and forward rules, but does not explain the difference between the two versions of the backward rules. It seems that the huge difference in the number of rules really made the difference—6 versus 982 and 32,511 for the 29- and 187-relation subalgebras (see Table 3).

Finally, the point not shown in Fig. 4a for `jena-bw-29` at 140 intervals corresponds to 1314 s. Also in the same figure, the bump at 190 intervals for `jena-bw-builtin` is explained by the average degree of that problem group, 98 (see Table 4), which is higher than the average degree of the surrounding groups. This also explains the bump at 140 in Fig. 4b.

187-relation Subalgebra. In Fig. 4b, the larger number of relations in the subalgebra contributed to amplify the differences between the rulesets. The two forward rulesets had almost the same performance and hit the 900s threshold with graphs of size 50. The points are not shown in Fig. 4b but both, `jena-fw-187` and `jena-fw-builtin`, took on average about 5000 s to answer the 100 questions over 50 intervals. The results of the backward ruleset without the built-ins, `jena-bw-187`, were even worse. It hit the 900 s threshold with just 40 intervals. Actually, 89 of the 100 runs of `jena-bw-187` over 40 intervals failed with a stack overflow error, which usually means that recursion was too deep.

---

[12] In [4], the authors also report being able to reason over 500 intervals under 150s using HermiT, but the exact type of reasoning they consider is not clear and their problem set, which was derived from a dataset of dates of marriages, seems to be easier than the one we are using here.

The clear winner was again the backward ruleset with the custom builtins, `jena-bw-builtin`, which was able to keep the average time below 900s for graphs with up to 160 intervals. This result together with that of Fig. 4a, demonstrate not only the generality of our approach but also its greater scalability when combined with backward-chaining. At the same time, both results also make evident the limits of rule-based reasoning for this type of application (we will have more to say about this in Sect. 6).

5   Related Work

The two papers [4,5] of Batsakis et al. are our principal references. In both papers, the authors present SWRL-based implementations of path-consistency for a tractable fragment of Allen's IA (the 29-relation subalgebra). They also deal with the Point Algebra and RCC (other qualitative calculi for time and space), related quantitative extensions, and the representation of temporal knowledge, which are not our focus here. Two other works by some of the same authors are [28] and [3]. The former extends SOWL, an ontology for spatiotemporal information, with SPARQL primitives for qualitative reasoning, including support for the basic interval relations. Reasoning itself is handled by CHRONOS, introduced in [3], which combines an OWL reasoner with an external Allen's IA reasoner which implements path-consistency. In a sense, the external reasoner of CHRONOS plays the role of our rules plus custom built-ins.

At least two other works use rules for reasoning in Allen's IA. In [29], the authors define ALLEN+, an ontology for representing and reasoning about time. ALLEN+ uses SWRL for reasoning over sets of basic Allen relations, but it adopts an approach which does not coincide with usual definitions and algorithms of Allen's IA—for instance, the authors do not consider tractable subalgebras or the path-consistency algorithm. The second work, [1], is similar. It presents an ontology of time and uses SWRL for reasoning over (extended) basic Allen relations. It also adopts a nonstandard reasoning algorithm. Neither [29] nor [1] present performance evaluations of the proposed rulesets.

The ideas of using sets of JEPD relations to represent uncertainty and of operating these sets using converse, intersection, and composition, which are central to Allen's IA, are also adopted by many other qualitative calculi, including spatial calculi such as RCC. The methods of reasoning in these calculi are thus quite similar to those of Allen's AI. This means that the approach we describe here can be adapted to rule-based qualitative spatial reasoning of the type described in works such as [5] and [15].

6   Conclusion

We presented an approach for practical rule-based qualitative temporal reasoning using Allen's IA. Reasoning in tractable subalgebras of the IA is usually done through path-consistency, a constraint propagation algorithm whose formulation using rules requires $O(n^2)$ rules for a subalgebra with n relations. The approach we propose here avoids this quadratic growth in number of rules by moving the IA composition table from rules to custom built-ins. With this idea, we were able to outperform other rule-based reasoners and more traditional implementations of path-consistency. An additional contribution of the paper is the dataset used in the evaluations, which is publicly available under an open-source license.

As we mentioned at the end of Sect. 4, despite the speed-up enabled by our approach, the results of Fig. 4 highlight the limits of rule-based reasoning for this type of application. The same graphs that caused the rulesets of Fig. 4 to exceed the 15 min threshold are easily handled by specialized solvers, such as GQR [12], which can solve them using path-consistency in no more than a couple of seconds. The main reasons for such a difference in performance are twofold. First, specialized solvers use a matrix representation which allows them to manipulate interval graphs much more efficiently. Second, the triangle operations implemented by such tools actually replace an edge in the graph (instead of adding a new one). Adding a new edge, as it's done in the Horn-clause formulation of path-consistency, has the immediate drawback of increasing the number triangles that need to be considered in subsequent iterations.

We are currently investigating how nonmonotonic reasoning can be used to circumvent this last problem. Also, in the spirit of CHRONOS [3], we are investigating how to combine matrix-based reasoners, such as GQR, and distributed reasoners, such as [23], with the rule-based approach, so that multiple solutions can be combined to reason over RDF/OWL data.

Acknowledgments. This work was partially supported by the DARPA KAIROS program.

References

1. Achich, N., Ghorbel, F., Hamdi, F., Métais, E., Gargouri, F.: Approach to reasoning about uncertain temporal data in OWL 2. Procedia Comput. Sci. **176** (2020)
2. Allen, J.F.: Maintaining knowledge about temporal intervals. Commun. ACM **26**(11) (1983)
3. Anagnostopoulos, E., Batsakis, S., Petrakis, E.G.M.: CHRONOS: a reasoning engine for qualitative temporal information in OWL. Procedia Comput. Sci. **22** (2013)
4. Batsakis, S., Petrakis, E., Tachmazidis, I., Antoniou, G.: Temporal representation and reasoning in OWL 2. Semant. Web **8**(6) (2016)
5. Batsakis, S., Tachmazidis, I., Antoniou, G.: Representing time and space for the semantic web. Int. J. Artif. Intell. Tools **26**(3) (2017)
6. van Beek, P.: Reasoning about qualitative temporal information. Artif. Intell. **58** (1992)
7. Beek, P.V., Cohen, R.: Exact and approximate reasoning about temporal relations. Comput. Intell. **6**(3) (1990)
8. Cox, S.J.D., Little, C.: Time ontology in OWL. Candidate Recommendation, W3C, March 2020
9. Drakengren, T., Jonsson, P.: Towards a complete classification of tractability in Allen's algebra. In: Proceedings of the 15th IJCAI (1997)

10. Dylla, F., et al.: A survey of qualitative spatial and temporal calculi: algebraic and computational properties. ACM Comput. Surv. **50**(1) (2017)
11. Forgy, C.L.: Rete: a fast algorithm for the many pattern/many object pattern match problem. Artif. Intell. **19**, 17–37 (1982)
12. Gantner, Z., Westphal, M., Wölfl, S.: GQR: a fast reasoner for binary qualitative constraint calculi. In: Proceedings of the AAAI WS on Spatial and Temporal Reasoning (2008)
13. Glimm, B., Horrocks, I., Motik, B., Stoilos, G., Wang, Z.: HermiT: an OWL 2 reasoner. J. Automat. Reason. **53**(3) (2014)
14. Golumbic, M.C., Shamir, R.: Complexity and algorithms for reasoning about time: a graph-theoretic approach. J. ACM **40**(5), 1108–1133 (1993)
15. Holzmann, C.: Rule-based reasoning about qualitative spatiotemporal relations. In: Proceedings of 5th International Workshop on Middleware for Pervasive and Ad-Hoc Computing: Held at the ACM/IFIP/USENIX 8th International Middleware Conference. ACM (2007)
16. Horridge, M., Bechhofer, S.: The OWL API: a Java API for working with OWL 2 ontologies. In: Proceedings of the 6th International Conference OWL: Experiences and Directions. CEUR-WS.org (2009)
17. Horrocks, I., Patel-Schneider, P.F., Boley, H., Tabet, S., Grosof, B., Dean, M.: SWRL: a semantic web rule language combining OWL and RuleML. W3C member submission, W3C, May 2004
18. Krokhin, A., Jeavons, P., Jonsson, P.: Reasoning about temporal relations: the tractable subalgebras of Allen's interval algebra. J. ACM **50**(5), September 2003
19. Ladkin, P.B., Maddux, R.D.: On binary constraint networks. Technical report. KES.U.88.8, Kestrel Institute (1988)
20. Ladkin, P.B., Reinefeld, A.: Effective solution of qualitative interval constraint problems. Artif. Intell. **57**(1) (1992)
21. Ligozat, G.: Qualitative Spatial and Temporal Reasoning. Wiley, Hoboken (2012)
22. Llorens, H., Chambers, N., UzZaman, N., Mostafazadeh, N., Allen, J., Pustejovsky, J.: SemEval-2015 task 5: QA TempEval: evaluating temporal information understanding with question answering. In: Proceedings of the 9th International Workshop on Semantic Evaluation. ACL, June 2015
23. Mantle, M., Batsakis, S., Antoniou, G.: Large scale distributed spatio-temporal reasoning using real-world knowledge graphs. Knowledge-Based Syst. **163** (2019)
24. Milea, V., Frasincar, F., Kaymak, U.: tOWL: a temporal web ontology language. IEEE Trans. Syst. Man Cybern. **42**(1) (2012)
25. Nebel, B.: Solving hard qualitative temporal reasoning problems: evaluating the efficiency of using the ORD-Horn class. Constraints **1** (1997)
26. Nebel, B., Bürckert, H.J.: Reasoning about temporal relations: a maximal tractable subclass of Allen's interval algebra. J. ACM **42**(1) (1995)
27. Sirin, E., Parsia, B., Grau, B.C., Kalyanpur, A., Katz, Y.: Pellet: a practical OWL-DL reasoner. J. Web Semant. **5**(2) (2007)
28. Stravoskoufos, K., Petrakis, E.G.M., Mainas, N., Batsakis, S., Samoladas, V.: SOWL QL: Querying spatio-temporal ontologies in OWL. J. Data Semant. **5** (2016)
29. Terziyan, V., Kaikova, O.: Ontology for temporal reasoning based on extended Allen's interval algebra. Int. J. Metadata Semant. Ontol. (2016)
30. The Apache Software Foundation: Apache Jena (2021). https://jena.apache.org/. Accessed 03 Nov 2021
31. Villain, M., Kautz, H.: Constraint propagation algorithms for temporal reasoning. In: Proceedings of the AAAI Conference on Artificial Intelligence (AAAI 1986). AAAI Press (1986)

Logic Rules Meet Deep Learning: A Novel Approach for Ship Type Classification

Manolis Pitsikalis[1]([⊠]) [iD], Thanh-Toan Do[2] [iD], Alexei Lisitsa[1] [iD],
and Shan Luo[1] [iD]

[1] Department of Computer Science, University of Liverpool, Liverpool, UK
{e.pitsikalis,a.lisitsa,shan.luo}@liverpool.ac.uk
[2] Department of Data Science and AI, Monash University, Clayton, Australia
toan.do@monash.edu

Abstract. The shipping industry is an important component of the
global trade and economy, however in order to ensure law compliance and
safety it needs to be monitored. In this paper, we present a novel Ship
Type classification model that combines vessel transmitted data from the
Automatic Identification System, with vessel imagery. The main components of our approach are the Faster R-CNN Deep Neural Network and a
Neuro-Fuzzy system with IF-THEN rules. We evaluate our model using
real world data and showcase the advantages of this combination while
also compare it with other methods. Results show that our model can
increase prediction scores by up to 15.4% when compared with the next
best model we considered, while also maintaining a level of explainability
as opposed to common black box approaches.

Keywords: Object detection · Classification rules · Fuzzy rules

1 Introduction

Nowadays, the combination of deep learning with logic has been attracting a
lot of attention for numerous reasons. On the one hand, deep learning has been
used extensively in different applications, such as object detection [18,19] and
language analytics tasks [3,13] with a lot of success. On the other hand, logic
approaches have been used widely in tasks where explainability is required, such
is the case in certain medical tasks [11], or where expert knowledge is available
and needs to be encoded into a model [5]. However, logic approaches typically
provide crisp predictions over symbolic data, and it is often the case that human
experts are required to express the knowledge into some form of logic. On the
other hand, although deep learning approaches can handle unstructured data
such as text and images, their black box nature makes them inadequate for
tasks where explainability is a key requirement. For these reasons, there is a
need for a model that combines the advantages of deep learning with those of
logic based approaches. In this paper we propose a model that combines deep
learning with logic rules, applied in the shipping domain, for the task of ship
type classification.

S. Moschoyiannis et al. (Eds.): RuleML+RR 2021, LNCS 12851, pp. 203–217, 2021.
https://doi.org/10.1007/978-3-030-91167-6_14

Shipping, since the ancient years, has been a very important component of global trade and economy. However, there are many cases where ships are found to be involved in illegal activities that are possibly dangerous or harmful to the environment. In order to ensure law compliance and safety, shipping needs to be monitored. Today, there is abundance of Maritime data. Systems such as the Automatic Identification System (AIS[1]), a system that allows the transmission of both dynamic spatio-temporal data and static identity data from vessels, CCTV imagery from stationary cameras placed in ports or from cameras in Drones, Satellite Aperture Radar (SAR) images, data from RADAR systems and so on, provide valuable information for the maritime monitoring task. Ships or in general maritime vessels are divided into ship types based on their characteristics and purpose, for example there are fishing vessels, search and rescue vessels, cargo vessels and so on, consequently different regulations apply to each ship type. In order to promote security and abidance to regulations the process of classifying and validating a vessel's type needs to be automated using the data available.

In the context of this paper, we aim to combine two data sources in order to perform ship type classification as illustrated in Fig. 1. We use static vessel transmitted AIS data and a collection of images pre-linked with the AIS records. The main components of our approach are the Faster-RCNN deep neural network and a Neuro-Fuzzy model leveraging convolutional deep features of the former along with AIS information. We evaluate the presented model using real world data and compare it with other algorithms available. The contributions of this paper are:

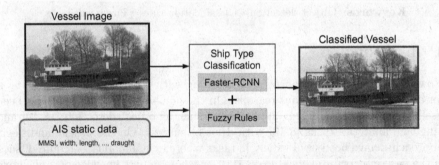

Fig. 1. Pipeline of the Ship Type Classification system.

- a novel classification model that combines images with structured contextual data, in our case vessel images and AIS data for ship type classification,
- a Neuro-Fuzzy approach that can be used to improve classification accuracy in object detection and maintain a level of explainability when additional data is available.

---

[1] http://www.imo.org/en/OurWork/Safety/Navigation/Pages/AIS.aspx.

The paper is organised as follows. In Sect. 2 we present work related to our approach. In Sect. 3 we present material needed for the presentation of our work. Next, in Sect. 4 we describe our methodology, while in Sect. 5 we present our experimental setting and analyse the experiments we performed in our evaluation. Finally, in Sect. 6 we focus on future work and discuss our findings.

2 Related Work

In this section we present works related to the ship type classification task, the combination of logic rules and neural networks and finally the fuzzification of logic rules.

In the recent years, Ship Type classification has attracted a lot of interest. D. Nguyen et al. in [14] present an architecture capable of performing ship type classification and anomaly detection using AIS trajectories. They use an embedding block based on Variational Recurrent Neural Networks (VRNNs) [2] to transform the irregularly shaped AIS data into 10-min sampled structured regimes. Then using the regimes of the embedding block, they perform specific tasks such as trajectory reconstruction, ship type classification, anomaly detection etc. In our approach, instead of using complete trajectories, we choose to use only the information transmitted over the static AIS messages, since complete trajectories are not always available and require a bigger amount of transmitted AIS messages over a period of time. U. Kanjir et al., in another work [9] provide an overview of the available methodologies for vessel detection and classification using SAR imagery along with the most important factors affecting the accuracy of the aforementioned task. According to their overview, the ship detection task comprises of three steps. The first step is to detect whether a vessel exists in an image; the second step is to identify its type, while the third step is the unique identification of the vessel, i.e., finding a unique identifier such as the Maritime Mobile Service Identity (MMSI) number or the International Maritime Organisation (IMO) number. Their analysis focuses on the optical sensors used, the different detection workflows used for detecting vessels in images, the classification methods used, the metrics for evaluation and finally on the importance of combining different types of data sources for better results. We focus on the two first steps of U. Kanjir's et al. ship detection methodology, which are the 'detection of a ship in an image' and 'the identification of its type'.

When it comes to Logic in Neural Networks, Z. Hu et al. in [8], present a way of harnessing knowledge from logic rules in a teacher-student model setting. The goal of their approach is to transfer the human knowledge provided by the rules into the network parameters. They evaluate their rule-knowledge distillation approach in certain Natural Language Analytics tasks and their results show that their approach manages to improve the accuracy compared to other methods. However this approach does not allow any learning in the aspect of the logic rules, since they remain constant during training. In another work, G. Marra et al. [12], integrate first order logic rules with deep learning in both training and evaluation settings. The approach of G. Marra et al. allows the learning of the weights of the neural network and the parameters of the integrated logic rules that are used for reasoning. In order to render the rules suitable for integration they replace conjunction and disjunction with the t-norm and s-norm equivalents. In our approach, we fuzzify the logic rules, with the use of the sigmoidal membership function and use weighted exponential means for the approximation of conjunction and disjunction. The fuzzified rules are then integrated into the neural network architecture, whereby the weights of the disjunction operation are learned.

M. Tsipouras et al. in [20] present a fuzzy model created using rules extracted from a C4.5 Decision Tree that they later fuzzify in a similar way as we do in this paper. They evaluate their optimised fuzzy model on medical data and their results show that they achieve comparable accuracy with an ANN approach. Compared to our approach, instead of using one Decision Tree to extract the logic rules, we use a set of one-vs-all CART classifiers since this method produces specialized rules for each class [6] in our problem. Moreover, we treat our fuzzy model as a way of integrating two sources of information, in the training step the initial fuzzy model is created using one source of information while the parameters of the fuzzy model are computed using both sources, then in the evaluation step both sources of information are required to make a prediction.

3 Preliminaries

The main components of our approach are a Fuzzy model created by extracting rules from a set of Decision Trees, and the Faster R-CNN deep neural network [19]. In what follows, we present the necessary background for our approach.

Decision Tree classifiers are probably the most widely known classifiers in Machine Learning. In their simplest form, they use a binary tree structure, that when traversed in accordance to a part of an input set they produce a conclusion. In our approach we use the Classification and Regression Trees (CART) [1]. The tree growing process of CART tree starts from the root node, containing all the data instances, and recursively continues to its child nodes by choosing at each node the split among all possible univariate splits that makes the instances of its child nodes the purest. Common splitting criteria include the Gini criterion and the Twoing criterion. A node stops splitting when one of the following conditions is satisfied. The node is pure, i.e., all its instances have the same label; the values of the instances in the node are the same; the depth has reached a user specified depth; the number of the instances in the node are less than a user specified threshold or if its splits results in a child node containing a number of instances less than a user defined threshold. Thus, the tree growing process is completed when no further splits can be performed.

Fuzzy Logic as opposed to Boolean Logic produces values ranging from 0 to 1 instead of crisp 0 and 1. However, crisp values can be converted to fuzzy values with the use of fuzzy membership functions. For example, a fuzzy membership function for the comparison of two numbers such as $a > b$ that transforms the True (1) or False (0) result to a value $\in (0, 1)$ can be the sigmoidal membership function $f(a; b, s)$ with a center at b, a slope parameter s and the value of a. Moreover, the logical connectives of conjuction and disjunction in a Logic Formula can be replaced with their fuzzy equivalents such as min and max respectively.

Faster R-CNN [19] is a deep neural network that is used for object detection, that is, the process of identifying and locating objects in images or videos. The architecture of Faster R-CNN consists of a Convolutional Network for feature extraction–usually a pre-trained version of well known image classification network such as ResNet50 [7], a Regional Proposal Network (RPN) that is used for the generation of Regions of Interest (RoIs), and finally a Classification and Regression Network that takes input convolutional features from a RoI pooling layer applied on the features from the Convolutional Network and the ROIs. In our approach we extract convolutional features from the output of the RoI pooling layer of a pretrained Faster R-CNN network corresponding to the detected objects in the input images.

4   Methodology

Here, we present our methodology of combining the information of two data sources of different format—the first source contains images while the second one contains numerical structured data describing attributes of vessels—in order to achieve higher prediction scores and add explainability to the final model.

4.1   Rule Extraction and Fuzzification

As mentioned before the first stage of our method is the extraction of logic rules in Disjunctional Normal Form (DNF). For each class label y, we train a Decision Tree model using the CART algorithm for binary classification where the positive class is y and the remaining are negative. Then, for each class y we parse the corresponding *tree* and recursively create a rule, by adding conditions expressing the path from the root to leaf nodes where the label is y. Therefore, a condition C_i included in the body of the rule concerning label y is expressed as:

$$C_i = (x_1 \ op \ v_1) \wedge \cdots \wedge (x_k \ op \ v_k) \tag{1}$$

where v_i are the values obtained during the splitting process of the tree training; x_i are the values of the attributes on which the constraints are applied and op is either '$>$' or '$\leq$'. A rule R_i for a specific class y_i has the following form:

$$IF \ C_1 \vee \cdots \vee C_n \ THEN \ y_i \tag{2}$$

For the Fuzzification of the rules, we apply the sigmoidal membership function (3) in the comparisons $c_{ij} \in C_i$ so that each comparison c'_{ij} yields a value in $[0, 1]$.

$$f_>(x; s, v) = \frac{1}{1 + e^{-s(x-v)}} \text{ for } x > v \text{ and,} \tag{3}$$

$$f_\le(x; s, v) = \frac{1}{1 + e^{-s(v-x)}} \text{ for } x \le v$$

The s parameter defines the slope of the sigmoid curve while the v parameter defines the 'center' of the curve (see Fig. 2). Moreover, as seen in Eq. (4), for each class rule R_i we add a weight w_i in each of the conditions C_i where $w_i \in [0, 1]$ and $\sum_{i=0}^{n} w_i = 1$.

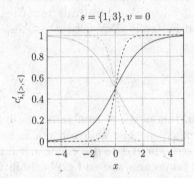

Fig. 2. Plots of $c'_{i,>}$ (blue) and $c'_{i,<}$ (red) with s set to 1 and 3 (continuous and dashed lines respectively) for $x \in [-5, 5]$. (Color figure online)

$$IF \ w_1 C_1 \vee \cdots \vee w_n C_n \ THEN \ y_i \tag{4}$$

Finally, we replace the logical connectives of conjunction and disjunction with their Weighted Exponential Mean approximation [4] as depicted in Table 1, min' and max' respectively. For the experimental results presented in Sect. 5 we have set the level of andness and orness to 'medium high' $r = -5.4$ for conjunctions and $r = 5.4$ for disjunction by taking into consideration the results of the ablation study presented in the same section. Consequently, the truth value of a rule R_i is produced by computing the max' of all the conditions C_i as follows:

$$R_i(x; W, S) = \max' \left\{ w_1 \min'\{c'_{11}, \cdots, c'_{1k}\}, \ldots, w_n \min'\{c'_{n1}, \cdots, c'_{1z}\} \right\} \tag{5}$$

where W is a vector containing the weights of the conditions and S is a vector containing the slope parameters of the sigmoid membership functions included in each C_i. Finally, to make a class prediction, we produce the R_i values for each class y_i and produce the simplex vector by applying $L1$ normalisation on the vector $F_c = \{R_1, \ldots R_m\}$ where m is the number of classes.

Table 1. Approximation of conjunction and disjunction using Weighted Exponential Means. An analysis of the effects of r for WEM can be found in [4].

Notation	WEM
$c_1 \wedge \cdots \wedge c_n$	$\frac{1}{r}\ln\left(\frac{1}{n}\sum_{i=0}^{n} e^{rc_i}\right), r \in \{-14.0, -5.4, -2.14\}$
$w_1C_1 \cdots \vee w_nC_n$	$\frac{1}{r}\ln\left(\sum_{i=0}^{n} w_i e^{rC_i}\right), r \in \{2.14, 5.4, 14.0\}$

4.2 Neuro-Fuzzy Combination

In the previous Section, we mentioned that each class rule R_i accepts as parameters a set of weights W for the weighted max approximation and a set of slopes S for the sigmoid membership functions included in the conditions of the rule. Here, we present how we combine the Fuzzy Model described in Sect. 4.1 with a Neural Network into a single model. The architecture of our combined model is illustrated in Fig. 3.

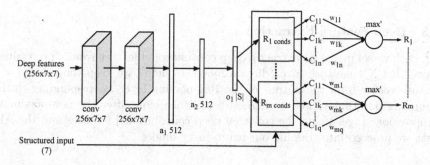

Fig. 3. Architecture of the Neuro-Fuzzy network. The upper branch receives deep features extracted from the RoI pooling layer of a Faster R-CNN model when given a vessel image, while the lower branch receives AIS data (Structured data) that is then given to the different fuzzified rules $R_{i\,conds}$.

In our approach we aim to perform ship type classification by combining the information included in the images of the vessel with the information included in the characteristics of the vessel transmitted over AIS. For this reason, the architecture of our model has two inputs. The first one is the deep convolutional features extracted from the RoI pooling layer of a pre-trained Faster R-CNN model, while the second input includes the values of the AIS fields. In the upper branch of Fig. 3 we use two convolutional layers, where the output of the second layer is flattened and given as input to a fully connected layer a_1 with 512 neurons followed by the fully connected layer a_2, with batch normalization, dropout and ReLu activation, and finally the o_1 layer which has Leaky ReLu as an activation function and yields an output equal to the size of S, i.e., the vector containing the slope parameters of the rules.

Then, using the output of the o_1 layer, along with the rules input (AIS fields) we can now compute the values C_{ij} included in each $R_i, i \in [1, m]$ (see the R_i *conds* blocks in Fig. 3). Next, for each R_i *conds* we create the vector $\{e^{rC_{i1}}, \ldots, e^{rC_{in}}\}$ and feed it into a log activated layer, with bias set to 0 and normalised weights, that computes the approximation of weighted disjunction as follows:

$$R_i = \frac{1}{r} \ln \left(\sum_{j=0}^{n} w_{ij} e^{rC_{ij}} \right) \tag{6}$$

where w_{ij} are the weights of the input and r is the orness level. Finally, all R_i are fed through a *softmax* layer that outputs a probabilistic vector F.

We train the complete neuro-fuzzy model using the cross entropy loss L (Eq. (7)) over F and the one-hot ground truth label $y = \{y_c\}_1^m$.

$$L = -\sum_{c=1}^{m} y_c \log(f_c), \quad F = \{f_1, \ldots f_m\} \tag{7}$$

4.3   Deep Feature Extraction

For each vessel image we extract a deep convolutional feature from a pre-trained Faster R-CNN network in prediction mode. In detail we keep the $256 \times 7 \times 7$ feature vector from the output of the RoI pooling layer, corresponding to the bounding box that yields the highest confidence score after the non-maximum suppression stage. Using the collected deep convolutional features and the AIS data we proceed into training our neuro-fuzzy model.

5   Evaluation

In this section, we present the characteristics of the datasets we use for our experimental evaluation, the experimental settings for the training of our models and finally the prediction scores of the evaluated models.

5.1   Dataset

We construct our dataset using the AIS records from the maritime dataset presented in [17]. In the context of the presented experiments, we use only the 'MMSI', 'to_bow', 'to_stern', 'to_starboard', 'to_port', 'width', 'length' and 'draught' fields of the static AIS messages (see Table 2 for a description of those fields). Moreover, using the 'MMSI' value we collect up to 5 images for each vessel from the IHS Markit World Register of Ships (v12) and the ShipScape photographic library. The collected images contain one vessel per image and have been annotated using the ship type field of the AIS messages and the manual

Table 2. Description of the retained AIS fields.

AIS Field	Description
MMSI	The Maritime Mobile Service Identity number
To {bow, stern, starboard, port}	Distance from the AIS transceiver to the {bow, stern, right side, left side} of the vessel
Draught	The vertical distance between the waterline and the bottom of the hull
Width	The width of the vessel (to bow + to stern)
Length	The length of the vessel (to starboard + to port)

Table 3. Number of instances per class.

Shiptype	Vessels	Images
Cargo	2412	11185
Tanker	864	3950
Other	53	229
Passenger	42	199
Tug	32	139
Total	3403	15702

selection of the bounding box of each ship. Note that there are more images than distinct vessels, since each vessel may have up to 5 images. Using the retained AIS fields and the collected images we create an Image classification centred dataset IC by computing the following natural join:

$$I \underset{\text{I.MMSI=A.MMSI}}{\bowtie} A \tag{8}$$

where I is the image table with the fields 'Image_ID', 'MMSI' and 'df' corresponding to the deep feature of the image while A is the table with the mentioned AIS fields. However, there is also another way of looking at the classification problem. While in the previous case the problem is image centralised, in the current case we focus on the vessels, therefore we create a vessel centred dataset VC by grouping and averaging the deep features per vessel MMSI as follows:

$$A \underset{\text{A.MMSI=I.MMSI}}{\bowtie} \gamma_{\text{MMSI, avg(df)}}(I) \tag{9}$$

The number of different vessels and images per vessel type are presented in Table 3. Note that the numbers presented in Table 3 correspond to records that have images available; records that are incomplete are not used in the experiments. Additionally, we remove all instances of ship types that do not have more than 20 different vessels.

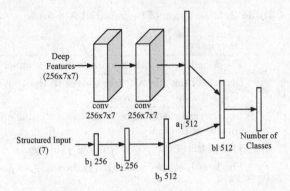

Fig. 4. Architecture of the baseline model. Here, in contrast with the model of Fig. 3, AIS data is given as input to the b_1 layer of the lower branch, while the combination of the different data sources is achieved using the bilinear layer bl.

5.2   Baseline Model

In addition to the Neuro-Fuzzy model presented in this paper, we create the baseline model of Fig. 4 which retains the convolutional branch of the neuro-fuzzy model up to layer a_1 and adds a second branch that accepts as input the AIS fields. The additional branch has one input layer with 7 input neurons and 256 output neurons, followed by two fully connected layers (b_2, b_3) with batch normalization, dropout and ReLu activation. The output of layers a_1 and b_3 is then given as input to the bilinear layer (bl), which has batch normalization, dropout and ReLu activation. Finally, the output of layer bl is fed into a fully connected output layer with *softmax* activation that yields the class prediction.

5.3   Experimental Setup

We extract the IF-THEN rules of the Neuro-Fuzzy model with the methodology of Sect. 4.3 using 75% of table A (minus the 'MMSI' field) and train a Faster R-CNN model, with 'ResNet-50' [7] network as backbone using the corresponding images. Then, we extract the deep feature corresponding to each image using the methodology presented in Sect. 4.3 and create the datasets IC and VC. Finally, we train both the Neuro-Fuzzy model presented in Sect. 4 and the baseline model on the created datasets IC and VC and evaluate them separately.

All models were implemented using PyTorch [16] and were trained for 100 epochs using the Adam optimiser [10] and with learning rate set to 1e−4. The weight decay for Faster R-CNN was set to 5e−4, while for the remaining models weight decay was not applied. The batch size was set to 4 and 32 when training the Faster R-CNN model and the Neuro-Fuzzy/Baseline models respectively. Plots of the losses per model are illustrated in Fig. 5.

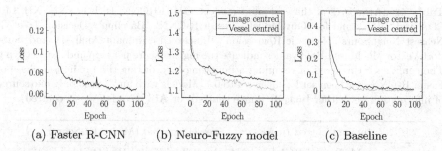

(a) Faster R-CNN   (b) Neuro-Fuzzy model   (c) Baseline

Fig. 5. Plots of the Faster R-CNN (a), the Neuro-Fuzzy model (b) and the baseline (c) losses per epoch number on the Image and Vessel centred (when applicable) training datasets.

5.4   Experimental Results

We evaluate our model on both Image and Vessel centred datasets. In the first case we use the mean Average Precision Metric presented in [15], with interpolation over all recall levels while in the second case we use the macro F1-Score. Some example detections of the Neuro-Fuzzy model are illustrated in Fig. 6. The results of our evaluation are presented in Table 4 and show that the combination of vessel transmitted AIS information along with Imagery using the Neuro-Fuzzy model of this paper yields better results than using each data source separately and using both sources in the baseline model in both Image and Vessel centred datasets. However, although data fusion proves to improve prediction scores, we attribute the low prediction scores to the class imbalance of the dataset, since the lowest mAP and F1 scores where produced by the 'Other' ship type which

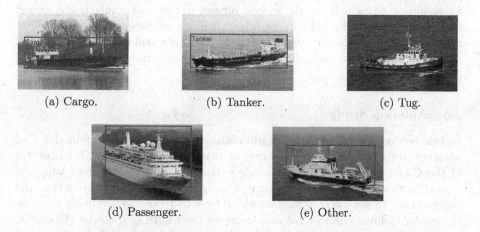

(a) Cargo.   (b) Tanker.   (c) Tug.

(d) Passenger.   (e) Other.

Fig. 6. Example detections. The bounding boxes are produced by the Faster R-CNN network while the detected labels are produced from the Neuro-Fuzzy model of this paper.

Table 4. mAP scores of the evaluated models. OM, FRCNN, B, DT, kNN, NB, LR, LDA and SVM stand for 'Our Model', 'Faster R-CNN', 'Baseline', 'Decision Tree', 'k Nearest Neighbours', 'Logistic Regression', 'Linear Discriminant Analysis' and 'Support Vector Machines'. Bold values indicate the highest score per ship and dataset type. The confidence threshold of retaining a bounding box, during the prediction phase of Faster R-CNN, has been set has been set to 0.7. Models with an '*' used only one source of information i.e., either Images (Image centred) or AIS records (Vessel centred).

	Image Centred (mAP)			Vessel Centred (Macro F1-Score)							
	OM	B	FRCNN*	OM	B	DT*	kNN*	NB*	LR*	LDA*	SVM*
Cargo	91	92	**94**	**97**	97	88	91	74	86	84	82
Tanker	87	84	**93**	94	**95**	72	71	46	46	38	10
Other	**9**	**9**	**9**	**37**	23	27	30	0	22	0	0
Passenger	94	**97**	84	88	**94**	37	22	46	0	28	0
Tug	**67**	59	60	88	18	80	**89**	82	40	22	88
All	**69.6**	68.2	68.0	**80.8**	65.4	60.8	60.6	49.6	38.8	34.4	36.0

expresses a diverse spectrum of vessels but has very few examples in the present case. Moreover, in the image centred dataset, although the score difference is not that significant, our model compared to the other two offers to some degree explainability since a classification decision can be tracked through the rules included in the Neuro-Fuzzy system. An example of an extracted rule and its corresponding fuzzified version used for the classification of the 'Tug' shiptype is presented in Table 5. Table 5 shows that the fuzzified version of condition (e) has the highest weight in the disjunction approximation, while also having the highest accuracy in its crisp form on the full dataset, the same behaviour is observed for condition (d) which has the second biggest weight and similarly the second highest accuracy in the full dataset. The remaining weights although they don't match in order their accuracy on the full dataset, they still manage to generalise and reflect a more accurate view of the whole dataset rather than the training dataset.

5.5   Ablation Study

In this section we present our ablation study on the Neuro-Fuzzy model. Our ablation study evolves around the importance of the max depth (D) parameter of the CART models used for the rule extraction, and the different values of r used in the weighted exponential means approximation for conjunction and disjunction. We set the D parameter for all trees to 10 and we gradually decrease it in order to limit and in most case decrease the length of the rules. Moreover, for each D setting we train the Neuro-Fuzzy model using different levels for andness and orness (r). The results, presented in Table 6, show that small rules

Table 5. Example of an extracted logic rule for the 'tug' shiptype and its fuzzified version included in the trained Neuro-Fuzzy system. 'l', 'w', 'd', 'te', 'to' and 'tb' stand for the 'length', 'width', 'draught', 'to stern', 'to port' and 'to bow' fields of the AIS messages. The first two columns of the upper part of the table correspond to the rule accuracy, i.e., true positive instances over total instances covered by the rule on the training and full versions of the vessel centred dataset.

		Extracted rule	
Train	Full	Conditions	Symbol
		IF	
1	0.26	$(l \leq 27.5 \wedge te \leq 16.0 \wedge d > 3.75 \wedge to > 3.5) \vee$	(a)
0.9	0.54	$(l \leq 57.5 \wedge w \leq 24.0 \wedge d > 3.75 \wedge l > 27.5) \vee$	(b)
1	0.5	$(l \leq 72.5 \wedge l > 57.5 \wedge te > 52.0 \wedge d > 5.0) \vee$	(c)
1	0.57	$(l \leq 76.5 \wedge l > 72.5 \wedge te > 52.0) \vee$	(d)
1	1	$(tb \leq 32.5 \wedge te \leq 106.5 \wedge l > 76.5 \wedge tb > 31.5)$	(e)
		THEN Tug	

	Fuzzified rule	
	Formula	Symbol
$R_{Tug} = \max' \left\{ \begin{array}{l} \\ \\ \\ \\ \\ \end{array} \right.$	$0.1799 \ \min'\{f_{\leq}(l; s_{11}, 27.5), f_{\leq}(te; s_{12}, 16.0),$ $f_{>}(d; s_{13}, 3.75), f_{>}(to; s_{14}, 3.5)\},$	(a)
	$0.1035 \ \min'\{f_{\leq}(l; s_{21}, 57.5), f_{\leq}(w; s_{22}, 24.0),$ $f_{>}(d; s_{23}, 3.75), f_{>}(l; s_{24}, 27.5)\},$	(b)
	$0.1089 \ \min'\{f_{\leq}(l; s_{31}, 72.5), f_{>}(l; s_{32}, 57.5),$ $f_{>}(te; s_{33}, 52.0), f_{>}(d; s_{34}, 5.0)\},$	(c)
	$0.2242 \ \min'\{f_{leq}(l; s_{41}, 76.5), f_{>}(l; s_{42}, 72.5),$ $f_{>}(te; s_{43}, 52.0)\},$	(d)
	$0.3835 \ \min'\{f_{\leq}(tb; s_{51}; 32.5), f_{\leq}(te; s_{52}, 106.5),$ $f_{>}(l; s_{53}, 76.5), f_{>}(tb; s_{54}, 31.5)\}$	(e)

produced by $D = 4$ setting tend to give lower scores. On the other side, over fitted rules (max height set to 10) produce high scores but sacrifice performance due to the increase of parameters. The best score was produced using a depth set to 6. The study shows that 'medium high' levels of andness and orness, i.e., $r = -2.14, +2.14$ produce worse results than the 'high' and 'very high' settings. This is because in the 'medium high' setting the model tends to over fit on the training data thus yielding the best training accuracy but loses generalisation. In the 'very high' setting the model produces better results however the best score is produced using the 'high' setting.

Table 6. F1-Macro scores of the Neuro Fuzzy model produced on the validation set of the Vessel Centred dataset using different parameters for r and D. The lower part of the table contains the number of comparisons and conditions included in the extracted rules of each model.

	$D = 4$	$D = 6$	$D = 8$	$D = 10$
Very high $r = 14$	72	74	73	76
High $r = 5.4$	74	81	78	77
Medium high $r = 2.14$	69	71	72	76
# comparisons	60	264	607	1126
# conditions	18	58	110	178

6   Conclusions and Future Work

We presented a methodology that can be used to combine AIS data with vessel Imagery along with the advantages of our Neuro-Fuzzy model over the baseline model and using each data source separately as show cased by the experimental evaluation. We believe that the logic rules extracted by the decision trees add information over the dependencies between the AIS fields, and thus providing additional information in the combined Neuro-Fuzzy model. Although our methodology has been applied in the maritime domain, we believe that it can be also applied in other domains where multiple sources of information are available.

For future work, we aim to evaluate our Neuro-Fuzzy approach when there is uncertainty or missing fields in the input data, while also investigating further the explainability of our model. Moreover, we want to extend our methodology, so that it handles multiple vessels in an image by automatically linking the AIS transmitted information with the corresponding vessel in the image.

Acknowledgements. This work has been funded by the Engineering and Physical Sciences Research Council (EPSRC) Centre for Doctoral Training in Distributed Algorithms at the University of Liverpool, and Denbridge Marine Limited (https://www.denbridgemarine.com), United Kingdom.

References

1. Breiman, L., Friedman, J., Olshen, R., Stone, C.J.: Classification and Regression Trees. Wadsworth and Brooks, Monterey (1984)
2. Chung, J., Kastner, K., Dinh, L., Goel, K., Courville, A., Bengio, Y.: A recurrent latent variable model for sequential data. In: NIPS, pp. 2980–2988. MIT Press, Cambridge (2015)
3. Collobert, R., Weston, J.: A unified architecture for natural language processing: deep neural networks with multitask learning. In: ICML, pp. 160–167. Association for Computing Machinery, New York (2008). https://doi.org/10.1145/1390156.1390177

4. Dujmović, J.J., Larsen, H.L.: Generalized conjunction/disjunction. Int. J. Approx. Reason. 423–446 (2007). https://doi.org/10.1016/j.ijar.2006.12.011

5. Grosan, C., Abraham, A.: Rule-based expert systems. In: Grosan, C., Abraham, A. (eds.) Intelligent Systems. ISRL, vol. 17, pp. 149–189. Springer, Heidelberg (2011). https://doi.org/10.1007/978-3-642-21004-4_7

6. Hashemi, S., Yang, Y., Mirzamomen, Z., Kangavari, M.: Adapted one-versus-all decision trees for data stream classification. IEEE Trans. Knowl. Data Eng. **21**, 624–637 (2009). https://doi.org/10.1109/TKDE.2008.181

7. He, K., Zhang, X., Ren, S., Sun, J.: Deep residual learning for image recognition (2016). https://doi.org/10.1109/CVPR.2016.90

8. Hu, Z., Ma, X., Liu, Z., Hovy, E., Xing, E.: Harnessing deep neural networks with logic rules. In: ACL, Berlin, Germany, pp. 2410–2420. Association for Computational Linguistics (2016). https://doi.org/10.18653/v1/P16-1228

9. Kanjir, U., Greidanus, H., Oštir, K.: Vessel detection and classification from spaceborne optical images: a literature survey. Remote Sens. Environ. 1–26 (2018). https://doi.org/10.1016/j.rse.2017.12.033

10. Kingma, D.P., Ba, J.: Adam: a method for stochastic optimization (2014)

11. London, A.J.: Artificial intelligence and black-box medical decisions: accuracy versus explainability. Hastings Cent. Rep. **49**(1), 15–21 (2019). https://doi.org/10.1002/hast.973

12. Marra, G., Giannini, F., Diligenti, M., Gori, M.: Integrating learning and reasoning with deep logic models. In: Brefeld, U., Fromont, E., Hotho, A., Knobbe, A., Maathuis, M., Robardet, C. (eds.) ECML PKDD 2019. LNCS (LNAI), vol. 11907, pp. 517–532. Springer, Cham (2020). https://doi.org/10.1007/978-3-030-46147-8_31

13. Mikolov, T., Sutskever, I., Chen, K., Corrado, G., Dean, J.: Distributed representations of words and phrases and their compositionality. In: NIPS, pp. 3111–3119. Curran Associates Inc., Red Hook (2013)

14. Nguyen, D., Vadaine, R., Hajduch, G., Garello, R., Fablet, R.: A multi-task deep learning architecture for maritime surveillance using AIS data streams. In: IEEE DSAA, pp. 331–340 (2018). https://doi.org/10.1109/DSAA.2018.00044

15. Padilla, R., Netto, S.L., da Silva, E.A.B.: A survey on performance metrics for object-detection algorithms, pp. 237–242 (2020). https://doi.org/10.1109/IWSSIP48289.2020.9145130

16. Paszke, A., et al.: Automatic differentiation in pytorch (2017)

17. Ray, C., Dréo, R., Camossi, E., Jousselme, A.L., Iphar, C.: Heterogeneous integrated dataset for maritime intelligence, surveillance, and reconnaissance. Data in Brief, p. 104141 (2019). https://doi.org/10.1016/j.dib.2019.104141

18. Redmon, J., Divvala, S., Girshick, R., Farhadi, A.: You only look once: unified, real-time object detection (2016). https://doi.org/10.1109/CVPR.2016.91

19. Ren, S., He, K., Girshick, R., Sun, J.: Faster R-CNN: towards real-time object detection with region proposal networks, vol. 28 (2015)

20. Tsipouras, M., et al.: Automated diagnosis of coronary artery disease based on data mining and fuzzy modeling. IEEE Trans. Inf. Technol. Biomed. **12**(4), 447–458 (2008). https://doi.org/10.1109/TITB.2007.907985

An Evaluation of Meta-reasoning over OWL 2 QL

Haya Majid Qureshi[✉][iD] and Wolfgang Faber[iD]

University of Klagenfurt, Klagenfurt, Austria
{haya.qureshi,wolfgang.faber}@aau.at

Abstract. There has been increasing interest in enriching ontologies with meta-modeling and meta-querying for the past few years. Unfortunately, the Direct Semantics for OWL2 and SPARQL does not support meta-constructs in a satisfactory way: While meta-axioms (involving identifiers used both as a class and an individual) can be syntactically expressed using punning, different occurrences of the same identifier will be treated as different entities. For example, GoldenEagle used as an instance of EndangeredSpecies and also as a class containing individuals, will be treated as two separate, unrelated entities. Meta-queries (for example, asking for classes that also occur as individuals) are not allowed at all in SPARQL under the Direct Semantics Entailment Regime. To overcome this, a new semantic flavour for SPARQL, called Meta-modeling Semantics Entailment Regime (MSER), has been introduced. In previous work, Cima et al. have proposed a reduction from OWL 2 QL (a light-weight profile of OWL 2) and associated meta-queries in SPARQL to query answering over Datalog rules. In this paper, we experiment with various logic programming tools that support Datalog querying to determine their suitability as back-ends to MSER query answering. These tools stem from different logic programming paradigms (Prolog, pure Datalog, Answer Set Programming). Our work shows that the Datalog approach to MSER querying is practical also for sizeable ontologies.

Keywords: Meta-reasoning · SPARQL · Datalog

1 Introduction

For the past few years there has been an urge for enriching ontologies with meta-modelling and meta-querying. Meta-modelling allows for expressing meta-concepts (classes are instances of other classes) and meta-properties (relation between meta-concepts), and therefore makes conceptual modelling more flexible, as argued for instance in [1,17]. Meta-querying ports this idea to queries as well, allowing the use of the same variable in positions of different types.

The de-facto standard language for ontologies, OWL 2, syntactically allows for meta-modelling by means of Punning[1], using the same name for ontology

---

[1] http://www.w3.org/2007/OWL/wiki/Punning.

S. Moschoyiannis et al. (Eds.): RuleML+RR 2021, LNCS 12851, pp. 218–233, 2021.
https://doi.org/10.1007/978-3-030-91167-6_15

elements of different type (most notably, class and individual). However, the prevalent Direct Semantics (DS) does not interpret punning in the way intended by meta-modelling, as it will interpret the different occurrences of the same name as different entities.

To remedy these limitations, Higher-Order Semantics (HOS) was introduced in [13] for DL-Lite$_\mathcal{R}$, which is a low-complexity family of Description Logics. DL-Lite$_\mathcal{R}$ forms the basis for the OWL 2 profile OWL 2 QL, which is geared towards Ontology-Based Data Access (OBDA) that focuses on querying ontologies with less complicated axioms, but in combination with larger amounts of data. Query answering tasks in DL-Lite$_\mathcal{R}$ and OWL 2 QL require logarithmic space with respect to data complexity [18]. The interpretation structure of HOS follows Hilog-style semantics, which allows the elements in the domain to have polymorphic characteristics. Data complexity of HOS stays in $\mathbf{AC}^0$ for answering unions of conjunctive queries. In subsequent work [14,15] HOS is referred to as Meta-modelling Semantics (MS), we will adopt this terminology in this paper as well.

Similar considerations apply to meta-querying as well. SPARQL is the de-facto standard ontology query language. The logical underpinning for SPARQL queries over OWL 2 QL ontologies is defined by the *Direct Semantics Entailment Regime* (DSER) [7]. As the name implies, DSER relies on the Direct Semantics for ontologies and therefore imposes typing constraints on both the ontologies and queries that make meta-querying impossible. To remedy this, the Meta-modelling Semantics Entailment Regime (MSER) was proposed in [3], which does allow meta-modelling and meta-querying using SPARQL over OWL 2 QL.

In [3] a reduction from query-answering over OWL 2 QL to Datalog queries is provided, and experimental results using two Datalog engines, Logicblox and Rdfox, are reported. Datalog is an attractive target, as it has received increased academic interest with renewed tool support over the last few decades, see for instance [4,10]. In this work, we continue the line of [3] and explore several other tools that are capable of answering Datalog queries, relying on diverse foundations and techniques. Indeed, [3] have used Logicblox and Rdfox (which we also include in our analysis for reference), but it turns out that other tools perform very well, too, especially in meta-modelling scenarios, which were not considered in the performance analysis reported in [3]. In [16], meta-modelling and meta-querying in OWL 2 QL under MSER is discussed and evaluated as well, however the tested implementations do not rely on the Datalog characterization of [3].

The main contributions of this work can be summarised as follows:

- We implemented the rewriting/reductions of [3] and adapted it to support several languages of tools that extend Datalog (Prolog, Answer Set Programming).
- We evaluated the performance of the Datalog-based MSER approach using various tools as backends that support Datalog.
- In the evaluation, we considered both meta-modelling ontologies and meta-queries.

- The evaluation showed that the Datalog-based MSER approach is effective also for sizeable ontologies.

Concerning the structure of the remainder of this paper, Sect. 2 introduces the background notions like OWL 2 QL, SPARQL, MSER, and Datalog. Section 3 recalls the rewriting technique presented in [3]. Section 4 illustrates the series of experiments we have carried out using the LUBM and MODEUS ontologies and present a detailed discussion about the experiments. Section 5 concludes the paper with a brief discussion and pointing out the future work.

2   Background

In this section we recall the preliminary notions that are needed for the rest of the paper, in particular OWL 2 QL under the Meta-modelling Semantics (MS), SPARQL, and Datalog.

2.1   OWL 2 QL Under the Meta-modelling Semantics

We start by recalling some basic elements that are used to represent knowledge in an ontology: *Concepts*, a set of individuals with common properties, *Individuals*, objects of a domain of discourse, and *Roles*, a set of relations that relate the individuals. Based on these elements, the OWL 2 QL vocabulary V constituted by the tuple: $V = (V_N, V_C, V_{OP}, V_{DP}, V_I, V_{DT}, L_{QL})$. In V, V_N is a set of Internationalised Resource Identifiers (IRIs), the set of names of all entities in the ontology plus the keywords of OWL 2 QL; V_C, V_{OP}, V_{DP}, V_I and V_{DT} are subsets of V_N used to denote the entities of type concept names, object property names, data property names, individuals, and datatypes; and L_{QL} denotes the set of literals in OWL 2 QL. An OWL 2 QL Knowledge Base $\mathcal{O}$ is a pair $\langle T, A \rangle$, where T is the TBox (non-assertional axioms) and A is a ABox (assertion axioms). Sometimes $\mathcal{O}$ is also considered as the union of T and A, and it is assumed to be finite. The axioms allowed in an OWL 2 QL ontology are listed in the α columns of Table 1 (in Description Logic syntax).

The Meta-modelling Semantics (MS) [13] is based on the idea that every entity in V_N may simultaneously have more than one type, so it can either be a class, or an individual, or data property, or an object property or a data type. To formalise this idea, the Meta-modelling Semantics had been defined for OWL 2 QL as follows. The meta-modelling semantics for $\mathcal{O}$ over V is based on the notion of interpretation structure, constituted by a tuple $\mathcal{I} = \langle \Delta, \cdot^I, \cdot^C, \cdot^P, \cdot^D, \cdot^T, \cdot^{\mathcal{I}} \rangle$, where Δ is the disjoint union of the two non-empty sets: $\Delta = \Delta_o \cup \Delta_v$, and Δ_o is the object domain, and Δ_v the value domain; $\cdot^I : \Delta_o \to True, False$ is a total function for each object $d \in \Delta_o$, which indicates whether d is an individual; if $\cdot^C, \cdot^P, \cdot^D, \cdot^T$ are undefined for some d, then we require $d^I = True$; $\cdot^{\mathcal{I}}$ is a function that maps every expression into Δ_o and every literal into Δ_o; all functions $\cdot^C : \Delta_o \to \mathcal{P}(\Delta_o)$, $\cdot^P : \Delta_o \to \mathcal{P}(\Delta_o \times \Delta_o)$, $\cdot^D : \Delta_o \to \mathcal{P}(\Delta_o \times \Delta_v)$, and $\cdot^T : \Delta_o \to \mathcal{P}(\Delta_v)$ are partial.

The semantics of logically implied axioms are defined in accordance with the notion of axiom satisfaction with the interpretation $\mathcal{I}$. Moreover, $\mathcal{I}$ is said to be a model of $\mathcal{O}$ if it satisfies all axioms of $\mathcal{O}$. Finally, an axiom α is said to be logically implied by $\mathcal{O}$, denoted as $\mathcal{O} \models \alpha$, if it holds for every model of $\mathcal{O}$.

2.2 SPARQL

As query language, for simplicity we consider conjunctive SPARQL queries, restricted to **SELECT** queries. It is sufficient for our purposes to describe result forms by set of variables.

A conjunctive *SPARQL* query q is of the form

$$SELECT\ ?v_1\ \cdots\ ?v_n\ WHERE\ \{\ t_1\ .\ \ldots\ .\ t_m\ \}$$

where $?v_1 \cdots ?v_n$ is a space-separated sequence of query variables and $t_1.\ldots.t_m$ is a sequence of triples separated by dots, where triples are either elements of V_N or SPARQL variables. All $?v_i$ must occur in $t_1.\ldots.t_m$.

Given an ontology $\mathcal{O}$ and a conjunctive SPARQL query q as above, then the answers to q are the tuples $\langle ?v_1\sigma, \ldots, ?v_n\sigma \rangle$, where σ is a substitution that maps all query variables in q to elements of V_N such that $\mathcal{O} \models t_i\sigma$ for all $1 \le i \le m$ under the Meta-modelling Semantics.

This is the standard behaviour of SPARQL queries, but here we explicitly use MS as the underlying semantics and we also allow meta-queries.

For instance,

$$SELECT\ ?y\ WHERE\ \{\ ?x\ \textit{rdf:type}\ ?y\ .\ \ ?y\ \textit{rdf:type}\ ?z\ \}$$

will return all classes that are themselves members of another class.

2.3 Datalog

Datalog is a declarative query language rooted in logic programming. A Datalog program is a finite set of rules, where a rule r has the form

$$h \leftarrow b_1, \ldots, b_n.$$

In r, h is the rule head and $b_1, \ldots, b_n$ is the rule body. Each of b_i and h are atoms of the form $p(t_1, \ldots, t_n)$, where p is a predicate symbol and t_i are *terms* that can be *constants* or *variables*; n is the arity of p. We say that r is a fact if it has an empty body and omit the symbol $\leftarrow$ in that case. The body can be thought of a conjunction. Rules need to satisfy safety in order to be domain independent, so each variable occurring in the rule head must also occur in the rule body.

For a Datalog program P, the Herbrand Base $HB(P)$ consists of all atoms that can be formed using predicates and constants in P. An interpretation $I \subseteq HB(P)$ consists of those atoms that are true in I. A rule r is satisfied if $h \in I$ whenever $\{b_1, \ldots, b_n\} \subseteq I$, and an interpretation I is a model of a program P

if all of its rules are satisfied. the semantics of P is given by the subset-minimal model of P.

A conjunctive query $q_1, \ldots, q_n$? consists of atoms as in Datalog rules, and the answers with respect to a program P are those substitutions σ (mapping variables in the query to constants) such that $\{q_1\sigma, \ldots, q_n\sigma\} \subseteq M$ for the subset-minimal model M of P.

3   Query Answering Under MSER to Datalog Evaluation

In this section, we recall query answering under the Meta-modelling Semantics Entailment Regime (MSER) from [3]. This technique reduces SPARQL query answering over OWL 2 QL ontologies to the Datalog query answering. Note that here we do not consider ontologies containing data properties for the sake of simplicity. The main idea of this approach is to define (i) a translation function τ mapping OWL 2 QL axioms to Datalog facts and (ii) a fixed rule base $\mathcal{R}^{ql}$ that captures inferences in OWL 2 QL reasoning.

The reduction employs a number of predicates, which are used to encode the basic axioms available in OWL 2 QL. This includes both axioms that are explicitly represented in the ontology (these will be added to the Datalog program as facts resulting from the mapping τ) and axioms that logically follow (these will be derivable by the fixed rules $\mathcal{R}^{ql}$). In a sense, this representation is closer to a meta-programming representation than other Datalog embeddings that translate each axiom to a rule.

Table 1. τ Function

	α	$\tau(\alpha)$	α	$\tau(\alpha)$
$\mathcal{P}_{\mathcal{O}}^{ql,\mathcal{T}}$	$c1 \sqsubseteq c2$	isacCC(c1, c2)	$r1 \sqsubseteq \neg r2$	disjrRR(r1,r2)
	$c1 \sqsubseteq \exists r2^-.c2$	isacCI(c1, r2, c2)	$c1 \sqsubseteq \neg c2$	disjcCC(c1,c2)
	$\exists r1 \sqsubseteq \exists r2.c2$	isacRR(r1,r2,c2)	$c1 \sqsubseteq \neg \exists r2^-$	disjcCI(c1,r2)
	$\exists r1^- \sqsubseteq c2$	isacIC(r1,c2)	$\exists r1 \sqsubseteq \neg c2$	disjcRC(r1,c2)
	$\exists r1^- \sqsubseteq \exists r2.c2$	isacIR(r1,r2,c2)	$\exists r_1 \sqsubseteq \neg \exists r2$	disjcRR(r1,r2)
	$\exists r1^- \sqsubseteq \exists r2^-.c2$	isacII(r1,r2,c2)	$\exists r1 \sqsubseteq \neg \exists r2^-$	disjcRI(r1,r2)
	$r1 \sqsubseteq r2$	isarRR(r1,r2)	$\exists r1^- \sqsubseteq \neg c2$	disjcIC(r1,c2)
	$r1 \sqsubseteq r2^-$	isarRI(r1,r2)	$\exists r1^- \sqsubseteq \neg \exists r2$	disjcIR(r1,r2)
	$c1 \sqsubseteq \exists r2.c2$	isacCR(c1,r2,c2)	$\exists r1^- \sqsubseteq \neg \exists r2^-$	disjcII(r1,r2)
	$\exists r1 \sqsubseteq c2$	isacRC(r1,c2)	$r1 \sqsubseteq \neg r2^-$	disjrRI(r1,r2)
	$\exists r1 \sqsubseteq \exists r2^-.c2$	isacRI(r1,r2,c2)	irref(r)	irrefl(r)
	refl(r)	refl(r)		
$\mathcal{P}_{\mathcal{O}}^{ql,\mathcal{A}}$	c(x)	instc(c,x)	$x \neq y$	diff(x,y)
	r(x, y)	instr(r,x,y)		

The function τ used to encode the OWL 2 QL assertions α as facts is summarised in Table 1. For a given ontology $\mathcal{O}$, we will denote the set of facts obtained by applying τ to all of its axiom as $\mathcal{P}_{\mathcal{O}}^{ql}$; it will be composed of two portions $\mathcal{P}_{\mathcal{O}}^{ql,\mathcal{T}}$ and $\mathcal{P}_{\mathcal{O}}^{ql,\mathcal{A}}$, as indicated in Table 1.

The fixed Datalog program $\mathcal{R}^{ql}$ can be viewed as an encoding of axiom saturation in OWL 2 QL. The full set of rules provided by authors of [3] are reported in online repository mentioned in Sect. 4. We will consider one rule to illustrate the underlying ideas:

$$\text{isacCR(c1,r2,c2) :- isacCC(c1,c3), isacCR(c3,r2,c2)}$$

The above rule encodes the following inference rule:

$$\mathcal{O} \models c1 \sqsubseteq c3,\ \mathcal{O} \models c3 \sqsubseteq \exists r2.c2 \Rightarrow \mathcal{O} \models c1 \sqsubseteq \exists r2.c2$$

In other words, if c1 is a subclass of c3 and c3 is a subclass of everything that has an r2-successor in c2, then also c1 is a subclass of everything that has an r2-successor in c2.

Finally, the translation can be extended in order to transform conjunctive SPARQL queries under MS over OWL 2 QL ontologies into a Datalog query. For example, consider the following query that retrieves all triples $\langle a, b, c \rangle$, where a is a member of class b that is a subclass of c:

```
SELECT ?x ?y ?z WHERE {
        ?x rdf :type ?y.
        ?y rdfs :SubClassOf ?z
}
```

then it can be translated to a Datalog query

$$\text{instc(X,Y), isacCC(Y,Z)?}$$

In general, these queries will be translated into a rule plus an atomic query to account for projections. The previous example will be translated to

$$\text{q(X,Y,Z)} \leftarrow \text{instc(X,Y), isacCC(Y,Z).}$$
$$\text{q(X,Y,Z)?}$$

The slightly modified query
```
SELECT ?y WHERE {
        ?x rdf :type ?y.
        ?y rdfs :SubClassOf ?z
}
```
will accordingly be translated to

$$\text{q(Y)} \leftarrow \text{instc(X,Y), isacCC(Y,Z).}$$
$$\text{q(Y)?}$$

4 Experiments

In this section we describe the experiments that we have conducted, including the tools we used, the ontologies and queries we considered, and report on the outcomes. All material is available at https://git-ainf.aau.at/Haya.Qureshi/mhf-algo-testing.

4.1 Tools

We have implemented the translation of ontology axioms summarised in Table 1 in Java. We should point out that this implementation is not optimised and serves as a proof of concept. For the Datalog back-end, we have used six tools in our experiments. These tools stem from different logic paradigms like Prolog, pure Datalog, Answer Set Programming and Hybrid-Knowledge Bases. In the following, we briefly describe each of these tools.

RDFox[2] is an in-memory, scalable, centralised data engine for Resource Description Framework (RDF) data models. The tool supports the current standard querying language SPARQL 1.1. It also allows for reasoning and representing knowledge in rules, supporting materialisation-based parallel Datalog reasoning. RDFox uses parallel reasoning algorithms to support Datalog reasoning over RDF data. It had already been used in the performance analysis reported in [3].

LogicBlox[3] is another state-of-the-art Datalog engine to unify the models of the program and allow applications to automate and enhance their decision making via a single expressive declarative language. For this purpose, the authors have introduced an extended form of Datalog called *LogiQL*, which is expressive enough to allow coding of entire applications. LogicBlox implements many deductive database techniques, among them a magic set technique. Also this tool had been used in [3].

XSB[4] is a logic programming engine and language rooted in Prolog. It supports Prolog's standard functionality, and features a powerful technique called tabling, which significantly increases its applicability. In 'large classes of programs, also covering Datalog, tabling avoids infinite loops and meets known optimal complexity for query answering. Since it relies on a top-down technique, its internals are significantly different from RDFox and LogicBlox.

Clingo[5] is an ASP system used to ground and solve logic programs. Answer Set Programming (ASP) [2] is a declarative programming paradigm that applies non-monotonic reasoning and relies on the stable model semantics [6]. Over the past decades, it has attracted considerable interest thanks to its accessible syntax, expressiveness and efficient systems implementations. Clingo exhibits exceptional performance in numerous domains, including industrial, robotics and biomedical applications [5].

---

[2] https://www.oxfordsemantic.tech/product.
[3] https://developer.logicblox.com/.
[4] https://xsb.com/.
[5] https://potassco.org/.

DLV[6] is another ASP system with particular emphasis on Disjunctive Logic Programming. It offers several front-ends with high expressivity intending to capture the practical problems in the presence of incomplete knowledge. It is a general-purpose system that can deal with extensive input data, hard search, and problems of relatively high complexity. Contrary to Clingo, DLV implements a magic set technique for query answering.

NoHR[7], the Nova Hybrid Reasoner allows to query a combination of DL ontologies and non-monotonic rules in a top down fashion. It is a variant of [11] based on the well-founded semantics for logic programming and stays in polynomial time complexity (when used with polynomial-complexity ontologies). *NoHR* combines the capabilities of many DL reasoners like *ELK*[8], *Hermit*[9], *Konclude*[10] with **XSB**. We have included NoHR because we wanted to assess the overhead it produces with respect to XSB, as the agenda for our future work includes leveraging hybrid tools like NoHR for meta-modelling and meta-querying.

4.2   Tool-Specific Settings

In this section we provide a brief overview of the experimental setup of the tools considered in this work. We have used the set of inference rules $\mathcal{R}^{ql}$ reported online and the translation of ontology axioms as specified in Table 1, produced by our implementation. One observation is that the tools slightly differ in the Datalog syntax they require and thus needed minor adjustments. For instance, LogicBlox uses <- instead of :-, and also variables are denoted in different ways in the various input languages.

RDFox needed some major adjustments. We have first used tuple tables, which RDFox provides for importing external data from relational databases and making it compatible with RDF. In particular, we have written atoms with binary predicates as triples and other predicates as tuple tables. Queries in RDFox are already in SPARQL, but we needed to use TT for the non-binary predicates. However, this setup turned out to be very slow, orders of magnitudes slower than the results reported in [3].

We then contacted the authors of [3] who sent us the code they used in their experiments. Indeed, they only used triples and used Skolem functions for representing atoms with non-binary predicates as triples. The way to write Skolem functions had also changed in RDFox in the meantime, which meant that we also needed to make some slight updates there with the help of the RDFox team.

The encoding is as follows: An atom R(x,y,z) is re-written as BIND(rdfox: SKOLEM("f",x,y,z) AS ?T3) ⇒ T1(t3,x), T2(t3,y), and T1(t3,z), where

---

6 https://dlv.demacs.unical.it/.

7 https://nohr.di.fct.unl.pt/documentation.html.

8 http://www.cs.ox.ac.uk/isg/tools/ELK/.

9 http://www.hermit-reasoner.com/.

10 https://www.derivo.de/en/products/konclude/.

`rdfox:SKOLEM` creates a Skolem term with functor `"f"` and parameters `x,y,z` and then bound the Skolem term to a variable `?T3` via the built-in predicate `BIND`. The following rule shows the translation of one of the property axioms of Department0 from the LUBM ontology.

```
    :instr1[?T,"takesCourse"],
      :instr2[?T,"UndergraduateStudent385"],
        :instr3[?T,"Course41"] :-
rdfox:SKOLEM("f","takesCourse","UndergraduateStudent385","Course41"
,?T).
```

For querying, we of course need to incorporate the `:inst*` in the query as well, for example:

SELECT $?y$ WHERE {
       $?T$: $instr1$ "$takesCourse$".
       $?T$: $instr2$ "$UndergraduateStudent385$".
       $?T$: $instr3$ $?y$
}

Concerning XSB, at first we used regular tabling and declared all predicates like this:

$$:- table\ p/n.$$

The query execution was quite slow, so we contacted the XSB development team, and got the suggestion to use subsumptive tabling instead. This allows for better reuse of previously computed answers, and is declared as:

$$:- table\ p/n\ as\ subsumptive.$$

We noticed that the execution for subsumptive tabling was much faster than for standard tabling.

XSB and RDFox are the only tools for which we applied any manual optimisations, all other tools received the same input, except for variations due to language syntax.

4.3   Experiment Datasets

This section describes the ontologies used in the experiments. We often refer to the ontologies as datasets.

Datasets: Our experiments are based on the widely used Lehigh University Benchmark (LUBM) dataset [9] and Making Open Data Effectively USable (MODEUS) Ontologies[11]. Instead of creating a new benchmark from scratch, we decided to build our experiments on top of the **LUBM** and **MODEUS** datasets and queries.

The **LUBM** datasets describe a university domain with information like departments, courses, students, and faculty. This dataset comes with 14 queries

---
[11] http://www.modeus.uniroma1.it/modeus/node/6.

with different characteristics (low selectivity vs high selectivity, implicit relationships vs explicit relationships, small input vs large input, etc.).

The **MODEUS** ontologies describe the *Italian Public Debt* domain with information like financial liability or financial assets to any given contracts [16]. It comes with 8 queries. These queries are pure meta-queries as they span over several levels of the knowledge base. MODEUS ontologies are meta-modelling ontologies with meta-classes and meta-properties.

Problem Sizes: Although **LUBM** is a fairly simple ontology, it captures existentially quantified knowledge. It comes with a predefined data generator to generate random sizes of $\mathcal{A}$, which can be used to test the system ability of handling data of varying sizes. We have used LUBM(1) consisting of 43 classes, 32 properties and 10334 axioms and LUBM(9) consisting of 43 classes, 32 properties and 79501 axioms. In **MODEUS**, there are four ontologies: The first ontology **MEF_00** contains 93 classes, 11 properties, 26298 individuals, 163884 axioms. The second ontology **MEF_01** contains 93 classes, 11 properties, 33301 individuals, 205902 axioms. The third ontology **MEF_02** contains 98 classes, 11 properties, 26302 individuals, 163991 axioms. The fourth ontology **MEF_03** contains 98 classes, 11 properties, 30304 individuals, 188003 axioms.

4.4   Results

We ran all experiments on Ubuntu 20.04.2 LTS x86_64 with an Intel Xeon E5645 processor with 32 GB of RAM. For simplicity, we have not included queries that contain the data properties in our experiments.

We have not explicitly mentioned the translation time of the ontology axioms. It takes up to several seconds for the MODEUS ontologies because the translation implemented in this work is a prototype and not optimised. We believe that a more streamlined implementation should have negligible runtime for the ontologies considered here.

We next report the results on different datasets, first LUBM with standard queries, followed by meta-queries over LUBM, then moving towards meta-modelling.

LUBM with Standard Queries. In Table 2 we have reported the results for two different $\mathcal{A}$ sizes of the LUBM ontology. All times reported in these tables are in seconds and include loading the Datalog program including facts and rules and answering the query. The best performance for each query is highlighted in boldface.

We can observe that performance is generally good. We can see, however, that NoHR generally introduces significant overhead, which we did not really expect on this scale. It is not fully clear to us yet what causes this; the ontology part is empty and therefore we would have expected performance to be similar to XSB. It might be that the tabling strategy is to blame, but this is just a conjecture. There is one instance in which XSB is slower than NoHR (q9 on LUBM(9)),

Table 2. LUBM with standard queries under MSER (execution times in seconds)

	q1	q2	q3	q5	q6	q7	q9	q10	q11	q12	q13	q14
						LUBM(1)						
RDFox	3.10	3.06	3.07	3.07	3.10	3.10	3.11	3.07	3.09	3.10	3.09	3.08
LogicBlox	0.46	0.50	0.46	0.43	0.42	0.41	0.41	0.41	0.42	0.42	0.41	0.41
XSB	0.46	2.36	0.33	**0.13**	**0.11**	0.71	28.22	0.46	**0.10**	**0.10**	0.45	**0.11**
Clingo	0.27	0.27	0.27	0.27	0.27	0.27	0.27	0.27	0.27	0.27	0.27	0.27
DLV	**0.21**	**0.22**	**0.21**	0.21	0.21	**0.22**	**0.22**	**0.21**	0.21	0.22	**0.21**	0.21
NoHR	48.53	51.35	47.73	49.44	49.22	48.56	63.14	47.29	48.80	48.64	50.74	49.00
						LUBM(9)						
RDFox	55.73	55.33	57.12	55.55	57.33	56.30	56.46	55.99	58.10	56.86	55.78	57.18
LogicBlox	**0.42**	**0.42**	**0.42**	**0.43**	**0.51**	**0.42**	**0.43**	**0.43**	**0.41**	**0.41**	**0.41**	**0.49**
XSB	20.03	420.1	14.782	18.1	1.13	32.38	15143	20.03	9.62	1.48	19.87	1.12
Clingo	2.13	2.14	2.15	2.13	2.15	2.13	2.16	2.13	2.14	2.15	2.15	2.15
DLV	1.43	1.48	1.43	1.43	1.41	1.46	1.49	1.43	1.42	1.45	1.43	1.41
NoHR	2742	3013	2658	2876	2717	2688	10714	2788	2785	2767	2705	2635

but performance on this query is generally bad and a different indexing strategy might be the cause for this artefact.

Across all queries and ontology sizes, LogicBlox exhibits the most regular performance with roughly the same execution time for all queries, independent on the ontology size, which is quite remarkable. Also DLV and Clingo have very regular performance, but the time is affected slightly by the size of the dataset. RDFox is also regular across different queries, but is quite a bit affected by the size of the dataset. XSB shows varying performance also with different queries over the same ontology. While it is the fastest system on some queries over LUBM(1), it is among the slowest on other queries. This becomes more pronounced for LUBM(9), where XSB is still quick for a few queries, but really slow on others.

LUBM with Meta-queries. We have also considered the meta-queries $mq1$, $mq4$, $mq5$, and $mq10$ from [12] as they contain variables in-property positions and are long conjunctive queries. We have also considered two special-case queries $sq1$ and $sq2$ from [3] to exercise the MSER features and identify the new challenges introduced by the additional expressivity over the ABox queries. Basically, in special-case queries, we check the impact of DISJOINTWITH and meta-classes in a query. For this, like in [3], we have introduced a new class named $TypeOfProfessor$ and make $FullProfessor$, $AssociateProfessor$ and $AssistantProfessor$ an instance of this new class and also we define $FullProfessor$, $AssociateProfessor$ and $AssistantProfessor$ to be disjoint from each other. Then, in $sq1$ we are asking for all those y and z, where y is a professor, z is a type of professor and y is an instance of z. In $sq2$, we have asked for different pairs of professors.

It can be seen in Table 3 that the overall performance of meta-query evaluation is similar to the one in Table 2. LogicBlox has again the most regular performance (with only one outlier). Clingo and DLV have regular performance over varying queries over the same ontology, but are slightly affected by the

Table 3. LUBM with meta-queries (execution times in seconds)

	mq1	mq4	mq5	mq10	sq1	sq2
LUBM(1)						
RDFox	3.10	3.07	3.07	3.07	3.24	3.12
LogicBlox	1.20	0.48	0.66	0.48	0.49	0.51
XSB	4.06	**0.08**	0.30	0.37	0.26	0.23
Clingo	0.29	0.27	0.27	0.27	0.30	0.27
DLV	**0.22**	0.21	**0.24**	**0.21**	**0.21**	**0.21**
NoHR	42.65	36.06	39.83	37.54	34.30	36.85
LUBM(9)						
RDFox	56.90	57.15	56.83	57.32	56.48	55.28
LogicBlox	**0.59**	**0.49**	**1.32**	**0.55**	**0.50**	**0.48**
XSB	11.55	11.57	11.57	10.39	29.03	29.42
Clingo	2.38	2.14	2.20	2.14	2.21	2.22
DLV	1.59	1.48	1.63	1.46	1.43	1.38
NoHR	2585.64	2508.12	2478.39	2497.81	2449.69	2494.37

ontology size. Similar comments apply to RDFox, but it is overall slower and performance deteriorates more. XSB and NoHR show somewhat more regular performance here, but it still varies over queries and deteriorates with the ontology size.

MODEUS Queries. Table 4 shows the second part of the experiments, where we used the four MODEUS ontologies. Both LogicBlox and Clingo were not able to compute answers with the given resources.

LogicBlox took more than 3 h and was still increasing memory and disk space consumption. The tool created huge amounts of "workbooks". We conjecture that the ontology causes many rules to be applicable and that, different from the LUBM scenario, the magic set technique is not effective for some reason here, which would have the potential to curb these inferences. It might be connected to the meta-modelling axioms in the MODEUS ontologies and the meta-queries posed.

Clingo, on the other hand, produces an error while grounding which indicates that the system ran out of identifiers for ground atoms. Apparently the problem gives rise to a ground program that is too large for Clingo. It is interesting, though, that there was no out-of-memory error before this happened. Unfortunately there seems to be no way of circumventing this. Clingo does not employ any magic set technique, which could have helped in this case.

It is clear that DLV is the best overall performer in Table 4. Its performance is very regular and consistently quick. We assume that the magic set technique implemented in DLV as a huge impact here; but it is not clear to us why Log-

Table 4. MODEUS with meta-queries (execution times in seconds)

	mq0	mq1	mq2	mq3	mq4	mq5	mq6	mq8
MEF-0								
RDFox	1616.38	1621.34	1614.11	1589.49	1560.19	1581.07	1578.59	1579.52
XSB	23.70	22.71	27.53	23.37	19.64	29.54	38.57	19.32
NoHR	315.42	391.33	1166.03	339.13	130.07	604.46	174.88	122.51
DLV	**7.29**	**7.91**	**10.13**	**7.36**	**6.39**	**8.12**	**6.52**	**6.33**
MEF-1								
RDFox	2665.04	2675.29	2664.07	2578.67	2620.52	2574.85	2621.15	2617.17
XSB	142.84	137.12	137.26	138.19	135.47	139.08	150.74	136.09
NoHR	451.52	645.25	1806.51	501.93	262.71	982.62	298.18	253.02
DLV	**9.08**	**9.99**	**12.8**	**9.23**	**7.90**	**10.18**	**7.97**	**7.88**
MEF-2								
RDFox	1621.40	1598.74	1576.13	1602.90	1606.77	1598.88	1576.26	1576.96
XSB	23.93	22.83	28.30	23.75	19.56	29.80	41.00	19.77
NoHR	317.89	489.96	1220.96	350.82	131.16	628.47	176.83	123.22
DLV	**7.34**	**8.08**	**10.68**	**7.48**	**6.33**	**8.17**	**6.49**	**6.32**
MEF-3								
RDFox	2387.96	2417.88	2436.00	2381.75	2422.03	2386.42	2427.03	2414.71
XSB	42.39	40.10	47.30	41.21	35.99	49.55	60.11	36.96
NoHR	373.41	566.01	1772.28	422.93	170.77	904.71	219.16	167.49
DLV	**8.94**	**9.71**	**12.89**	**9.12**	**7.75**	**10.30**	**8.13**	**7.87**

icBlox (which is also supposed to implement one) cannot profit from it. A possibility is that different sideways information passing strategies (SIPS) are used.

XSB also shows comparatively regular performance, but less so than DLV. It is interesting to see that XSB cannot profit more from its top-down strategy; it is possible that tabling is actually slowing it down in these examples. As in the LUBM experiments, NoHR suffers from quite severe overhead compared to XSB, but it is actually less pronounced here than for the LUBM queries.

Finally, RDFox is actually the worst performer in this benchmark (not considering Clingo and LogicBlox). Already for LUBM it was not performing as well as we oped, even though we used a specifically optimised program. Still, it appears that the "triples with Skolem term solution" performs better than the native Datalog encoding, but still creates a lot of overhead in the system. We suppose that the system is optimised towards traditional triple stores and not this kind of triples.

There are also some considerations concerning the nature of the MODEUS ontologies. (1) As mentioned earlier, the MODEUS dataset consists of meta-layers, which appear to cause many tools to do more inferencing, (2) the meta-queries consist of different layers of classes, instances and properties, which span over several layers of the dataset, and (3) lastly, we think the presence of many *disjoint* axioms causes especially many inferences.

We have also tried the only other OWL 2 QL reasoner that supports the Meta-Modelling Semantics that we are aware of, MQ-Mastro[12]. It allows meta-querying over ontologies that contain meta-modelling. MQ-Mastro offers two query evaluation algorithms, NAIVE and Lazy Meta-Grounding (LMG) [16]. We have used LMG as it is a generalisation of NAIVE based on lazy grounding. The system comes with a Graphical User Interface (GUI) and unfortunately we did not succeed to run it in batch mode, so we were not able to accurately measure its execution times. The results are somewhat mixed: loading and preprocessing took several minutes, but once this was done, answering queries is practically instantaneous.

So for scenarios in which a lot of queries are to be answered over the same ontology, or in which the ontology can stay loaded, MQ-Mastro might be a better choice, but in most other scenarios the Datalog approach can work better.

5 Discussion and Conclusion

In this paper we provided both a brief theoretical background and an evaluation of a method for answering SPARQL queries over OWL 2 QL ontologies under Meta-Modelling Semantics via a reduction to evaluating Datalog queries. Related to this work are [8,12,19], which consider OWL 2 QL ontologies under DSER and show that it is decidable and can be reduced to Datalog evaluation. However, those works do not consider meta-modelling and meta-querying. In [13,14], the authors overcome the limitations of querying over OWL 2 QL ontologies via introducing the Meta-modelling Semantics and show that their proposed algorithm tackles the untyped querying problem in PTime w.r.t. data and ontology complexity.

Our work is based on [3], which presented the reduction to Datalog, argued its correctness, and analysed complexity. The main contribution of our paper is that it expands the performance analysis in [3] considerably. On the one hand, we do consider the MODEUS ontologies that involve meta-axioms, and on the other and we evaluate more tools that support Datalog query answering.

Indeed, our experiments show that especially DLV, but also XSB appear to be promising back-ends for meta-querying over OWL 2 QL ontologies. Surprisingly, neither RDFox nor LogicBlox coped very well with the MODEUS ontologies that involve meta-modelling, while LogicBlox performed very well on LUBM queries. Also, RDFox does not seem to be a particularly good fit for this particular kind of application. Also Clingo seems to be not particularly well-suited for query answering of this particular kind. Lastly, the overhead created by NoHR appears quite prohibitive in this scenario. While we did not expect it to perform better than XSB, we hoped to be using it for future work.

---

[12] http://www.modeus.uniroma1.it/modeus/node/6.

This future work is to use hybrid reasoning for answering meta-queries. The idea would be to translate only parts of the ontology to Datalog and do some of the reasoning with ontology tools. Having originally targeted NoHR for this, the results of the experiments show us that the reasons for NoHR's performance need to be explored carefully before continuing in this direction. Also, we intend to test lazy grounding systems such as *Alpha* [20] in the future.

References

1. Brasileiro, F., Almeida, J.P.A., Carvalho, V.A., Guizzardi, G., et al.: Expressive multi-level modeling for the semantic web. In: Groth, P. (ed.) ISWC 2016. LNCS, vol. 9981, pp. 53–69. Springer, Cham (2016). https://doi.org/10.1007/978-3-319-46523-4_4
2. Brewka, G., Eiter, T., Truszczyński, M.: Answer set programming at a glance. Commun. ACM **54**(12), 92–103 (2011)
3. Cima, G., De Giacomo, G., Lenzerini, M., Poggi, A.: On the SPARQL metamodeling semantics entailment regime for OWL 2 QL ontologies. In: Proceedings of the 7th International Conference on Web Intelligence, Mining and Semantics, pp. 1–6 (2017)
4. De Moor, O., Gottlob, G., Furche, T., Sellers, A. (eds.): Datalog 2.0 2010. LNCS, vol. 6702. Springer, Heidelberg (2012). https://doi.org/10.1007/978-3-642-24206-9
5. Gebser, M., Kaminski, R., Kaufmann, B., Schaub, T.: Answer Set Solving in Practice. Synthesis Lectures on Artificial Intelligence and Machine Learning. Morgan and Claypool Publishers (2012)
6. Gelfond, M., Lifschitz, V.: The stable model semantics for logic programming. In: Kowalski, R., Bowen, K. (eds.) Proceedings of the Fifth International Conference and Symposium of Logic Programming (ICLP 1988), pp. 1070–1080. MIT Press (1988)
7. Glimm, B., et al.: Using SPARQL with RDFS and OWL entailment. In: Polleres, A. (ed.) Reasoning Web 2011. LNCS, vol. 6848, pp. 137–201. Springer, Heidelberg (2011). https://doi.org/10.1007/978-3-642-23032-5_3
8. Gottlob, G., Pieris, A.: Beyond SPARQL under OWL 2 QL entailment regime: rules to the rescue. In: Twenty-Fourth International Joint Conference on Artificial Intelligence (2015)
9. Guo, Y., Pan, Z., Heflin, J.: LUBM: a benchmark for owl knowledge base systems. J. Web Semant. **3**(2–3), 158–182 (2005)
10. Huang, S.S., Green, T.J., Loo, B.T.: Datalog and emerging applications: an interactive tutorial. In: Proceedings of the 2011 ACM SIGMOD International Conference on Management of Data, pp. 1213–1216 (2011)
11. Knorr, M., Alferes, J.J., Hitzler, P.: Local closed world reasoning with description logics under the well-founded semantics. Artif. Intell. **175**(9–10), 1528–1554 (2011)
12. Kontchakov, R., Rezk, M., Rodríguez-Muro, M., Xiao, G., Zakharyaschev, M., et al.: Answering SPARQL queries over databases under OWL 2 QL entailment regime. In: Mika, P. (ed.) ISWC 2014. LNCS, vol. 8796, pp. 552–567. Springer, Cham (2014). https://doi.org/10.1007/978-3-319-11964-9_35
13. Lenzerini, M., Lepore, L., Poggi, A.: A higher-order semantics for OWL 2 QL ontologies. In: Description Logics (2015)
14. Lenzerini, M., Lepore, L., Poggi, A.: Answering metaqueries over HI (OWL 2 QL) ontologies. In: IJCAI, pp. 1174–1180 (2016)

15. Lenzerini, M., Lepore, L., Poggi, A.: A higher-order semantics for metaquerying in OWL 2 QL. In: Fifteenth International Conference on the Principles of Knowledge Representation and Reasoning (2016)
16. Lenzerini, M., Lepore, L., Poggi, A.: Metaquerying made practical for OWL 2 QL ontologies. Inf. Syst. **88**, 101294 (2020)
17. Motik, B.: On the properties of metamodeling in OWL. J. Log. Comput. **17**(4), 617–637 (2007). https://doi.org/10.1093/logcom/exm027
18. Motik, B., et al.: OWL 2 web ontology language profiles. W3C Recommendation 27, 61 (2009)
19. Poggi, A.: On the SPARQL direct semantics entailment regime for OWL 2 QL. In: Description Logics (2016)
20. Weinzierl, A.: Blending lazy-grounding and CDNL search for answer-set solving. In: Balduccini, M., Janhunen, T. (eds.) LPNMR 2017. LNCS (LNAI), vol. 10377, pp. 191–204. Springer, Cham (2017). https://doi.org/10.1007/978-3-319-61660-5_17

cl-psoatransrun: An Efficiently Executable Specification of PSOA RuleML in Common Lisp

Mark Thom[1]([⊠])([iD]), Harold Boley[2]([iD]), and Theodoros Mitsikas[3]([iD])

[1] RuleML, Fredericton, Canada
[2] University of New Brunswick, Fredericton, Canada
[3] National Technical University of Athens, Athens, Greece
`mitsikas@central.ntua.gr`

Abstract. The open-source `cl-psoatransrun` system, a realization for reasoning in PSOA RuleML is discussed. `cl-psoatransrun`, written in Common Lisp follows the paradigm of functional programming for the central transformation steps, necessary for translating the object- and graph-oriented PSOA syntax to relational Prolog clauses. We describe the parsing of the PSOA RuleML presentation syntax, and we provide a detailed analysis of the transformation steps. `cl-psoatransrun` can serve as an alternative of the reference implementation PSOATransRun, providing both fast translation times and feature parity. Additionally, the flexibility of the transformation functions provides an ideal environment for developing the PSOA RuleML specification.

1 Introduction

The active development of a rule language poses a series of challenges. The specification of the language drives the development of the systems implementing it. Technical limitations of the programming languages and the tools used for these implementations often hinder the development of the specification. During the development of PSOATransRun [13], a reasoner for the multi-paradigm – particularly, graph-relational – data and rule language Positional-Slotted Object-Applicative RuleML (PSOA RuleML) [4,5], we were limited by the rigidity of its toolchain of Java and ANTLR. This prompted us to search for an alternative toolchain to assist us in the concurrent development of the specification and the implementation of PSOA RuleML language. Consequently, we developed `cl-psoatransrun`, a realization of the PSOA RuleML rule and data language written in Common Lisp (CL). `cl-psoatransrun` currently targets XSB Prolog and Scryer Prolog as client logic engines. Serving as a second realization of PSOA RuleML, it is a parallel implementation effort to the PSOATransRun system, the latter being implemented primarily in the Java programming language.

In Memoriam Harold Boley, who passed away before the composition of this manuscript. All faults and inaccuracies belong to his co-authors.

© Springer Nature Switzerland AG 2021
S. Moschoyiannis et al. (Eds.): RuleML+RR 2021, LNCS 12851, pp. 234–249, 2021.
https://doi.org/10.1007/978-3-030-91167-6_16

CL is well-known for its productivity, performance, and expressive power [8]. Its powerful meta-programming capabilities have enabled the CL community to keep the decades-old CL programming language at pace with the latest innovations from the object-oriented, reflective and functional programming communities, each of whose paradigms is natively supported by CL. There is a rich history of implementing other languages in CL, an attraction again owed to its nearly unrivaled support for meta-programming.

`cl-psoatransrun` was created to harness these strengths to allow for the fast implementation of, and experimentation with, the syntax and semantics of PSOA RuleML, a language with many planned but as-yet fluid or incomplete features. CL has long had efficient native support for many present and planned features of PSOA RuleML, most prominently in its support for symbolic computation and functional programming. This confluence of features greatly reduces the effort required to implement PSOA RuleML in CL as compared to that required in languages lacking those features.

CL's functional programming sub-language is especially applicable to the transformation stages used to compile PSOA programs into Prolog programs, so that they may be loaded into a client Prolog system and queried against. These stages were originally defined in the formal language of recursive functions and their semantics-preserving properties proved in [12]. As such, one can closely transcribe these transformations into a suitably equipped (functional) programming language such as CL where they can be realized as plain parameterized functions.

For these reasons, we consider `cl-psoatransrun` to be a declarative, executable and efficient specification of PSOA RuleML. "Efficiency" refers here to both machine execution time and the number of source lines of code (SLOC) composing `cl-psoatransrun`. Our (primarily) functional style of implementation is not only tersely expressive but also compiles down to highly performant native code produced by the free open source CL compiler Steel Bank Common Lisp (SBCL) [2]. The KB and query translation and execution times of `cl-psoatransrun` often considerably undercut those of the primarily Java-based PSOATransRun; we give benchmarks comparing the performance of PSOATransRun and `cl-psoatransrun` on a few publicly available PSOA RuleML KBs in a later section of this paper.

The rest of the paper is organized as follows: Sects. 2 and 3 provide an overview of the PSOA RuleML presentation syntax and the `cl-psoatransrun` system, respectively. The parsing of the PSOA Presentation Syntax (PS) is discussed in Sect. 4. Section 5 describes the functional implementation of Abstract Syntax Tree (AST) transformations while Sect. 6 discusses how the resulting transformed ASTs are translated to Prolog queries, whose (Prolog) solutions are pretty-printed back to PSOA PS. Section 7 presents an overview of `cl-psoatransrun` performance. Finally, Sect. 8 concludes the paper and proposes future research directions.

2   PSOA RuleML Presentation Syntax Overview

PSOA RuleML allows for an atom to be with or without an Object IDentifier (OID)—typed by the predicate—while the predicate arguments (descriptors) can be tupled, slotted, or tupled and slotted. Moreover, a descriptor can be either dependent on the predicate and attached to the OID, or independent, attached only to the OID [5].

A fact concerning a purchase involving three parties can be represented e.g., as a relationship (i.e., a single-tupled atom without OID):

```
purchase(John Mary Fido)
```

where the tuple `John Mary Fido` serves as an abridged form of the predicate-dependent tuple `+[John Mary Fido]`. The general form of a dependent-tupled-only atom is as follows:

$$\textbf{Oidless:}\quad \text{f}(\, +\, [\text{t}_1 \,\ldots\, \text{t}_n])$$
$$\textbf{Oidful:}\ \text{o\#f}(\, +\, [\text{t}_1 \,\ldots\, \text{t}_n])$$

The `purchase` predicate can be alternatively represented using dependent slots:

```
purchase(buyer+>John seller+>Mary item+>Fido)
```

In this case, the three slots (or alternatively, unordered key-value pairs) are dependent on the predicate, coupled to a system-generated Skolem constant OID.

A variant of the above with an OID could be as follows:

```
transaction200#purchase(buyer+>John seller+>Mary item+>Fido)
```

The general form of this multi-slotted atom is

$$\textbf{Oidless:}\quad \text{f}(\text{p}_1\text{+>}\text{v}_1 \,\ldots\, \text{p}_k\text{+>}\text{v}_k)$$
$$\textbf{Oidful:}\ \text{o\#f}(\text{p}_1\text{+>}\text{v}_1 \,\ldots\, \text{p}_k\text{+>}\text{v}_k)$$

The general psoa atom form can homogeneously integrate relationships and frames, dependent and independent descriptors, and being multi-tupled. This form is shown in the following example, where he superscripts indicate subterms that are part of dependent ("+") vs. independent ("-") descriptors [5]:

$$\text{o\#f}(\, +\, [\text{t}_{1,1}^{+} \ldots\, \text{t}_{1,n_1^+}^{+}] \ldots\, +\, [\text{t}_{m^+,1}^{+} \ldots\, \text{t}_{m^+,n_m^+}^{+}]$$
$$-\,[\text{t}_{1,1}^{-} \,\ldots\, \text{t}_{1,n_1^-}^{-}] \,\ldots\, -\,[\text{t}_{m^-,1}^{-} \,\ldots\, \text{t}_{m^-,n_m^-}^{-}]$$
$$\text{p}_1^+\text{+>}\text{v}_1^+ \,\ldots\, \text{p}_{k^+}^+\text{+>}\text{v}_{k^+}^+$$
$$\text{p}_1^-\text{->}\text{v}_1^- \,\ldots\, \text{p}_{k^-}^-\text{->}\text{v}_{k^-}^-)$$

A PSOA Knowledge Base (KB) consists of clauses, mostly as ground facts and non-ground rules: While facts are psoa atoms, rules are defined – within `Forall` wrappers – using a Prolog-like *conclusion* `:-` *condition* syntax, where *conclusion* can be a psoa atom and *condition* can be a psoa atom or a prefixed conjunction of psoa atoms [14].

3   Architecture of `cl-psoatransrun`

A `cl-psoatransrun` session begins with the user submission of a PSOA RuleML KB to the evaluation loop beginning in the top left-hand column of Fig. 1. The KB must be specified in PSOA Presentation Syntax (PSOA PS). In the remaining sections of the paper, we will walk the figure in counter-clockwise order, starting with the parsing stage and ending with the pretty printing stage.

The read-eval-print-loop (REPL) reads queries against the PSOA RuleML KB loaded into the Prolog engine subprocess at startup. The first column of Fig. 1 describes the steps of the transformation and Prolog translation procedure for PSOA RuleML KBs and queries alike.

Queries are evaluated via communication with the Prolog client running a Prolog program that listens for query strings from the front end. After evaluating them, it returns solution strings in Prolog syntax. These are pretty-printed back to PSOA PS where they are printed to the screen by the REPL or compared against expected solution strings by the test suite mode.

The test suite mode programmatically loads test KBs to the Prolog engine and evaluates test queries present in an expected test directory structure. The testing process prints to standard output any discrepancies between the expected and evaluated query solutions.

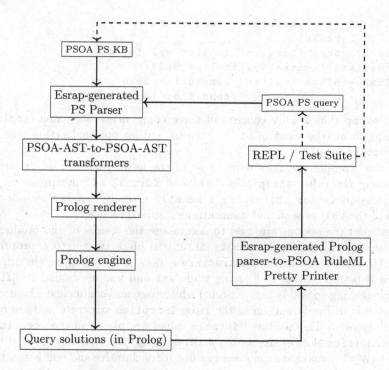

Fig. 1. The `cl-psoatransrun` system.

4 Declarative Parsing of PSOA RuleML KBs and Queries

Abstract syntax trees are initially produced from PSOA RuleML KBs by a parser declaratively specified in the domain-specific language (DSL) of the `esrap` parser generator library. The grammar of the `esrap` DSL resembles that of the familiar EBNF formalism for language grammars. As with all non-native CL libraries `cl-psoatransrun` uses, `esrap` is available via the Quicklisp library manager [1].

esrap form	EBNF rule	Rule description
(and E_1 E_2 ... E_N)	$E_1, E_2, ..., E_N$	Concatenation of rules $E_1, E_2, ..., E_N$
(or E_1 E_2 ... E_N)	$E_1 \mid E_2 \mid ... \mid E_N$	Disjunction of rules $E_1, E_2, ..., E_N$
(* E)	$\{E\}$	Greedy repetition of rule E
(? E)	$[E]$	Optional matching of rule E
(not E)	$-E$	Negation of rule E
"string"	"string"	Literal matching of "string"

esrap rules are defined as in the example:

```
(defrule implies
    (and head
         (* (or whitespace comment))
         ":-"
         (* (or whitespace comment))
         formula)
  (:destructure (head ws1 implies ws2 formula)
     (declare (ignore ws1 implies ws2))
     (make-ruleml-implies :conclusion head
                          :condition formula)))
```

An `esrap` rule usually consists of three components: its name (`implies`), matching form (the `(and head ...)` form) and an optional action (the final `destructure` form).

In the example, `implies` parses text of the form $<head>$:-$<formula>$ by naming the other `esrap` rules `head` and `formula` as subexpressions. The subexpression `(* (or whitespace comment))` greedily matches zero or more copies of the `whitespace` and `comment` rules/subexpressions.

`destructure` actions are used to decompose the results of `and` productions and then (most often in `cl-psoatransrun`) to place them into appropriately typed CL structures. In the `destructure` action of the example, the `implies` symbol is bound to the `":-"` string while `ws1` and `ws2` are bound to `NIL` values representing (possibly non-existent) whitespace and comments. These values play no role in the formation of the `ruleml-implies` structure and are consequently ignored. The `head` and `formula` values are placed in the `:conclusion` and `:condition` slots of the returned `ruleml-implies` structure.

Most of `cl-psoatransrun`'s `esrap` rules are declarative and purely functional as in the example but there are a few exceptions. For instance, side effects are used in the `prefix-list` production to populate the `*prefix-ht*` hash table. In

PSOA RuleML, some built-in predicates can only be accessed via a prefixed IRI (for example, built-in mathematical functions are available under the https://www.iso.org/standard/21413.html# IRI referring to the ISO Prolog standard). We found it most convenient to expand abbreviated predicates in RuleML KBs at parse time.

In the `prefix-list` production, the `*prefix-ht*` variable is declared special, making it a dynamically scoped variable whose value is automatically reset to NIL when the thread of execution leaves its defining scope. The `ruleml` production parses entire PSOA RuleML KBs, and the `*prefix-list*` is declared over it so that its value is dynamically accessible to the actions of all the PSOA grammar's other productions, which are run as functions further down the CL stack.

```
(defrule prefix-list
    (* (or prefix whitespace comment))
  (:around ()
    (declare (special *prefix-ht*))
    (let ((prefixes (esrap:call-transform)))
      (setf *prefix-ht* (prefix-list->prefix-ht prefixes))
      prefixes))
  (:lambda (prefixes)
    (remove nil prefixes)))
```

esrap's `around` actions allow code to be executed before and after subsequent transforms belonging to the production are called. The sequence of transforms following the `around` action are executed via the `(esrap:call-transform)` form. In `prefix-list`, the `lambda` action removing NIL from the list of parsed nodes `prefixes` is run and its return value is naturally that of `(remove nil prefixes)`. The `around` action transforms the list of prefixes to a hash table with prefix keys and IRI values using the `cl-psoatransrun` function `prefix-list->prefix-ht`, which is then bound to `*prefix-ht*`.

By decoupling parsing and transformation-functions into separate modules, `cl-psoatransrun` has several developments advantages over PSOATransRun, which uses the ANTLR parsing library both for parsing KBs and queries and implementing transformation-functions on them. Each transformation-function is realized in PSOATransRun as an ANTLR tree grammar containing each of the productions of the PSOA RuleML grammar. The transformations are specified as actions following the productions of the tree grammar to which they apply. It is too often the case that productions are untouched by a given transformation but must be specified for the tree grammar-transformations to work. This results in a great deal of redundant code that is duplicated each time a new transformation is added and whenever the PSOA grammar is expanded to include new productions. Additionally, the transformations themselves are implemented in a verbose and highly stateful style that is often difficult for even experienced PSOATransRun developers to understand, extend, and debug.

In `cl-psoatransrun`, esrap is used exclusively for parsing text to ASTs for later consumption by the transformation-functions. Its decoupling of parsing productions and transformation-functions is highly composable and allows a much narrower locality of focus in the transformations, eliminating the redundancy of PSOATransRun's ANTLR tree grammars.

5   Abstract Syntax Tree Transformations

The core of `cl-psoatransrun` is in its functionally defined transformations, the first series of which transform PSOA KBs to semantically equivalent PSOA KBs ready for direct translation to Prolog. These stages are described and motivated in Gen Zou's doctoral thesis and derived papers where the semantics preservation property of each transformation step is also proved mathematically [5, 12].

PSOA-to-PSOA transformation stages are realized in `cl-psoatransrun` as plain CL functions. Each is applied to a PSOA RuleML KB before being translated to Prolog. After being returned as the output of an `esrap` parse (which is executed as a call to a function of the `esrap` library), a PSOA RuleML KB abstract syntax tree (AST) is subject in the listed order to the following sequence of transformation-functions.

1. `rename-anonymous-constants`
2. `subclass-rewrite`
3. `embedded-objectify`
4. `unnest`
5. `objectify`
6. `skolemize`
7. `flatten-externals`
8. `separate-existential-variables`
9. `describe`
10. `split-conjunctive-conclusion`

Of these ten transformations, only `separate-existential-variables` is undocumented in the previously cited literature, as it was newly introduced to PSOATransRun and `cl-psoatransrun` by the authors of this paper in the summer of 2020 [3].

Describing its purpose naturally leads to a more germane discussion of how `cl-psoatransrun`'s transformation-functions are implemented in general. PSOA's `Exists` formula was introduced to offer lexically scoped logical variables. Often no counterpart concept exists in the target logic engine – for instance, in Prolog, all variables are dynamically scoped. Therefore, `separate-existential-variables` substitutes for every existentially qualified variable (that is, its declaration as a variable of the `Exists` clause and its occurrences in the `Exists` subformula) a uniquely named universally quantified variable on the condition side of a PSOA `Implies` formula or within a query (it is recognized in the theory of logic programming/theorem-proving method of resolution that query terms are in a "negative" context similarly to terms in facts and in implication conditions [6]). Since the logical proposition $P \rightarrow Q$ is equivalent to $\neg P \lor Q$, `separate-existential-variables` is a semantics-preserving transformation.

As with all of the other transformation-functions, it takes as input a node in the abstract syntax tree of-the PSOA RuleML KB or query and returns an appropriately transformed node when finished. The input node represents either a conjunctive query term or a KB rule or fact. In either case, the node is always a meaningful PSOA AST. Variables and symbols are the most common leaf types of PSOA ASTs. Composite nodes are typically specified as appropriately named CL structures. The specification of the node type for PSOA `Exists` formulas in `cl-psoatransrun` is

```
(defstruct (ruleml-exists (:include ruleml-ast-node))
  (vars nil :type list)
  formula)
```

An `Exists` clause consists of a list of variables and a subformula, which is reflected by the specification of its `cl-psoatransrun` type. We should also note that all AST node types inherit from the `ruleml-ast-node` supertype via the `:include` directive.

The strong dynamic typing of CL allows us to arrange AST nodes of different types freely while at the same time encoding enough information in the node types to drive the case analyses of the transformation-functions and to perform automated run-time type checks. This approach models the representation of composite types as algebraic data types as pioneered in statically-typed functional languages like Standard ML while greatly reducing the verbosity typically required by statically typed languages [10].

The standard functional programming approach to transforming a tree is to use recursion to walk the tree. As each node is encountered, a function given as an argument of the tree walker is applied to it. The results of the walk are assembled one output node at a time into a new tree by the tree walker. There are several well-known ways of abstracting this process to allow the caller to express a wide variety of tree transformations. Our tree walker, `transform-ast`, takes three arguments: the root of the tree, the *key* function κ and the *propagator* function ρ.

κ and ρ interact to define the action of the tree walker on the root argument. ρ is the most fundamental of the two in determining how the tree is traversed because it defines the recursion step. κ defines the transformation on the node built up from the results of ρ on the root node's children. We can look to how `ruleml-exists` nodes are handled in `transform-ast` to get a sense of how these steps are implemented at once:

```
(defun transform-ast (root κ ρ)
  (match root
    ...
    ((ruleml-exists :vars vars :formula formula)
     (funcall κ (make-ruleml-exists
                  :vars (mapcar ρ vars)
                  :formula (funcall ρ formula))))
    ...))
```

`match` is a pattern-matching macro provided by the (non-CL-native) `trivia` library. It dispatches execution to a patch of code cued by the type of `root` as identified by the first symbol of the matching s-expression pattern in each ()-enclosed patch; in the example, this symbol is `ruleml-exists`. `match` allows us to destructure `root` by its type, in this case assigning the variable names `vars` and `formula` to the `ruleml-exists` structure's slots of those (keyword) names.

The Lisp form following the matching s-expression defines what `transform-ast` does upon successfully binding the type of `root` and its contents to the pattern form. Here, ρ is called on the child nodes of `root`, the variable members of the `vars` list and the PSOA RuleML formula `formula`, and the results are packaged into a fresh `ruleml-exists` value, which is passed to κ. It is κ's job to change the type of `root` in the output tree if so desired. We emphasize that `transform-ast` is purely functional, meaning that it does not mutate its arguments.

It is sufficient to use `transform-ast` by specifying only the `root` and κ arguments, because ρ has the default value

$$\rho := (\texttt{lambda (term) (transform-ast } \kappa\rho\texttt{))}$$

This fixed-point definition of ρ (the value of which is the same on either side of its own defining equation) propagates both κ and itself to the direct children of its tree argument `term`. If κ preserves the types of its argument, then it when used with the default value of ρ produces a tree walker that preserves the structure of its input tree if not its contents.

In Fig. 2, we convey the operation of `transform-ast` pictorially by illustrating the action of a simple key function κ step-by-step on a PSOA RuleML AST. We will use the default (self-propagating) value of ρ.

For κ, we use the CL anonymous function

```
(lambda (term)
  (match term
    ((ruleml-const :contents "_")
     (funcall name-generator))
    (_ term)))))
```

It replaces anonymous constants (denoted with the _ identifier) with the constants produced by the externally instantiated `name-generator` generator function, the sequence _1, _2, ... while leaving all other nodes unchanged. Nodes of all other types (non-constant nodes and non-anonymous constants) are captured by the `match` macro's wildcard pattern _. Each step is fully shown in the root node of each graph and decomposed recursively into (downward) child nodes. The final graph shows the outcome of the tree transformation in a tree structurally identical to the original.

Starting from the top-left diagram, the root node is decomposed into the constituent parts of the PSOA RuleML atom structure represented in PSOA PS as p(_ c _). These are the root constant p and the dependent tuple of constants +[_ c _], whose children are its constant node contents. The top-left diagram is thus a visual representation of the atom prior to κ and ρ being applied.

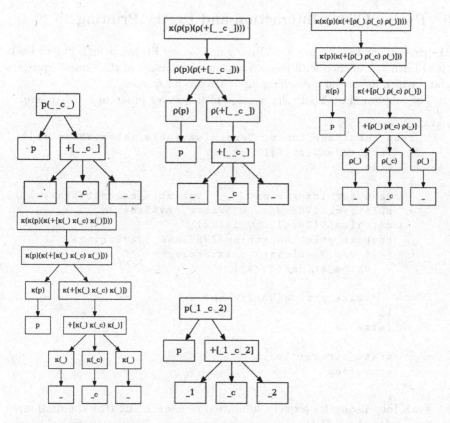

Fig. 2. Stepwise transformation of the Exists syntax graph by `transform-ast`

In the following diagram (to its right), ρ is applied to the internal parts of the atom after which κ is applied to the penultimate atom built from the two applications of ρ. Unlike in call-by-name functional programming languages such as Haskell, CL has call-by-value semantics, so that the two applications of ρ will be applied before κ is finally applied, since they determine the value passed to κ.

Next, ρ is applied to the constant nodes of the dependent tuple. $\rho(\mathrm{p})$ becomes $\kappa(\mathrm{p})$ since p is a constant with no child nodes for ρ to propagate itself to. This also describes what happens in the first diagram of the second row, where all ρ's have been replaced by κ's. Since CL's `mapcar` function applies its argument ρ (which in this example is κ) from left-to-right, `name-generator` is applied to the leftmost _ constant first, so that it is replaced by _1 in the final diagram, leaving _2 to substitute for the second _ constant.

6   Prolog Client Interaction and Pretty Printing

cl-psoatransrun supports XSB Prolog and Scryer Prolog as logic engine backends. Each is launched with its own customized version of the same server program, which listens on a blocking input stream for queries.

The loop for the XSB Prolog version of the server program is listed here.

```
eval_loop :-
    read_term(user_input, Term, [variable_names(VNNames)]),
    (  Term == end_of_file ->
       true
    ;
       read_term(user_input, _, [variable_names(UVNNames)]),
       split_vars(VNNames, UVNNames, RVNNames),
       catch(call(Term), _, false),
       compile_solution_string(RVNNames, VarString),
       (  ( var(VarString) ; VarString == "" ) ->
          write_string("Yes")
       ;
          write_string(VarString)
       ),
       false
    ;
       write_string("No"),
       eval_loop
    ).
```

eval_loop listens for a query submitted to user_input (the standard input stream) using the ISO Prolog predicate read_term [7]. The variable VNNames is bound to a list of pairs equating (Prolog atom) variable names as parsed by read_term to their Prolog variable counterparts in Term.

cl-psoatransrun stops the server by submitting end_of_file to the Prolog engine, which causes eval_loop to terminate. Otherwise, a second string is read from standard input identifying the variable names in the translated PSOA RuleML query that were generated by the transformation steps and not present in the original user-submitted query. cl-psoatransrun formats the variable names equated to their bindings in VarString using the server predicate compile_solution_string.

eval_loop uses several helper predicates to filter these variables out from the string of variable bindings it generates to submit back to cl-psoatransrun as a solution to the original query. The ISO standard predicate call is used to invoke Term as a query against the Prolog KB that was translated from PSOA RuleML and loaded into the Prolog engine by cl-psoatransrun. If the query has multiple solutions, Prolog will naturally backtrack to call(Term) and undergo the subsequent solution generation and submission process for every solution set.

The PSOATransRun implementation uses the InterProlog third party library to communicate with its Prolog subprocesses. cl-psoatransrun's approach neatly sidesteps the need for any intermediaries by leveraging the built-in features of (ISO) Prolog in a way that is agnostic to the PSOA RuleML implementation with which it communicates. All that is required of the PSOA RuleML implementation is the ability to parse the simplified Prolog notation the Prolog server program uses to convey solution sets back to it. At the time of this writing, PSOATransRun and `cl-psoatransrun` both do this, allowing for a future experiment with direct communication between PSOATransRun and the Prolog engines. Stripping the server functionality down to its strict necessities contributes to the fast query execution performance of `cl-psoatransrun` relative to PSOATransRun, as seen in the next section.

Once `cl-psoatransrun` parses the Prolog-notated solution sets to its PSOA AST representation, it pretty prints the AST back to PSOA PS, which it prints to standard output (in the REPL case). The pretty printer is written using CL's highly expressive native DSL for pretty printing, the Common Lisp Pretty Printing System [11], and produces readable machine-generated PSOA PS syntax.

7 Benchmarks

The benchmarks given in this section were gathered over the PSOATransRun test suite available at https://github.com/RuleML/PSOATransRunComponents/tree/master/PSOATransRun/test.

The test suite was administered on a desktop PC with an Intel i5-7500 processor running at 3.40 GHz with 8 GBs RAM on Arch Linux 5.12.12; PSOATransRun was run on OpenJDK 16.0.1 and `cl-psoatransrun` on SBCL 2.1.1.

The KB columns list the time it took for the test suite KB (of the row) to be translated from PSOA RuleML and loaded into XSB Prolog by the benchmarked PSOA RuleML realization (of the column). Similarly, the Queries columns list the time it took for the test case queries to be translated to Prolog from PSOA RuleML, run on the Prolog engine, and translated back to answer bindings in PSOA RuleML. All running time measurements are given in milliseconds.

Test case	`cl-psoatransrun`		PSOATransRun	
	KB	Queries	KB	Queries
betweenObjRel-groundfact	0.502	13.432	0.793	687.283
betweenObjRel-nongroundfact	0.505	5.12	1.231	274.516
betweenObjRel-rule-v1	1.566	6.34	2.780	322.384
betweenObjRel-rule-v2	1.839	3.044	9.786	198.966
class_membership	0.915	0.402	1.200	3.321
constant_variation	1.447	21.681	1.549	216.845
discount	1.599	1.258	1.339	44.822
empty-tuples	6.885	5.375	21.863	152.738

(*continued*)

(*continued*)

Test case	cl-psoatransrun		PSOATransRun	
	KB	Queries	KB	Queries
external-function1	0.199	3.035	0.305	159.140
external-function2	2.002	1.391	5.626	54.271
external-isopl-function	0.761	11.93	1.052	242.649
external-isopl-predicate	0.764	5.544	1.085	155.387
external-predicate1	0.234	1.667	0.273	56.597
external-predicate2	2.08	1.128	6.128	42.955
factorial1	2.059	2.023	1.627	70.937
factorial2	2.525	14.472	2.942	62.978
factorial3	1.169	1.032	4.525	97.57
family1	1.142	1.068	2.256	55.276
family2	1.802	5.603	2.942	62.978
function_application_as_slot_filler	0.732	2.817	1.747	104.911
ground-rule	1.643	1.958	3.089	61.300
mixed-use-of-oids-in-psoa-terms	1.572	1.456	4.579	14.629
multi-slot_psoa_fact	0.379	1.738	0.654	52.637
multi-valued_slot	0.967	6.7	1.478	68.882
multiple_entailment	0.499	0.84	0.870	6.316
music_album	2.203	14.072	2.007	117.490
nested_atoms1	1.198	5.463	6.646	213.525
nested_atoms2	14.309	0.851	1.912	50.980
objectification	0.558	0.963	0.802	47.328
own	1.237	1.88	1.656	99.052
passive_function	0.354	1.246	1.016	47.062
physics-comparison	37.216	51.196	173.415	706.027
physics-datetime	74.518	6.181	292.849	181.261
psoa-abridged-constants1	0.663	0.725	0.990	14.170
psoa-abridged-constants2	1.031	3.173	1.648	49.809
psoa-atom-dependency1	0.867	4.983	1.122	274.935
psoa-atom-dependency2	1.136	1.54	215.178	19.890
psoa-atom-dependency3	1.454	6.576	1.958	194.364
psoa-atom-dependency4	1.175	3.582	1.767	152.952
psoa-atom-dependency5	1.489	6.234	3.696	148.594
psoa_facts_with_slots_and_tuples	1.316	36.168	2.633	103.996
psoa_terms_test	1.846	5.696	2.242	158.221

(*continued*)

(*continued*)

Test case	cl-psoatransrun		PSOATransRun	
	KB	Queries	KB	Queries
recursive_frame_rule	1.90	9.955	13.742	66.730
recursive_rule	1.902	1.605	2.884	4.946
slotribution1	1.252	1.357	1.187	48.143
slotribution2	1.637	1.393	1.871	94.311
startup	1.954	1.582	2.337	54.679
subclass-axiomization	1.34	1.333	1.479	54.682
subclass-bird	1.444	4.222	3.128	149.682
subclass-test1	0.608	1.96	2.336	104.820
subclass-test2	1.201	3.4	1.604	122.025
transfer	1.422	6.692	8.071	320.426

As seen above, `cl-psoatransrun` is on average about 2.16 times faster when translating a KB (after removing the outlier test `psoa-atom-dependency2`), and on average 33 times faster when executing a query.

8   Conclusions

The CL programming language offers a number of compelling advantages. In `cl-psoatransrun`, the most impactful of these have been incremental compilation, interactive development, and its (native and library-based) DSLs for generating high-level feedback in the form of ASTs pretty-printed to PSOA RuleML PS and programmatically drawn syntax graphs for AST nodes.

CL's strong support for meta-programming has allowed the historically stable core language, ANSI-standardized in 1994 [9], to keep pace with later innovations not present in the original language through library extensions. The highly expressive and computationally efficient pattern matching of the `trivia` library is one such extension that has contributed greatly to the declarativity of the `cl-psoatransrun` codebase. In addition to all this, `cl-psoatransrun` compiles down to very fast executable native code generated by the Steel Bank Common Lisp compiler.

Since so much of `cl-psoatransrun` is written in mostly functional style, its parts are inherently highly modular and composable. We expect these features to assist us greatly in proceeding through the items of the PSOATransRun Development Agenda at a heightened but still rigorous pace.

The Scryer and XSB Prolog servers can be used by any front-end capable of initializing them atop their compatible Prolog engine as a subprocess. The servers assume nothing about the front-end, requiring only that the front-end follows the simple text-based protocol outlined in Sect. 6 of this paper. The servers are compact Prolog programs, whose lengths measure at approximately

120 SLOC each. They obviate the need for third-party libraries to intermediate communication between a PSOA RuleML realization and its Prolog engine.

As advantageous as the approach of `cl-psoatransrun` has been to PSOA RuleML implementation overall, it presents several drawbacks that will take work to address. Like logic programming, functional programming remains a difficult subject for many and is often inadequately taught to computer science students. We have tried to amelioriate this by extensively documenting `cl-psoatransrun` here, in the RuleML wiki report of [3], and in the `cl-psoatransrun` source code. Once the source code of `cl-psoatransrun` has been studied and adequately understood by a human reader, they should ideally be left with the impression that realizing a PSOA RuleML system is fairly straightforward if the mathematical character of its core transformation and client logic engine translation processes in particular is properly appreciated. All that is required of the front-end's implementation language is that it can express that character directly and unobtrusively.

References

1. Quicklisp Common Lisp Library Manager. http://www.quicklisp.org/
2. Steel Bank Common Lisp. http://www.sbcl.org/
3. The cl-psoatransrun System: An Efficiently Executable Specification of PSOA RuleML in Common Lisp. http://wiki.ruleml.org/index.php/The_cl-psoatransrun_System:_An_Efficiently_Executable_Specification_of_PSOA_RuleML_in_Common_Lisp
4. Boley, H.: PSOA RuleML: integrated object-relational data and rules. In: Faber, W., Paschke, A. (eds.) Reasoning Web 2015. LNCS, vol. 9203, pp. 114–150. Springer, Cham (2015). https://doi.org/10.1007/978-3-319-21768-0_5
5. Boley, H., Zou, G.: Perspectival Knowledge in PSOA RuleML: Representation, Model Theory, and Translation. CoRR abs/1712.02869, v3 (2019). http://arxiv.org/abs/1712.02869
6. Fitting, M.: First-Order Logic and Automated Theorem Proving. Graduate Texts in Computer Science, 2nd edn. Springer, Heidelberg (1996). https://doi.org/10.1007/978-1-4612-2360-3
7. ISO/IEC 13211–1: Prolog - Part 1: General core (1995)
8. Khomtchouk, B.B., Weitz, E., Karp, P.D., Wahlestedt, C.: How the strengths of Lisp-family languages facilitate building complex and flexible bioinformatics applications. Briefings Bioinform. **19**(3), 537–543 (2016). https://doi.org/10.1093/bib/bbw130
9. Miller, F.P., Vandome, A.F., McBrewster, J.: Common Lisp: Lisp (Programming Language), Programming Language, American National Standards Institute, Specification (Technical Standard), Free and Open Source Software, Programming Paradigm. Alpha Press (2010)
10. Milner, R., Tofte, M., Macqueen, D.: The Definition of Standard ML. MIT Press, Cambridge (1997)
11. Waters, R.C.: A common lisp pretty printing system. Technical report, Massachusetts Inst of Tech Cambridge Artificial Intelligence Lab (1989)
12. Zou, G.: Translators for interoperating and porting object-relational knowledge. Ph.D. thesis, University of New Brunswick. (2018)

13. Zou, G., Boley, H.: PSOA2Prolog: object-relational rule interoperation and implementation by translation from PSOA RuleML to ISO prolog. In: Bassiliades, N., Gottlob, G., Sadri, F., Paschke, A., Roman, D. (eds.) RuleML 2015. LNCS, vol. 9202, pp. 176–192. Springer, Cham (2015). https://doi.org/10.1007/978-3-319-21542-6_12

14. Zou, G., Boley, H., Wood, D., Lea, K.: Port clearance rules in PSOA RuleML: from controlled-English regulation to object-relational logic. In: Proceedings of the RuleML+RR 2017 Challenge, vol. 1875. CEUR, July 2017

Leveraging the Power of IDP
with the Flexibility of DMN:
A Multifunctional API

Simon Vandevelde[1,3]([✉]), Vedavyas Etikala[2,3], Jan Vanthienen[2,3],
and Joost Vennekens[1,3]

[1] Department of Computer Science, KU Leuven, De Nayer Campus,
J.-P- De Nayerlaan 5, 2860 Sint-Katelijne-Waver, Belgium
{s.vandevelde,joost.vennekens}@kuleuven.be
[2] Leuven Institute for Research on Information Systems (LIRIS), KU Leuven,
Leuven, Belgium
{vedavyas.etikala,jan.vanthienen}@kuleuven.be
[3] Leuven.AI - KU Leuven Institute for AI, 3000 Leuven, Belgium

Abstract. Decision Model and Notation (DMN) models are user-friendly representations of decision logic. While the knowledge in the model could be used for multiple purposes, current DMN tools typically only support a single form of inference. We present DMN-IDPy, a novel Python API that links DMN as a notation to the IDP system, a powerful reasoning tool, allowing the knowledge in DMN models to be used to its fullest potential. The flexibility of this approach allows us to build intelligent tools based on DMN unlike any other execution engine.

Keywords: Decision model and notation · Knowledge base paradigm · IDP · API · Python

1 Introduction

The Decision Model and Notation standard [10], designed by the Object Modeling Group (OMG), is a user-friendly, table-based notation for modeling decision logic. Its main goals are to make decision knowledge readable by everyone involved in the decision process (business people, IT experts), and to be executable. Since its start in 2015, DMN has quickly gained popularity in both industry [4,9,13] and academia [1,5].

Typically, DMN is used to automate day-to-day business decisions. Most DMN tools therefore focus on supporting the required functionalities for this specific use.

However, we believe that more ambitious uses of DMN are also possible. In particular, the knowledge that is contained in a DMN model could be used to

This research received funding from the Flemish Government under the "Onderzoeksprogramma Artificiële Intelligentie (AI) Vlaanderen" programme.

© Springer Nature Switzerland AG 2021
S. Moschoyiannis et al. (Eds.): RuleML+RR 2021, LNCS 12851, pp. 250–263, 2021.
https://doi.org/10.1007/978-3-030-91167-6_17

build knowledge-based AI systems, that can implement various sorts of intelligent behaviour. Consider, for instance, a cobot tasked with assisting an operator in product assembly. It seems likely that the domain knowledge that such a cobot would need can be expressed in DMN, and, moreover, doing so would allow the domain knowledge to be written and maintained directly by the operators themselves, instead of requiring programmers or knowledge engineers as middle men.

To actually implement such a system, the functionality of typical DMN tools does not suffice. For instance, the cobot would need to figure out which sensor input is necessary for specific operations, and such functionality is typically not available. In an effort to allow DMN models to be used in a more flexible way, a translation from DMN to the FO($\cdot$) language was presented in [5]. FO($\cdot$) is an extension of classical first-order logic, which serves as the input language for the IDP Knowledge Base System [6]. Following the approach of [7], IDP allows the same knowledge base to be (re-)used for different forms of logical inference, facilitating the development of flexible knowledge-based tools. The work of [5] allows the powerful logical inference algorithms of IDP to be applied to DMN models as well. However, to build truly useful intelligent systems, this alone does not suffice: it is also necessary to combine these different inference tasks in a suitable way. Moreover, this should be done using the concepts and terminology from the original DMN model (instead of those from the FO($\cdot$) theory that the DMN model is translated to behind the scenes).

To make this possible, we present the DMN-IDPy API: a versatile Python API that combines DMN as a notation with the IDP system as a reasoning engine. It aims to deliver the building blocks required to unlock more powerful and flexible uses for DMN models. In this way, the API facilitates the creation of systems that exhibit intelligent behavior, based on the user-friendly structure and format of DMN models.

This work is similar in spirit to previous work on the PyIDP API [16], which exposes the functionality of IDP to Python programmers, allowing also the knowledge base itself to be represented in a pythonic syntax, rather than the usual syntax of FO($\cdot$). The difference to our work is that we now bring DMN into the mix to allow the knowledge to be maintained by domain experts, rather than Python programmers.

This paper is structured as follows. First, we elaborate on some background in Sect. 2. Next, we go over all functionalities of our DMN execution API in Sect. 3. Afterwards, Sect. 4 showcases a possible application of the API, in the form of a naive chat bot. We also briefly touch on the concrete implementation of the API itself in Sect. 5. Lastly, we compare our implementation to the current state-of-the-art in Sect. 6, and we conclude in Sect. 7.

2   Background

This section elaborates on the DMN standard, the current execution methods supported by the state-of-the-art DMN tools and the IDP system.

2.1 DMN

The Decision Model and Notation (DMN) standard provides a user-friendly notation for (business) decision knowledge. It consists of two main components: the Decision Requirements Diagram (DRD), and decision tables. The DRD is a graph representing the *decision flow* throughout the DMN model. It shows a graphical overview of which decision tables are present, how they connect, which input variables are used, which data sources are needed, and more. Figure 1a shows an example of a DRD with three decision tables, as represented by the rectangles, and four input variables, as represented by the ovals. The arrows between them represent the flow of information, e.g., the value of *BMI* is defined by the value of the inputs *Weight* and *Length*.

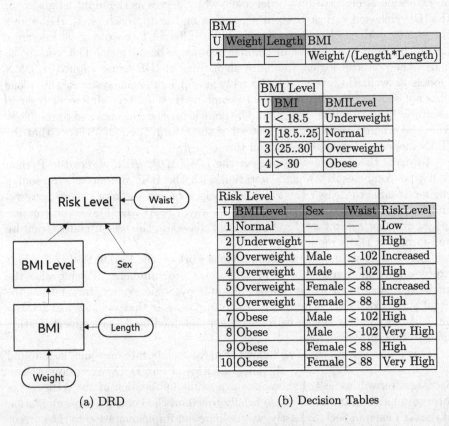

BMI		
U	Weight	Length	BMI
1	—	—	Weight/(Length*Length)

BMI Level		
U	BMI	BMILevel
1	< 18.5	Underweight
2	[18.5..25]	Normal
3	(25..30]	Overweight
4	> 30	Obese

Risk Level				
U	BMILevel	Sex	Waist	RiskLevel
1	Normal	—	—	Low
2	Underweight	—	—	High
3	Overweight	Male	≤ 102	Increased
4	Overweight	Male	> 102	High
5	Overweight	Female	≤ 88	Increased
6	Overweight	Female	> 88	High
7	Obese	Male	≤ 102	High
8	Obese	Male	> 102	Very High
9	Obese	Female	≤ 88	High
10	Obese	Female	> 88	Very High

(a) DRD   (b) Decision Tables

Fig. 1. Decision tables and DRD for the BMI running example.

The second main component consists of decision tables, as shown in Fig. 1b. Every decision table contains one or more input variables and one or more output variables, each corresponding to a column. A decision table defines the value of the output variables in term of the value of the input variables. Each row of the table corresponds to a decision rule. We say that a rule *fires* whenever the actual value of the input variables match the values listed in its cells. The way in which the inputs define the output depends on the *hit policy* of the table. This hit policy can either be single hit (such as *U(nique)*, *F(irst)*, *A(ny)*) or multiple hit (such as *C(ollect)*, *C+* and *C<*). If multiple rows fire at the same time, the hit policy specifies how these rows are combined to determine the value of the output variable.

The example DMN model shown in Fig. 1 consists of three tables in total, defining BMI, BMI Level and Risk Level. For these decisions, it uses four different input parameters: the weight, length, sex and waist size of a person. In this example, all tables have the U hit policy, meaning that only a single row can fire per table. E.g., if the value of *BMI = 23*, the second row in the *BMI Level* table fires, thus assigning *Normal* to the decision variable *BMILevel*. A cell containing "—" signifies that the value of this variable does not matter. For instance, if the BMI Level is underweight, the Risk Level is always high, regardless of sex and waist size.

2.2 Execution Methods

Since the introduction of DMN by OMG, software companies such as Camunda [3], OpenRules [11] and Signavio [12] offer decision modeling software based on this standard. Besides assisting the user in modeling and verifying decisions, some of them also provide execution mechanisms for the models.

Such execution goes back to Decision Table Solvers [15]. Practically, most of these tools all support the same execution method: the *bottom-to-top* approach. This execution method requires the user to input a value for every input variable present in the model, after which the execution engine decides the value of all other variables. For example, supplying a value for *Weight*, *Length*, *Waist* and *Sex* to find the value of *Risk Level*. While this is considered the standard usage of a DMN model, some tools also support additional execution methods.

One such method is *reasoning on sub-decisions*: instead of evaluating every decision table in a model, it is sometimes preferable to evaluate only a specific subset of decisions. If we are only interested in the *BMI Level*, for example, we do not need to evaluate the *Risk Level* table. The advantage of reasoning on sub-decisions is that not all input variables must be known (i.e. *Waist* and *Sex* are irrelevant as long as we do not need to know the *RiskLevel*). Examples of tools capable of this execution method are Camunda and OpenRules, both of which can evaluate a decision table in isolation. By reasoning on a single table at a time, they allow only evaluating the tables necessary for a sub-decision.

Another alternative execution method is the *"wildcard" mode*, such as the one provided by Camunda and Signavio, in which users can evaluate a decision model with partial input values. For example, if the value of *Sex* is unknown, a wildcard value can be used instead, in which case the engine returns a set of all possible output values.

2.3   IDP

The IDP (Imperative Declarative Programming) system [6] is a powerful and flexible reasoning engine. As an implementation of the Knowledge Base Paradigm [7], it creates a clear distinction between knowledge and its use. Concretely, knowledge is stored in a so-called knowledge base (KB), written in an extended version of First-Order Logic (FO), called FO($\cdot$). As an example, (1) shows a possible FO($\cdot$) representation of the *BMI Level* table shown in Fig. 1b in the form of a conjunction of implications, as defined by the semantics of Calvanese et al. [2].

$$
\begin{aligned}
&(BMI < 18.5 &&\Rightarrow BMILevel = Underweight) \\
\wedge\,&(18.5 \leq BMI \leq 25 &&\Rightarrow BMILevel = Normal) \\
\wedge\,&(25 < BMI \leq 30 &&\Rightarrow BMILevel = Overweight) \\
\wedge\,&(30 < BMI &&\Rightarrow BMILevel = Obese)
\end{aligned}
\tag{1}
$$

In FO($\cdot$), we represent each DMN variable by a constant c, with for every such constant a list of possible values $poss(c)$. A total assignment assigns to every constant precisely one value $c^I \in poss(c)$. A partial assignment assigns to every constant a non-empty subset $c^{\mathcal{I}} \subseteq poss(c)$ of its possible values $poss(c)$.

To reason on the knowledge in a KB, the IDP engine supports various inference tasks; three of these are used in this paper. To start, there is the *model expansion* task: given an assignment of values to some of the variables, compute an assignment to the other variables such that the knowledge base is satisfied. If the given variables are precisely the "input" variables of the model, this boils down to the standard "bottom-to-top" execution. However, we can also assign a value to a decision variable and then compute corresponding values for the input variables. *Propagation* is the second inference task implemented in our API. Here, after assigning values to some variables, the IDP system generates (in-)equalities of the form $c\theta v$ with c a variable, v a value from $poss(c)$, and θ a comparison operator, that are now implied by the KB. E.g., if we add $BMI < 30$ to (1), propagation will automatically derive that $BMILevel \neq Obese$. The final inference task used in this work is *optimization*, which allows us to find a solution with the lowest/highest value for any given term.

Note that by using these inference tasks, we can do more than just bottom-to-top calculation. Indeed, the IDP system has no sense of direction: any variable can be used as "input" by assigning it a value. In this way, we can also use DMN tables "backwards", by going from the output variable to the input variables.

The motivation behind using the IDP system is twofold: firstly, the semantics as defined by Calvanese et al. [2] can be unambiguously translated to FO($\cdot$), and secondly, there is already a strong basis of papers describing the connection between DMN and IDP [5,8,14].

3   API Features

This section aims at showcasing the features of the DMN-IDPy API. For every feature, we briefly mention what it is, why it is important and we show a short code snippet to show it in action.

3.1   Bottom-Up Decision Calculation

Our API can be used to provide the same "bottom-to-top" functionality as standard DMN tools. In the example shown in Fig. 1, this corresponds to setting the values for *Weight, Length, Sex* and *Waist* in order to then calculate the decisions in the following order: *BMI* → *BMILevel* → *RiskLevel.*

```
spec = DMN('bmi.dmn')
spec.set_value('weight', 74)
spec.set_value('length', 1.79)      →
spec.set_value('sex', 'Male')
spec.set_value('waist', 90)
```

```
>>> spec.model_expand(1)
Model 1
===========
riskLevel:={->Low}
waist:={->104}
BMILevel:={->Normal}
bmi:={->23.09540900720951}
sex:={->Male}
weight:={->74}
length:={->1.79}
```

3.2   Reasoning with Incomplete Information

Instead of requiring all input variables to have values assigned to them in order to run the execution, we also allow reasoning on DMN models with incomplete information. This functionality can e.g. be used to calculate the value of one or more sub-decisions without requiring the values of all input variables, thereby reducing the number of necessary operations. For example, if we are merely interested in the value of *BMILevel*, we should be able to perform this decision using only *Weight* and *Length* as inputs.

```
spec.set_value('Weight', 74)
spec.set_value('Length', 1.79)      →
spec.propagate()
```

```
>>> spec.value_of('BMI')
23.09540900720951
```

By supporting reasoning with incomplete information, every DMN model that consists of more than one table can directly and efficiently be used for multiple purposes by reasoning on sub-decision trees.

3.3 Relevance

One of the goals of our API is to allow *generic* tools to be built, by avoiding the need to hard-code which variables must be assigned a value and in which order this should happen. To this end, it allows to query on the fly which variables are relevant for making a certain decision. For example, because *BMI* is defined by *Length* and *Weight*, these latter two variables should both be known in order to decide the value of *BMI*. By implementing this functionality in the API, tools can be built with a more generic nature.

Note that by "inputs" we do not only mean the inputs of a decision table, but rather all *upstream* variables needed for a decision to be made. For example, while the *BMI Level* table only has one input variable, that variable in turn has two input variables. So, in reality, there are three dependencies for *BMI Level*, but at two different levels of the DRD. In the API, we show the number of *node hops* necessary to reach the variable to clearly denote this difference. This information is generated from the DMN file, without making use of the IDP system.

```
>>> spec.dependencies_of('BMILevel')
{'BMI': 0, 'Weight': 1, 'Length': 1}

>>> spec.dependencies_of('BMILevel')
 {'BMILevel': 0, 'BMI': 1, 'Weight': 2, 'Length': 2,
  'Sex': 0, 'Waist': 0}
```

As mentioned in Sect. 3.2, this can help optimize the required operations needed to decide a variable's value.

3.4 Multidirectional Reasoning

In our goal to get as much use out of a single DMN model as possible, the ability to reason on decisions in any direction is the functionality that results in the most mileage. Instead of only calculating in the direction of the arrows in the DRD (bottom-to-top), we can reason in the other direction as well. Among other things, it then becomes possible to calculate the input variables of the model based on the top-level decision.

To do this, the API supports directly assigning values to the decision variables. For example, if the value for BMI is already known beforehand, we can directly assign that value to the decision variable and use it to derive the value of BMI Level.

```
spec.set_value('BMI', 31)          →     >>> spec.value_of('BMILevel')
spec.propagate()                          Obese
```

For an example of multidirectional reasoning, consider a person who just used the model to calculate that they are overweight, and now wants to query what their weight should be in order to reach a BMI of 25. By entering their length and their desired BMI value, the tool can calculate the weight required to reach their goal.

```
spec.set_value('BMI', '25')
spec.set_value('Length', 1.79)      →      >>> spec.value_of('Weight')
spec.propagate()                           80.1025
```

Here, only a single value for *Weight* remains, because we set both *BMI* and *Length*. However, if we only set *BMI*, multiple values for *Weight* (and *Length*) are still possible, and no equality *Weight* $= x$ can be propagated. Indeed, instead of a single solution, we now have a *solution space*.

There are multiple ways to traverse this solution space in order to find a single solution. Assigning values to more variables will decrease the size of the space, possibly up until the point where there is only one solution left. If there are no variables left and there are still multiple solutions possible, we can generate solutions via IDP's model expansion inference (as demonstrated in the example in Sect. 3.1). Alternatively, we can search for the solution with the maximal/minimal value for a specific variable, as further explained in the Sect. 3.7.

3.5 Known Variables

Because of the API's interactive approach, where any variable can be assigned a value at any time, it is important to be able to keep track of which variables are known, i.e., have been assigned a value either by the user or by the reasoning engine via propagation. Consider for instance a case where a user has calculated their BMI level as demonstrated in Sect. 3.2, by entering their length and weight. If they want to calculate their risk level afterwards, they should only have to enter their sex and waist, as that is the only information that is still missing for this decision.

```
                                           >>> spec.is_certain('BMI')
spec.set_value('Length', 1.79)             True
spec.set_value('Weight', 79)        →      >>> spec.is_certain('Sex')
spec.propagate()                           False
```

3.6 Variable Type and Values

Every variable in a DMN model has a data type, such as *Int*, *Float*, *String* or other. Intuitively, these denote the type of data that a variable represents. To avoid errors such as assigning a numerical value to a variable of data type *String*, the API allows querying a variable's type via *type_of*.

String is a special case of data type: where *Int*, *Float*, etc. are considered to have infinite ranges, *String* is often limited to a predefined list of possible values. Indeed, it makes sense that only those values that appear in a table can be assigned to a variable. E.g., in the BMI example the variable *Sex* can only be assigned values *Male* or *Female*. To prevent assigning impossible values to a string variable, the API can give a list of all possible values by either returning the variable's predefined list, or, if no list was predefined, by returning a list of all string values which appear at least once for that variable.

```
>>> spec.type_of('Sex')
String
>>> spec.possible_values_of('Sex')
['Male', 'Female']
```

3.7 Optimization

Optimization allows us to find the solution with the highest, or the lowest value for any given numerical variable. Consider a patient that has just entered their weight and length to find out that they have an *Overweight* BMI Level. A logical next question would be: "What should my target weight be if I want to have a normal BMI Level?". To answer this, they can enter their length and set the value of *BMI Level* to *Normal*. If they then maximize the value of *Weight*, the system will calculate the maximum weight that still results in a normal BMI Level.

```
>>> spec.set_value('Length', 1.79)
>>> spec.set_value('BMILevel', 'Normal')
>>> spec.maximize('Weight')
Model 1
==========
RiskLevel:={->Low}
Waist:={->104}
BMILevel:={->Normal}
BMI:={->25}
Sex:={->Male}
Weight:={->80.1025}
Length:={->1.79}
```

4 Application Example

To truly showcase the power of combining DMN as a modelling tool and IDP as a reasoning engine, this section sketches a possible implementation for a naive chat bot, implemented in less than 25 lines of Python. Its main goal is to allow users to calculate any of the intermediary or top-level variables of a DMN model. In order to achieve this, the bot goes through a few steps. First, it fetches the list of variables and asks the user which variable should be calculated.

```
spec = DMN(sys.argv[1], auto_propagate=True)
vars = spec.get_outputs() + spec.get_intermediary()
req_var = input('Which_variable_to_calculate?_{}\n>'.format(variables))
```

Next, the program finds out which input variables should be known in order to make this calculation. Input variables without any effect on the value of the requested variable are not included.

```
deps = spec.dependencies_of(req_var)
missing_vars = [x for x in deps if x in spec.get_inputs()]
print("\nThe_following_variables_are_still_unknown:")
print(missing_vars)
```

Finally, it loops over every unknown variable and queries the user for its value. Important here is that we ask a different question, based on the data type of the variable. Indeed, the user should be aware of the data type of the variable that is being queried. If the program requests the value of a *String*-based variable, it should also supply the user the list of possible values. Similarly for numerical variables, the user should be notified if the variable is an integer or a float.

```
for var in missing_vars:
    # Ask for the variable's value. Based on var type, ask different question.
    var_type = spec.type_of(var)
    if var_type in ['Real', 'Int']:
        msg = "Value_for_{}_({})_unknown.\n>".format(var, var_type)
    else:
        pos_vals = spec.possible_values_of(var)
        msg = "Value_for_{}_unknown.\n"\
            "Possible_values:_[{}]\n>".format(var, pos_vals)
    value = input(msg)
    spec.set_value(var, value)

    if spec.is_known(req_var):
        break

req_var_val = spec.value_of(req_var)
print('Calculated_value_for_{}:\n{}'.format(req_var, req_var_val))
```

Note that at the end of every loop cycle, the program checks whether the variable is known yet. While this might not make much sense at first, because the program specifically fetched the list of necessary inputs for the decision, there are cases where not all inputs might be necessary. Consider for example the decision table for *RiskLevel*. Here, if the values for *Weight* and *Length* are queried first and they lead to a BMI Level that is neither overweight nor obese, then the values of *Sex* and *Waist* will have no impact on this decision.

```
>>> python bot.py bmi.dmn
Which variable to calculate? ['RiskLevel', 'BMILevel', 'BMI']
> Risk Level
The following variables are still unknown:
['Weight', 'Length', 'Sex', 'Waist']
Value for Weight (Real) unknown.
> 79
```

Value **for** Length (Real) unknown.
\> 1.79
Calculated value **for** Risk Level:
Low

While this implementation uses the BMI example, it is not limited to it. Indeed, by supplying a different DMN model when invoking the program, the chat bot can be used for different purposes. For example, after inserting a DMN model designed to calculate personal taxes, the chat bot is capable of reasoning in that problem field without having to change any code.

5   Implementation

This section briefly elaborates on the implementation of the DMN-IDPy API. To transform DMN models to input for the IDP system, it uses a tool developed in [1,14]. This tool accepts DMN models that are either in XML format (as specified by the DMN standard), or in the form of an Excel spreadsheet.

When using the API, a few internal steps are performed. To begin, as soon as a specification is entered, it is translated internally into the FO($\cdot$) format of the IDP system. This translation is done based on the decision table semantics as defined by Calvanese et al. [2], i.e., every table is represented by a conjunction of material implications. To run the IDP system, we use the *idp-engine*[1] Python package.

Whenever a variable is assigned a value, the underlying IDP specification is updated to represent this change. If the user invokes the *propagation* method, the API immediately runs IDP's propagation inference and updates the values of the other variables accordingly. Similarly, if they invoke the model expansion function, the API triggers IDP's model expansion inference.

The PyDMN-API library is available to download via the Python Package Index[2]. Furthermore, there is also a practical usage guide for the API available online[3]. Note that the API does not (yet) support the full DMN standard. Currently, it is capable of reasoning on tables with the following hit policies: *U*, *F*, *A*, *C+*, *C<* and *C>*. It supports the *Int*, *Float*, *Boolean* and *String* data types, but not e.g. the *Date* type. There is also no support for boxed expressions.

6   Comparison

To the best of our knowledge, there is no other approach that offers such a flexible yet powerful use of DMN models. While there exist tools that support more than exclusively the bottom-to-top calculation, none are capable of performing all features discussed in this work. Table 1 shows a comparison of the functionalities of DMN-IDPy, the OpenRules API and the Camunda API.

---

[1] https://pypi.org/project/idp-engine/.

[2] https://pypi.org/project/cdmn/.

[3] https://cdmn.readthedocs.io/en/latest/DMN_guide.html.

As expected, all compared APIs support the bottom-to-top execution. Additionally, they all also support reasoning on incomplete information, but only up to a varying degree. Both OpenRules and Camunda are capable of using incomplete information by reasoning on sub-decisions, as they allow the evaluation of a single decision table isolated from the rest of the DMN model. Thus, it is possible to e.g. use the Risk Level model to only calculate a patient's BMI, as discussed in the example in Sect. 3.2. However, as the API's only allow reasoning on either the entire model or a single specific table, attempting to reason on a sub-decision consisting of multiple tables (e.g. *BMI* followed by *BMILevel*) requires quite a bit of extra overhead: for each table, we would need to (a) manually supply the inputs, (b) evaluate, and (c) extract the outputs to use as inputs for the next table. In our API, no such workarounds are needed, as it suffices to enter all input values followed by calling the propagation inference. As such, the process of using sub-decisions with DMN-IDPy is much more streamlined.

The wildcard mode, as featured in e.g. Camunda, is possible in DMN-IDPy by leveraging its ability to reason on incomplete information. After entering a partial set of input values, we can generate all remaining solutions using the model expansion inference.

Neither OpenRules nor Camunda support multidirectional reasoning or optimization.

Table 1. Comparison between functionalities of DMN-IDPy, and state-of-the-art DMN execution engines. (X = full support, o = partial support)

	DMN-IDPy	OpenRules	Camunda
Bottom-to-top	X	X	X
Incomplete Information	X	o	o
Wildcard mode	X		X
Multidirectional Reasoning	X		
Optimization	X		

The main downside of our approach is the efficiency of the reasoning engine itself. Where other engines have specific optimized algorithms to perform the bottom-to-top calculation, we use a general purpose reasoning engine. As such, our calculation times will often be a magnitude higher compared to the other state-of-the-art engines. However, we feel that we make up for it with the increased flexibility that the API offers.

7   Conclusion and Future Work

While DMN models are most often used for bottom-to-top calculations, they can be used in many more scenarios. For this to be possible however, DMN needs to be supported by a flexible reasoning tool. In this paper, we present a Python

API that enables the IDP reasoning system as an execution engine for DMN. This way, it provides the building blocks necessary to construct intelligent tools based on user-friendly DMN models. The main additions of the API are:

- Support for reasoning in any direction (e.g. going in the other direction of the DRD);
- Support for reasoning on incomplete data (allowing for sub-decision calculations);
- Addition of the optimization of variable values.

In order to showcase DMN-IDPy in action, we created a naive implementation of a chat bot in under 20 lines of Python code. The implementation is generic in the sense that it can be used with any DMN model, without having to change a line of code.

In future work, we will look into extending the API to support more of IDP's inference tasks. Moreover, we will also develop a more extensive, real-life application based on our API to further research its usefulness in a more realistic setting.

References

1. Aerts, B., Vandevelde, S., Vennekens, J.: Tackling the DMN challenges with cDMN: a tight integration of DMN and constraint reasoning. In: Gutiérrez-Basulto, V., Kliegr, T., Soylu, A., Giese, M., Roman, D. (eds.) RuleML+RR 2020. LNCS, vol. 12173, pp. 23–38. Springer, Cham (2020). https://doi.org/10.1007/978-3-030-57977-7_2
2. Calvanese, D., Dumas, M., Laurson, U., Maggi, F.M., Montali, M., Teinemaa, I.: Semantics, analysis and simplification of DMN decision tables. Inf. Syst. (Oxford) **78**, 112–125 (2018)
3. Camunda Services GmbH: Camunda DMN Decision Engine (2013–2021). https://camunda.com/
4. Car, N.J.: Using decision models to enable better irrigation decision support systems. Comput. Electron. Agric. **152**, 290–301 (2018)
5. Dasseville, I., Janssens, L., Janssens, G., Vanthienen, J., Denecker, M.: Combining DMN and the knowledge base paradigm for flexible decision enactment. In: Supplementary Proceedings of the RuleML 2016 Challenge, vol. 1620. CEUR-WS.org (2016)
6. De Cat, B., Bogaerts, B., Bruynooghe, M., Janssens, G., Denecker, M.: Predicate logic as a modeling language: the IDP system. In: Declarative Logic Programming: Theory, Systems, and Applications, pp. 279–329. ACM Books (2018). https://doi.org/10.1145/3191315
7. Denecker, M., Vennekens, J.: Building a knowledge base system for an integration of logic programming and classical logic. In: Garcia de la Banda, M., Pontelli, E. (eds.) ICLP 2008. LNCS, vol. 5366, pp. 71–76. Springer, Heidelberg (2008). https://doi.org/10.1007/978-3-540-89982-2_12
8. Deryck, M., Hasić, F., Vanthienen, J., Vennekens, J.: A case-based inquiry into the decision model and notation (DMN) and the knowledge base (KB) paradigm. In: Benzmüller, C., Ricca, F., Parent, X., Roman, D. (eds.) RuleML+RR 2018. LNCS, vol. 11092, pp. 248–263. Springer, Cham (2018). https://doi.org/10.1007/978-3-319-99906-7_17

9. Hasic, F., Vanthienen, J.: From decision knowledge to e-government expert systems: the case of income taxation for foreign artists in Belgium. Knowl. Inf. Syst. **62**(5), 2011–2028 (2020). https://doi.org/10.1007/s10115-019-01416-4
10. Object Modelling Group: Decision model and notation (2021). http://www.omg.org/spec/DMN/
11. OpenRules Inc.: OpenRules Decision Manager (2003–2021). https://openrules.com
12. Signavio GmbH: Signavio Process Manager (2009–2021). https://www.signavio.com/
13. Sooter, L.J., Hasley, S., Lario, R., Rubin, K.S., Hasić, F.: Modeling a clinical pathway for contraception. Appl. Clin. Inform. **10**(5), 935–943 (2019). https://doi.org/10.1055/s-0039-3400749
14. Vandevelde, S., Vennekens, J.: A multifunctional, interactive DMN decision modelling tool. In: Proceedings of BNAIC/BeneLearn 2020, pp. 399–400 (2020)
15. Vanthienen, J., Dries, E.: Illustration of a decision table tool for specifying and implementing knowledge based systems. Int. J. Artif. Intell. Tools **3**, 267–288 (1994)
16. Vennekens, J.: Lowering the learning curve for declarative programming: a python API for the IDP system. In: Lierler, Y., Taha, W. (eds.) PADL 2017. LNCS, vol. 10137, pp. 86–102. Springer, Cham (2017). https://doi.org/10.1007/978-3-319-51676-9_6

Technical Communication Papers

Eliminating Harmful Joins in Warded Datalog+/−

Teodoro Baldazzi[1]([✉]), Luigi Bellomarini[2], Emanuel Sallinger[3,4],
and Paolo Atzeni[1]

[1] Università Roma Tre, Rome, Italy
[2] Banca d'Italia, Rome, Italy
[3] TU Wien, Vienna, Austria
[4] University of Oxford, Oxford, UK

Abstract. We provide a rewriting technique of Warded Datalog+/−
settings to sustain decidability and data tractability of reasoning tasks
in the presence of existential quantification and recursion. To achieve
this behaviour in practice, reasoners implement specialized strategies
which exploit the theoretical bases of the language to control the effects
of recursion, ensuring reasoning termination with small memory foot-
print. However, as a necessary condition for such exploitation, the setting is required to be in a "normalized form", essentially without joins
on variables affected by existential quantification. We present the Harmful Join Elimination, a normalization algorithm of Warded Datalog+/−
that removes such "harmful" joins, supporting the tractability of the
reasoning task as well as the full expressive power of the language. The
algorithm is integrated in the Vadalog system, a Warded Datalog+/−
-based reasoner that performs ontological reasoning in complex scenarios.

1 Introduction

Among the requirements for a *Knowledge Representation and Reasoning* (KRR)
language, full support for recursion and joins as well as existential quantification are essential to guarantee the expressive power needed for knowledge graph
traversal and ontological reasoning [4]. Warded Datalog$^\pm$ [12], a member (technically, a *fragment*) of the Datalog$^\pm$ family [8], covers these requirements offering a good tradeoff between expressive power and computational complexity,
with conjunctive query answering being PTIME-complete in data complexity. It
is implemented in the Vadalog system, a state-of-the-art reasoner. While the
favourable computational characteristics of the fragment bode well for efficient
implementations, a workable algorithm handling the interplay between existen-
tials and recursion is highly needed. Consider the following example.

Example 1. Let Σ be a set of warded rules, based on a real reasoning setting [5]:

$$\text{Company}(x) \rightarrow \exists p \, \text{PSC}(x, p). \tag{α}$$

$$\text{PSC}(x, p), \text{Controls}(x, y) \rightarrow \text{PSC}(y, p). \tag{β}$$

© Springer Nature Switzerland AG 2021
S. Moschoyiannis et al. (Eds.): RuleML+RR 2021, LNCS 12851, pp. 267–275, 2021.
https://doi.org/10.1007/978-3-030-91167-6_18

$$\text{StrongLink}(x, y) \rightarrow \exists p \text{ PSC}(x, p). \tag{γ}$$
$$\text{PSC}(x, p), \text{PSC}(y, p) \rightarrow \text{StrongLink}(x, y). \tag{ρ}$$

For each company x there exists a "person of significant control" (psc) p (rule α); for each company y controlled by x, p is a psc (rule β); if x and y have a common psc, they share a "strong link" (rule ρ) and vice versa (rule γ). Consider, as ontological reasoning task, the query Q: "what are all the entailed StrongLinks?" and the database D={Company(HSBC),Company(HSB),Controls(HSBC,HSB)}. ∎

The semantics of Σ over D is defined via the *chase* [16], which adds new atoms to D, possibly involving freshly generated symbols (technically, *labelled nulls*) [8] to satisfy the existentially quantified variables, until all the existential rules are satisfied. In Example 1, we generate PSC(HSBC, ν_0) and PSC(HSB, ν_1) from D by applying α, PSC(HSB, ν_0) via β, StrongLink(HSBC,HSB) via the join on ν_0 performed by ρ, and so on. Due to the recursion involving ρ, γ, and β, an infinite set $\bigcup_{i=2,...}\{\text{PSC}(\text{HSBC}, \nu_i), \text{PSC}(\text{HSB}, \nu_i)\}$ would be generated, giving rise to a non-terminating $chase(D, \Sigma)$. However, the set of strong links is finite (only the pairs with constants) and a small portion of $chase(D, \Sigma)$ is needed to answer Q.

To practically ensure reasoning completion, reasoners resort to *termination strategies*. Specifically, the Vadalog system adopts the *isomorphism termination strategy* [4]: isomorphic copies of the facts (i.e., same constants and bijection between the labelled nulls) are suppressed, hence the chase steps starting from them are not performed and the descending facts are not generated. The properties of the warded fragment ensure that such facts would be in turn isomorphic copies of others already in the chase—being their origins isomorphic—, thus uninformative for query answering, upholding the correctness of the approach.

Yet, it has been proved [5] that, to apply the strategy and enable a reasoning algorithm, a set of warded rules must be expressed in a "harmless" form (namely, in *Harmless* Warded Datalog$^\pm$), without joins between variables affected by existential quantification. The propagation of labelled nulls in the chase execution, up to the join arguments, would otherwise hamper the application of the termination strategy: it is the case of PSC(HSB, ν_0) in our example, which is isomorphic to PSC(HSB, ν_1) and yet cannot be suppressed without blocking the activation of ρ with PSC(HSBC, ν_0), essential to generate StrongLink(HSBC,HSB).

In this short paper, we investigate the theoretical foundations of the *normalization* techniques aiming at eliminating such "harmful" joins, and show that a set of warded rules can be equivalently expressed in Harmless Warded Datalog$^\pm$. An extended version of this work with full proofs and experimental evaluations can be found online as part of the IWARDED project [3].

Contribution. In particular, we provide the following contributions.

- We present novel theoretical bases for Warded Datalog$^\pm$ and discuss the NORMALIZATION problem of rewriting a set of warded rules into a harmless version that is equivalent with respect to the reasoning task.
- We enable the practical application of the isomorphism termination strategy by proposing the HARMFUL JOIN ELIMINATION (HJE) algorithm, the first normalization technique for Warded Datalog$^\pm$.

Overview. Section 2 provides preliminary concepts relevant for our work. Section 3 introduces the normalization problem. Section 4 presents the HJE algorithm. Section 5 analyzes related work. Section 6 concludes the paper.

2 Vadalog and Datalog$^\pm$

The Vadalog system adopts VADALOG, a language that is essentially an implementation of Warded Datalog$^\pm$. To guide our discussion, we briefly recall notation and terminology. A VADALOG program is a set of facts and rules. An *existential rule* is a first-order sentence $\forall \bar{x} \forall \bar{y} (\varphi(\bar{x}, \bar{y}) \rightarrow \exists \bar{z}\ \psi(\bar{x}, \bar{z}))$, where φ (the *body*) and ψ (the *head*) are conjunctions of atoms over the respective predicates. In this context, we omit universal quantifiers and denote conjunction by comma.

Given a set Σ of rules, a position $\pi[i]$ (i.e., the i-th term of a predicate π, with $i = 1, \ldots$) is *affected* if (i) π appears in a rule ρ of Σ with the i-th term that contains an existentially quantified variable or, (ii) there is a rule ρ of Σ such that a *frontier variable* (i.e., universally quantified and appearing in the head) is only in affected body positions and in $\pi[i]$ in the head of ρ. A variable x is *harmful*, with respect to a rule, if x appears only in affected positions, otherwise it is *harmless*. A rule that contains a harmful variable is a *harmful rule*. In Example 1, α and γ are existential rules, while β propagates the affected position PSC[2] and ρ has a join between the harmful variables p (*harmful join*).

Given a database D and a pair $Q = (\Sigma, Ans)$, where Σ is a set of rules and Ans an n-ary predicate, we define the evaluation of Q over D as the set of tuples $Q(D, \Sigma) = \{\bar{t} \in dom(D)^n \mid Ans(\bar{t}) \in chase(D, \Sigma)\}$, where $\bar{t}$ is a tuple of constants. We denote *reasoning task* as the task of finding a database instance J such that: (i) $\bar{t} \in J$ if and only if $Ans(\bar{t}) \in Q(D, \Sigma)$ and (ii) for every other instance J' such that $\bar{t} \in J'$ if and only if $\bar{t} \in Q(D, \Sigma)$, there is a homomorphism from J to J' [4]. We define *chase graph* $\mathcal{G}(D, \Sigma)$ as the directed graph having as nodes the facts from $chase(D, \Sigma)$ and an edge from a node n to a node m if m is obtained from n (and possibly other facts) by applying a chase step, i.e., a rule in Σ [7].

3 Normalizing Warded Datalog$^\pm$

VADALOG's termination strategy is based on Warded Datalog$^\pm$ syntactic restrictions (namely, *wardedness* [11]), which ensure that, given two isomorphic facts n and n', it is sufficient to explore n, pruning the descending portions of the chase graph rooted in n'. Yet, recent work [5] shows that harmful joins are required to be removed first, as pruning a chase graph on the basis of isomorphism between facts with labelled nulls could hamper the activation of the join on such nulls.

Normalization Problem. To apply the isomorphism termination strategy, without restricting VADALOG expressiveness to joins between harmless variables, we propose a technique to rewrite sets of warded rules into an equivalent form without harmful joins. Two sets of rules are considered equivalent if they have the same meaning [1]. Given the many notions of semantics proposed in the literature [9], we follow a practical approach and define the meaning of a set Σ of rules in an operational way via the chase, so that Σ and Σ' are equivalent if $chase(D, \Sigma) = chase(D, \Sigma')$ modulo fact isomorphism, for every database D.

We define the *normalization problem* for the set Σ of Warded Datalog$^\pm$ rules as the task of finding an equivalent set Σ' of Harmless Warded Datalog$^\pm$ rules.

Causes of Affectedness. Let $\rho \in \Sigma$ be a *harmful join rule*, of the form (without loss of generality [4]): $A(x_1, y_1, h), B(x_2, y_2, h) \to \exists z\ C(x, z)$, where A, B and C are atoms. By definition of harmful variables, we state that Σ includes $i \geq 1$ sets of rules $\Gamma_{Ai} = \{\sigma_1, \ldots, \sigma_s\}$ ($s < |\Sigma|$) for A, each containing: (i) one *direct* cause of affectedness, that is, an existential rule which causes a position to be affected, of the form σ_1: $A_1(x, y), R_1 \to \exists h\ A_2(x, y, h)$ (α and γ in Example 1); (ii) $s - 1$ *indirect* causes of affectedness, that is, rules propagating such affected position from σ_1 to ρ. They are of the form σ_k: $A_k(x, y, h), R_k \to A_{k+1}(x, y, h)$, $1 < k \leq s$, $A_{s+1} = A$ (β in Example 1). $A_1, \ldots, A_s$ are atoms, $R_1, \ldots, R_s$ are (conjunctions of) atoms not containing h (by definition of warded fragment [11]). Σ also contains $j \geq 1$ sets Γ_{Bj} for B. In Example 1, we observe that the atoms in the harmful join in ρ belong to the same predicate PSC. To distinguish them, we adopt the notation PSC_1, PSC_2 (in order of appearance in ρ). The sets of causes for PSC_1 are: $\Gamma_{PSC_11} = \{\alpha\}$, $\Gamma_{PSC_12} = \{\alpha, \beta\}$, $\Gamma_{PSC_13} = \{\gamma\}$, $\Gamma_{PSC_14} = \{\gamma, \beta\}$. Indeed, PSC_2 features the same sets of causes. Let $X_{ij} = \Gamma_{Ai} \cup \Gamma_{Bj}$ be a set which contains the causes from Γ_{Ai} and Γ_{Bj}, labelled after the set they belong to. For instance, in our example $X_{22} = \{\alpha_{\Gamma_{PSC_12}}, \beta_{\Gamma_{PSC_12}}, \alpha_{\Gamma_{PSC_22}}, \beta_{\Gamma_{PSC_22}}\}$ from Γ_{PSC_12} and Γ_{PSC_22}.

Harmful Unfolding Tree. To remove ρ from Σ and solve the normalization problem, we first determine how labelled nulls activating the harmful join are propagated along X_{ij} and their impact in terms of meaning on the chase. For this purpose, we introduce the structure *harmful unfolding tree* (hu-tree).

It is based on the *unfolding* and *folding* operations [1]. Let ρ be a rule $A, B \to C$, where A and C are atoms and B is an atom or a conjunction of atoms, and let σ be a rule $R \to A'$, where A' is an atom and R an atom or a conjunction of atoms. Let A' be unifiable with A by substitution θ. The result of unfolding ρ at A with σ ($\texttt{unfold}(\rho, A, \sigma)$) is the rule τ: $(B, R \to C)\theta$. If the head of σ contains an existentially quantified variable h, we replace h with a *Skolem atom* $f_{h\sigma}$ in τ. The symbol f denotes an injective, deterministic and range disjoint function that calculates the values for existentially quantified variables, to control the identity of labelled nulls [5]. Let ρ be a rule $A, B \to C$, where C is an atom and A and B are (conjunctions of) atoms, and let σ be a rule $A' \to R$, where R is an atom and A' is an atom or a conjunction of atoms. Let A' be unifiable with A by substitution θ. The result of *folding* ρ into σ ($\texttt{fold}(\rho, \sigma)$) is the rule τ: $(B, R \to C)\theta$.

The hu-tree T for the harmful join rule ρ in Σ is a structure that composes ρ along all the possible sequences of causes propagating the affected position to it. Intuitively, a *u-node* is a node in T resulting from unfolding its parent with a cause from the set X_{ij}, whereas a *f-node* is a node in T resulting from folding a u-node with its ancestors to handle recursive causes. We declaratively define the hu-tree T for $\langle \Sigma, \rho \rangle$ as a rule-labelled tree, where:

1. *the root of T is labelled by ρ;*
2. Φ *is a (partial) function from rules × causes to atoms, whose value for a rule μ and a set X_{ij} of causes is an atom I in the body of μ;*
3. N, *labelled by a rule ν, is a u-node in T iff:*
   (a) *there exists a u-node M, labelled by μ, and a cause $\sigma_{\Gamma_{Hk}} \in X_{ij}$ ($H \in \{A,B\}$, $k \in \{i,j\}$) such that $\nu = \mathtt{unfold}(\mu, \Phi(\mu, X_{ij}), \sigma_{\Gamma_{Hk}})$ and*
   (b) *there does not already exist a u-node in T labelled by ν and*
   (c) *the cause $\sigma_{\Gamma_{Hk}} \in X_{ij}$ has not already been unfolded in T;*
4. O, *labelled by a rule o, is a f-node in T iff:*
   (a) *there exists a u-node N, labelled by a rule ν, and a recursive cause $\sigma_{\Gamma_{Hk}} \in X_{ij}$, such that $\nu = \mathtt{unfold}(\mu, \Phi(\mu, X_{ij}), \sigma_{\Gamma_{Hk}})$ and*
   (b) $o = \mathtt{fold}(\mathtt{unfold}(\nu, \Phi(\nu, X_{ij}), \sigma_{\Gamma_{Hk}}), \mu)$.

The hu-tree does not contain cycles and each node only has one parent, as all the nodes have distinct labels (3b). T is finite, as each cause $\sigma_{\Gamma_{Hk}}$ is removed from the set X_{ij} it belongs once unfolded (3c) and the recursive causes in X_{ij} are handled via folding (4). A deterministic order of the unfolded causes is applied. By design, Φ prioritizes the first atom in the harmful join, in order of appearance in ρ: unfoldings with causes from Γ_{Ai} are applied before those from Γ_{Bj} in X_{ij}. Causes are unfolded from indirect to direct ones in X_{ij}, as the affectedness propagation is walked backwards from ρ up to the direct cause: if two or more causes in the same Γ_{Hk} feature the same predicate as head, their order of unfolding depends on the distance from its direct cause (in terms of chase steps) and other parameters.

Harmful Unfolding Path. We define the *distance from harmlessness* ($\mathtt{dh}_{ij}$) as the cardinality of X_{ij}. Intuitively, $\mathtt{dh}_{ij}$ is equal to the number of edges of the *hu-path* (i.e., a root-to-leaf path) T_{ij} in T for $\langle \Sigma, \rho \rangle$. Let the *maximum distance from harmlessness* ($\mathtt{mdh}$) of ρ be the max of $\mathtt{dh}_{ij}$ for ρ (i.e., the height of T).

Figure 1 shows the hu-path T_{22} of T for Example 1, derived from unfolding ρ at PSC_1 and PSC_2 with the causes in $\Gamma_{PSC_12} = \{\alpha, \beta\}$ and $\Gamma_{PSC_22} = \{\alpha, \beta\}$. Atoms are renamed for space reasons. The $\mathtt{dh}_{22} = 4$ of T_{22} is the cardinality of the above set X_{22}. Moreover, note, for instance, the recursive $\beta_{\Gamma_{PSC_12}}$ of X_{22}. By definition of hu-tree, the recursion is covered in T as follows. First, the u-node N is unfolded again with $\beta_{\Gamma_{PSC_12}}$. Then, the result is folded into N itself and a f-node is generated, labelled by the rule $\mathtt{Strong}(v_1, y), \mathtt{Cont}(v_1, v_2) \rightarrow \mathtt{Strong}(v_2, y)$ and linked to N via a new

$$PSC(x,p), PSC(y,p) \rightarrow Strong(x,y).$$
$$\downarrow \beta_{\Gamma_{PSC_12}}$$
$$PSC(v_1,p), Cont(v_1,v_2), \quad (N)$$
$$PSC(y,p) \rightarrow Strong(v_2,y).$$
$$\downarrow \alpha_{\Gamma_{PSC_12}}$$
$$Comp(v_1), Cont(v_1,v_2), PSC(y,p),$$
$$f_{pa}(v_1) \rightarrow Strong(v_2,y).$$
$$\downarrow \beta_{\Gamma_{PSC_22}}$$
$$Comp(v_1), Cont(v_1,v_2), PSC(v_3,p),$$
$$Cont(v_3,v_4), f_{pa}(v_1) \rightarrow Strong(v_2,v_4).$$
$$\downarrow \alpha_{\Gamma_{PSC_22}}$$
$$Comp(v_1), Cont(v_1,v_2), Comp(v_3),$$
$$Cont(v_3,v_4), f_{pa}(v_1), f_{pa}(v_3) \rightarrow Strong(v_2,v_4).$$

Fig. 1. Hu-path T_{22} for Example 1.

branch: apart from the technical side, this is intuitively justified as such rule covers the activation of the harmful join in ρ on nulls propagated from the recursion of $\beta_{\Gamma_{PSC_1}2}$ in the chase.

4   Harmful Join Elimination Algorithm

Harmful Join Elimination is a rewriting algorithm designed to solve the normalization problem. Let Σ be a warded set with one or more harmful join rules ρ. The algorithm produces a new set Σ', replacing ρ with harmless rules that cover the generation of all the facts derived in $chase(D, \Sigma)$ from the activation of ρ, thus ensuring equivalence of Σ' with Σ while $\Sigma' \in$ Harmless Warded Datalog$^\pm$. Algorithm 1 provides the pseudo-code for HJE(Σ), divided into three phases.

Back-Composition. First, a *back-composition* phase is applied to cover the activation of ρ on labelled nulls, propagated along its causes of affectedness. For each ρ, its hu-tree T is built from all the sets X_{ij} (line 5), by performing mdh iterations. At each iteration, every hu-path T_{ij} that has not already reached its leaf (i.e., some causes in X_{ij} can still be unfolded) is extended with a new u-node, labelled by the result of unfolding its parent with the next $\sigma \in X_{ij}$, according to the priority discussed in Sect. 3 (line 13). If one or more causes in X_{ij} are recursive, folding occurs (line 17). The resulting leaves are added to Σ'.

Grounding. Then, a *grounding* phase is applied (line 19) to cover the activation of ρ on ground values, propagated from rules $\pi \in \Sigma$ that are not causes of affectedness. It employs the Dom(h) [5] atom to ensure that the harmful variables in ρ bind only to ground values in the domain. It proceeds as follows.

1. For A in ρ, add to Σ' the following rules (and the corresponding ones for B):
   Dom$(h), A(x_1, y_1, h) \rightarrow A'(x_1, y_1, h)$.
   $A'(x_1, y_1, h) \rightarrow A(x_1, y_1, h)$.
   $A'(x_1, y_1, h), B(x_2, y_2, h) \rightarrow \exists z \ C(x, z)$.
2. For each π whose head unifies with the atom $H \in \{A, B\}$ in the body of ρ, add to Σ' the rule π', resulting from renaming H in π with H'.
3. For each π whose head unifies with the atom $I \in$ body of a cause σ of ρ, add to Σ' the rule $\pi' = \mathtt{unfold}(\mu, I, \pi)$, where $\mu \in T$ results from unfolding σ.

Specifically, step 1 makes use of Dom(h) to prevent the propagation of labelled nulls up to the harmful variable h in A, B. Step 2 covers the direct propagation of ground values from the rules π to ρ. Step 3 covers the indirect propagation of ground values from π to ρ along the causes of affectedness: by definition of hu-tree, the results of unfolding ρ up to σ are already present in T, thus it is sufficient to apply an additional unfolding of such u-nodes with π itself to cover the propagation from π to ρ. Now, ρ is removed from Σ'.

Cleanup. Finally, a *cleanup* phase is applied (line 20). Possible duplicate rules are eliminated from Σ', as well as rules that never activate. If the functions of the Skolem atoms in a rule (derived from unfolding a direct cause in T) respect injectivity and range disjointness, they are unified and removed, otherwise the rule is dropped from Σ'. The latter occurs, for instance, if the direct causes in the same X_{ij} differ, as the Skolem atoms ($f_{p\alpha}, f_{p\gamma}$ in Example 1) cannot be unified due to range disjointness.

With reference to Example 1, Fig. 2 shows the results of applying HJE to Σ. Specifically, we provide the new rules added to Σ' at the end of HJE, some of which are merged for space reasons: δs are added by grounding, whereas τs and ηs are T leaves derived from unfoldings and foldings (respectively), after Skolem cleanup. For instance, τ_4 derives from the leaf of the hu-path T_{22} illustrated in Fig. 1.

$$\begin{aligned}
\text{Dom(p),PSC(x,p)} &\rightarrow \text{PSC}^{\cdot}\text{(x,p)}. \quad (\delta_1) \\
\text{PSC}^{\cdot}\text{(x,p)} &\rightarrow \text{PSC(x,p)}. \quad (\delta_2) \\
\text{PSC}^{\cdot}\text{(x,p),PSC(y,p)} &\rightarrow \text{Strong(x,y)}. \quad (\delta_3) \\
\text{Comp(x)} &\rightarrow \text{Strong(x,x)}. \quad (\tau_1) \\
\text{Comp(x),Cont(x,y)} &\rightarrow \text{Strong(x,y),Strong(y,x)}. \quad (\tau_{23}) \\
\text{Comp(x),Cont(x,y),Cont(x,z)} &\rightarrow \text{Strong(y,z)}. \quad (\tau_4) \\
\text{Strong(x,y),Cont(x,w),Cont(x,z)} &\rightarrow \text{Strong(w,z)}. \quad (\tau_5) \\
\text{Strong(x,y),Cont(x,z)} &\rightarrow \text{Strong(x,z),Strong(z,x)}. \quad (\tau_{67}) \\
\text{Strong(x,y)} &\rightarrow \text{Strong(x,x)}. \quad (\tau_8) \\
\text{Strong(x,y),Cont(x,z)} &\rightarrow \text{Strong(y,z),Strong(z,y)}. \quad (\eta_{12}) \\
\text{Strong(x,y),Cont(y,z)} &\rightarrow \text{Strong(x,z),Strong(z,x)}. \quad (\eta_{34})
\end{aligned}$$

Fig. 2. HJE output for Example 1.

Algorithm 1. Harmful Join Elimination.

```
1:  function HARMFUL-JOIN-ELIMINATION(Σ)
2:      P ← all harmful join rules in Σ; Σ' = Σ
3:      for ρ in P do
4:          T ← empty hu-tree with ρ as root                          ▷ BACK-COMPOSITION phase
5:          Γρ ← all Xij from ΓAi, ΓBj for ρ in Σ                     ▷ all sets of causes of affectedness for ρ
6:          Q ← queue with ρ enqueued
7:          mdh = max(|Xij|) with Xij in Γρ
8:          for dh ← 1 to mdh do                                       ▷ build hu-tree T for ρ
9:              μ = Q.dequeue()
10:             for Xij in Γρ do
11:                 if dh ≤ |Xij| then
12:                     σ = Xij.next()                                 ▷ next cause, from indirect to direct
13:                     ν = unfold(μ, Φ(μ, Xij), σ)
14:                     Q.enqueue(ν)
15:                     Tij ← Tij ∪ {ν}                                ▷ update hu-path Tij at depth dh with u-node ν
16:                     if inRecursion(σ, Xij) then
17:                         T ← T ∪ {fold(unfold(ν, Φ(ν, Xij), σ), μ)} ▷ f-node for recursive causes
18:             Σ'.add(T.leaves())
19:             add grounding rules for ρ to Σ'; Σ'.remove(ρ)          ▷ GROUNDING phase
20:         simplify Skolem atoms and deduplicate rules in Σ'          ▷ CLEANUP phase
            return Σ'
```

Correctness and Complexity. By definition of unfolding and folding, it can be proved that Σ' is a harmless warded set of rules; equivalence to Σ is easily derived as a generalization of proofs in the Datalog context [17]. The normalization problem is solved by HJE, as it can be constructively shown that for every Σ there exists a Σ' [3]. We close Example 1 by listing the output facts of the reasoning task, via isomorphism termination strategy: StrongLink(HSBC,HSBC), StrongLink(HSBC,HSB), StrongLink(HSB,HSBC), StrongLink(HSB,HSB).

The algorithm shows an exponential behaviour with respect to the number of causes of affectedness. Intuitively, this is due to the worst-case generation of a distinct hu-path in the hu-tree for each subset of the causes. Yet, such exponential blowup is data independent and it does not affect the performance of reasoning tasks. We consider a more in-depth discussion regarding complexity outside the scope of this paper and it can be found in the extended version [3].

5   Related Work

The growing interest towards Datalog$^\pm$-based languages, to be adopted as logical core of reasoning systems, determined the research and the development of novel approaches to sustain termination of reasoning tasks [6,7], particularly relevant in the presence of recursion and existential quantification [8].

Specifically, the Harmful Join Elimination algorithm can be compared, by interpreting the rules as queries, to the class of methodologies for *query rewriting*. Regarding Datalog, the current literature encompasses both rewriting from distinct formalisms, such as *Regular Path Queries* [10] and *Description Logics* [2], and Datalog translation into specific fragments, such as *Plain* from *Disjunctive* [14], *Guarded* [13] and *Linear* [1], which partially inspired this work.

In particular, several methods have been devised for rewriting Datalog$^\pm$ members with existential rules [15,18]. Yet, the HJE algorithm is, to the best of our knowledge, the first technique developed for the translation of sets of Warded Datalog$^\pm$ rules into an equivalent Harmless Warded Datalog$^\pm$ version.

6   Conclusion

To ensure termination of VADALOG reasoning settings with harmful joins in practice, it is required to first normalize them into an equivalent harmless version. Motivated by this condition and by the fact that such a rewriting technique for the underlying Warded Datalog$^\pm$ is not covered in the existing literature, we discussed the normalization problem and we contributed the Harmful Join Elimination, a normalization algorithm integrated in the Vadalog system.

Acknowledgements. This work was supported by the EPSRC programme grant EP/M025268/1 VADA and the Vienna Science and Technology Fund (WWTF) grant VRG18-013.

References

1. Afrati, F., Gergatsoulis, M., Toni, F.: Linearisability on datalog programs. Theoret. Comput. Sci. **308**(1–3), 199–226 (2003)
2. Ahmetaj, S., Ortiz, M., Simkus, M.: Polynomial datalog rewritings for expressive description logics with closed predicates. In: IJCAI, pp. 878–885 (2016)
3. Baldazzi, T., Bellomarini, L., Sallinger, E., Atzeni, P.: iWarded: a system for benchmarking datalog+/-reasoning (tr). arXiv preprint arXiv:2103.08588 (2021)
4. Bellomarini, L., Benedetto, D., Gottlob, G., Sallinger, E.: Vadalog: a modern architecture for automated reasoning with large knowledge graphs. IS (2020)
5. Bellomarini, L., Sallinger, E., Gottlob, G.: The vadalog system: datalog-based reasoning for knowledge graphs. VLDB, **11**(9) (2018)

6. Berger, G., Gottlob, G., Pieris, A., Sallinger, E.: The space-efficient core of Vadalog. In: PODS, pp. 270–284 (2019)
7. Calì, A., Gottlob, G., Lukasiewicz, T.: A general datalog-based framework for tractable query answering over ontologies. In: PODS, pp. 77–86 (2009)
8. Calì, A., Gottlob, G., Lukasiewicz, T., Marnette, B., Pieris, A.: Datalog+/-: a family of logical knowledge representation and query languages for new applications. In: 2010 25th Annual IEEE LICS, pp. 228–242. IEEE (2010)
9. van Emden, M.H., Kowalski, R.A.: The semantics of predicate logic as a programming language. J. ACM 23(4), 733–742 (1976)
10. Francis, N., Segoufin, L., Sirangelo, C.: Datalog rewritings of regular path queries using views. arXiv preprint arXiv:1511.00938 (2015)
11. Gottlob, G., Pieris, A.: Beyond SPARQL under OWL 2 QL entailment regime: rules to the rescue. In: IJCAI (2015)
12. Gottlob, G., Pieris, A., Sallinger, E.: Vadalog: recent advances and applications. In: Calimeri, F., Leone, N., Manna, M. (eds.) JELIA 2019. LNCS (LNAI), vol. 11468, pp. 21–37. Springer, Cham (2019). https://doi.org/10.1007/978-3-030-19570-0_2
13. Gottlob, G., Rudolph, S., Simkus, M.: Expressiveness of guarded existential rule languages. In: PODS, pp. 27–38 (2014)
14. Kaminski, M., Nenov, Y., Grau, B.C.: Datalog rewritability of disjunctive datalog programs and non-Horn ontologies. Artif. Intell. 236, 90–118 (2016)
15. Kónig, M., Leclere, M., Mugnier, M.L.: Query rewriting for existential rules with compiled preorder. In: IJCAI, pp. 3006–3112 (2015)
16. Maier, D., Mendelzon, A.O., Sagiv, Y.: Testing implications of data dependencies. ACM Trans. Database Syst. 4(4), 455–469 (1979)
17. Tamaki, H., Sato, T.: Unfold/fold transformation of logic programs. In: ICLP, pp. 127–138. Uppsala University (1984)
18. Wang, Z., Xiao, P., Wang, K., Zhuang, Z., Wan, H.: Query answering for existential rules via efficient datalog rewriting. In: IJCAI, pp. 1933–1939 (2020)

Learning Decision Rules or Learning Decision Models?

Christian de Sainte Marie[✉]

IBM France Lab, Bâtiment Lisp 2 rue d'Arsonval, 91400 Orsay, France
csma@fr.ibm.com

Abstract. In this position paper, we discuss the reasons for the lack of success of rule learning, as witnessed by the quasi-absence of commercial applications, and what can be done to revive the domain and possibly to kick-start the kind of explosive development that statistical Machine Learning and Neural Networks have experienced over the past 15 years. The root cause of the problem is well-known, and it is not the rule learning algorithms themselves: if the representation language to which a rule learning algorithm has access – often only the representation model of the input data – is not appropriate to represent the decision rules, the algorithm has no way to generate a decision ruleset that generalizes well. Feature generation and other methods that have been proposed to augment the data representation language are useful, but we argue that the focus should be on discovering the conceptual model that underly the decision. We claim that this amounts to discovering the structure of decisions, that is, to learn decision models. We outline some potentially fruitful research directions, and how this topic is central to neuro-symbolic learning.

Keywords: Rule learning · Concept discovery · Decision modeling · Neuro-symbolic learning

1 Introduction

Learning rules from precedents has been a subject since Artificial Intelligence emerged as a research domain in the 50's. Rule-based systems have been mainstream in commercial decision assistance and automation at least since the 90's, e.g. as business rules management systems. Still, rule learning from data is nowhere close to be as successful as other Machine Learning techniques such as Neural Networks (NN), be it in terms of scientific, technical, social or commercial impact: none of the main commercial business rules management systems offers even the simplest rule learning capability, for instance.

In this paper, we examine what, we believe, are the reasons why learning rules from precedents has not been more successful, and what these reasons tell us about potentially fruitful research directions.

Let us start with a look at another machine learning technology, namely Neural Networks. The bases for most of modern machine learning technology existed essentially already in the early 90' (see e.g. [1]). Of course, progresses were made after that, but why

© Springer Nature Switzerland AG 2021
S. Moschoyiannis et al. (Eds.): RuleML+RR 2021, LNCS 12851, pp. 276–283, 2021.
https://doi.org/10.1007/978-3-030-91167-6_19

is it that we had to wait until the second half of the 2000's to witness the rebirth of Artificial Intelligence in the guise of (NN-based) Machine Learning and that explosive growth of scientific results, technology and applications? One usual answer to that question is that what unlocked the domain was the new availability (and affordability) of both data and computing power. But there was something else, otherwise (i) the onset of modern AI would have started earlier, and (ii) the affordable access to data and computing power should have benefited to symbolic ML as much as it did to statistical ML. That something else, which is to be found, at least for an important part, in Hinton's et al. paper [2], was a way to train arbitrarily deep neural networks by training each layer independently.

The situation of rule learning– and more generally of symbolic learning – is comparable to that of neural networks in the early 2000's: the technology and the algorithmic basis for learning rules from precedents, essentially existed already in the early 90's, e.g. CN2, FOIL, RIPPER [3], or decision trees, e.g. C4.5 [4], and improvements since then focused on performance and handling noisy data, but no breakthrough like Deep Learning has happened yet in symbolic learning to unlock the field.

In Sect. 2, we explain with an experiment what we believe is the main lock that holds rule learning from progressing at the same speed as neural networks and other kinds of statistical machine learning, and why decision rule learning should now focus on generating the best hypotheses space rather than on generating the best hypotheses in the given representation space. In Sect. 3, we outline some consequences of this change of focus on research directions and priorities. In Sect. 4, we point to relevant related work. Finally, in the conclusion, we propose a new interpretation of decision model, in view of our previous analysis, that justifies the title of this paper.

2   What is the Problem?

Rule learning algorithms can only learn rules that are accessible in their hypotheses space [5]. As obvious as this statement may seem, we believe that this is the root cause of the lack of success of rule learning technology.

Indeed, in the absence of additional knowledge, the representation language that is accessible to the rule learning algorithm to generate the conditions of candidate rules is made of straightforward tests on the input data attributes: rule learning algorithms typically generate hyper-rectangles in the input data space as Boolean combinations of tests that compare the value of an attribute of the tested instance in the input data space with a constant value in the domain of that attribute.

For instance, consider the simple example of learning rules to automate the decision to accept or reject loan applications from customers, based on customer details collected on their application forms. In the "miniloan" use case from the IBM ODM tutorial [6]. the data that is required for the sample ruleset to make the decision is the applicant and loan identifiers, the requested amount, interest rate and duration of the loan, and the revenue and credit score of the applicant[1].

---

[1] Typically, additional data such as the applicant home address, household etc. will be available, some of it completely unrelated to the decision at hand and making the learning problem more difficult. However, this simple example will be enough for our purpose.

A simple experiment will help make our point clear. We generated instances in the "miniloan" input space described above, with a uniform distribution, and we labelled them using the "miniloan" ruleset. Then we trained a decision tree with the instances[2]. Here is a typical example of a rule extracted from the decision tree[3]:

```
if CreditScore > 199 and ApplicantIncome <= 17020 and
LoanAmount <= 118303
then "Reject" loan request
```

The performance on the test set is acceptable (score >97% with 4,000 training instances), but the rules learnt do not generalize well, in the sense that adding new data points to the training set will generate additional rules: indeed, the size of the decision tree grows linearly with the number of training instances (see Fig. 1a, below).

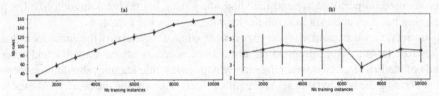

Fig. 1. Number of rules learnt as a function of the number of training instances, when the decision tree is trained on: (a) the initial representation of the instances; (b) *blue*: the representation learnt from a trained 5-5-5-3 multi-layer perceptron[4]; *red*: the initial representation augmented with repayment amount and debt to revenue ratio. (Color figure online)

One way to explain this is because, in the general case, the conceptual model that is required to make the decision is not the same as the conceptual model that is relevant to represent the data: in our credit approval example, it may make sense for a bank to describe loan requests with the attributes listed above, but when it comes to approve or reject them, one will probably rather think in terms of the reimbursement capacity of the applicant, of the sustainability of that capacity over the duration of the loan etc. A simplified meaningful rule of thumb for approving a loan could be:

If the Applicant is Reliable and Capable of Paying the Terms, Then Approve the Loan
We can see the traces of such a rule in our example, above: the test on 'CreditScore' checks the applicant reliability, the pair of tests on 'ApplicantIncome' and 'LoanAmount' checks the repayment capacity. But except for the credit score attribute, which is readily available in the input data, the hypotheses space does not contain a compact and robust representation for the concepts related to reimbursement capacity, for instance, such as that of periodic repayment amount and debt to revenue

---

[2] We used Scikit Learn DecisionTreeClassifier, which is an optimised version of the CART algorithm [7] and Scikit Learn MLPClassifier for the further experiment, reported below. In both cases, the performance is computed using the classifier "score" method on a test set.

[3] Each leave in a decision tree defines a rule, where the condition is the conjunction of the tests along the path and the leave specifies the corresponding decision.

[4] Other configurations produce similar results. See: https://github.com/cfmrsma/RuleML21.

ratio. When the decision tree is trained, instead, on instances that include these additional features, the number of rules remains constant as soon as the number of training instances has been sufficient for the algorithm to learn the initial "miniloan" rules (Fig. 1b, red line).

The well-known tendency of rule learning algorithms to overfit the training data with large number of rules, especially in the presence of noise, and the brittleness of the learnt rulesets are consequences of trying to approximate the decision rules in an inappropriate representation space. In addition, in the absence of an explicit representation of the relevant concepts, the rules cannot be easily interpreted from a decision maker or business point of view.

These problems are not specific to our decision tree algorithm: any rule learning algorithm will exhibit them in one form or another, including ones using completely different approaches to candidate rule generation, such as column generation [8].

Another simple experiment will help clarify our point that an appropriate change of representation can be learnt that decorrelates the number of rules from the number of training instances (thus relieving our primary symptom that the problem is the representation space rather than the learning algorithm). We trained a multi-layer perceptron with the same training instances as our initial decision tree, then we retrieved and discretized, for each training instance, the values of the nodes in the last hidden layer of the neural network, and we trained a decision tree in that transformed representation space. Figure 1b clearly shows that, with the learnt representation, the number of rules does not depend on the number of training instances (with similar performance).

We have stated earlier that the root cause of the lack of success of rule learning was that rule learning algorithms can only learn rules that are accessible in their hypotheses space. More precisely, the problem is that rule learning algorithms focus on generating the best candidate rules in their hypotheses space, which is of course required. But to be useful – and thus to be more widely used – they will have to focus also on generating the best hypotheses space for the decision problem at hand.

3   Research Directions and Approaches

We claim that the focus of rule learning, and more generally symbolic learning, should move to discovering the best hypotheses space, which requires discovering concepts and learning representations. The capability to learn representations is what made the success of Deep Learning and other statistical learning approaches, and it is what is missing for rule learning to succeed; with the difference that, here, we need to learn symbolic representations.

By learning symbolic representations, we imply (i) discovering the concepts that are useful or required to learn good decision rules and (ii) grounding these concepts in the input data space. This, in turn, requires a definition of what are good decision rules as well as research on how it can be measured; the same holds for what makes a concept useful or required to learn good rules. The next question is: how to learn those symbolic concepts? And, finally, how to ground them in the input space, that is, how to define them in terms of the observed features.

Understanding What Makes a Good Rule Good and a Useful Concept Useful

Ideally, we want to learn rules that are both correct and necessary. A rule is (i) correct if it proposes the correct decision in all instances that satisfy its condition, regardless of their other features: such rules will explain past decisions, propose the correct decision in future cases and permit counterfactual reasoning and what-if analyses; (ii) necessary if it cannot be replaced by a more general rule, covering, in the input space, more instances of interest with respect to the decision: such rules are more likely to rely on features that are essential to the decision. We want to learn a ruleset that covers the whole input space[5], but we also want to learn rules that generalize as much as possible, in the sense that they cover as many instances of interest as possible.

In addition, we want to learn rules that make sense to the user: indeed, ease of modification by the decision authority is, beside auditability and traceability, one of the most important motivations for rule-based decision automation or assistance.

In short, we want rules and rulesets that are compact, robust, necessary, general and understandable, all of which characterize explanations with a high explanatory power [9]: indeed, what makes a rule good is its capacity to explain a decision.

Therefore, we propose that the measure of the quality of a rule or ruleset (its goodness), and the objective that we want a learning algorithm to maximize for the learnt ruleset, should be its explanatory power. Let us stress, here, that we are not seeking high explanatory power because we want to use rules as a mean to provide explainable decisions, but that explanatory power seems to be an adequate measure of the good properties that we want from our decision rules, whatever the reasons why we want to use a rule-based approach: from the point of view of rule learning, the capacity of good rules to provide good explanations is a (much appreciated!) side benefit.

Our proposal does not offer ready-made solutions, but it may indicate fruitful new research directions. A good test for explanatory power could be, for instance, the capacity of a rule to explain noisy data away: a rule with a high explanatory power is robust to noise because it is "truer than the data", in the same sense that, in physics, theory is stronger than measurements[6]: if your instrument measures a force between two macroscopic masses that disagrees with Newton's attraction law, you will suspect your instrument, not Newton. In the same way, if the rule says that loans to reliable applicant with the capacity to reimburse are to be approved, if there is data about an applicant who satisfied the condition and was rejected, one should be able to conclude that either the data about the applicant is wrong, or the rejection was a mistake.

Learning a Useful Conceptual Model

The possibility to learn good rules depends critically on the rule representation space, as shown also by our simple experiment above: per the proposed criterion for rule goodness, rule learning requires the identification or discovery of the features or concepts that contribute most to the explanatory power of a rule, e.g. the features that are inherent to (or constitutive of) the different decisions in the problem at hand.

In the absence of further knowledge, the conceptual model that is most useful to learn or discover would be the, possibly latent, variable model that best explains the

---

[5] More precisely: the part of the input space that is relevant with respect to the decision at hand.

[6] That is, until measurements break the theory, and the theory must be changed, of course....

relations between input data and observed decisions. We will not review here the abun-
dant literature on identifying latent variables and on learning representations (but see
[10]). Let us only stress that learning causal representations [11] might prove especially
important, since our proposed definition of a useful concept may well boil down to that
of a causal variable in a decision... It might also be useful to revisit earlier work on
induced generalization structures such as formal concept analysis [15].

Grounding Symbolic Concepts

The reader will have noticed that there is no restriction to learning *symbolic* representations in the text above. Indeed, once a useful latent feature has been identified, it can
be assigned a symbol, and that symbol used to learn rules – symbolic rules – as any
other symbol in the representation language used by the learning algorithm, as we did
in the experiment described above. If identified as a node in the hidden layer of a neural
network, that feature is specified implicitly by its grounding in the input data.

If an explicit definition of the symbols is required, approaches such as symbolic
regression [ref] can be applied. Symbolic representations and their explicit definitions
can also be learnt bottom up from the data: constructive induction, predicate invention,
pattern mining (see review in [12]), and automated feature construction (see e.g. [13])
are important research topics in the proposed change of focus in rule learning.

Let us, however, notice that an explicit definition is not always required: the explicit
semantics of symbols that have only a sub-symbolic grounding (e.g. in a neural network)
would be defined by their use in a knowledge base. Garnelo et al. describe interesting
preliminary work in that direction [14]. That approach to the combination of symbolic
and sub-symbolic AI seems like a worthy research direction to us.

Once symbols have been identified, the concept discovery process can be iterated
to identify another layer of concepts (lower or higher level, depending whether a top-
down or bottom-up approach is used), each layer being defined in terms of lower layers,
until the most basic concepts can be meaningfully defined in terms of the input features.
Indeed, in most cases, we expect that the conceptual model that is useful to explain a
decision will be a graph structure where higher level concepts are defined in terms of
lower-level ones.

4   Related Works

The subject matter of this paper is, obviously, closely related to the research on feature
generation, representation learning, representation change, neuro-symbolic learning, as
well as to approaches to combine logic and neural networks, and probably machine
learning in general, and we have tried to make that relation clear by referencing relevant
work and surveys in the previous sections.

But we are aware of only few articles that analyze the missing link between symbolic
learning and success, as we do in this paper. Two recent papers put the same stress as we do
on learning higher-level representations and how it could unlock the progress of symbolic
learning. Kramer [12] reviews techniques to learn symbolic higher-level representations
and concludes, as we do, that they are useful both to improve symbolic learning and as
a first step towards converging symbolic and sub-symbolic learning, because they are
able to learn structures of symbolic representations with different levels of abstraction.

Fürnkranz et al. [16] focus on learning structured rule sets as a way to avoid artificial rule ordering mechanisms such as weights and claim that learning auxiliary concepts is useful for that purpose.

Kramer's and Fürnkranz et al. conclusions are close to ours, and so is probably their initial thinking as well. However, neither goes as far as claiming, as we do, that learning the appropriate structured conceptual models is a general requisite for successful symbolic learning and should therefore become the focus of this community.

Let us also stress that Bengio et al. review on representation learning [10] is extremely relevant to (and congruent with) the analysis presented here, although it is concerned with sub-symbolic representations: discovering the useful representations is a necessary step and, as we have claimed above, the grounding step may be separated from the discovery step, when symbolic grounding is required – and it is not necessarily required.

Finally, recent works on differentiable logics (e.g. [17]) may open different doors to make symbolic learning benefit from the advances in neural networks.

5   Revisiting Decision Modeling as a Conclusion

We are referring here to decision modeling as a method used by business analysts for identifying, specifying, analyzing and communicating decision, separately from (and possibly in conjunction with) the specification of business processes [18]. The method and a notation for decision models are the subject of the Decision Model and Notation standard [19]. An important characteristic of Decision Models is that they enforce a clean separation between the structure of a decision and the decision logic; that is, between the data requirements for a decision, and the decision rules.

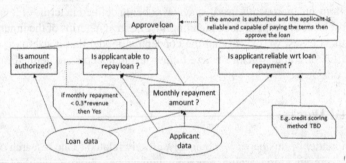

Fig. 2. A DMN decision model for the "miniloan" example [6]. Input data is represented as rounded forms, decisions as rectangles, decision logic as rectangles with two cut angles; plain arrows represent data flows, dashed arrows represent knowledge flow.

Figure 2 shows a DMN decision model for our loan approval example. Not surprisingly, the structure of the sub-decisions matches exactly the conceptual model that is required to explain the decision and to make it in a reasoned way (as opposed to making it on a purely statistical basis). We claim that this is an essential property of decision models: each sub-decision represents a required concept, and the associated decision logic specifies how that concept is grounded in other concepts, down to the input data.

A decision model does not only specify the conceptual model that is required to make a decision: it specifies also the chain of representation changes that ground that decision into the input data.

The introduction of decision modeling is a major paradigm shift in the decision automation industry, as it shifts the focus from the decision rules to the complete decision structure. We claim that the same shift is necessary to the success of symbolic (decision logic) learning, and that the symbolic learning research community should move its focus from rule learning to learning decision models.

References

1. Haohan, W., Bhiksha R.: On the origin of deep learning. arXiv:1702.07800 (2017)
2. Hinton, G.E., et al.: A fast learning algorithm for deep belief nets. Neural Comput. **18**, 1527–1554 (2006)
3. Furnkranz, J.: Separate-and-conquer rule learning. Artif. Intell. Rev. **13**(1), 3–54 (1999)
4. Quinlan, J.R.: C4.5: Programs for Machine Learning. Morgan Kaufmann Publishers (1993)
5. Mitchell, T.: Generalization as Search. Artif. Intell. **18**, 203–226 (1982)
6. https://github.com/ODMDev/odm-for-dev-getting-started
7. Breiman, L., Friedman, J.H., Olshen, R.A., Stone, C.J.: Classification and Regression Trees. 1st edn. Routledge (1984). https://doi.org/10.1201/9781315139470
8. Dash, S., Günlük, O., Wei, D.: Boolean decision rules via column generation. In: 32nd Conference on Neural Information Processing Systems (NeurIPS 2018) (2018)
9. Miller, T.: Explanation in artificial intelligence: insights from the social sciences. Artif. Intell. **267**, 1–38 (2019)
10. Bengio, Y., et al.: Representation learning: a review and new perspectives. IEEE Trans. Pattern Anal. Mach. Intell. **35**, 1798–1828 (2013)
11. Scholkopf, B., et al.: Toward causal representation learning. Proc. IEEE **109**, 612–634 (2021)
12. Kramer, S.: A brief history of learning symbolic higher-level representations from data (and a curious look forward). In: IJCAI (2020)
13. Sondhi, P.: Feature construction methods: a survey (2009)
14. Garnelo, M., et al.: Towards deep symbolic reinforcement learning. ArXiv abs/1609.05518 (2016)
15. Ganter, B., Wille, R.: Formal Concept Analysis: Mathematical Foundations. Springer, Berlin (1999). https://doi.org/10.1007/978-3-642-59830-2
16. Fürnkranz, J., et al.: Learning structured declarative rule sets - a challenge for deep discrete learning. ArXiv abs/2012.04377 (2020)
17. Shindo, H., et al.: Differentiable inductive logic programming for structured examples. In: AAAI (2021)
18. Fish, A.: Melding process models and decision models. Modeling decision-making processes. https://dmcommunity.files.wordpress.com/2016/06/decisioncamp2016-alanfish.pdf
19. OMG, Decision Model and Notation. https://www.omg.org/spec/DMN

Author Index

Printed in the United States
by Baker & Taylor Publisher Services